GLOBALIZATION AND ORGANIZATION

DUE FOR RETURN

Globalization and Organization

World Society and Organizational Change

GILI S. DRORI, JOHN W. MEYER,
AND HOKYU HWANG

Editors

OXFORD
UNIVERSITY PRESS

OXFORD
UNIVERSITY PRESS

Great Clarendon Street, Oxford OX2 6DP

Oxford University Press is a department of the University of Oxford.

It furthers the University's objective of excellence in research, scholarship,
and education by publishing worldwide in

Oxford New York

Auckland Cape Town Dar es Salaam Hong Kong Karachi
Kuala Lumpur Madrid Melbourne Mexico City Nairobi
New Delhi Shanghai Taipei Toronto

With offices in

Argentina Austria Brazil Chile Czech Republic France Greece
Guatemala Hungary Italy Japan Poland Portugal Singapore
South Korea Switzerland Thailand Turkey Ukraine Vietnam

Oxford is a registered trade mark of Oxford University Press
in the UK and in certain other countries

Published in the United States by Oxford University Press inc., New York

© Gili S. Drori 2006

Published in the United States by Oxford University Press Inc

The moral rights of the author have been asserted
Database right Oxford University Press (maker)

First published 2006

British Library Cataloguing in Publication Data
Data available

Library of Congress Cataloguing in Publication Data
Data available

Typeset by SPI Publisher Services, Pondicherry, India
Printed in Great Britain
on acid-free paper by Biddles Ltd., King's Lynn, Norfolk

ISBN 0-19-928453-9   978-019-928453-5
ISBN 0-19-928454-7 (Pbk.)   978-019-928454-2 (Pbk.)

1 3 5 7 9 10 8 6 4 2

1004902358

Foreword

The studies reported in this book reflect common efforts with a considerable history. We, and our collaborating authors, have benefited from our long-term links to the research tradition in the sociology of formal organizations, particularly at Stanford University. Much of the work reported here was done at Stanford, and by researchers in continuing communication with one another.

The roots of these efforts go back to the 1970s. At that time, research on formal organizations—which had blossomed in the previous two decades—had a distinctive cast. Organizational scholarship then focused on organizations as what organizations claim to be, namely efficient modern systems for tightly controlling and coordinating complex activities. The technical nature of the work involved naturally dictated the right ways to organize. Size and complexity of the work activity produced more organization(s), and made possible new efficiencies. As a matter of practice and policy, these accounts seemed fairly convincing.

Nevertheless, rapidly expanding traditions of theoretical and empirical work raised many questions that the organizational scholarship of the period could not ask or answer. The field of organizational scholarship identified empirical patterns that seemed anomalous in the dominant traditions. Organizations often do not control what they do very tightly; and organizations frequently make decisions that are ill informed, vague, and rhetorical, and commonly unimplemented in practice. Further, these decisions have a shadowy character, as organizations routinely copy patterns of the past or of more admired organizations. Some organizations—and even whole categories, or types, of organizations—survive for long periods of time with no evidence of efficiency or effectiveness. With these findings now revealed, too many little 'academic sins' seemed embedded in the confident rationalism of organization theory of the time.

Worse than the sins, perhaps, organization theory was uninspiring; research questions did not seem to be interesting or important. The focus on the influence of funding or size failed to lead to new propositions, and thus research was stagnating, whereas interesting phenomena visible in the rapidly expanding organizational systems of the time were not dealt with, or explained, or even noticed.

The result was an explosion of intellectual and research innovations, a good many centering on the organizations research community at Stanford

University. Many of these innovations are summarized and interpreted else-where (for example, in Scott 1998, 2001). Together, they shared some funda-mental elements, which also serve as the core to our broad project here.

For one thing, it was clear that organizations are creatures of their envir-onments in ways that go beyond the organization theories of the earlier period. They are created and constrained (and sometimes fragmented) by power structures in these environments (Pfeffer and Salancik 1978). The dynamics of organizational populations are in large part determined by changes in the resource, rule, and competitive structures of the environments (Hannan and Freeman 1977). Further, organizations are constituted and reconstituted by the knowledge systems and cultural frames of these envir-onments (Meyer and Rowan 1977, DiMaggio and Powell 1983). Finally, because organizations operate (or are embedded) in inconsistent and mul-tiple environments, organizations and their decisions are far removed from any models of clear and determinate rationalistic action. In a phrase that became famous, decisions come out of a 'garbage can' in which all sorts of ingredients are thrown perhaps by accident (Cohen, March, and Olsen 1972).

All these lines of thought suggest a core idea. Because environments in modern society have much homogeneity, despite some multiplicity and internal inconsistency, organizations may reflect that homogeneity more than the detailed technical variations in what they do. This central idea, developed in several different ways, opened up the intellectual terrain, literally and figuratively, for the field of organizational theory that has flourished since the 1970s. Moreover, developments in theory building and research design in the social sciences in general since the 1970s made it increasingly appealing to study large samples of organizations across a wide range of environments in disparate places (even countries), social sectors, and ultimately across time periods. These developments made possible and necessary the examination of large-scale variations in environments. Many studies effectively showed the important impact of environmentally produced variation among organiza-tions and populations of organizations. Thus, a first core point lies in the background of our work:

1. Organizations tend to reflect models in their environments. Such models evolve over time. Organizations often tend toward homogeneity within particu-lar environments and time periods.

Many studies also pointed to something beyond the tendency toward organizational homogeneity within particular environments: across widely varying environments, organizations displayed more similarities than seemed plausible. And perhaps even more significant, organizations tend to change in similar ways over time. The fundamental implication is that modern social environments may be organized on a much larger scale than the network of transactions or the particular local environment in which organizations are embedded. The scale is often built around national culture and law and sometimes is seen to extend beyond national borders and cultures, made up of global ideologies, models, and rules. Thus, a second core point in the background of this book derives from ideas about the rising importance of the world polity, or world society (Meyer et al. 1997):

2. The environments that support and impact organizations are often organized at very large-scale levels, and increasingly at the world level. National and increasingly global movements provide a context for organizing.

In the current volume, we integrate the theoretical awareness of these two central points with a perspective on 'globalization'—the general modern sensibility and reality that has now entered common parlance. The term 'globalization' has multiple meanings, as we discuss in the chapters of the book. One meaning is simply transactional interdependence. Another, more important for our purposes, is a highly developed social awareness of global interdependence. A third, perhaps still more important but too often overlooked in both popular and scholarly discussions, is the awareness that the logics and scripts that constitute modern actors and action are global in scale and meaning. It is commonly perceived that we live as humans in a global society, and our actions have global meanings and definitions.

If people imagine they live in a global society structured in highly rationalized modern terms—economy, polity, culture, education, health—then it makes sense that (a) they would try to adopt similar organizational forms. Further, (b) innovations, changes, and fashions in organization would sweep around the world. And, most fundamentally, (c) the structural forms that seemed to make sense to them would have characteristics celebrated in modern organizational theory—characteristics that contrast sharply with older organizational arrangements. Thus, a third core point underlying our work further develops the sociological discussion of 'world society', or the 'world polity' (Drori et al. 2003):

3. Preferred models of social organization arise out of the increasing awareness of an expanding world society. They centrally stress the continued expansion and penetration of formal organization throughout the world.

The studies in our book flow out of these core themes. We study a broad wave of global organizational expansion and the diffusion of specific elements that embody the modern ideology of expanded organizations. We study these issues over time, across countries, and across social sectors. In Part I, we look at the social and ideological movements of recent decades that create the groundwork for organizational expansion everywhere. Part I attends to global waves of rationalistic scientization, worldwide emphases on the competence of rather professionalized human actors, and the extraordinary modern faith in the applicability everywhere of managerial principles of governance.

Then in Part II, we pull together studies of the spread of specific components of the modern ideology of expanded organizations around the world. We look at the success of the worldwide movements for reformed accounting and for 'standards'. We analyze the global expansion of management education, 'empowering' forms of personnel training, and notions of the corporation as a social citizen. We examine the impact of modern organization theory on a sector with a millennium of built-in inertia, namely the university. In each case, we see a worldwide movement and its widespread impact on local settings.

But we do not interpret these materials as simply showing arbitrary changes in fashion. There is clear directionality here: toward the creation of expanded organizational structures and controls in a society seen as global. As the world emerges more fully as one 'place', one could imagine a single integrated controls system, something resembling a state. That clearly does not happen. What does happen is the global expansion of more lateral, webbed, and diffuse control systems, built around common ideologies. Thus we argue in this book that the outcome result is the expansion of organization. And, such organization is of a particular kind: rationalized and empowered.

These arguments and the studies in this book build on a common frame that has evolved over several decades, and through long-term scholarly interactions among our participants. There is plenty of diversity here, in topics, forms of data, and interpretations of the materials. But there is much more of a common perspective than ordinarily occurs in collections of more disparate studies.

The individual studies acknowledge specific intellectual (and sometimes funding) debts. Here, we acknowledge more collective ones—help and support, advice and criticism, over the long pull from our colleagues. We start by thanking Francisco Ramirez and the broad circle of the members of the Comparative Workshop at Stanford University. We presented most of this work, in both early and late stages, before this group and the final product benefited much from their comments and guidance. We also thank the intellectual community of Scancor (Scandinavian Consortium for Organizational Studies) and its related colleagues: Woody Powell, in particular, helped us think through this set of issues. We thank our colleagues Marie-Laure Djelic, Kerstin Sahlin-Andersson, and Marc Ventresca who, in organizing workshops to discuss neo-institutional work on global and organizational trends, inspired this project. David Frank provided insightful comments to our initial proposal. Mark Granovetter has been a friendly critic as a dissertation committee member for several of the contributors. And over many years, Nils Brunsson, James March, and W. Richard Scott have contributed a great deal to the development of our work.

Important in pulling this book project together was the sponsorship of David Musson at the Oxford University Press. David's gentle and invaluable comments help translate the ideas in the book to address its intended audience. We thank him for such guidance. We also thank Matthew Derbyshire, Tanya Dean, Lizzie Suffling, Anita Petrie, Claire Abel, and Maggi Shade of Oxford University Press for their diligent editorial work.

We thank our research assistants who labored to compile data for this work and to help edit the volume to its final shape. For such work, we thank Mark Bekheit, Eric Kramon, Barbara Barath, and Colin Beck. We also thank Stanford University's Freeman Spogli Institute for International Studies (formerly, the Stanford Institute of International Studies), and especially its director Coit Blacker, for sponsoring these students' work through S-IIS Undergraduate Research Internship over several quarters.

Last, we thank our families for bearing with us through the intense times that come with composing a challenging piece of work as this.

GSD, JWM, HH
Stanford, February 2006

Contents

Tables, Figures, and Appendices

Tables

Figures

Appendices

Abbreviations

AAU	Association of African Universities
ABAMEC	Association for Analysts of Brazilian Banks and Capital Markets
AC	anti-corruption
AIDI	Accounting Information Disclosure Index
ANSI	American National Standards Institute
ASEAN	Association of Southeast Asian Nations
ASQ	American Society for Quality
AUTM	Association of University Technology Managers
BEE	Black Economic Empowerment
CACG	Commonwealth Association for Corporate Governance
CA	collective action
CEO	chief executive officer
CIFAR	Center for Financial Analysis and Research
CR	corporate responsibility
DGQ	German Association for Quality
DIN	German Standards Institute
DOL	Department of Labor
DQS	German Society for Certification of Quality Assurance Systems
EC	European Commission
ECGI	European Corporate Governance Institute
EEC	European Economic Community
EOQC	European Organization for Quality Control
EOTC	European Organization for Testing and Certification
FEBRABAN	Brazilian Federation of Banks
FTE	full-time equivalents
GATT	General Agreement on Tariffs and Trade
GBRC	Global Business Reference Center
GCGF	Global Corporate Government Forum
GC	Global Compact
GDP	gross domestic product
GI	governance improvement
GNP	gross national product
GRECO	Group of States against Corruption to Monitor European anticorruption Convention
GRI	Global Reporting Initiative
IAOS	International Association of Official Statistics
IASC	International Accounting Standards Committee
IAUP	International Association of University Presidents

ICA	International Council for Information Technology in Government Administration
ICGN	International Corporate Governance Network
ICT	information and communications technology
IEC	International Electrotechnical Congress
IFAC	International Federation of Accountants
IGLU	Institute for University Management and Leadership
IGO	international governmental organization
ILO	International Labour Organization
IMF	International Monetary Fund
IMHE	Institutional Management in Higher Education
INGO	international nongovernmental organization
IP	intellectual property
ISO	International Standards Organization
JSE	Johannesburg Stock Exchange
KI	knowledge and information
LE	political leadership
MBA	Master of Business Administration
MBO	management by objectives
MDC	management development center
MDG	Millennium Development Goals
MNCs	multinational corporations
MNE	multinational enterprises
NAFTA	North American Free Trade Association
NBEET	National Board of Employment, Education and Training
NICs	newly industrialized countries
OECD	Organisation for Economic Cooperation and Development
PEST	political, economic, social, and technological
PUMA	public management service
R & D	research and development
SDC	Sustainable Development Committee
SDO	Standards Development Organization
SHD	sustainable human development
SMEs	small/medium-sized enterprises
SRI	socially responsible investing
SWOT	strengths, weaknesses, opportunities, and threats
TI	Transparency International
TRIPs	Trade Related Aspects of Intellectual Property agreements
UIA	Union of International Association
UNDP	United Nations Development Programme
UNESCO	United Nations Education, Science and Culture Organization
UNRISD	United Nations Research Institute for Social Development
UN	United Nations
WIPO	World Intellectual Property Organization
WTO	World Trade Organization

Introduction

Gili S. Drori, John W. Meyer, and Hokyu Hwang

The intensification of global interdependencies and the consolidation of the global as a social horizon—both captured in the now popular term *globalization*—have provided fertile ground for the creation of new organizations and the expansion of existing ones. With globalization, much human activity has spawned a growing set of universalized rules and standards. The older protective armor provided by the sovereign national state and society has weakened, so much local activity become linked into the global web of organizations and institutions. In this context, both risk and opportunity are now conceived as worldwide, and forms of behavior and action are assessed in global terms. The result has been a worldwide explosion of organizations and organizing. This book provides an analysis of how and why this expansion has happened.

The global expansion of the formal organization, the focus of this book, is generally perceived and defined in the modern social world. We, as researchers, do not impose our definition on an innocent phenomenon, decoding some components of social life as something *we* decide to call organization. Organizations as social entities, and the term *organization*, are common creatures of our time. Every imaginable social group—economic, ethnic, political, religious, educational, medical, or scientific—is likely to claim explicitly and self-consciously to be an organization. What they mean by claiming to be organizations and what they are distancing themselves from through this claim are main keys to understanding this great social movement. In modern life and usage, the core meaning of the term *organization* seems to sharply focus on the idea of *actorhood*. The organization is a collective actor, not simply a servant of some other sovereign such as a state, a profession, or an owning family. An organization in this sense is to be seen as distinct from, and in partial opposition to such traditional structures as bureaucracy, professional association, family or family firm, and perhaps other structures. Although formal organizations have existed during much of human history—universities are thought to be the oldest form of formal organizations (Clark 1998; Krücken and Meier, Chapter 10), the organization as a sovereign actor that is constructed principally on the notion of actorhood seems to be a new idea. The sheer scope and extent of this phenomenon are unique only to the contemporary, rapidly globalizing era. The theme of this book is that modern globalization—in politics, culture, and identity rather than economic (ex)change—is central to the transformation of many social entities into organized actors.

I.1. OBSERVING THE PATTERN

It is easy enough to observe instances of organizational expansion around the world. Various labels and phrases, such as *the organizational revolution* and the *rise of managerialism*, depict and capture the tenor of the general phenomenon. More specific terms may be employed in specific sectors and fields: the new public management in the public sector (Olson, Guthrie, and Humphery 1998), the relative decline of the individual practitioner in law (Heinz et al. 2001), or academic capitalism or the multiversity in higher education (Slaughter and Leslie 1997; Kerr 2001), for instance.

While the common use of the term 'expansion' means increase and spreading out, or profusion and proliferation, we distinguish among several dimensions to describe this phenomenon more accurately. First and most obviously, the number of entities calling themselves organizations is increasing dramatically. This is true in local communities and in national societies around the world: Paget (1990) describes the increase in civil society organizations in the United States; Barr et al. (2003) document the increase in NGOs in Uganda; Thomas (2004) explores the increase in cooperatives in Italy. The expansion is also occurring in international life, with an explosion of regional and global organizations and international and transnational organizations (Boli and Thomas 1997, 1999; Salamon et al. 1999; Anheier and Cunningham 2001). And as a global phenomenon this expansion is evident in the nonprofit and for-profit sectors (Boli and Thomas 1997, 1999; Chandler and Mazlich 2005, respectively), as well as the governmental and nongovernmental sectors (Diehl 1997; Boli and Thomas 1997, 1999, respectively).

Second, the social arenas that are being filled with organizations greatly multiply. Highly elaborated organizations were once found only in a few sectors linked closely to the state and church, and in a few large-scale capitalist countries. Now, the fields of education, medicine, development, and science are filled with organizations. So are communal life and groups that once had informal structures—the family, local government, ethnic community, gender and sexuality, and all sorts of recreational activities (to mention only the few examples about sexuality and culture, Frank and McEneaney 1999; Boyle 2002).

Third, increasingly formal organizational rules and elaborate role specifications penetrate extant social organizations (Edelman 1990, 1992; Dobbin et al. 1993; Sutton et al. 1994). Older safety or environmental concerns produce detailed departmental structures, as do research and development (R & D) and all sorts of personnel matters. Rights and responsibilities are organizationally defined in a highly detailed manner and describe various roles and the relationships among them, such as doctor and patient, teacher and student, employer and employee, public servant and citizen, and for that matter husband and wife. Traditional family, professional, or bureaucratic structural forms are rapidly morphing into formal, manageable, and empowered organizations.

These patterns are clear: organizations and organizing expand. We can observe our religious congregation transforming into a nonprofit organization. Similarly, our children's schools adopt performance criteria and overwhelm their procedures with the rising notion of governance. And corporations expand their core for-profit mission to add various duties such as worker's training (Luo, Chapter 9) and corporate responsibility (CR) (Shanahan and Khagram, Chapter 8). And, thus, fears about the decline of community, as in Robert's Putnam's observation (2000) about the decline of community organizing in the United States, are reinterpreted by Skocpol (2004) as simply a change in the *nature* of organizing (from members-based voluntary associations to advocacy-focused professionalized organizations) rather than a decline in volume. In these various instances, the social world is being recast as a web of organizations (Coleman 1974; Perrow 1991; Scott 2003).

The observable changes are evident in many spheres—economic, political, community—and at many levels—national, sub-national and supranational. Following are some examples that illustrate the point.

On the national level, numbers of business corporations are multiplying in countries around the world. As a good many data were collected for Organisation for Economic Cooperation and Development (OECD) countries during the 1990s, we show these as an example for this national-level trend. Figure I.1 shows the dramatic rise in the number of domestic firms in Sweden, Turkey, Holland, Hungary, and Greece in 1988–2002.[1] A similar trend of organizational expansion in the economic field is also evident for sub-national

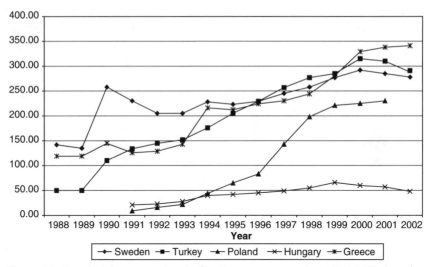

Figure I.1 Organization expansion in five European countries, 1988–2002 (number of domestic companies, in thousands)

units. Figure I.2 illustrates an equally dramatic increase in the number of corporations in the American state of California in 1960–2000.[2] And other available data show similar changes in other fields at the global level. Figure I.3 shows quantitative data on various forms of organizational units of a noneconomic nature: nation-states (a constitutive organizational form during the

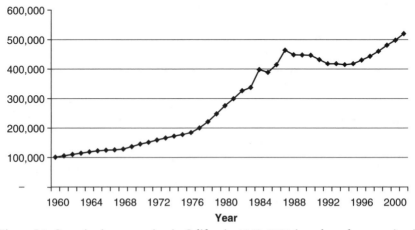

Figure I.2 Organization expansion in California, 1960–2001 (number of corporations)

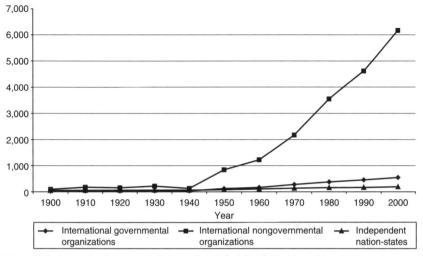

Figure I.3 Organization expansion at the global level, 1900–2000

modern era), international governmental organizations (IGOs), and international nongovernmental organizations (INGOs).[3] The intensification in global formation of international nongovernmental organizations and of international intergovernmental organizations is well documented (Carroll 1992; Boli and Thomas 1997, 1999; Diehl 1997; Salamon et al. 1999; Beckfield 2003; Roberts 2005). The works comment on the timing of the international tendency toward organizing, and show much expansion in numbers of formal organizations since the end of the nineteenth century, with a sharp acceleration after World War II. The twentieth century is also the era of the formalization of global trade in organizational terms: in the short but intense decade of the 1990s, the number of multinational corporations (MNCs) grew from about 37,000 to 63,000 in 2002 (Chandler and Mazlich 2005: 2).

Although the data are presented here for illustrative purposes only, they reveal something of the intensity of the changes. The rates of expansion are very dramatic: in California, for example, the number of registered corporations grew from 101,081,000 in 1960 to 520,056,000 in 2001. The rates of growth are even more astonishing for European countries (most probably, we will argue, a result of Europeanization). The number of listed domestic companies in Sweden grew from 142 in 1988 to 278 in 2004, doubling in fourteen years. At the margins of Europe, Turkey's numbers grew from 50 in 1988 to 288 in 2002, and Poland's from 9 in 1991 to 230 (!) in 2002. Barr et al. (2003) claim that 3,500 nongovernmental organizations were registered in Uganda alone in 2000. These cases reflect the global trend of formal organization.

Much modern organizational research calls attention to the expansion of specific types of organizations. Riddle (1989) notes the rapid postwar expansion in numbers of universities around the world. Scott et al. (2000) give a detailed account of the massive organizational crystallization in the health care field in California. Other researchers call attention to the explosive expansion of particular organizational departments and roles (e.g. Edelman 1990, 1992; Dobbin et al. 1993; Sutton et al. 1994). And others focus specifically on the corporate, for-profit world of organizations (Jones 2005; Chandler and Mazlich 2005).

The identification of the pattern is not new. Alexis de Tocqueville, in *Democracy in America*, compiled impressions of his travels in America during 1831–2, and recorded the American propensity to organize social life into associations. He traced the phenomenon, in theoretical insight that is central to this book, to the relative statelessness of nineteenth-century American society. In our discussion of the effects of modern globalized but statelessness society, we use the same imagery.

Since Tocqueville, others have documented and commented on the phenomenon of expanding formal organization in the United States (Coleman 1974, 1990; Perrow 1991), Europe (e.g. Thomas 2004), and the developing world (e.g. Barr et al. 2003). Speaking in Tocquevillian terms, Lester Salamon (1987, 1994) argues that this global 'associational revolution' is as significant today as was the rise of the nation-state several centuries ago.

In the prolific body of work documenting the dramatic expansion of formal organization, we have attempted to discuss the reasons for the expansion of formal organizations and the possible causes for the timing of the process. Most such attempts focus on particular times, places, and/or types of organizations. The common explanatory factor has been a rise in the complexity of social life during the twentieth century's period of high modernity. The intricacies of and intense demands from the modern systems of production, trade, and exchange, and more generally the complex and differentiated division of labor functionally require that the management and coordination of increasingly complex systems be modernized, rationalized, and differentiated. With the goal of enhancing system efficiency and capacity (e.g. Kerr et al. 1960), organizational modernization is seen as driven by technical requirements. Therefore, increased organizational buildup is seen as a mechanical, even if nominal, solution to problems of management and social order.

Sometimes the same story is told in a more critical vein to emphasize the way the complexity of the modern world makes organizational expansion, power, and monopoly natural outcomes. This version sometimes emphasizes the efficiency and effectiveness of the exploitive potentials of organizations, as in the Marxian tradition (Burawoy 1979, 1985). But in extreme cases, the argument can simply be, as in the old 'mass society' criticism of modernity, that modern techniques and interdependencies enable expanded exploitive capacities, efficient or not (as the discussions of the rise of the modern state in Tilly 1990).

The conventional explanations of organizational expansion in terms of expanded social complexity leave open many questions. Why does expansion occur in countries, regions, and social sectors that seem not to have much changed in complexity? For instance, does the modern religious congregation really face an expanded set of technical tasks requiring many offices and committees? How about the modern elementary school and district? or, the modern medical practice? Or the government of a developing country built around an elementary economy? Our work in this book addresses these issues. First, we describe the features of the global organization trend as cultural phenomena. Second, we suggest that it is cultural forces in particular that accelerate the rate of organization and propel it worldwide.

I.2. THE EXPLANATORY PROBLEM

Explanations of the expansion of organization in the modern period, whether they focus on the general expansion or on specific types of organizations or organizational components, tend to emphasize globalization as a causal factor. It often takes little theoretical creativity to suggest such explanations, since organizers and organizations themselves commonly make the case at the top of their voices. So reformers who propose to transform a traditional firm into an organization routinely invoke globalization and its competitive pressures as justification. More surprisingly, so do reformers who want to turn schools and universities, or government agencies, or hospitals into 'real' organizations. The underlying idea is that some sort of direct or indirect global competitive pressures require change.

This emphasis on intensified exchange and competition is common in various conceptions of globalization. Social scientists routinely invoke the nation-state, the multinational corporation, or the nongovernmental association and describe globalization as intensification of exchange and competition among them (most bluntly in the work of such political scientists as Robert Koehane and Joseph Nye Jr. 2000). Many scholars of globalization have long relied on the imagery of a world of competing social units. They define globalization as the intensifying exchanges among social units, or *transference*, as termed by Jens Bertelson (2000). Further, they do so with very little attention to collective structure or culture.

Conceptions of globalization as intensified exchange and competition—always economic, sometimes also military—treat the expansion of organizational structure as functionally necessitated by competitive pressures. The implication is that more highly organized units proliferate in response to increased demands from a rapidly modernizing competitive context that poses a variety of functional problems. In describing the role, if not utility, of international organizations, Kenneth Abbot and Duncan Snidal argue,

[International organizations] allow for the centralization of collective activities through a concrete and stable organizational structure and a supportive administrative apparatus. These increase the efficiency of collective activities and enhance the organization's ability to affect the understandings, environment, and interests of states (1998: 5).

In other words, organizations proliferate because proliferation is required by considerations of efficiency and effectiveness in a complex and competitive global context. Organization, thus, is the natural outcome of complex and modern global competition.

These functional accounts are fiercely debated and realists like those mentioned are sometimes challenged. Most vocally, neo-Marxists challenge the notion of functional need by recasting it as capitalist interests: it is capitalist and class considerations, they argue, that expand the reaches of organizations because those are molded to serve the perpetuation of existing power structures (Wallerstein 2000; Sklair 2001). Such critics expect organizational expansion to correspond with a growth in capacity and complexity. Hence, from this critical viewpoint, the globalization of organizations is expected to correspond with the global reach of capitalist economy. In this sense, several scholarly traditions—realist, neoliberal, and neo-Marxist—share the expectation that the expansion (in numbers and in global reach) of organizations corresponds with intensifying complexity and modernization of social systems.

But these expectations are obviously challenged by empirical observations. The pattern of expansion does not seem to be related to any comparable increase in the complexity of social life. Hence, while classic sociological theories of change would lead to the expectation that organizational proliferation is related to an increase in social complexity, modernization, or demands for modern management, these expected causal relations are not confirmed by what we know about this era. Rather, the rate of organization far exceeds the rate of growth in the fields that we would regard as demonstrating need or complexity.

Again, for illustrative purposes, we chart some data on organizational expansion on measures of increased demand or modernization—the size of the population and the volume of economic activity in terms of gross domestic product (GDP). The expectation is rather simply put: we investigate whether organizational expansion is related to an increase in the complexity of our life (*a*) because there are more of us (population; Ehrlich 1971) and it is easier to manage us through organizations, or (*b*) because we operate economically in a more complex way (produce more) and thus need more structure and organization in our lives. For these illustrative purposes, Figure I.4 displays global-level data, Figure I.5 displays several national-level data, and Figure I.6 displays California data. These charts show that there is little relationship between the rates of growth in the number of organizations, economic production, and population size. We recalibrated the data so that they are scaled by their state in year of origin to allow a comparison of data from various scales onto the same 'map'. The charts show that in most cases the rate of organization far exceeds the rates of growth in both simple measures of demand or needs.[4]

The pattern is rather compelling: in all social units reviewed here—global, national, or sub-national—the rate of change in organization is higher than the rates of social change in modernization- or complexity-related functions. If indeed the growth in organization is not related to increased modernity or intensifying complexity, what would explain this worldwide tendency? Why would the proliferation of organizational units outpace the expansion of other measures of expanding social life? And, specifically, why would organizational proliferation increase at a more rapid rate than those of the factors that we

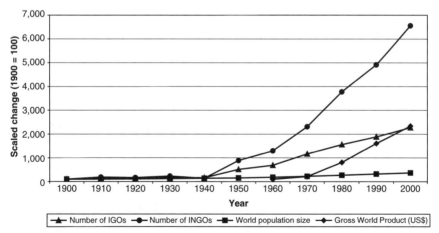

Figure I.4 Organization expansion compared with economic and population growth at the global level, 1900–2000 (IGOs and INGOs vs. World Pop and Gross World Product (US$))

commonly think of as their causes such as growth in the size of our economic
capacity or the size of the public market they serve.

This is more than a disagreement on the interpretation of empirical patterns, or even on the measurement of global trends. Rather, the debate extends
to the conception of modern globalization. The data imply that the expansion
of organizational forms is not merely an economic matter, in contrast with the
essentially economistic conception of globalization (as argued by, e.g.
Chase-Dunn 1998; Wallerstein 2000; Sklair 2001; Jones 2005). The overall
data also show that organizational expansion is not experienced only in
particular economic or political sectors, since many types of organizations
grow and grow in under many conditions.

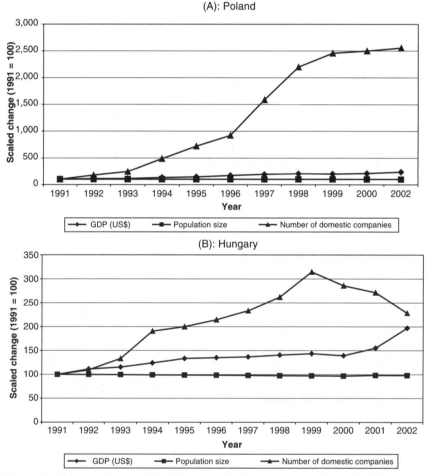

Figure I.5 Organization expansion compared with economic and population growth
at four European countries, 1988–2000

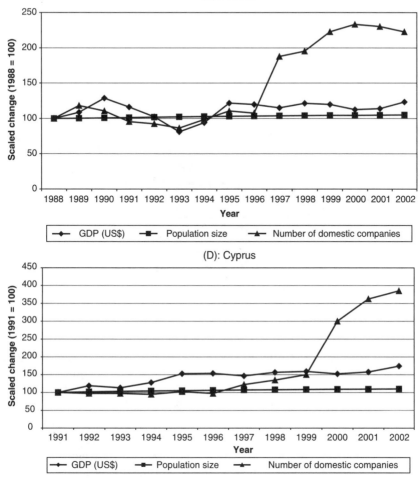

Figure I.5 (*continued*)

The problem is easier to solve if we envision modern globalization as a broadly cultural and political process (Appadurai 1996; Giddens 2000; Ritzer 2004*a*). Globalization is a multifaceted process whose essence extends beyond the economic, rational, and proactive rationales that are often used to define and explain it. Globalization involves the diffusion of cultural practices and commodities—from consumption of media like TV programs and Hollywood movies to norms like human rights and environmentalism. In its modern

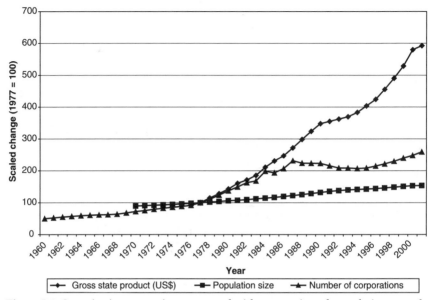

Figure I.6 Organization expansion compared with economic and population growth in California, 1960–2001 (Number of corporations with Gross State Product and population)

form, we argue, globalization provides cultural ideologies and legitimization, demanding and facilitating the organizational reconstruction of much social life.

This approach to globalization defines our explanation of its relationship with the trend of organization. This book is devoted to (*a*) explaining the primarily cultural and global forces that compel this tendency toward formal organization and (*b*) describing the features of this worldwide tendency toward formal organization. We argue that the nature of globalization is such as to encourage these tendencies toward formal organizations.

I.3. THE CAUSAL FACTORS

We see three particular features of globalization as fueling the modern pattern of expanded organization: (*a*) the rise of the global as the relevant social horizon, (*b*) rationalization and standardization processes, reinforced through the expanding globalized institutions of science and expertise, and (*c*) a culture of actorhood and empowerment, carried by the rapidly expanding and globalized educational institutions. These dimensions of globalization, we argue, create a real or imagined society on a world scale, calling for organizational mobilization at lower levels. They also undercut many older forms of social organization that were rooted in the boundedness and sovereignty of the world's nation-states that once held a monopoly of legitimate authority.

(a) The emergence of the term 'globalization' describes global processes as unitary, sweeping, and continual (Guillén 2001). The related notion that society is global—rather than national, ethnic, or familial—is new. In earlier periods of expansion of global exchange, the boundaries of perceived society corresponded to national or religious boundaries (as in 'American society' or 'Western society'). In the later part of the twentieth century, the relevant social horizon came to encompass the globe. Trade, social welfare, and violence are now assessed and measured globally (Hwang, Chapter 3), and are calculated in terms of the needs and problems of people across the globe. Conceptions of world society and world culture, much like global trade and international diplomacy before them, have come to describe the current scope of social affairs (Meyer et al. 1997; Drori 2005).

It is all a matter of high awareness, with massive quantities of the literature calling attention to globalization. Much of this discussion sees globalization as economic in character, and the sense that the world is dominated by expanded trade and investment is part of the colloquial meaning of the term *globalization* (see, e.g. Ohmae 1990 for an academic analysis as well as Wolf 2004 for essay-like statement). Broader conceptions of globalization call attention to expanded political and social networks of organizations (Held and McGrew 1999, 2002a, 2002b; Axford and Huggins 2000). But there is also an extended awareness—central to the arguments of this book—that globalization is a cultural and social matter of a broader sort (Meyer et al. 1997; Drori et al. 2003, portraying a world society view, as well as other emphases on the cultural qualities of globalization in Appadurai 1996; Castells 1996–98). In fact, even the most narrowly economistic analyses reinforce the point: in celebrating or decrying the broad and global changes that are required to adapt to the brave new economic world, they also dramatically assert these conditions. And even these narrowly economistic views clearly undercut any notion that the nation-state itself can autonomously sustain more traditional organizational forms.

(b) Increasingly, world society has emerged and has been recognized as a primary locus of rationalization (Meyer 1987). Rationalization refers to

(1) continuing efforts to systematize social life around standardized rules and schemes that explicitly differentiate and then seek to link means and ends; (2) the ongoing reconstruction of all social organization—both social activities and social actors, ... as means for the pursuit of collective purposes, these purposes themselves subject to increasing systematization (Jepperson 2002a: 257).

The global expansion of science and scientized knowledge systems as social and cultural institutions greatly accelerates rationalization, constructing new social domains for responsible and empowered human actorhood.

Rationalization builds legitimate arenas for organizing and formal organization (Drori et al. 2003; Meyer and Drori, Chapter 2). In this sense, rationalization creates, on a global scale, both 'new organizational elements, and new social nodes around which formal organizations can form' (Jepperson 2002*a*: 234). It also undercuts the realities and mythologies of national cultural uniqueness on which so many older social organizational forms depended: once something like medical practice becomes rationalized on universalistic and scientific bases, it is difficult to sustain professional and organizational forms devoted to 'Swedish medicine' or 'American medicine'.

(c) While rationalization opens up new social frontiers to be organized, empowered 'actors' are mobilized to pursue their 'interests' (Meyer and Jepperson 2000). Actorhood is 'the principle that social life is built up of actors— human individuals, organizations, and national states with valid interests that others are to respect, and with the capacity (i.e. agency) to validly represent those interests in activity' (Meyer and Jepperson 2000; Drori et al. 2003: 30 also express this idea). In today's world, with the rise of the global as a relevant social horizon, individual actorhood—and as a corollary, organizations as free association among empowered individuals—takes on added significance. The acephalous character of the modern global polity and the rise of a global human rights movement contribute to the expansion of both individual and organizational actorhood. Empowered individuals, associations, and polities reconstructed as agentic human actors are to solve the problems of a world perceived as a risk society. Naturally, revolutions of organizational expansion follow.

These three features of globalization, both cultural and structural in character, imprint concrete institutions, practices, and behaviors. A great world society is commonly perceived as a central locus of our activity. It is filled with rationalization—scientific and professional principles apply everywhere. And it is filled with people and groups perceived to possess the rights and capacity to mobilize and act authoritatively and effectively and in large-scale terms. In this way, global culture manifests itself in expanded organization, and also in the defining features of what we, in common with contemporary global discourse, call organizations. And in the same sense, much of the sovereignty and legitimacy of older national and local cultures are undercut so that their capacity to sustain more traditional organizational forms is weakened.

I.4. THE FEATURES OF MODERN ORGANIZATION

The nature of globalization affects the shape of the organizational forms that so fiercely expand and proliferate, while creating the social forms that we now call 'organizations', and undercutting older forms (like 'bureaucracy'). There is much scholarly agreement that formal structures dramatically changed by the end of the twentieth century. Works documenting the changes and explaining their nature have focused on corporations (the various contributions to DiMaggio 2001) and political regimes (Huntington 1991; various contributions to Diamond and Plattner 2001). It is common to describe such changes as fundamental, breaking from earlier patterns of organization and behavior. Powell, for example, in his assessment of the change in the design of corporations and thus in the landscape of labor (2001), highlights the following changed features: networking rather than hierarchical structure, experimentation and learning rather than command structures, cross-sector and cross-firm fertilization rather than innate expertise, and flexibility rather than career trajectory. 'What is apparent', concludes Powell (2001: 68), 'is how rapidly the social technology of organizing work had changed'.

Spelling out the dimensions especially distinctive to the modern conception of *organization* is in a sense a focus of this book as a whole. Here we indicate the general field of view.

The contemporary organization carries on several properties in common with the older organizational forms that managed collective activities in earlier periods. In common with the old family enterprise, the modern organization has boundaries characteristic of ownership, and a concentration of decision-making authority that comes under the general heading of unified sovereignty. Along with traditional professional organizations in education, medicine, religion, and law, the modern organization has some clearly defined, certified, and empowered personnel. In common with classic bureaucracies, the modern organization shares a good deal. Roles and relationships tend to be formalized—articulated explicitly, and often in written form. They tend to be universalistic—organized around general principles. And they tend to be rationalized—built around explicit causal theories of what is to happen. The rationalization describes both means–ends relationships, or how purposes are to be achieved, and a control system, or how local activities are ultimately under the control of organizational sovereignty.

The modern organization is, however, distinguished from all its predecessor forms in a number of respects. (*a*) The degree and scope of rationalization in the modern organization are much greater than in the traditional bureaucratic form. A wide variety of activities and issues, such as the environment, innovation, safety, personnel matters, all sorts of operational details, and funding flows, are brought under at least nominal organizational control, with specified responsibilities and powers. Explicit descriptions of how these responsibilities will be carried out are incorporated. Both the detailed control of the organization as sovereign, and the numbers and ranges of causal processes over which this control is to be exercised expand greatly. (*b*) The degree and scope of personnel professionalism in the modern organization vastly exceed those of the traditional professional organization. All sorts of people, not just the core professionals, are educated, trained, and credentialed. They are explicitly thought to be capable of exercising discretion on behalf of the organization. Responsibilities are also much greater—modern personnel are thought to be capable of all sorts of judgments. (*c*) Sovereignty and authority are much more widely distributed in the modern organization than in the traditional family firm or bureaucracy. There is a great deal of 'management' inside the modern organization; many of the personnel— sometimes all of them—are part of what could be called management. And, Westphalian sovereignty (including current infringements on its principle of nonintervention, as in having jurisprudence transcend borders) is enjoyed today not only by states but also extended to international and transnational organizations. For this goal of sovereignty, organizations wear the protective armor of rationalization and formalization.

Thus, the modern organization is highly rationalized, formalized, and coordinated around unified sovereignty, but in a way that would once have seemed odd. The organizational members are to participate actively in the rationalization and formalization of the organization and are to help make the organization dynamic, adaptive, innovative, and so on. They are not relatively inert agents of an external sovereign or role specification. But they do so as sovereign actors with rights and responsibilities. Actorhood not just of the organization, but everybody in it, it seems, is the most central feature of the modern organization.

The contrast with the classic conception of bureaucracy elaborated by Max Weber may be especially useful. Beyond Weberian structural prerequisites of explicit and predictable rules, roles, and imperative authority, the modern organization has a whole set of new standards of appropriateness. And these standards can undercut elements of the old ones. The new standards of appropriateness are built around professionalized or scientific knowledge, the expanded human rights, capacities of participants, and principles of rationality. In this sense, today's organizations control their own formalization and rationalization, with clear marks of transcended boundaries: corporations engage in socially responsible initiatives, while nonprofit organizations hire professional managers to manage their community-based affairs (Powell, Gammal, and Simard 2005); and neither one of these archetypes is bureaucratic in the traditional sense. Social interaction becomes less explicitly formal: teamwork is encouraged, social events are routine, and the organization often takes on itself a friendly mascot in addition to its logo. The informality of the formerly formal organization often takes the structure of 'soft' rule-making; emphasis on the naturalness of rules and procedures and on their voluntary nature permits the organization to take a less formal and explicit forms.

Prevalent approaches to the transformation of modern organization regard expansion and change as a response to functional needs or requirements that are driven by specific (and growing) uncertainties in particular social conditions. In this book, we focus instead on the institutionalization of modern organization itself as an abstract and deeply cultural form. It is the cultural standing of this form as a social institution rather than as a solution mechanism that accounts for its ubiquity in the contemporary world. In other words, expanded organization, on its various forms and with its various features, appears in environments whose functional needs and complexities are clearly not the main driving forces behind modernization.

Several recent scholarly projects have emphasized the nontechnical aspects of the globalization of management: example are the volumes edited by Sahlin-Andersson and Engwall (2002), Djelic and Quack (2003), and Sahlin-Andersson and Djelic (2006). These impressive scholarly collections emphasize the carriers: namely, the actors who carry the message of the rationalization of cultural themes and the social groups (mostly professional) that serve as agents in the globalization of managerial rationalization. They thus focus on the network connections among groups as the conduits through which the notions diffuse worldwide. Our work develops this line of argumentation further and focus specifically on the cultural themes themselves, as they are advanced by professional groups and associations. The most important issue, we think, rests with the cognitive and normative background to the global processes of organizing rather than with the actors that carry the message. Without a mooring in the cultural sea of world society, it is not obvious why rationalizing organizational reforms has such strength worldwide. The advocacy and efficacy of standardization rest on the cultural foundations of scientization and rationalization, and the advocacy of formalization rests on modern agency and personhood.

In summary, modern conceptions of markets and social action, as organized on a global scale, have produced the rapid and worldwide diffusion of formal organization. Activity is seen in terms of very general norms, and the traditional buffering provided by local (national) states and other institutions is weakened. There are now global prescriptions on a great variety of issues, from how to structure and manage a national economy to what to teach school-age children, and to how to define a family. The global system is a rationalistic one, and expanded formal organization is the standard response. This volume centers on the phenomenon of formal organization, discussing its roots and exploring its various dimensions.

I.5. PREVIEW OF CHAPTERS

This book has two main parts. Part I examines the aspects of globalization that fuel the global proliferation of formal organization. Part II offers illustrative descriptions of the features of this tendency of formal organization.

Part I begins with a comprehensive review of the abstract argument. In Chapter 1, we set out the general theoretical arguments underlying all our studies. Modern globalization is perceived as having a number of dimensions. Actual international interdependencies expand, and so do worldwide perceptions of interdependence. Older local and national structures that provided buffering from global forces are weakened in the face of a rationalized world culture. Nature is scientized to an extraordinary degree, and the analyses involved are brought into human life through expanded education. Universal law-like principles of human rights expand, transcending local memberships and cultural principles. As a result, there is an explosion in the rationalized formal organization of human activity, and models of such organizations sweep around the world in waves. Organization expands on many dimensions: managerialized principles of governance, elaborated accounting of resources, rationalized forms of personnel counting and selection and training, and detailed measurement of achievements. Organization grows in many new domains: schools and universities become 'organizations' as do hospitals and traditional governmental bureaucracies and traditional production systems. Organizational numbers and scale grow, and rationalization is endemic.

Building on this foundation, we add discussions of several key features of the global culture that carries formal organization. In Chapter 2, Gili Drori and John Meyer pose scientization as a major change in the modern global environment that produces the rise and rationalistic elaboration of formal organizing. Science globalizes activity, spreading a rationalizing logic. Linked to greatly expanded educational systems, this logic makes organizing both more necessary and much easier. And because modern scientific and educational expansions cover great proportions of modern populations, they change the character of organizations, moving them from the classic hierarchical bureaucracies of early modern states and industries to the 'complex organizations' of the contemporary world. In this sense, the scientization of the world (*a*) sets the parameters for organizing and (*b*) shapes the actors who are to take an active role in organizing.

Also central to the culture of globalization is the rise of a modern mode of management. We devote two chapters to two components—planning and governance—since they directly link with organizations. In Chapter 3, Hokyu Hwang observes that for most of the second half of the twentieth century, state planning was the dominant model of national development. Under globalization, however, the idea of a sovereign and autonomous planning state has declined. This decline has been accompanied by both upward and downward shifts in development planning away from the state. The upward shift recasts cognitive frames of development from the national to the world stage; and the world is increasingly depicted as an 'imagined community' in Anderson's terms (1991), reflected in the emergence of world level data that construct the world as an integrated collectivity. Shifting downward is the locus of planning: sub-state level entities are constructed as rational actors or organizations. Government agencies become autonomous organizations as in the new public finance management, and organizations become more and more the locus of planning and strategy. In short, globalization weakens the authority of the state, creates worldwide cognitive frames, and builds up sub-state level entitles as legitimate actors and organizations.

In Chapter 4, Gili Drori posits that although curbing corruption was long a policy focus, a more generalized and global concern with 'governance' emerged in the 1990s. Rationalized forms of governance and organizational 'actorhood' (in both the public and the private sectors) are emphasized. Global concern with corruption has increased, and governance has emerged as a solid global field of action with a web of transnational organizations and national agencies. Particular notions of governance are advanced by the work of these transnational organizations, carrying themes of actorhood and efficiency. With the weakened capacity of states and societies to resist global pressures for standard governance, waves of reform sweep the world.

Chapters 1 through 4, then, form a base for the contributions in Part II. Together, these first four chapters illustrate the central dynamics and impact of the globalization of modern organizations. The chapters in Part II, in turn, highlight particular aspects of modern organizational life in particular sectors.

In Chapter 5, Hyeyoung Moon and Christine Min Wotipka analyze (*a*) the global rise of professional management education as manifested by business schools and the Masters of Business Administration (MBA) and its global model of organizational actorhood and (*b*) the resultant legitimization of rational formal organization as a standard and universal format. The chapter focuses on the worldwide spread of business education in general and the MBA in particular, as increasingly seen as necessary for the administration of private corporations and public agencies, for-profit and not-for-profit businesses, large and small organizations.

In Chapter 6, Peter Mendel focuses on the legitimizing and standardizing machinery of global standards. First, this chapter describes the development of the ISO 9000 standards and the construction of a formal accreditation system from the confluence of two globalizing movements—global managerial culture and pressures for international standardization. Second, the chapter presents an analysis of the diffusion of ISO 9000 certificates in 129 countries from 1992 to 1998. The chapter substantiates the role of global managerial culture in stimulating general demand for organizational reforms. At the same time, the findings underscore the impact of national contexts—in particular, political cultures and styles of rationality—in mediating the diffusion of organizational ideas and practices, with notable differences between developed and developing countries. The influence of European integration and the effect of a country's role within the world system on organizational adoption of reforms also demonstrate the necessity of placing global managerial culture within the context of a wider and already expanding world polity.

In Chapter 7, Yong Suk Jang focuses on the global expansion of modern accounting as a dimension of expanded organizational rationality. Accounting is far more than a technical device, and it is deeply embedded in world cultural and institutional environments. With data on a large, cross-national sample of organizations, the chapter documents the global increase in organizational conformity to the norm of expansive accountability and examines how models of accountability and transparency flow from nation-states and world society to organizations. The chapter presents analyses of the factors that encourage the worldwide spread of transparent accounting—economic, political, cultural, and organizational globalization.

In Chapter 8, Suzanne Shanahan and Sanjeev Khagram observe that talk of CR can now be found almost everywhere. Relevant policies and practices are, however, highly variable, as might be expected with any globalizing institution. Corporate responsibility is the subject of popular discourse, state policy debate, strategizing in firms, and activist mobilization. In the abstract, however, a set of baseline responsibilities is emerging, to which companies are increasingly thought to be accountable, and CR is depicted more and more as a constituitive feature of contemporary business. The chapter examines dramatic geographical, sectoral and firm-level variations in philosophies, policies, and practices within the broad umbrella of CR. Firm practices depend on a mix of transnational embeddedness, state–business–society relations, sectoral reputation, firm ideology, and local mobilization.

In Chapter 9, Xiaowei Luo analyzes the worldwide development and spread of a 'human resources' culture. Historically, formal training programs took the form of apprenticeships or vocational education. The new model of in-house human resource development that emerged after World War II supports the features of professional management, of participatory and empowered individuals, and of organizational actorhood. This new model of formal training now extends worldwide in an abstract model of human resource development and is related to rising ideas about the rationalization of management and governance. Moreover, the management consulting industry has played an important role in the globalization of the regime of human resource development.

In Chapter 10, Georg Krücken and Frank Meier explore the particular case of the university and focus on its transformation into an organizational actor. Traditionally, universities are described in two distinct ways. First, they are seen as embedded in highly variable national systems. Second, universities were distinguished from other organizations because of their lack of a coherent organizational structure. Both characteristics have come under increasing pressure over the last few years. Globalization forces seem to erode distinct national systems and give way to new, more uniform concepts of organizational actorhood. And increasingly, universities emulate models originating in other organizational domains, most notably in business organizations. Thus, universities are now expected to demonstrate strong leadership, professionalize management, and incorporate accountability and efficiency criteria in their routine administrative procedures. They are also expected to design and propagate clear-cut profiles; and formulate explicit goals and mission statements. It is an open question whether universities only ritually adopt new and globally diffusing concepts and models stressing their actorhood, whether they are making fundamental changes in their institutional identities and actual organizational practices.

To conclude the volume, we summarize the findings and highlight paths for future work in the field of organizations and globalization. We show that in the various contributions to this volume, a single theme emerges: globalization produces a world of agentic, empowered, rationalized, standardized, and professionally managed organizations. These organizations not only share a form of operation but also ideologies of sovereignty and actorhood. We note that the rise of culturally defined standardized organizational forms on a worldwide scale, and the highly elaborated forms of organizations involved, is often criticized as embodying a new controlling human Leviathan—as in Weber's fears of an 'iron cage'. Our own arguments do not lead in this direction. Modern organizational forms are embedded in cultural understandings as much as is concentrated power. And modern organizational forms, however rationalized, involve the most elaborate controls over the degree of their control over social life. Seen macroscopically, there is a great deal of irrationality in the rationalization of the modern system.

NOTES

1. Data on the total number of listed domestic companies were compiled from the World Bank, World Development Indicators (WDI) database.
2. Data on the total number of listed corporations were compiled from the State of California's Franchise Tax Board, Economic and Statistical Research Bureau.
3. Data on the total number of IGO and INGO were compiled from UIA (2002), Figure 5.1.1.
4. World population data were compiled from US Census Bureau, International Database; world GDP, national GDP, and national population data were compiled from WDI database; data on California's gross state product and population were compiled from RAND Corporation's files.

Part I

Globalization and Expanded Models of the Organized Actor

1

World Society and the Proliferation of Formal Organization

John W. Meyer, Gili S. Drori, and Hokyu Hwang

> Americans of all ages, all conditions, and all dispositions constantly form associations. They have not only commercial and manufacturing companies, in which all take part, but associations of a thousand other kinds, religious, moral, serious, futile, general or restricted, enormous or diminutive.
>
> Alexis de Tocqueville, *Democracy in America* (1836, Volume 2, Chapter V)

Alexis de Toqueville, in his commentary on nineteenth-century America, noted the tendency of Americans toward the organizational structuring of social life (1969 [1836]). Today, this tendency is shared across societies worldwide, and for some of the same reasons that mobilized American society over two centuries ago. The core thesis of this book is that main dimensions of what came to be codified in the term 'globalization' promote formalized associations or organizations. In the current period, images and realities of a world society arise and intensify so that it becomes more and more routine to discuss social life in a global frame rather than a national or local one. In addition, dominant social orientations value formal and rationalized arrangements, infusing them with a sense of empowerment. As a result, schools, hospitals, charitable enterprises, business firms, and government agencies are seen in light of global standards calling for expanded formal and agentic organization. In this modern context, the term 'organization' takes on distinctive meaning: bounded, rationalized, purposive, and differentiated structures, with elements of sovereignty as autonomous actors (Brunsson and Sahlin-Andersson 2000).

Globalization is a cultural process that extends beyond the actual expansion and intensification of worldwide interdependencies. It encourages the structuring of social life around expanded modern models of organization in two ways. On the one hand, globalization has weakened the meaning and legitimacy of older solidarities upon which more traditional collective entities relied. In the new vision, the sovereignty and boundaries of older national and state structures attenuate, along with classic bureaucracies, established professional structures, or family firms that depended on national society. The emergent global cosmopolitan world is a stateless society, in which networks of purposive organizations, rather than a centralized authority structure, coordinate and manage activities.

On the other hand, new forms of identity, based on an imagined world society (Drori 2005), come into cultural dominance. An expanded notion of the capacities and rights of human persons spreads, along with the idea that these rights and capacities are universal and provide a basis for global solidarity (Ramirez and Meyer 2002; Lauren 2003). Similarly, expanded scientized pictures of a universal and lawful nature in which these humans live and act spread around the world and provide common global frames and rules governing action (Drori et al. 2003). Finally, there is an expanded sense that humans, informed about the rules of nature, can find rational bases for cooperative and collective action to address their problems (Meyer and Jepperson 2000). These rational bases are understood to have a universalistic character. They are objectively true, and true everywhere, so that it is possible to prescribe rational organizational forms even in unfamiliar or distant contexts (Meyer 2002). Associated with this trend is a sharp rise and expansion in the world's educational systems, specifically in the social sciences that define the collective rationalities of action (Wong 1991; Drori and Moon forthcoming; Frank and Gabler forthcoming).

The product of these broad changes—both the weakening of the traditionally bounded nation-state and the strengthening of a universalistic cosmopolitan world—has been an explosion of contemporary structuration (Giddens 1984; Turner 1991) around the conception of an organization as a core social 'actor' (Brunsson and Sahlin-Andersson 2000). Older structures are transformed; thus, firms, schools, hospitals, and government agencies become organizations. Organizations arise in the interstices that were informally arranged, and familial, ethnic, or loose working arrangements are now recast into the framework of the modern organization. And organizations develop in areas not previously structured at all, as with many aspects of international life now activated by associations (Boli and Thomas 1997, 1999). Further, newly emerging social concerns, such as environmental issues or digital divides, become structured in this formal and organized way from their inception (Frank et al. 1999; Drori 2005).

In this chapter, we develop the argument that the rise of a self-conscious(ly) global society is a main source of the contemporary organizational revolution. This society creates a cultural field or 'safe' environment (Drori and Meyer, Chapter 2) in which modern formal organizations can readily form, prosper, and expand in numbers and functions. And it creates a highly analyzed and analyzable environment, in which formal organizing becomes a necessary obligation. In pursuing of this matter, we first discuss (Section 1.1) the evolving conceptions of the forces that produce and define 'organizations' in modern organizational theory. After discussing recent theoretical orientations, we discuss (Section 1.2) the nature of modern globalization, deriving our arguments from the conceptions of world society as a highly cultural enterprise. We then review (Section 1.3) the substance of the global cultural field that arises in this world society and (Section 1.4) the ways in which globalization and its cultural field facilitate organization-building in the modern vein. Finally, we consider (Section 1.5) the transformed qualities of the proper modern organization that arises in this new context—the definition of 'organization' that results and contrasts with older forms of formalized structure.

1.1. THEORIES OF THE RISE AND NATURE OF ORGANIZATIONS

Most modern thinking about organizations can, with a little effort, be traced back to Max Weber's writing on the economy and bureaucracy (1968/1924). This is often a way for modern theorists to legitimate their ideas. But the great scholar was of several minds in understanding the rise of modern formalized organizational structure. Different lines of modern organization theory are rooted in different 'versions' of Weber.

In the optimistic postwar period from which all modern organizational theory emerged, rationalized organizational structure was seen as, for better or worse, a 'higher' form of structuring of social activity (see Scott 1998 for a review). Long-term competitive evolution and increasing socio-technical complexity demanded more and more rationalization and standardization. Organization thus arises and dominates because it is a more efficient and effective way to produce and control important activities. From this point of view, organizations are very real and muscular technical enterprises: sharply bounded from their environments, tightly controlled and coordinated, and driven by logics of efficiency. The high form of this vision, of a closed and stable system, is impressively laid out in Thompson (1967), relying on features of scientific management (Taylor 1911), mechanistic operations (Burns and Stalker 1961), goal-directed systems (Pfeffer 1982), and obviously Weber's conception of bureaucracy. The 'society of organizations' may not be desirable or attractive (Coleman 1975; Perrow 1986), and Weber had worries that humanity was coming under the control of an 'iron cage' (DiMaggio and Powell 1983). Nevertheless, it is an inevitable consequence of progress. Complementing this view of organizations is a particular perspective on globalization. From this viewpoint, globalization is seen as mostly economic, though the same perspective could see past changes as driven more by political and military competition. Modern globalization expands organization, as a mode of operation, because of the increasing complexity and scale of economic, technical, and political interdependencies (e.g. Blau 1970; Perrow 1970, 2002; Blau and Schoenherr 1971). Organizations expand where these interdependencies strike, not elsewhere.

More recently, organizational theory has been dramatically transformed by lines of argument which de-emphasize pictures of organizations as naturally evolving from the pressures of technical complexity, and as tightly coherent enterprises designed for this sort of competition (see Scott 2003). Organizations, in this newer view, are deeply interdependent with, and constructed in, social and cultural environments. This draws on Weber's alternative vision of the organization as devolving from broad Western sociocultural rationalization, and of formal organization as an ideological project as much as a means to coordinate work. Environments create political and social resource pressures which build organizations quite apart from efficiency considerations (Pfeffer and Salancik 1978; Freeland 2001; see review in Fligstein and Freeland 1995). They give advantages to some organizational forms and stigmatize others (Hannan and Freeman 1989; Carroll and Hannan 1999). And above everything else, they create cultural forms and meanings that make organization seem the natural and legitimate way to do almost everything (Meyer and Rowan 1977; DiMaggio and Powell 1983; March and Olsen 1989). From this point of view, organizations may not be so tightly controlled, bounded from environments, or muscularly efficient. Indeed, they may be built up to such an extent that they lack much internal coherence, and are often 'loosely coupled' (March and Olsen 1976; Weick 1976; Meyer and Rowan 1977).

The arguments in this book follow from this latter line of reasoning in modern organization theory. In the version employed here, the underlying ideas are called sociological institutional (or neo-institutional) theory (Powell and DiMaggio 1991; Scott 2000; Jepperson 2002a; Hasse and Krücken 2005). In this line of theory, globalization is seen to have a strongly cultural component, and the rise of modern organization is an incorporative response to the cultural models of the wider environments.

It should be stressed that the issues involved here, in the contests among organizational theories, are not only theoretical. At issue are different pictures of what modern organizations tend generally to be like: in the view taken in this book, they are often elaborated and ritualized, and they are framed as fashionable assemblies of rationalized stories or myths institutionalized in their environments. Also at issue are different pictures of where and how these organizations form: in our view, they are found as much where the environmental myths of rationalization penetrate as where actual interdependencies do. One such overriding modern myth, impacting viewpoints on organizations and their proliferation, is about globalization.

1.2. MEANINGS OF GLOBALIZATION: THE CULTURE OF INTERDEPENDENCIES

In colloquial and polemic discussions, globalization has a clear core meaning. The idea, conveyed in both 'popular' literature (Wolf 2004; Friedman 2005) and scholarly work (Beck 2000; Giddens 2003; Ritzer 2004*a*, 2004*b*), is that local people and activities, in any particular setting, are increasingly affected by events that are distant and large in scale. Mostly, this idea envisions local dependence on long-distance economic transactions (Chase-Dunn 1998; Keohane and Nye 2000). And so modern social, political, and cultural globalizers often claim to be 'anti-globalization', meaning that they are proponents of global control over economic power (Mander and Goldsmith 1996; Houtart and Polet 2001; Bhagwati 2002).

Further, there is the notion that globalized economic transactions can occur in great waves, or traumatic shocks, and that these cycles can overwhelm and destabilize local customs and traditions (Wallerstein 2000). The long-distance transactions have something of an arbitrary or unpredictable quality—much like powerful natural disasters. Human societies, the overall story has it, are increasingly exposed to high and potentially dangerous uncertainty: we live in a 'risk society' (Beck 1992) and social crises of this era are global (Ritzer 2004*a*).

There are variations on the core story. Perhaps the great world economic forces that beset particular societies with uncertainty are not arbitrary, but are controlled by problematic world powers (Chase-Dunn 1998; Wallerstein 2000; Went 2003). The forces of world capitalism, or specifically the interests of some dominant powers (Sklair 2001), lead to decisions that overpower weaker and more peripheral societies. In this account, there remains massive uncertainty or risk at the bottom of the world stratification systems, though it is produced by more order and certainty in the boardrooms at the top.

Chaotic and two-tiered globalization, of the sort depicted in these accounts, is very far from the reality of modern world society. If it were the dominant strand, indeed, we would find a very different set of organizational outcomes than what we observe in empirical reality. Societies shattered by massive random events, or controlled events perceived as random and arbitrary, would react with defensive retreat and prayer, not organizational assertions. The tone of social action would be that of subdued submission rather than empowered claims. Organizations, most modern theories have it, arise in response to (and to control) uncertainties, but uncertainties that can be understood, rather than random or arbitrary shocks, and therefore can be managed, or even resisted, rather than tolerated or endured.

Indeed, a striking feature of modern world society is precisely that it is filled with articulate and self-conscious discussion and conceptualization. The term *globalization* is in the air (Guillén 2001), and this colloquial term is employed with elaborate and rationalized analysis, far removed from fatalistic conceptions. The world is painted as controlled or managed, for better or worse, by the economic power of (MNCs) (e.g. Sklair 2001; Shamir 2004; Chandler and Mazlich 2005; Jones 2005) and intergovernmental financial and trade organizations (e.g. Sinclair 1994; Finnemore 1997; Friedrichs and Friedrichs 2002; Barnett and Finnemore 2004; Jackson 2005). In this picture, there is indeed a world economy with common or easily translatable currencies, production measures, exchanges, investments, technical standards, and the like (Wallerstein 2000; Wolf 2004). Capital, labor, or technology can be shifted about, and data on the actual or potential shifts are readily at hand from international for-profit and public agencies (such as Business International and the World Bank). Based on these data and analyses, strategies and models for national, regional, or corporate development are drawn. Similarly, there is an elaborately analyzed world political order, filled with detailed information on states and their relationships and interdependencies, and the threats these may pose (Diamond 1993). And these data provide the basis of the advocacies for democracy and nation-building regimes (Diamond 2005).

Similar elaborated models of reality, based on elaborate data, are developed for other social domains. There is a world ecological system with increasingly elaborate measures of all sorts of properties of the common air, water, flora, fauna, minerals, and the structures organizing all these, and with a celebrated script of systemic features in the Gaia hypothesis (Lovelock 1988). There is a world health system, with similarly detailed specifications of biological information—from disease to mortality to nutrition (see Inoue 2003 for a review). And the status of the world's human people, as they study, labor, and live, is recorded in great detail, and subsequently curious cultural matters (such as female genital cutting, see Boyle, McMorris, and Gomez 2002) become subject to global discussion and regulation in human rights terms. The same elaborated emphases on global interdependencies are found for the issues of law (Baudenbacher 2003), justice and morality (De Greiff and Cronin 2002), or identity (Gerhards and Haceknbroch 2000; Arnett 2002; Bruner 2002). Overall, more and more social issues are conceived and described as global in nature, drawing on the increased intensity of worldwide exchanges and interferences (Ritzer 2004*a*).

These more intense interdependencies add to the general confusion, and theoretical muddling, about the system. The terms *international, transnational,* and *global* are frequently used interchangeably (even though analytically they connote distinct relations, between and across national borders, transcending national borders, and relating to the canopy at the 'higher' level of reference, respectively). In our work globalization is a two-tiered process, enhancing internationality and transnationality by the diffusion of models worldwide while also consolidating the global (Drori et al. 2003). In this view, modern globalization has three important properties beyond the increased magnitude of actual international interdependence to which much attention is called. Each of these properties contributes to the increased amount of organizing that occurs throughout the world.

First, whether international interdependencies in fact expand or not (and there are active debates on economic and environmental predictions, for instance), they are perceived and analyzed with greatly enhanced intensity, and are seen as extraordinarily consequential. Any analysis of a national economy or polity must now take into account its close linkages with the world outside it. But in the same way, local weather talk—the humdrum chatter of daily life—now includes components about global warming and El Niños. Local unemployment is seen as having global explanations, as do local crime rates or problems with schooling. Discussions and analyses abound, along with proposals for increased organizational management. Thus, modern globalization involves an articulated awareness that we live in a common world susceptible to detailed rationalized analysis.

Second, modern globalization involves much world-level influence on, and sometimes management of, local societies. Societies incorporate world standards to surprising degrees (McNeely 1995; Meyer et al. 1997*a*, 1997*b*). They respond to global scrutiny and criticism, both of which become increasingly legitimate. A proper modern sociologist can prescribe appropriate solutions to address gender inequality to any society on earth. Similarly, proper medical professionals can tell any society anywhere in the world about correct procedures and standards. The same principle holds for every sector of social life: there are standards about how to do democracy, economic growth, equality, welfare, education, health, trade, labor, or any other substantial modern institution. A society that organized its schools, for instance, under traditional forms of physical discipline, would come under severe criticism. Thus, common—and highly rationalized—models of society arise around the globe and are employed as standards everywhere (Mendel, Chapter 6; Brunsson and Jacobsson 2000).

Third, modern globalization involves an increased sense that the world itself is a society—an analyzable and manageable social system. We have, or perceive, a world economy, political order, world ecology, health and education problems, and so on. We even envision a world defense order against internal terrorism and disorder and external asteroid attacks. Increasingly, data are organized to describe properties of world society as a whole: aggregated for the world, one can easily find educational statistics (e.g. world student enrollment, by gender, and by level of schooling), economic statistics (world oil reserves, economic production, and unemployment), ecological statistics (global temperature changes, deforestation, and waste accumulation), health data (worldwide malaria cases, immunization and infant mortality rates), and so on (Hwang 2003, Chapter 3). These world data serve as a rational and scientific basis for mobilization, and world policies are organized to deal with the problems involved—to solve global health, educational, economic, or security problems.

The multidimensionality and wide scope of social matters that are perceived to be shared worldwide makes the world seem as a whole—a society of its own. This awareness goes beyond the functions and interdependencies that are imposed by intensifying exchange, to frame a common understanding of universal qualities and transnational rights. The world seems unified, much like Anderson's imagined community (1991), with a world culture (Drori 2005) and a sense of community (Etzioni 2004). When nation-states are involved, they take the role of carriers of world models and norms and are under pressure to conform to standards of good global citizenship. So the world models discussed earlier (environmentalism, social justice, health, and others) are edited to depict a world of nation-states that are, or should be, on their best global behavior. And when the perspective shifts to the point of view of the nation-state itself, a central modern idea is that it is and perhaps should be heavily influenced by the wider global system, with openness as a core world virtue, economically, politically, medically, educationally, and culturally. A country's economy is expected, under these assumptions, to be open to the world for trade and inspection (of, e.g. transparency), as its political system should be visible to the carriers of democracy (mostly publicly, from former American presidents).

Globalization, in short, has mythic properties in the modern system. And, while this grand reputation is not in contradiction with the organizational importance of states, it is certainly inconsistent with the myth of the primordiality of the national state.

1.2.1. The Decline of the Primordiality of the National State

During the period of high modernity, roughly between 1800 and 1940, the national state was the most celebrated collective entity with ontological standing in world society (Thomas et al. 1987). Increasingly built on individual citizenship (Marshall 1964), the nation-state came to be seen as the evolutionary triumph of human society rather than the murderously mobilized mistake it might have seemed in medieval (or postmodern) eyes (compare Tilly 1990 with Almond and Powell 2000). In many models, the nation-state rode society into the battle for progress, though in some liberal societies, as in the American case, society retained stronger sovereignty (Jepperson 2002b). In essentially all cases, the rise of the nation-state involved the rise of nationalism, or notions of imagined society united in, and expressed by, the state: the title 'nation-state' indicates the cohesion of a nation within the boundaries of a sovereign state (Anderson 1991).

Nationalism reflects the political fact that in a period of intense conflict and expansion, the national state took on quite demonic mythic powers, rooted in ethnic, religious, or historical features of the nation, or based on the state structure itself. Increasingly, the state could be seen as appropriately managing almost every aspect of society—economy, polity, educational system, medical system, knowledge system, and so on. Interestingly, every domain on which the myth of the state left its imprint, dramatically increased its formal organizational structure, though in forms appropriate to the distinctive qualities of particular state models (Jepperson 2002b). And in society, traditional organizational forms directly reflected the sovereignty of the ideal state.

A great deal of posturing was involved in the claims of nationalism and the sovereign authority of the state. The imagined unity and coordinated control never did really achieve complete reality in even the nominally highest forms. The nation-state indeed was something of a dramatic invention (Anderson 1991; Hobsbawm 1993), whether in Meiji Japan, Wilhelminian Germany, or nineteenth-century France (Weber 1976). But as a myth, the nation-state was able to mobilize a great deal of competitive energy—economically, politically, and militarily. Empires spread, economies grew, and some very impressive wars resulted.

Globalization, with its dominating images of national society as penetrated by, responsible to, and judged by world society, undercuts much of the support structure for the national state as demonic actor in world history. Heroic masculinity resulted in mutually destructive war (McEneaney and Meyer 2000); national identity became racism (Greenfeld 1992); economic autarchy became economic disaster (Sachs 1992); and educational nationalism became an assault on the neighborhood (Frank et al. 2000; Schissler and Soysal 2005). The institution of the nation-state comes, then, under attack from all sides: from the global polity, the market, and the empowered individual. In weakening the myth of the national state and its mobilizing charisma, a number of the core organizational forms associated with this state were similarly undercut.

We may note here three properties of the core myth of the national state. Each of them was fundamentally reconstructed in the postwar period by myths of globalization.

First, the national state was rooted in a territorial conception analogous to property. There could be scientized analyses of this property, with mappings and measurements, and either sentimental or resource-oriented assessments, but the boundaries of it and its ontological status had an arbitrary quality (Wilford 1981; Ventresca 1996). Attempts to justify it (as with the mystique about the hexagonal shape of France) moved quickly to the transnational. As property, the national state could be organized around individual or family property, or as public bureaucratic administration—two of the favorite forms of organization in the national state.

Second, the national state was rooted in an exclusive and comprehensive conception of citizenship rather than in the traditional notions of community and family. Every person, in principle, could be a citizen of one and only one national state, and all national states had a definite population of citizens. Again, these citizens could be measured and counted, and their properties, assessed (as in the famous vision of Quetelet or in human capital terms; see Ventresca 1996), but at the boundary, the ontological definition of a population had (and has) an arbitrary and circumscribed quality. As population, the people of a national state lent themselves readily to conceptions of individual rights, but also to bureaucratic management—and thus two of the forms of governmentality of the nation-state period (Foucault 1991).

Third, the national state was rooted in a conception of unified sovereign purpose, vested variously in national and state centers (Jepperson 2002*b*). The state was what we would now call a unitary rational actor, possessed of competence in the several senses of that term. To carry out its mission as an actor, it had bureaucratic forms, and was filled with professionals (and the universities from which these sprang) who had access to the mysteries of knowledge necessary for proper service to the sovereign.

An example of the modern weakening of the autonomous state is the globally changed attitude toward migration. The notion of the 'brain drain', or the loss of national leadership and human resources, has been replaced at the age of globalization by the idea of 'brain circulation', acknowledging the natural mobility of human resources and the spin-off benefits of human labor (Saxenian 2002). In this changing attitude toward migration, there is a recognition of the weakening of the charisma and sovereignty of the state: migration is beyond the control of the state; national boundaries (physical and conceptual) are porous; citizens are more than bundles of human resources; and finally, national advantages need not be fortressed but can come from exchanges with the world. The literature on 'global tribes', praising their adaptability, addresses these notions directly (e.g. Aneesh 2005); so do the literatures on economic niches and the management of trade (e.g. Wolf 2004). Together, the autonomous, bounded nation-state is recast in the global web of resource flows, highlighting the mythology of globalization and world society.

1.3. VISIONS OF WORLD SOCIETY: THE CULTURE OF GLOBALIZATION

The national state, as primordial integrating principle though not as practical organization, greatly weakened at the end of World War II. The disasters of the war (and the earlier Great War), the experience of a global depression, the Cold War, the prospect of nuclear catastrophe, and the breakdown of the colonial system undercut the picture of the core national states as great unitary heroes, or actors, in world history. Through these tribulations, the nation-state became a practical entity more than a primordial one. As a service structure, it was supposed to aid the development of both old societies and new social entities rather than to maintain entirely autonomous purposes.

Causal relationships between the rise of global social interdependencies and the visions of global culture run both ways. (*a*) The consciousness of global interdependence on multiple fronts led to widespread efforts to envision a global society. Exactly as Tocqueville noted in his analyses of the rise of an integrated, though stateless, American society in the nineteenth century, people developed and tried to institutionalize models of association on the global level built on reconstructed principles. Thus, the culture of postwar globalization was in some measure a deliberate construction, in an attempt to build workable ideologies of social control in a stateless world. It was quickly understood that a real world state was not feasible, and Tocquevillian alternatives were obviously available. (*b*) Globalization, of course, has a very long history. Its modern conceptions have clear roots in medieval Christendom, and in a variety of conceptions that derive from Christendom (e.g. the

Westphalian vision of a world of national states). The institutionalized modern world culture has its roots in that long history (e.g. Lauren 2003), and it is carried by various organizations whose constitutive myths are themselves anchored in this cultural framework (see Finnemore 1996; Drori 2005).

First among the global cultural principles is the idea that the world is made up of individual human persons, with rights and powers of all sorts (Meyer and Jepperson 2000; Ramirez and Meyer 2002; Lauren 2003). These individuals transcend the corporate bodies—most strikingly, national states, but also familial and ethnic constructions—of the nation-state period (Frank and Meyer 2002). The rights of such individual human persons, in symbolic principle, challenge and often supercede those of the older groupings—as in the case in regards to the practice of female genital cutting, for example (Boyle et al. 2002). To make this vision work in a complex and expanding world society, the individual persons—now carrying almost the whole right and responsibility for virtuous action (Meyer and Jepperson 2000)—have enormously expanded notions of rights, duties, and entitlements. This picture of the human person is made sacred, and in the modern human rights tradition, both sanctity and moral responsibility rest within each individual. These expanded capacities and rights extend all the way down in human society to formerly obscure populations in terms of age, race, ethnicity, class, and gender (Frank and Meyer 2002). And, increasingly, such expanded rights, and their implied capacities, are confirmed in law, both formal and 'soft'.

A simple indicator of this sweeping change, as well as the primary socializing mechanism that leads to this result, is the extraordinary global expansion in education in the current period (Meyer, Kamens, and Benavot 1992; Schofer and Meyer 2005). Worldwide, 20 percent of the relevant age cohort is blessed with some tertiary education—a figure that would have been inconceivable in most core countries at any point in the high period of the nation-state. Modern schooled persons are seen as having a natural capacity to act rationally and cooperatively in organized collective action, and expanded and changed organizations are a natural consequence. As creatures of natural law, rather than the positive law of the state, they have extraordinary standing and capacity. Through this link, modern education results in modern organization: Stinchcombe (1965) noted that the spread of modern organization rests in part on the enormous modern expansion of mass education. More recent changes create a world in which enormous numbers of people are, by schooling, empowered as potential organizational managers: the modern world is made up of empowered human persons, not simply members or citizens.

Second, replacing the nation-state model of the physical world as a bounded territory is the universalized vision of the world as an ecosystem

(Frank et al. 1999). This is true in terms of economic resources, environmental sustainability, and social migration. The world and its units are scientized entities: every aspect of the world and its units are analyzable in terms of universalistic laws (Drori et al. 2003). Science in practice, as in logic, blossoms to an extraordinary degree in every society, and in every social sector. It provides basic rationalized meta-legal structures in terms of which the empowered individual persons can negotiate their interactions. People everywhere can work out scientifically the best ways to accomplish ends and the interdependencies associated with these technologies. Globalization lies behind the cultural expansion of science, and scientization facilitates universal perspectives and regulation (Drori et al. 2003). And both globalization and its cultural component of scientization work to enable and empower much modern organizing (Drori and Meyer, Chapter 2). If the world surrounding an issue is scientized (categorized, ordered, codified, and universally lawful), and if the uncertainties it contains can and must be analyzed and responded to rationally (analyzed and modeled into patterns), then organization of that issue—any issue—is a very natural consequence.

Third, in place of the nation-state model rationalized around a sovereign state, we now have the global conception of a more abstract and universal rationality. There are generally right ways to do things, carried, among others, by social scientific professionals whose instructions have widespread and rapidly increasing authority. There are correct ways to bring about health, schooling, economic development, and democratic politics and the principles of bringing those things about apply everywhere. The laws involved are partly rooted in (social) scientific claims, but they clearly transcend ordinary scientific standards and procedures: like modern economic theory or democratic theory, they rely in good part on a natural law principle of logical rationality that has its Western roots in medieval celebrations of Greek philosophy. The key point for our arguments here is that these principles and models are universal—not seen as linked to racial, historical, religious, or accidental virtues of particular peoples.

In summary, globalization, while certainly involving world-reaching concrete interdependencies, also involves the consolidation of a world culture and its related assumptions. Here we emphasize three of these: the role of the empowered individual human person, the notion of scientized universality, and the sense of the social authority of rational models. These principles reflect a change from older notions of nation-statehood, or familiar, racial, or gender-based organizing principles, or from older logics of religion and traditional rules. Modern organizing follows from the institutionalization of this expansive set of principles.

1.3.1. A Note on Hypothetical Worlds

Modern globalization is by no means mainly linked to regression and anomic disorder, despite its portrayal as a world of problems (Wallerstein 1974, 2000; Ritzer 2004*b*). If it were, we would find little modern organization and a great deal of retreat to communities of various sorts—familial, ethnic, national, racial, regional, or religious. We do find such events, and they are played up as omens by popular interpreters, but these are not by any means dominant. Modern terrorists, for instance, are generally not defenders of traditional community; rather, they are themselves salesmen of made-for-TV visions of alternative global normative orders.

The globalized world society is obviously not a centralized state system, simply replacing the nation-state with a similar structure, one or two higher levels of aggregation. Even the European Union, by far the strongest of the modern regional associations, is not much like a nation-state (Fligstein 1996*a*). World society is prominently stateless, with very little of any strong sovereign center (see Wallerstein 1974 for the most extensive discussion). If it were, we would undoubtedly see the organizational forms associated with the national state replicated on a larger scale and a higher level. We would see the classic top-down bureaucracy, reflecting the will of its lord. We would see the traditional corporate structures of professional organizations (e.g. in education, medicine, law, guilds, and industrial cartels), supported by state protections. And, we would see global versions of the old family firm, with power held as a matter of personal property by established status groups protected by the state (see Djelic 1998 for examples). All of these kinds of organizational forms can readily be found in the world, but they are not the dominant forms of the modern rationalized organizational system.

In cultural terms, the globalized world society is much different than the model of the nation-state. World culture, because of its emphasis on universal values, does not celebrate its boundaries, although the dramatization of geographical, cultural, and political boundaries is a core cultural practice of nations and states. World culture, while celebrating nation-statehood as one of its constitutive myths, still shows a more communal picture than that drawn by the nation-state model. Lacking a clear center of power and an obvious mechanism for enforcement, global institutions (such as the United Nations; Drori 2005) emphasize a universal cultural base of shared norms and core values (such as human rights, anti-slavery, equality, and satisfaction of basic needs). Further, most of those norms and values *in their generalized form* are not contested. In this way, global institutions rely on a distinct picture of global society: universalistic, guided by set of core norms, and operating through 'soft laws'.

1.4. ENTER THE ORGANIZATION

The literature on formal organization tends to read its subject far back into history, giving it more continuity than it might deserve. Examples are found in the Church, old empires, monasteries, and guild societies (see Kieser 1987, 1989, for examples; Scott 2003 for an overview). In some ways, this is useful, since the components of the modern organization certainly have their histories in earlier forms of rationalization. But images of continuity can be carried too far, and can lead us astray. The classic older forms of rationalized structuration are meaningfully distinct from the modern 'organization'. These transitions are widely recognized in the literature (Chandler 1962, 1977; Freeland 2001; Scott 2003).

Bureaucracy provides a good example. The term was once the core label for rationalized formal structures, and was treated as an ideal type by Weber and Fayol. Everything required for efficient operation seems to be included: clear hierarchies, divisions of labor, professionalized personnel, sharp boundaries against unofficial society and the environment, explicit rules, and markedly defined authority. Imperative authority was the essence (Weber 1968). The ideal form bureaucracy was a clockwork machine, tuned perfectly to carry out the will of its sovereign, and to accomplish clearly defined ends.

The academic literature on formalized organization commonly used the term 'bureaucracy' without much apology (Merton 1940/1957, Gouldner 1954; Blau 1955; Selznick 1957; and so on). Today, the term 'bureaucracy' has almost disappeared from this literature—a book or academic course on bureaucracy would almost certainly be discussing a historical form (e.g. the Prussian bureaucracy) or a defective systems in a Third World country (e.g. the Indian bureaucracy). Today's connotation involves 'red tape' problems with effectiveness, implementation, and binding hierarchical differentiation: the inert consistency that was a central virtue of the classic bureaucracy has now become a social problem.

What has changed so that in every text where the term bureaucracy might once have appeared we would now find the term organization? Fundamentally, what has changed is the nature of sovereignty: the modern organization is an actor, not an instrument. In classic bureaucracy, the sovereign is the ultimate external authority and decision-maker—the structure exists to serve the decisions of the sovereign. As such, classic bureaucracy depended on the legitimated authority and capacity of the state, or some other external principale.

This essentially changes with the modern organization. True, it has external owners, stakeholders, and the like, who have partial sovereignty, and to whom the organization is accountable. But the organization itself is the accountable, responsible, and authoritative decision-maker. In the terms of Brunsson and Sahlin-Anderson (2000), the organization is an 'actor' rather than a passive instrument of an external actor. Extending beyond the legal dimension, this actorhood is expressed, for example, in the organizations speaking in a singular voice: corporation A denies this, organization Z decides that (see Mendel, Chapter 6). Actorhood of this sort is also a feature of workers and participants in such organizations: they are responsible for and initiators of the organization's tasks rather than servants of an executive head; and, they draw their authority to be proactive from guidelines and 'soft laws' rather than from commands or directives, much in line with Wilensky's notion (1964) of the 'professionalization of everybody'.

All the cultural forces we have discussed above work to produce this end. We have an expanded rationalized and scientized environment, the absence of charismatic or primordial national states and of any larger world state, the celebration of universalized rationalities, and the rise of the modern empowered (but in a sense standardized) individual endowed with authority and capacity. This cultural system encourages and facilitates coordinated, collaborative, and rational human action.

Whether in the public or private arena, and in any social sector or industry, organization is possible and desirable. Empowered and rational people can be brought together in a managed and rationalized structure to take purposive collective action on many fronts in a scientized environment. This sort of 'professionalization of everybody' brings us together: we can plan innovation, manage safety, calculate products, scientifically analyze needed supplies, create professionalized and rational personnel, labor relations, and governmental relations systems, and so on. We can coordinate it all and unify it around shared collective purposes, making rational decisions in ways accountable to our stakeholders.

With globalization, the same historical trajectory describes the evolution of the private familial organization held as personal property. Over time, sovereignty is split between ownership and managerial control (classically discussed by Berle and Means 1932), and the decision-making, managed organization appears. Actorhood, once centrally located in owners and family heads, shifts to the organization itself, to the managers who operate it, and even to the workers or participants. The tendency is worldwide, and is understood to reflect what we here call globalization, or the expansion of the rationalized environment (e.g. markets) in which the organization operates (Meyer 1996, 2002). There is much dispute on the exact markets and/or political processes that produce the evolution, but there is certainly agreement on the overall character of the change (Chandler 1977; Fligstein 1990; Weick

1995; Freeland 2001). This process is evident in recent changes to the for-profit corporation: it is no longer organized around family ownership and family-like relationship between owners and workers. Rather, the corporation is a social actor, carrying responsibility to its social environment (Shanahan and Khagram, Chapter 8) and to its workers' life plan (Luo, Chapter 9). And it is managed in a standard form (Mendel, Chapter 6) by professional managers (Moon and Wotipka, Chapter 5) and professional groups (Jang, Chapter 7).

Precisely the same sorts of change describe the evolution of the organizations centered on the old high professions—the school or university (see Slaughter and Leslie 1997; Aronowitz 2001; Kirp 2004), the clinic or hospital (see Scott et al. 2000), and the religious community (see Monahan 1993; Chaves 2004). These structures shift away from the older forms of domination by the high professionals involved: they are now rationalized, organized, and administered as themselves purposive actors. In this form, actorhood shifts from the professional community to the organization. This process is most evident in the life of the university (Krücken and Meier, Chapter 10), where the 'ivory tower' is handed over to managers of educational systems (Slaughter and Leslie 1997; Aronowitz 2001; Kirp 2004).

Alongside the old professional structures, many newer ones emerge as well, taking the modern organizational forms—engineering firms, consulting firms, architectural firms, accounting firms, etc. In each case, whatever diffuse authority the professions had is now restructured as organizational actorhood, and built around notions of organized strategy and decision.

1.4.1. The Universalization and Diffusion of the 'Organization'

The rise of the modern organization is a general cultural matter of far-reaching consequences. It functions as a modern myth, replacing in part the myth of the national state and society. As an ideological model it is extremely general: it can be applied in any social sector—to public or private for-profit or nonprofit activities. It can be prescribed for any society in the world, whose government should be made up of transparent agencies, whose private sectors should be efficiently organized, and whose schools and hospitals should be well managed. Independent of specific context, in short, organization is what Tyack (1974) called 'the one best system'.

The universalism of the formal organization follows from the modern global environment (Meyer 1983). Globalization itself suggests a common and unified world. The associated scientization of the natural environment clearly underscores the notion that universal laws are in place everywhere—the uncertainties that these law-like patterns create are standard, and the means to most effectively deal with them are also standardized. In the same way, the universalization of notions of the empowered individuals entitled to human rights, further reinforced by the expansion of universal schooling, clearly suggests common frames by which these human persons can form organizations. And finally, the universalistic principles of social rationality and rationalization create common building blocks for the construction of standardized and expanded organizations.

All this means that it is extremely easy, under modern conditions, for the principles and practicalities of modern organization to spread anywhere. If the conditions for organizing are seen as universal and standardized everywhere, diffusion can be overwhelming (Strang and Meyer 1993). Whole industries arise and spread the principles of organization. Large-scale consulting firms carry common policies and programs everywhere, and local firms copy them (Ernst and Kieser 2002; Kipping and Engwall 2002; Ruef 2002). Whole professions arise around expansive rationalizing programs, often rooted in themselves-standardized business schools (see Moon and Wotipka, Chapter 5; Jang, Chapter 7). Professors of accounting, or safety engineering, or quality control, or organizational management, or strategy, can talk to each other anywhere in the world, and professional associations facilitate the conversations. Similarly, in every industry, associations form and carry (nominally) best practices to the far corners of the world.

A new interdisciplinary academic field of entrepreneurship emerges to study the creation of new businesses and the entrepreneurs who create new organizations. Entrepreneurship courses have become an integral part of management curricula in most business schools. And there has been a proliferation of specialized conferences and journals, books, and research centers in recent decades (Aldrich 2004). The celebration of entrepreneurship underscores the idea that creating new organizations is the source of innovation, and is an engine of economic growth and social change (Romanelli and Schoonhoven 2001). Moreover, the recent rise of entrepreneurship as an academic field reinforces the notions that individuals have the capacity to engage in creative activities and at the same can be routinely taught entrepreneurship in a standardized manner (Hwang and Powell 2005). A budding organizer can, in short, find scripted, standard and elaborate principles of organization at every hand.

Much of this cultural material is structured in what amount to social movements—great schemes for progress in accounting, management, quality control, and so on. Hence, modern doctrines of organization spread in a New Public Management movement (e.g. Olson, Guthrie, and Humphery 1998). A quality circles movement is partly superceded by a movement for standards (Brunsson and Jacobsen 2000). In dimension after dimension, in this globalizing era, organizational reform is in the air (Brunsson and Olsen 1998).

We take all this diffusion to be natural, in a world already globalized in our minds. It does not seem so natural in even very recent historical perspective. A few years ago, Guillén (1994) published a most impressive study of the spread of modern management doctrines to some Western countries (the United States, Britain, Germany, and Spain) in the decades up into the 1970s. Framed by the question of how various models of management did or did not spread among these countries, Guillén stressed how deeply management ideologies and models, and their diffusion, depended on political, economic, and cultural features of those countries. In his view, diffusion was a partial and slow and constrained enterprise, by no means to be taken for granted. But while global variation indeed persists, even with the power of globalization, more than a few recent studies show a trend of change. Alvarez, Mazza, and Pederson (2005) collect studies showing how management ideas flow rapidly even through mass media. Czarniawska and Sevon (1996) similarly assemble studies assuming diffusion—and treat what were for Guillén real barriers as translation and editing problems as management and organizational models flow around the world.

1.5. PROPERTIES OF THE CONTEMPORARY 'ORGANIZATION'

One can find a wide range of innovations and reforms floating about in modern organizational theories and ideologies. It is possible to imagine that there is no coherence—just a random collection of fashions of reform, set loose by accident and flowing through a communication system (Abraham-son 1991, 1996a, 1996b; Brunsson and Olsen 1998). There is enough truth to this imagery to sustain interesting lines of diffusion research. But for our purposes, it is more useful to look for common elements among them.

Today, there are indeed more common elements among various organizations and organizational settings than in the past. The standardization and universalization of the interpreted environment, and the rise of ideologies of agentic actorhood, mean that common principles of the managed organization take hold everywhere. General organizational literatures (over and above schools, say, in particular), both academic and popular, proliferate. Abstract processes are defined, and can be seen in operation anywhere: for example discussions of innovation, and of R & D, rather than of the exploration of specific techniques. A language of organizing, close to the mind of a universal and very rational God, and far from any particular local reality, comes into place: talk of 'dashboard performance indicators', measurable outcomes, accountability, and transparency sweeps through. One can find it in business schools, other components of the university, and in consulting firms. But one can also find it within organizations themselves, which routinely incorporate abstract and inflated notions of managerial agency. From innovation systems and entrepreneurship training, to a quality department and a strategic plan, we can find the artifacts of organizational actorhood anywhere from a non-profit agency delivering meals to seniors (Hwang and Suarez 2005) to a gigantic national defense (previously war) department.

We can see the common elements of the modern 'organization' most clearly if we contrast them with traditional bureaucracies, professional organizations, and family firms. First, the contemporary organization is a sovereign actor, with agency (Meyer and Jepperson 2000). Agency means the legitimate capacity to make decisions pursuing organizational goals. The legitimacy is general in character, implying a general right and capacity to do something called management, beyond any specific technical competence at a particular line of work. Managerial agency (like any form of legitimated sovereignty) can be seen as a legitimated balance between autonomous authority and schooled accountability and responsibility (Foucault 1991).

Second, organizations, as rational actors, tend to have and to talk about their own legitimated goals. They acquire these goals, again, in a legitimated trade-off with their environments for resources. In this way, they differ from more traditional organizational forms that serve the goals of an external sovereign such as an owner or a professional mission. It would have been hubris for a more traditional organization to claim its own goals: a medieval university was a university rather than an organization, and thus it did not announce organizational goals. Modern organizations are, however, experts at producing mission statements for both internal and external consumptions.

Third, the modern organization tends to have elaborately spelled out technical structures, by which claimed goals are to be accomplished. It is not all delegated to a professional, or a simple assembly-line technology, or traditional competencies. There is a good deal more explicit differentiation around organizational goals than would be found in traditional structures. These new tools of organizing are 'management tools', and they, by definition, regard the organization as a standard creature. Since World War II, there have been several general fashions around management tools—for example, those of planning (Hwang, Chapter 3) and governance (Drori, Chapter 4), but all tend to regard the organization as a sovereign, manageable, and standard entity.

Fourth, the organization explicitly tracks the resources employed and deployed in pursuit of the claimed goals. Elaborate counting and accounting take place. Elements formerly taken for granted (such as donated goods and services or product satisfaction) are reported and accounted (as in counting attendance at social functions or compiling ratings for satisfaction). Again, we have the property of a rational actor, deliberately and forcefully assembled. Note how distinct this is from more traditional organizational forms, in which many resources are buried in taken-for-granted assumptions, traditional professional roles and chains of imperative authority.

Fifth, the organization incorporates persons as individuals. It lists and names them as in organizational charts, and keeps track of their properties. They have real roles and responsibilities, and are seen to be capable of fulfilling them. This new mode of governance, relying heavily on the knowledge of the participants, is a 'soft' control structure (Robertson and Swan 2004; Drori, Chapter 4). Furthermore, participants are not simply objects of social control. The modern organization incorporates them as persons with rights, and it is unlikely to employ physical controls and punishments. Rather, their mode of incorporation is itself rationalized and modeled, yet again assuming a relationship with organizational goals, performance, and spirit.

Sixth, the organization incorporates these member-individuals as participants in its decision structures. That is, even far down in the hierarchy, individuals are supposed to have the rights, obligations, and capacities to participate in organizational decisions and activities (Mintzberg 1989). In this respect, the modern organization is theoretically less manageable than more traditional hierarchical forms, in which most individuals are seen as passive automatons and objects of control. This point is made clear in Hofstede's (1980) contrasting of 'organization' with 'bureaucracy'. The obligation to acknowledge the personhood of workers is, then, an extraordinary rationalization of the modern environment (with science, rationality, and individualism everywhere), and it lowers the formal rationality of organizational structures (Meyer 1983).

Seventh, the organization has clear symbolic boundaries defining the limits of its actorhood. At every boundary are images of formal contracts and accountabilities. Statistics can be kept to capture who is and who is not part of the organization and when. Other statistics define resources as part of, or outside, the organizational domain. In practice, as always, everything tends to be blurred: nonprofit organizations form 'circles of friends' for fund-raising purposes, and corporations count family members and dependents as eligible for the corporate health plan. But the social form of the organization as actor is preserved and intensified: increasingly there are clear definitions of what is and what is not corruption or donation.

1.5.1. The Dialectics of Organizational Actorhood

Operating in a scientized and rationalized global environment, organization is easy—and necessary—to produce in many local situations. Everything is structured to make it easy. Training programs spit out managerial capabilities and orientations, the babble of organizational talk is everywhere, and all sorts of interests and constituents demand that social settings now be organized. Older underpinnings of authority in profession and state are weakened, but new ones are ready to hand. Facilitating supplies of organizing materials are found on a global scale in rapidly expanding consulting firms, business school instruction, and all sorts of professional and nongovernmental organizations (see the papers in Sahlin-Andersson and Engwall 2002; Djelic and Quack 2003). No one is now surprised if a baby-sitting cooperative among some parents, or a religious congregation, or an elementary school is found to have an organizational structure, with officers, committees, goals, annual reports, and the like. Such groups are encouraged by the members, sponsors, and advising consultants to organize. And around the world, more and more people 'intuitively' know just how to do it, as a matter of standard social form; and, if they do not know off hand, there is likely to be an organization—from professional fund-raising agency to consultancy group to training center—to sponsor their transition into the modern form.

This means, of course, that the organizations claiming to be distinctive agentic actors and decision-makers are in fact under a great deal of social and cultural control (Foucault 1991; Meyer and Jepperson 2000). It was Tocqueville's fundamental insight about American society that the free American individual is caught in a network of socializing and associational structures and brought under the control of a civic culture that makes democracy orderly rather than anomic. In the same way, the modern world of organizations is a relatively tamed world, compared with the older world of conflicting national polities and cultures. Large corporations are conformists as well as leviathans, and so are huge national medical and educational systems.

A first core point here is that there is a highly scripted quality to the social form of the rationalized formal organization. There are standardized ways to outline goals and plans, map organizational resources, or define decision structures and control systems. The implication is that all this standardization means that choices, decisions, and actions are themselves rather highly standardized. In Michel Foucault's terminology (1991), this is another instance of the dialectics of *Omnes et Singulatim*: acceptance of action scripts creates both totalizing and individualizing tendencies in modern entities, including organizations, in ways similar to Robertson's notion (1994) of 'universalism of particularism'. Agency, in other words, is a role more than a unique reality (Meyer, Boli, and Thomas 1994). As the modern organization acquires the agency central to its existence, it much sacrifices any unique soul (Meyer and Jepperson 2000).

A second core point is that the scripted character of the organization and its components means that contemporary organizations are a good deal less rational in structure and action than might have been assumed from the rationalization of organization as a social form. They are, in a phrase emphasized in sociological institutionalist thought, loosely coupled (Meyer and Rowan 1977). To be done properly, goals must look good although they may be far removed from any more real purposes of organizations. Similarly, individual participation in decision-making processes must be structured as a matter of form; it is unclear, however, that the form really takes bite as a matter of reality. The same is true of the other elements of organizing: depicted resources may not in fact be available for use, and decision sovereignty may be disconnected from any sort of implementation in reality (Brunsson 1989). Structures of innovation, standards, quality, safety, or environmental management may or may not function in any coordinated way. Real implementation can, in fact, create a cost to the ritualized affirmation of the institutionalized form (Shenhav and Kamens 1991; Kim, Jang, and Hwang 2002).

A third core point is that the rationalization of organizational structures within the highly rationalized context of contemporary societies creates inconsistencies between the postured rationality of the organization as actor and its embeddedness in an already rationalized society. What does it mean for a hospital or school organization to make claims about its treatment choices, if these choices are already determined by external scientization? The chosen treatments are enactments more than chosen action. What does it mean for an organization to claim the involvement of its individual members in coherent decision structures if these persons already have their rights, capacities, and responsibilities guaranteed in the political and cultural environment? The individuals may be as much scripted conformists as authentic participants. What does it mean for an organization to claim structural rationality, when its properly rationalized structure is a copy of a form taught in the nearby business school? Again what appears to be action and decision can best be read as enactment.

Overall, the infusion of a contemporary organization by all these external rationalities, or the construction of the organization out of these rationalities, makes the organization something very far from a coherent rational actor in reality. And, in fact, contemporary organizational structures look far from the simple rational bureaucratic forms celebrated by Weber, Fayol, or Taylor. Because they must incorporate already mobilized actor-individuals (again Wilensky's phrase [1964] 'the professionalization of everybody' comes to mind), they must blur their decision structures to accommodate the rights and capacities of these people. Complex participatory forms result, far from clear decision-structures (Hofstede 1980, 1994). Because organizations must incorporate or accede to an enormous amount of scientized and profession-alized knowledge (in natural or positive law), their own technical structures and technical choices have to be blurred. Because the requirements of exter-nally defined rationality and accountability are so highly developed, organ-izations must find ways to give deference to them. So maintaining standards becomes less important than maintaining membership in the International Standards Organization (ISO), for example. Accomplishing decision ration-ality is less important than employing the proper decision forms set out by an international consulting or accounting firm. Maintaining effective employee relations becomes less important than conforming to laws of rational person-nel management built into legal and professional environments (Edelman, Abraham, and Erlanger 1992; Dobbin and Sutton 1998). And so the institu-tion is sustained and further reified.

1.6. CONCLUSION

A highly rationalized cultural environment of globalization creates a fertile field for the rise of agentic organizations of a modern or postmodern form, and for the translation of older organizations into this form. Globalization, as a matter of culture more than exchange, builds up a model of a universalized and rationalized environment. This is variously written into scientific analyses of nature, legal, and moral analyses of individuals as possessed of universal rights and capacities, and into a whole set of doctrines about the rational structuring of social life. With this, a positive picture of a global world is painted. And older pictures of society as organized around primordial na-tional states and other communities are greatly weakened, along with the forms of rationalized organization associated with them: bureaucracy de-clines, as do older forms of professional guilds and firms built around families as property.

This context, culturally tamed no matter how complex, is an environment within which rational contemporary organizations—organizations structured as agentic social actors—become appropriate forms for all sorts of social activity, in every country and every social sector. These organizations—now accountable, responsible, and managed agentic decision-makers rather than the more inert organizations of the past—rise up everywhere. Because man-agement and agency are core features, and because these elements of actor-hood are universalized and globalized, organizations take on surprisingly common forms. They celebrate, in standardized ways, their goals, their technologies, their accounted resources, and their sharply defined boundaries. And they celebrate the highly participatory but centrally unified sovereign decision-structures. On all the dimensions of rational actorhood, they take on highly elaborated and scripted forms.

All this elaboration of rationally organized actorhood, however, involves a great deal of social, legal, scientific, and cultural control. And modern organizations, for all the pretenses of their boundaries, sovereignty, and actorhood, display an astonishing level sameness, and a considerable tendency to conformity. The carriers of these notions are key players in this process: consultants and professional managers aid the translation of organizational goals and practices into the standard scripts of organizational actorhood. In this process, the world of organizations may be unattractive, but it is a good deal less demonic, local, or authentic than its formal claims might appear.

2

Global Scientization: An Environment for Expanded Organization

Gili S. Drori and John W. Meyer[1]

Discussions of 'the knowledge society', 'knowledge work', and 'expertise' call attention to the generalized authority of professionalized knowledge, and its grip on modern (and especially postmodern) society. They emphasize the wide scope of the scientization of society. Science-based logics and practices have permeated almost all aspects of social life: they influence the ways we work, form relationships, and eat. Most relevant to the discussions in this volume, scientization acts as a basis for organizational formalization and proliferation. Scientization creates an environment in which organization becomes natural and necessary. It does this by supporting two main causal levers of organizing—the rationalization of activity in a tamed and analyzed environment, and the empowerment of human actorhood. This chapter describes and analyzes the rise of global scientization, and its effects on organizational expansion.

2.1. GLOBALIZATION AND SCIENTIZATION: 'IN SCIENCE WE TRUST'

While the meaning of, and motivation for, the rapid expansion of science is disputed,[2] there is no contention about how dramatic the expansion in activities has been. In a broad sense, scientific activity has grown since the late seventeenth century—but the explosive growth has occurred since World War II.

So, over the modern era, there is dramatic growth in the number of traditional science activities: the numbers of scientists and science-trained professionals (engineers, medical professionals, social scientists, and related professionals), scientific publications, and scientific conferences. In each case, there is a dramatically more rapid expansion since World War II (Barnes 1985; Ben-David 1990; Drori et al. 2003). This explosion in the volume of scientific activity is worldwide: universities, science education curricula, and governmental allocations for science policy have become standard features of the modern nation-state, regardless of country-specific features or requirements. Figure 2.1 (taken from Drori et al. 2003: 3) shows some illustrative indicators. Beyond state and public institutions, similar commitment to scientific progress has occurred among commercial firms: more firms than ever have in-house R & D operations, and more have contracted with universities to access their intellectual property (IP). And globalization has added a massive field of science to world society. The number of scientific international organizations has exploded. Some of these are professional scientific associations. Others are benevolent science organizations. Both governmental and nongovernmental organizations grow rapidly (Schofer 1999). Science becomes a whole new sector in both national and global societies.

With expansive growth science also brims over the traditional boundaries of scientific institutions (the university and professional scientific associations) to become incorporated in the activities of other social organizations and sectors. Science activities add new missions to other social organizations and institutions. As a result, organizations whose primary mission is not scientific add scientific components to their work: from corporate in-house R & D labs to forensic scientists in policing to educational professional advisory boards in school districts.

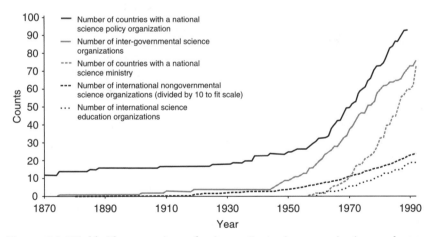

Figure 2.1 Worldwide expansion of science: Increasing organization and state structure, 1870–1995

Science, as foundational, also expands beyond the traditional groups of legitimated professional scientists. Arenas once reserved to the sole judgment of scientists now await professionalized science-based judgment from lay people under the assumption that people can all be scientifically literate (McEneaney 2003). Courts, family consultants, educators, and journalists all harness information, gathered according to scientific conventions and presented in scientific formats, to substantiate and support their practices. And the public audiences of these professional groups have grown accustomed to reviewing such scientific information: TV viewers can read synoptic maps to aid the weather person's predictions of tomorrow's climate conditions, jury members probe into the details of DNA research to consider criminal conviction, citizens study the intricacies of statistical error to contemplate the validity of predictions and results of political elections. The reliance of lay people on scientific tools, with an underlying assumption that the methodology involved in such increasingly complicated methods is available to all, reflects the scientization of contemporary society.

The scientization of society is quite a departure from science–society relations during earlier modern periods. The university, for instance, was then regarded as an 'ivory tower' (as in Wolfe's notion [1972] of the university as the 'home of science'). And scientists were seen as part of a distinct and cohesive social community, bound by unique normative rules and professional standards (Merton 1973). This special social standing of science emerged from its early modern roots, when science was considered a gentlemen's activity rather than a professional vocation (Wuthnow 1980; Toulmin 1990). Science was not seen as an occupation, and the term 'scientist' was not in use until around 1840 (McClellan in Schofer 1999). Even during the era of science's more rapid expansion after the late nineteenth century, scientific organizations were concerned primarily with the profession of science rather than with its application to social goals (Schofer 1999). Global science emerged principally for the sake of science. Only by the middle of the twentieth century did science orient its activities so elaborately toward social goals. Today, international science associations are increasingly defined as working to achieve a social good: organizations, such as the International Organization for Chemical Sciences for Development and the International Network of Engineers and Scientists for Global Responsibility, now focus on global social problems ranging from peace to environmental protection to poverty (Schofer 1999). Adding to this reorientation of science toward social goals is the intensive commercialization of scientific products that further reoriented science toward social needs. Capitalist pressures (Slaughter and Leslie 1997; Slaughter and Rhoades 2004) and funding crises (Gibbons et al. 1994; Nowotny, Scott, and Gibbons 2000) call for the traditional research universities to become entrepreneurial (Clark 1998) and to become integrated in the 'triple helix' production network between academia, government, and industry (Etzkowitch and Leydesdrof 2000).[3] All these pressures for reorientation of traditional science signal the socialization of science or the opening of social system to social fashions (norms, goals, needs, and demands).

The scientization of society and the socialization of science (Schofer 1999) are the 'yin and yang' of the tale of science–society relations, signaling the increasing interpenetration between science and society.[4] Evidence on the porousness of science–society boundaries ranges from the concrete and material (e.g. flows of funding, career tracks, and IP as in Powell and Owen-Smith 1998; Slaughter et al. 2002; Kleinman 2003) to the abstract and cultural (e.g. change in normative orientations of scientists as well as on the transfusion of norms across institutions, see Hacket 1990; Croissant and Restivo 2001; and Drori et al. 2003).

Expansion in the volume and scope of science activities has meant a change in the logic of operations in many parts of society. Scientization becomes a general cultural form. Science-based logics and practices permeate other social institutions: democratization, standardization, environmentalism, and developmentalism are social spheres that have been dramatically constructed or altered by the incorporation of scientific activities and logics (see Drori et al. 2003, particularly Chapters 10–13). This is most important for our discussion of scientization as a source for the global trend of organizational expansion, as we discuss later.

In summary, modern science has changed over time from a pastime for gentlemen to a professional vocation to a socially embedded institution. The interpenetration goes both ways: science is socialized, for better or worse, but society itself is scientized. This scientization is a core process in the hyper-organization of world society.

2.1.1. Explanations

The extraordinary explosion of science around the world has certainly received scholarly notice, but real explanations are poorly developed. Functional approaches to science, associated with Robert K. Merton (1938/1970, 1973; see also Zuckerman 1989; Cole 1992), tend to suppose that scientific expansion occurs because of its utility. Science is useful, particularly for modern economic, social, political, and military development. More critical traditions, clearly expressed in Sagasti (1973), Stepan (1978), and Aronowitz (1988), also suggest that science expands and globalizes because of its inherent utility, though they tend to be critical of the elites (e.g. capitalist) for whom science is useful. The utility of science is described, respectively, as satisfying the functional needs of society or as serving the interests of social elites (including the interests of scientists themselves).

In reaction to the intellectual difficulties of functionalism, as well as to the political stances sometimes involved, major modern traditions in the sociology of science (the 'social studies of science' schools) are much more skeptical about the functionality of science (see, e.g. Sarewitz 1996). But this tradition lacks a sustained explanation for the great overall scientific expansion of the modern period, and tends to fall back on the notion that the whole enterprise in partly the product of scientific interests themselves. There is no real explanation for the extraordinary putative success of the scientists in persuading world society to go along with the game.

The nature of the expansion of science defies functional and utilitarian theoretical expectations. First, science expands in societies where the functional utility of its cadre of expertise or institutions is unclear: African countries devote the highest share of their primary and secondary school hours to science and math instruction (Benavot 1992), science enrollments mushroom in developing countries as they do in the West (Ramirez and Wotipka 2001; Drori and Moon forthcoming), and science policy bodies are founded worldwide regardless of country-specific features (Finnemore 1993; Jang 2000).

Second, scientific investigations explore issues that are far from having direct and immediate rewards and thus are far from delivering direct benefits to societies or to ruling elites. Enormous scientific efforts are devoted to issues of little apparent utility. There are searches for ice on a moon of Jupiter and signals from the center of the galaxy. There are elaborate explorations of the origins of the human race or languages. There are major disputes over whether various animal species employ tools, use clear languages, or engage in rational calculation. Major social scientific conflicts occur over whether groups acquired their technologies internally or through diffusion.

The historical literature on the rise of science raises the same criticism of utilitarian and functional arguments. Scholars tend to be very doubtful about the importance of science for socioeconomic development before the current period (e.g. Barro 1991; Shenhav and Kamens 1991; Fuller and Robinson 1992; Drori 1993, 1998). And this skepticism is paralleled by doubts about whether socioeconomic development in fact drove the expansion of science.

Third, when science contributes directly to practice, it often does not benefit presumably dominant elites. On the contrary, scientific studies of global warming and workplace injuries, and the depiction of these as social problems, have taken many tolls on corporate pockets. In spite of the image of science as the 'fifth branch of government' (see Jasanoff 1990), scientists and science institutions are not the bearers of social power, as power is ordinarily conceived, but are rather increasingly dependent on society for funding and legitimacy.

So, while the justifications of science expansion are clearly utilitarian in tone, emphasizing its infinite usefulness and importance for the marketplace (Sarewitz 1996), science expands in directions of no direct efficacy to society in general or to particular groups in it. Scientization is a broad-ranging process: abstract and diffuse (rather than concrete and coupled), having porous boundaries (rather than distinct and insular), authoritative (rather than guided by need or subject to control), worldwide (rather than centered in particular countries or regions). And its dramatic growth occurs in a very specific period—since World War II. We need explanations of this growth that account for its concentration in this period as well as its global character and its diffuse and cultural form.

2.1.2. Globalization and Science

Much of the development of science since the seventeenth century can be analyzed as linked to the rise of the modern nation-state system (Wuthnow 1980; Toulmin 1990). Whether or not the sciences were useful to the economic purposes of the nation and the political and military aims of the state, science provided metaphors and ideologies for the rationalistic pretenses involved. But the range of scientific activities and professions involved was fairly limited by the same considerations.

World War II produced a fundamental change in the scheme of the competitive nation-state world. Closed, competitive, and corporate nationalism, with some of its ugly scientific accompaniments, was stigmatized deeply. Military might made competitive war unreasonable. Economic hardships of interwar period made competitive economic nationalist autarchy unattractive. The human disasters produced were overwhelming. The Cold War competition globalized the whole range of issues. And rapid decolonization, brought in part by the failures of nationalist corporatism, rewrote human society on a global scale.

A host of 'world-building' efforts followed. A whole international governmental and nongovernmental organizational system arose (Boli and Thomas 1999). Ideologies celebrating worldwide social and economic development took hold. Racisms and ethnocentric nationalisms were delegitimated.

It was obvious to almost everyone that a global world order was needed. But it was equally obvious that no world state or globalized version of the old national-state was possible. In this situation, directly analogous to

Tocqueville's 1836 analysis of stateless American society, all sorts of forces of social control—state, civil, political, military, economic, and ideological—searched for bases of a more universal rule-like social order outside of the nation-state system. In the absence of political possibilities, something akin to religion was needed.

In our view, science has been used to play that role in the postwar period, precisely as an older and more limited science had supported the rapid expansion of the nation-state system during the period of high modernity, from about 1800 to 1945 (Drori et al. 2003). In the absence of possibilities for much positive international law to provide for myths (and some actualities) of order, science—and faith in science—could pull law out of the Laws of Nature. This line of reasoning can help explain (*a*) the worldwide spread and organization of science, (*b*) the rapid period-dependence involved, (*c*) the very diffuse character of the science that expands, cutting across many fields and issues, and (*d*) the penetration of scientific authority far down into social life.

The sweeping rationalization of the whole natural (and social) environment of society generates a greatly expanded frame enabling and requiring organization in every society and institution. It does this by (*a*) expanding the possibilities for rational or rationalized action and by (*b*) expanding the capacities and responsibilities of humans as empowered actors.

2.1.3. Core Features of Scientization

In the following section we outline how the two core features of modern world culture, rationalization and empowered actorhood (see Meyer, Drori, and Hwang, Chapter 1) are constructed and expanded through scientization. These cultural foci are embodied in scientized activities and structures and legitimated in a scientized cultural logic.

(a) Rationalization. Scientization primarily carries the mission of rationalization. It provides tools for standardized strategies and methods, and by imposing an image of the world as an ordered creation makes rational management something of an obligation. The scientific approach to the natural world and subsequently to the social world is dominated by imagery of these worlds as decipherable. Armed with this perception, science challenges cultural conventions of disarray or mystery by carefully categorizing species, analyzing patterns, modeling behavior, and deriving laws. From Darwin's analysis of species and their evolution, to Durkheim's analysis of suicide rates and their cultural distribution, to Newtonian laws of gravitational motion—all such scientific breakthroughs seek regularity in the world, social and natural. In these ways, scientific work has cosmological qualities: it reflects the vision of world order and one's place in it, and thus it transcends the mundane truths of its discoveries per se. It turns inchoate uncertainties into rationalized and scripted ones. A fatalistic world of opaque terrors becomes comprehensible as a 'risk society' (Beck 1992), and thus as something humans can and should organize to deal with.

The cosmological nature of modern science is anchored in the scientific approach and its tools (Drori et al. 2003). Science assumes universality of patterns and thus derives law-like rules of regularity. In addition, scientific work is articulate and produces explicit scripts, formulae, models, and principles. The scientized scripts gain authority, derived from the faith in the scientific method, and thus can be applied and tested by others. One can see how this works, best, when it is applied without much actual data or analysis. We celebrate scientized scripts even when those are not more than awkward formulas of unquantifiable and untested data. For example, the World Bank, relying on the zeal of economists to formulate meaning in terms of equations, describes successful anti-corruption initiatives with an equation: GI & AC = F (KI, LE, CA), where, 'Successful Governance Improvement (GI) and Anti-Corruption programs (AC) are dependent on the public availability of Knowledge and Information (KI) plus Political Leadership (LE) plus Collective Action (CA).'[5] This scientized script has now become the basis of policy and action, with aura of the World Bank as a depository of expertise and knowledge on governance. Similar scientized scripts are prescribed to various problems, considering the effects of race on career trajectories, of watering patterns on bird migration, or of car emissions on weather patterns. Most important, they are used as standards for problem solving: various issues are more likely to be defined as problems and then tackled with solutions once they are defined in these schemes. In this way, scientization becomes the standard for defining a matter as a problem and for defining a solution. This tendency to scientize social problems is particularly evident in discussions of the 'risk society'.[6]

Scientized scripts have a dramatic standardizing power: relying on their assumptions of universal applicability, they are applied to very different contexts. For this reason, equations of education attainment from the United States, which have race as their prime independent variable, are applied then to data from Israel, the Philippines, and Japan, although race per se is less a social issue in these societies than ethnic origin. Similarity is imputed, nevertheless, drawing legitimacy from the scientific method itself. And similar assumptions about the validity of scientific theories and scripts across social context are taken for granted regarding economic development, democratization, disease contagion, and environmental degradation: they are understood to follow similar patterns and operate through similar mechanisms in Africa as in Asia. In this way, tools based on assumptions of universality reflect and further reinforce notions of universality.

To further allow the transfer of tools and methods, major enterprises of data compilation and analysis are taken in such soon-to-be-analyzed contexts (see Mendel, Chapter 6). Data compilation is a substantial classificatory labor: education statistics are broken by school level and year, demographics statistics by age and gender, and corporate statistics by sector (service, manufacturing; for-profit, not-for-profit). The social construction of such categories is clear, as is the rationalized character of the whole endeavor of public statistics (see Bowker and Star 1999). This rationalized activity has expanded from its origins in the concerns of a few statisticians to become an all-encompassing activity of governments, international organizations, corporations, and private structures. For example, Ventresca (1996) argues that the census has become an organizational norm, driven by the work of scientists but also by the powerful scientization of nonscience actors.

Through its rationalizing qualities, scientization is tightly linked with the global moves toward standardization. Standardization, or the creation of unitary criteria and measures, is nowadays a global enterprise. Rooted in late nineteenth century technical initiatives of engineering associations, it grew to encompass more and more social domains (see Loya and Boli 1999: 171–7; Drori et al. 2003: 282–4). In this transformation from technical to social, the global standardization movement grew beyond the concrete boundaries of standards organizations (Loya and Boli 1999: 176): standardization is created and advocated by organizations whose primary mission is not the setting of standards (e.g. manufacturers and professional associations) and standards have been formed for nontechnical matters, like the codification of production quality in ISO 9000 (Mendel, Chapter 6) or of ISO 26000 (Shanahan and Khagram, Chapter 8). Modern society is an 'audit society' (Power 1997): 'In addition to financial audits, we now hear of environmental audits, value of money audits, management audits, quality audits, forensic audits, data audits, intellectual property audits, medical audits, and many other forms.' These standardization efforts, in their application of technical and rational principles to categorize the world and impose further order, involve a great deal of scientized knowledge, logic, and authority. Indeed, more scientized societies are also societies relying on more formal standards for various activities: from compilation of information, to use of standards in corporate work, to more adherence to standard forms of governmental action (Drori et al. 2003: 287–90.) Scientization, in supporting the idea that a single set of rules and standards applies worldwide and that the natural and social worlds are governable by humans, encourages both the technical endeavor of standards-setting and the grip of the universalistic and taxonomic worldview.

(b) Actorhood. Science expands and empowers human actorhood. The categorizing work of science established classes and capacities of actors: 'when relying on science-based theories for evidence of their distinctiveness, their political voice is clearer' (Drori et al. 2003: 277). This effect goes beyond the strategic use of evidence to substantiate claims of the special or unique qualities of human individuals and associations. Science is a tool of empowerment, instilling and legitimating the agency of social categories seen as passive. This occurs in several ways. First, as with other dimensions of schooling, education in science transforms the former peasants of the world into citizens (and now, with global human rights, global ones). They have the expanded, generalized, and legitimated capacity to act, and their actions, now conceived as choices, legitimately matter in the world. Schooled persons can vote; whole political theories rest on the matter. They can make choices about work, investment, and a whole economic theory rests on it. They can make religious, cultural, and familial choices, and general ideologies of human rights gain power worldwide.

Second, science expansion provides legitimate tools for the action of empowered human actors. The putative knowledge carried by science provides justifications for the political, economic, and social choices of these actors. Ends are articulated, and means are provided for them. Purposes and reasons ground activity, and people become quite articulate in discussing them. Of course, as we emphasize in this chapter (and book), the choices of rationalized organizations are similarly empowered, and such organization can appear anywhere as touched by science.

In science, and in particular in the age of globalization, rationalization and actorhood come together in the seemingly contradictory process of the 'universalism of particularism' (Robertson 1994). The categories that are created as a result of the rationalizing and universalizing approach of science are then employed as a basis for construction of unique and particularist identities: calls for preservation and special protections that are based on the naturalist's creation of the category of 'endangered species' are similar to those claims made on behalf of women based on the social science attention to women's issues. Many other categories of persons are defined and empowered in the same way: children, the elderly, the handicapped, indigenous people, and all sorts of ethnic populations.

Of course, as Tocqueville (1969 [1836]) emphasized in discussing American society, the legitimation and empowerment of human actors are also a means of controlling them, and standards of human 'responsibility' are components of empowered actorhood and sovereignty. The line of thought, here, was emphasized by the classic American 'social control' theorists like Charles Horton Cooley, George Herbert Mead, and John Dewey, though these theorists tended to take quite a positive view of the virtues of the social controls involved. A much more skeptical contemporary view is famously put forward by Foucault (1980, 1991), and scholars who develop his arguments (Miller 1993; Hicks 2004). In either perspective, the point is made that categories of disenfranchisement are not much different than categories of power: the same societies that expand and celebrate education of actors also expand their categories of disabled 'special education' persons. And at the collective level, scales that celebrate national achievement, such as the Technology Achievement Index constructed by International Telecommunication Union to identify the 'winners' in the global IT race, also mark the 'losers'. They assume that all nation-states, because they are nation-states, are reasonable units to be scaled. The formula, with its categorizing and classifying authority, is an act of power. Scientific methodology is in this way a technology of power, and thus scientization is a prime example of governmentality (see Foucault 1991). The exercise of this kind power differs dramatically from instrumental or violent exercises of power; rather, it is more subtle and intricate in its permeation of social and private life. It is also mainly cultural in nature rather than directly political or based on wealth.

Overall, scientization has abstract and cultural features as well as concrete dimensions of science expansion (personnel, roles, activities, and networks). These various features constitute the two cultural pillars of scientization of society: rationalization and actorhood.

2.2. THE MEANING OF SCIENTIZATION

Alongside the observable expansion of numbers and scope of science-related activities and institutions, scientization also means the penetration of science-like activities and logics into everyday life. In its cultural forms, scientization conveys principles of universal order (universality, scripts) and proaction (constituted actorhood). Scientization, through these cultural features, acts to restate authority in terms of rationalization and empowered actorhood. Scientized authority is anchored in institutionalized myths of scientific knowledge and in the stature of experts who create and possess this knowledge. Thus, scientized authority is more expansive than most traditional forms of political and economic control. Science has many properties in common with religion, and can easily be seen as a rationalistic form of religion in the age of (modern) globalization.

With the rise of scientific authority (mostly expressed in the professions, see Moon and Wotipka, Chapter 5; Jang, Chapter 7), other authorities draw on its legitimacy for making judgments. Scientists are consulted on a regular basis for the sake of policymaking: science is Jasanoff's 'fifth branch of government' (1990). Science scripts, like the scientists who proclaim them, convey an epistemology of method and facts, systematic analysis and proof, order and verification. Armed with this rationalized image, scientization has come to substantially eclipse much of the authority of religious leaders, politicians, and administrative superiors. Based on scientific claims, all sorts of people and groups are empowered to take issue with the authority of more traditional leaders. And reliance on the legitimacy of science and scientized scripts has come to take some precedence over moral, political, or authoritarian judgments.

2.2.1. Examples

Contemporary society provides many examples of the extraordinary authority of the claims of science and scientists. We indicate a few here:

— Contemporary discussions about the definition of human (and other) life quickly involve scientific as well as religious and political analyses. When is a fetus a person? When is a dying person dead? Issues about euthanasia, abortion, or stem-cell research turn on such questions, and are now prominently addressed by science. Elaborate research generates scientific testimony to the public, courts, legislatures, and world governmental organizations. Questions formerly addressed by political, moral, religious, and economic authorities now receive scientific attention.

— In the same way, a whole array of issues about nonhuman life come under scientific authority and testimony. Grand issues about whether a given plant or animal is a species or a subspecies become important, as well as questions about how endangered it is, and whether it is important in the cycles of life. Narrow issues become important too—does a lobster feel pain on being boiled? The resolutions of such issues now occur through scientific authority.

— Very specific religious issues come to require scientific testimony. Consider the case of the Jewish elevator, where Rabbinical authority called scientific advise for aid—does the operation of an automatic elevator constitute Sabbath-violating work (see Drori and Meyer 2006)?

— Activities that might seem very dubious on common-sense grounds can take seem reasonable when rephrased in scientific models. Consider the PAM program of the American defense authorities, where econometric models of risk and bets (applied to the probabilities of assassinations, among other things) became the basis for security and political judgments (see Drori and Meyer 2006).

— In the same way, it is now common in the world to treat as legitimate exchanges of pollution rights so that poor and peripheral people and places become proper targets of pollutants. Obvious economic and scientific assessments of costs are involved.

— As a more extended example, consider how the Commonwealth of Virginia transformed formerly moral judgments into statistical plotting in the case of sentencing of nonviolent offenders. In 2000, Virginia started offering its judges information, as a part of each case before them, on the statistical probability that each such offender would return to a life of crime. Judges were then expected to include such predictions in their sentencing considerations. This Virginia sentencing technique was highly scientized: (*a*) The basis for the profile, or set of features of the typical nonviolent offender, was the statistical analysis of findings from a survey of 1,500 Virginia nonviolent criminals. (*b*) These findings identify clear patterns, commonly known to criminologists; for example, young and jobless men are at much higher risk of recommitting crime than older and employed women. Therefore, the rate of recidivism was calculated on the basis of personal and social characteristics: age, gender, employment, marital status, and the like. (*c*) Based on these calculations, the scale of recidivism propensity was calculated and while the proposed 'cutoff point' was changed several times,[7] it is used as a codified marker for judges to evaluate. The general goal was to have judges use these predictions as aid to shorten the duration of consideration. The intension was also explicitly to utilize scientific tools, in this case those commonly used for risk assessment: Richard Kern, the director of Virginia's state commission on sentencing, is quoted as saying that '[j]udges make risk assessments every day. Prosecutors do too. Our model brings more equity to the process and ties the judgments being made to science.'[8]

In this instance, the Virginia legislature and courts transformed moral judgment into scientific ones. This, of course, generates some stark inconsistencies: penalty judgments to be made by referring to social markers that are constitutionally protected as 'immutable characteristics' and thus prohibited from being used for differential treatment of any sort. This particular program folds all the characteristics of scientization and as a result serves as an exemplar case of the penetration of scientized logics and practices. It provides instances of three abstract and cultural features of scientization— the use of scientized scripts, the assumption of universalism, and the imputation of agentic actorhood. It also illustrates two concrete dimensions of science expansion—networking among scientists and the role of experts as advisors.

2.3. EFFECTS ON ORGANIZING AND ORGANIZATIONS

Scientization, and the practical and cultural foundation set by the expansion of science, makes the world a natural place for formal organization to rise. And it is through both concrete and abstract causal channels that scientization sets the basis for the expansion, proliferation, and globalization of organization. And scientization, through rationalization and the constitution of empowered human actorhood, and the combination of the two in professionalization, forms the particular core features of the current dominant models of organization. Figure 2.2 graphically presents these causal relations.

2.3.1. Scientization as Professionalization

On a very concrete level, scientization in the form of professionalization results in all sorts of specific roles and programs which create new organizations, but which press for entry into older ones: safety or environmental engineers, ergonomic specialists, psychologists in human resource capacities, economists with their projections, and so on and on (see Moore 1996). But very centrally, professionalization expands modern organizational hyper-managerialism—with extraordinary pictures of the modern organization as an empowered actor. Moon and Wotipka (Chapter 5) describe the expansion of management education. Professional education for managers, as is for the related administrative professions of accountants, is highly scientized and given to quantitative models. It is formal training in academic settings and draws on highly scientized programs for professional training, and on

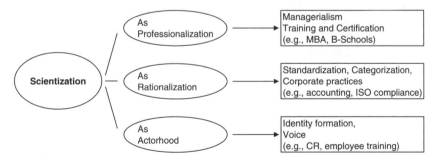

Figure 2.2 The Effects of Scientization on Organization

business as a field of research and scholarship. Management education also defines the role of management as a transnational social category: management is a generic role relevant for the running of an organization as such. Moon and Wotipka demonstrate that both national and world forces drive the worldwide institutionalization of professional management education. Among the first countries to establish professional management education, the characteristics of national environments (such as the business sector and the education system) are prime determinants, while over the duration of the globalization process the emphasis shifts from internal factors to external factors. At the current stage of the process, adoption of the management education model is primarily determined by embeddedness in world society.

The core theme of management education is the taming of uncertainties through rationalized procedures: everything from the volatility of financial markets to political conditions is tamed by careful analysis of predictive models and by the careful layout of management responses. 'Uncertainties are transformed from mysteries into risks that must be managed (the European version, see Beck 1992) or into opportunities for more effective action (the American version; see Peters and Waterman 1982)' (Drori and Meyer 2006; 31). This reframing of uncertainty in the running of organizations is captured in the term 'strategy' (turning the activity of management into statements about mission, the scanning of environment, planning, execution, and review). Strategy depends on something called 'analysis'. In some usages, this involves categorizing the environment of organizations into PEST (political, economic, social, and technological) or SWOT (strengths, weaknesses, opportunities, and threats) or numerous other coined tools. Even leadership is scientized: the notion of business leadership, for example, is drained of personal charisma by conceptions of entrepreneurship as a learned skill and by developing best practice models for leadership. In these ways, the availability of scientized tools of analysis and instruction as well as the availability of sites for learning encourage the constitution of organizations. Scientization, as a tool of professionalization, allows organizations to be manageable units and forms the cadre of managers as taking charge of this real and empowered social actor.

2.3.2. Scientization as Rationalization

Scientization facilitates the construction of the (chaotic) social and natural world as ordered. It identifies patterns, organizes evidence, and maps and models relations. Order is established with general laws, whether of gravity, natural selection, or market behavior. The scientific tendency to make sense of and order in the world is the cosmological essence of the whole science venture. And it is a prime tool of organizational rationalization.

Practices and procedures that arise in formal organizations reflect the broad tendency, in modern environments, to scientifically construct order. Two corporate operations that are highlighted in this volume—reliance on standards such as the ISO 9000 series (Mendel, Chapter 6) and accounting (Jang, Chapter 7)—express the grip of the 'audit society' on operations and logic of organization. In both these cases the organizational practice draws heavily from both global managerial culture and international standardization, both of which are rooted in scientization. ISO 9000 became the criteria and procedure for quality corporate management, as well as the most popular of all ISO standards. ISO 9000 directly influenced the expansion of organizational structure in many different countries and social sectors: it required existing corporations to create units for its assurance, encouraged a sector of accrediting bodies to certify compliance with ISO 9000, and its growing legitimacy required existing regulatory systems to adapt. In addition, ISO 9000 affected organizations through infusing compliant organizations with certain general management ideas (e.g. Walgenbach 2001): process management strategies, the disclosure of employee rights, and the importance of independent accountability. Accounting, in operationalizing expanded organizational rationalization, affects organizations in similar ways. Rather than being a strictly technical device for management, accountancy carries standard practices (e.g. book-keeping, review and audit, and professional certification) and conceptual frameworks (e.g. accountability and transparency, risk management). Overall, models of rationalized and scientized standardization and accountability have triumphed worldwide, constructing global models of expanded organizational rationality.

2.3.3. Scientization as Constituting Actorhood

Science has great taxonomic powers: the scientific endeavor requires classification into types, patterns, and models. This labor has ontological features, in constituting social units and setting the foundation for claims of uniqueness and empowerment. This directly affects organizations: it channels particular organizations to self-identify in scientized classifications. For example, UIA directories sort international bodies by their subject (health, education, and environment) as declared by members in their application forms. Since organizations only slowly change their formal goals and thus their declared subject-category, this declaration has feedback impact on identity declaration and thus on setting of goals and operations. Similarly, the classification of companies into sectors by economists imposes frames of reference on corporations.

Beyond the mere matter of classification and the imputed implication on self-identification of organizations, scientization also affects organizations by providing them with expectations, or a script, for actorhood. Two examples for such identity activation in organizations are described: human resource training (Luo, Chapter 9) and corporate responsibility initiatives (Shanahan and Khagram, Chapter 8). Luo (Chapter 9) describes how the new model of in-house human resource development that emerged after World War II asserted the centrality of professional management, participatory and empowered individuals, and organizational actorhood. As a result, according to a 1995 survey, 93 percent of US companies offered formal training to their employees and 70 percent of their employees, ranging from executives to production-line workers, took this opportunity to further their skills. This mode of training suggests a new engagement of workers in their company and a new role for companies. Similarly, the explosion in corporate responsibility initiatives suggests the onset of a moral and activist tone, once reserved to the state and public sector, into the for-profit, private sector. This process turns the corporation into a broad social actor, and extends beyond the legal dimensions of corporate liability and ownership. First, the corporate organization is no longer the sum of its components (workers or shareholders), but becomes a social entity: beyond its particular mission. Second, this new social entity acquires a character and a virtue, denoting civility and the extension of morality beyond primordial, or self-interested, drives. Through displaying responsibility towards its environment and taking a unitary persona, social responsibility is celebrated as a feature of a progressive corporation.

2.4. CONCLUSIONS

Formal organizations draw from the mythology, as well as from the methodology, of science. Scientized logics penetrated formal organizing, providing rationalized and empowering scripts of action. In addition to establishing concrete sets of practices and institutions, scientization helps form both the expectation of an ordered environment and of rational action, as well as the empowered social actors to lead such action. As a result, human endeavor is pressed to take formal responsibility for the management of more and more scientifically constructed uncertainties. It is to be done in a rational manner through purposive action by a purposive actor. In this way, scientization changes the basis for authority: no longer is it rooted in divine intervention, magical uncertainty, or political and economic coercion. Rather, authority rests in the hands of scripts of knowledge and in their professional carriers, and the expansion of these elements expands organizational authority and responsibility.

In the age of globalization, where science serves as the axis of rational modernity, 'cultural rationalization of this sort, rather than state formation at the global level, has taken a dominant place in world affairs' (Drori and Meyer 2005: 44). Scientization reflects this (post)modern form of authority. It is decentralized rather than emanating from a central source. It is diffuse, abstract, and loosely coupled rather than specific, concrete, and unitary. It draws on natural sovereignty rather than on divine, legal, or political authority.

Scientization does not mean the manipulative use of scientizaed truths for coercive purposes (in contrast, e.g., to Sagasti 1973 or Aronowitz 1988). While scientific tools are indeed tools of power and influence, it is unclear whose interests they clearly and directly serve. Contrary to these visions of science as a threat that can and should be tamed, scientization redirects the locus of action and the responsibility for action, within each social modern actor: in contemporary theory, we are all educated, knowledgeable social actors with a capacity and responsibility for action (Meyer and Jepperson 2000). The modern actor is to be something of a scientist.

The features of this scientized postmodern form of authority are distinctive:

— The authority is cultural rather than purely political or economic.
— It is powerful, but not coercive: 'soft power', anchored in mundane procedures; oriented to isomorphism, but in voluntaristic forms (Mörth 2004).
— It is diffuse, rather than hierarchical, and is built up around lateral communication systems rather than imperative authority (Luhmann 1995).
— It is empowering, activating, participatory (as in Wilensky's 'the professionalization of everybody', 1964).

It is not easy to decide who or what gains and loses with the extraordinary expansion of modern science, and its penetrative scientization. From the point of view of this book, though, one conclusion is obvious. Formalized organizational structure, in every locale and sector, expands enormously in the modern scientifically tamed environment.

NOTES

1. In this work we draw on our earlier writings on scientization: Drori et al. (2003) and Drori and Meyer (2005). The research was funded by grants from the Spencer Foundation, and from the Freeman Spogli Institute for International Studies in Stanford University.

2. The main contention is between those who regard scientific progress as paralleling and contributing to modernization (e.g. Inkeles and Smith 1974; Inhaber 1977) and those who regard science as a source of manipulative power and as an ideological mechanism (e.g. Mulkay 1983; Aronowitz 1988; Habermas 1993; Haraway 1996). Additional demarcations on the issue of the meaning of science are drawn between social constructivists (e.g. Callon, McKenzie) and realists (e.g. Merton, Ben-David).

3. On commercialization pressures on the traditional university, see also Wittrock and Elzinga (1985), Powell and Snellman (2004), and Croissant and Smith-Doerr (forthcoming).

4. See Scott (1998, 2001) for an account of increased social scientific awareness of interdependencies across organizational boundaries formerly conceived as relatively closed.

5. See, Drori, Chapter 4; source: http://www.worldbank.org/wbi/governance/about.html, accessed 1 June 2005.

6. And for more on the matter of the social construction of social problems, particularly on a global scale, see Ritzer (2004a).

7. Originally, Richard Kern, the director of Virginia's state commission on sentencing, and his staff calculated the cutoff point to be 35 (any score lower than 35 meant that the offender has a low propensity to re-offend and thus a judge is recommended to offer to him or her a sentence other than jail, like probation or house arrest). By July 2005 the cutoff point was adjusted to 38, based on recalculations of recidivism rates.

8. For more commentary on this Virginia program, see Bazelon 2005; Jenkins 2005.

3

Planning Development: Globalization and the Shifting Locus of Planning

Hokyu Hwang[1]

For the most part of the post-World War II period, state planning was the dominant model of development. The spread of the nation-state system constructed and legitimated the state as a dominant modern rational actor (Strang 1990; Meyer et al. 1997). Postwar efforts to bring about prosperity in the Third World propelled the state as the central locus of vision and action, and the state as such pursued progress on behalf of the nation and provided a blueprint for the nation's future in national development plans. State planning, however, has been in decline in the last few decades. With the breakup of even its most extreme form in the Soviet Union and Eastern European socialism, state planning has all but evaporated, and the Asian developmental states have been under pressure to reform themselves (Wade and Veneroso 1998; Wade 2000).

The apparent decline of state authority has elicited such gloomy observations as 'hollowing out' (Rhodes 1994) or 'the eclipse of the state' (Evans 1997) to mention a few. On the other hand, others have commented that 'governments have actually increased their involvement as they have embraced free trade' under globalization and liberalization (Fligstein 2005: 185; see also Vogel 1996). Although these two sets of observations are seemingly at odds with each other and suggest that the role of the state under globalization presents a complex set of problems and questions, the changing role of the state runs through both. I contextualize this debate in the broader processes of globalization in which the role of the state has been redefined with the decline of state planning and the concurrent rise of non-state actors—individuals and their voluntary associations.

First, I analyze the worldwide rise of state planning as the dominant model of development in the postwar period and show how the international development field facilitated the diffusion of state planning. In the second part, I document the expanding global conception of development and its manifestation in the content of national plans. As the notion of development narrowly conceived as economic growth expanded to include social justice, the content of national plans expanded accordingly. Moreover, in the current global conception of development, the people or individual humans take the center stage as the primary beneficiary and driving force of development. Third, I show the emergence of world-level data and the upward shift in the visions of development, which construct the world as an integrated social unit. Under globalization, the world is increasingly depicted as an 'imagined community', and world-level data on various development domains appear as the account and measures of progress. Fourth, I examine the decline of state planning and the rise of non-state actors. Accompanying the emergence of the world as an important unit of development, the locus of planning shifts downward to substate level entities that are increasingly seen as legitimate, rational actors. Finally, I summarize the materials presented in the chapter and discuss their implications.

3.1. THE GLOBAL DIFFUSION OF STATE DEVELOPMENT PLANNING

Development has been the primary goal of nation-states in the post-World War II period (Esteva 1992; Sachs 1992; Ferguson 1994; Escobar 1995; Evans 1995; Cooper and Packard 1997). Development—a central organizing and normalizing concept of the twentieth century—has served as a cognitive map of the world: modernization theorists associate advanced and developed countries with 'maturity' and underdeveloped and less developed ones with 'backwardness'; and similarly, world systems or dependency theorists label them, respectively, 'core' or 'center', and 'periphery' (Arrighi and Drangel 1986: 9). In short, development is seen as a continuum of progress. Beyond the classification of nation-states, however, the conception of development has also expanded significantly over time, particularly since the 1960s to include social justice such as quality of life, standard of living, poverty reduction, and individual empowerment to mention a few (Arndt 1987; Ferguson 1994; Leftwitch 2000; Sen 2000). Moreover, the notion that progression along the continuum of progress is possible, particularly through planning and active state intervention, has been at the heart of much development efforts—symbolized in national development plans (Escobar 1992).

Planning is an organized and rational attempt to select the best available alternatives to achieve specific goals. The idea of planning represents the modern belief that social change or progress can be achieved through scientific and rational application of knowledge. This belief has penetrated to various areas of modern life (Waterston 1965; Etzioni 1968; Inkeles 1976; Friedmann 1987). Around the idea of planning, one can also map the major ideological fault line of post-World War II geopolitics: the East–West divide. Although socialism and capitalism have been the two main contending models of development (Lindblom 1977; Berthoud 1992), the difference lies in the scope of state planning in the economy (March and Simon 1993 [1958]: 222), and the extent to which the state does so with relative authority and autonomy vis-à-vis other legitimate social actors. Even in Anglo-liberal societies, where seemingly the market is left to run its own course, 'laissez-faire is inevitably and continuously planned' by the state through its policies to securely reproduce stable markets (O'Riain 2000: 193; see also Polanyi 1944; Fligstein 1990, 1996; Block 1996). Planning then is not limited to planned economies or in the economic sphere, but is a more general characteristic of modern societies (Elliot 1958; Friedmann 1987). Further, planning is not an exclusive property of the state as it is becoming increasingly prevalent among other social actors such as corporations, nonprofits as well as individuals (Mintzberg 1994; Hwang and Suarez 2005).

National development plans embody these two notions of modernity and represent the legitimacy of the state as the primary actor to pursue collective goods in a rational and scientific way. Prior to World War II, the Soviet Union and a few other countries were involved in state planning. Since the war, however, as part of postwar reconstruction efforts in Western Europe and under the influence of the Soviet model in Eastern Europe, state planning landed on the European Continent (Djelic 1998). Further, the international development field made up of advanced industrial countries and international organizations zealously stimulated the spread of state planning worldwide through extensive loans and grants. Most first plan adoptions occurred between the end of World War II and the early 1970s. Especially, in the 1960s—the First UN Development Decade—various international organizations promoted state planning as the solution to Third World development problems (Esteva 1992; Chabbott 1998). As a result, Waterston (1965: 28) declared in the middle of the 1960s, 'the national development plan appears to have joined the national anthem and the national flag as a symbol of sovereignty and modernity' (see also Lewis 1966; Meyer, Boli-Bennet, and Chase-Dunn 1975).

Figure 3.1 shows the distribution of first national plan adoptions over time and the cumulative distribution of first adoptions. Between the late 1920s and the end of the 1980s, 135 countries adopted at least one national development plan with thirty-one countries adopting their first plans in the 1940s. In the 1950s and 1960s, twenty-nine and fifty-three countries, respectively, adopted

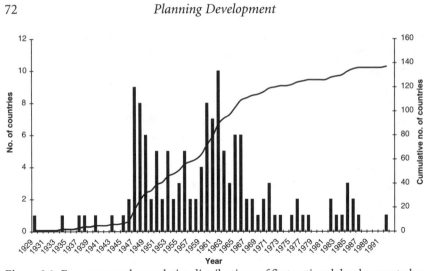

Figure 3.1 Frequency and cumulative distributions of first national development plan adoptions

national development plans. New adoptions dropped significantly after the peak in the 1960s. Only eight countries in the 1970s and fourteen countries in the 1980s adopted for the first time. This is not surprising given that most first adoptions had already occurred by that time with only a handful of newly independent countries adopting in the 1970s and 1980s. In short, there were two big waves of plan adoptions in the postwar period, reflecting the pattern of global diffusion of state planning from Europe to the rest. The first wave peaked immediately after the war, and the second in the mid-1960s. Eighteen European countries adopted first plans during the first wave, and twenty-six countries in Africa alone—half of all adoptions in the 1960s—adopted first plans during the second wave.

Underlying state planning and its worldwide diffusion was the belief that the state would provide the means to overcome obstacles to development and that state planning would stimulate systematic economic growth at a high and constant rate. This belief found strong theoretical support in socialism, Keynesianism, and development economics in socialist countries, advanced capitalist industrial countries, and the Third World, respectively.

The first instance of a modern national development plan was the Soviet Union's First Five-Year Plan adopted in 1929. To the Soviet leaders, in the context of direct competition with the capitalist world, planning was the primary means by which to pursue 'The material and technical basis of Communism and the highest standard of living in the world through the establishment of high and stable rates of growth and of optimal interrelationships in the development of the economy' (cited in Waterston 1965: 29). Through subsequent plans following the war, the Soviet Union, a relatively backward country, achieved impressive industrialization in a short span of time, rendering state planning as a viable model (Chang and Rowthorn 1995). The Soviet style of planning became a model in the Soviet satellites. Coupled with a democratic polity, it was embraced in a third way of economic development in the Third World—most notably in India, for instance (Singh 1995).

Keynesianism, on the other hand, provided a strong ideological as well as theoretical rationale for the interventionist conception of the state in capitalist societies (Hall 1989). First, new macroeconomic concepts based on the balance of aggregate demand and supply came into being and fundamentally changed the basic categories of economic discourse. Second, Keynesianism was influential through its particular set of policy prescriptions. Finally, Keynesian ideas articulated '... an image of the managerial state that endorsed a measure of state intervention but preserved the capitalist organization of production' (Hall: 366). According to Hirschman (1995), 'Prior to Keynes there simply was no respectable theoretical position between centralized planning and the traditional laissez-faire policies, with their denial of any governmental responsibility for economic stability and growth' (150).

Development economics played a similar theoretical and ideological role in the Third World. First, against the orthodox position, it was argued that underdeveloped countries were seen as distinct from advanced industrial countries, and therefore required a different path to industrialization. In other words, different theories and policies were necessary for underdeveloped countries: 'The long delay in industrialization, the lack of entrepreneurship for larger ventures, and the real or alleged presence of a host of other inhibiting factors made for the conviction that, in underdeveloped areas, industrialization required a deliberate, intensive, guided effort/by the state' (Hirschman 1981:10). Second, development economics was premised on the mutual-benefit assumption: expanded economic relations between advanced industrial countries and undeveloped countries were beneficial to both (Hirschman 1981). This led to a proposition that '...the core industrial countries could make an important, even an essential, contribution to the development effort of the periphery through expanded trade, financial transfers, and technical assistance' (12). This also reflected an increasingly integrated conception of the world economy (Meyer 1980). Jan Tinbergen (1967) echoed this view: 'It is, however, a matter of importance for the world as a whole that the poorer countries should become more prosperous. A world divided into halves, one poor and the other becoming continuously richer, cannot be a stable world—such a situation is sooner or later bound to result in conflict' (31). This integrated view of the world further fueled the expansion of the international development field.

The sweeping diffusion presented in Figures 3.1 attests to the rapid institutionalization of development planning as a taken-for-granted function and responsibility of modern state bureaucracy. Financial loans and grants from the advanced Western countries, international agencies as well as private foundations and development INGOs stimulated the worldwide diffusion of national development plans, particularly in the Third World. External aid directly affected the adoption of national development plans. For example, the United States based its foreign aid decisions on the evaluation of recipient countries' planning efforts; and in response, recipient countries adopted national development plans (Waterston 1965; see also Djelic 1998 for the Marshall Plan's role in Europe—particularly in France). Although political considerations were important in the decision-making process, 'Professional aid administrators tend to favour the countries which seem to be most effective in planning development' (Lewis 1966: 145). Although foreign economic assistance created external dependence in recipient countries, the state, through its control of external aid, enjoyed a significant level of autonomy vis-à-vis internal social groups at times (see Djelic 1998 for the case of France and Woo 1991 for the Korean developmental state).

Also important was the role of international agencies. The World Bank, for instance, was originally intended to provide long-term loans for post-World War II reconstruction in Europe, but later focused on development issues in the Third World (Block and Evans 2005; Osterfeld 1994). The World Bank provided countries with resident advisors and other means of assistance to help prepare and implement national development plans. By establishing regional and auxiliary agencies, the World Bank further stimulated the diffusion. In addition, many development agencies and organizations, in the business of finding development problems in the Third World, provided countries with ready-made development aid packages, which included expert advice as well as capital (Ferguson 1994). Chabbott (1998: 226–7) reports the exponential increase in the number of international nongovernmental development organizations based in OECD countries. Eighty percent of 2,152 development INGOs founded between 1900 and 1985 were established between 1946 and 1985. In the context of the post-World War II world polity, in short, states enacted the dominant global model regarding the appropriate role of the state to promote development, resulting in a high level of isomorphism (Meyer, Boli-Bennet, and Chase-Dunn 1975; Thomas and Meyer 1984; Meyer, Boli, and Thomas 1994).[2]

3.2. FROM ECONOMIC GROWTH TO HUMAN DEVELOPMENT

While the diffusion of state planning was worldwide in scope, the content of national development plans reflected the global conception of development. In this section, I document the evolution of global discourse on development and the changes in the content of national development plans in the postwar period. During this period, the conception of development has expanded from its initial narrow emphasis on economic growth to a more comprehensive conception in which social domains become an equally, if not more, important part of global development agenda. Further, the primacy of the state recedes as the people or human individuals take the center stage of development as the main driving force.

Arthur Lewis (1955), a prominent development economist and advocate of state planning, emphasized in his influential book, *The Theory of Economic Growth*: 'First it should be noted that our subject matter is economic growth, not distribution' (9). Lewis's emphasis on economic growth reflected the thinking of the 1950s. In the United Nations' report *Measures for the Economic Development of Under-developed Countries* published in 1951, for example, 'development was conceived primarily in terms of per capita real income, and its recommendations ... focused on technology, capital, planning, development of resources and aid' (Leftwitch 2000: 41). The dominant view was based on 'development orthodoxy' according to which development meant raising gross national product (GNP) or GNP per capita and industrialization, and the major roadblock to industrialization in the underdeveloped world was capital formation (Arndt 1987; Finnemore 1997; Easterly 2001). What was needed in generally capital poor Third World countries then was development aid and technical assistance. Indeed, in this period, states in developing countries undertook massive industrial infrastructure projects financed by external aid. Implicit in 'development orthodoxy' was that gains and benefits from increasing GNP or industrialization would trickle down to produce positive distributive and welfare consequences.

By the beginning of the 1960s, however, a more differentiated conception of development began to emerge, bringing social aspects to the forefront of development. In *The United Nations Development Decade: Proposals for Action*, the United Nations General Assembly declared the 1960s the First United Nations Development Decade and attempted to redefine development:

The problem of the underdeveloped countries is not just growth, but development.... Development is growth plus change. Change, in turn, is social and cultural as well as economic, and qualitative as well as quantitative.... The key concept must be improved quality of people's life (quoted in Esteva 1999: 13).

Despite or because of the initial focus on economic growth, state planning failed to upgrade the living standards and material conditions in many Third World countries. Consequently, equitable distribution emerged as a central issue since the 1960s. Within the United Nations, newly established institutions—such as the United Nations Research Institute for Social Development (UNRISD) and the United Nations Development Programme (UNDP) founded in 1963 and 1965 respectively—started to advocate for a 'unified approach' that incorporates both economic and social aspects of development. Similarly, the World Bank, under the leadership of Robert McNamara, brought forth 'poverty alleviation' through its antipoverty policies (Arndt 1987; Finnemore 1997). In the 1970s, the conception of development underwent further incorporation and redefinition. The International Labour Organization's (ILO) advocacy of 'Basic Human Needs' went beyond the conventional issues of economic redistribution and further expanded the notion of development. Development as systematic and steady provision of basic needs focused on the 'primary redistribution ... of income, assets, and power' (Leftwich 2000: 47).

After a period of retrenchment in the 1980s, the early 1990s witnessed the return of social concerns in development (Nelson 1992). Dealing with poverty in *World Development Report 1990*, for example, the World Bank argued that 'Progress in raising average incomes, however welcome, must not distract attention from this massive and continuing burden of poverty' (World Bank 1990: 1). The so-called 'Environment Report' (*World Development Report 1992*) emphasized the 'acceleration of sustained and equitable human and economic development' (Bartoli 2000: 11), and *World Development Report 1993* tackled health issues. Bringing back social dimensions to its development agenda, the World Bank brought back social dimensions to the table and attempted to redefine the role of the state in *World Development Report 1997*: 'the state is central to economic and social development, not as a direct provider of growth but as a partner, catalyst and facilitator' (World Bank 1997: 1). Although this acknowledgement of the positive role of the state signaled a shift away from the World Bank's previous call for a minimal state in the 1980s, this was not a ringing endorsement for the planning state either. In the 1990s, the state, while essential, does not carry the charisma of the planning state. Emerging is the participatory conception of development in which the 'people' take the center stage.

Human Development Report published annually by the United Nations Development Programme since 1990, embodied this new conception. UNDP defines human development as development 'of the people, by the people, and for the people':

Development of the people means investing in human capabilities, whether in education or health or skills, so that they can work productively and creatively, development for the people means ensuring that the economic growth they generate is distributed widely and fairly ... development by the people ... giving everyone a chance to participate (UNDP 1993: 3).

UNDP's people-centered approach emphasizes 'people's participation in development', particularly nongovernmental organizations (*Human Development Report 1993*). *Human Development Report 1994*'s main topic 'was "sustainable human development"; while the absolute priority of poverty reduction, productive employment, and social integration were again present, they were linked more to environmental regeneration' (Bartoli 2000: 13). *Human Development Report 1996* defined economic growth as a means to human development: 'Human development is the end—economic growth a means. So the purpose of growth should be to enrich people's lives' (*Human Development Report 1996*: 1).

The elaboration in the conception of development in international discourse as envisioned in sustainable human development was directly translated to actual national development plans in the 1990s. In Lesotho (1997: 70), 'Sustainable human development (SHD), the theme of this Sixth Plan, is based on the premise that the principal aim of development is the creation of an enabling environment in which all people in the nation may enjoy healthy and creative lives.' While Korea's Sixth Five-Year Economic and Social Development Plan (1989) did not explicitly invoke sustainable human development, it redefined the relationship between economic and social aspects of development:

The people of Korea are determined to speed the nation's economic development. Greater production is a prerequisite to higher living standards. The results of economic development should benefit people in all regions and all strata of society. At Korea's present stage of economic development, balanced development between social strata and between geographic areas should actually accelerate overall national development (31).

In short, there exists a positive feedback relationship between economic and social dimensions of development. This integrated view is a significant departure from the initial, narrowly economic conception of development.

Economic growth, once considered to be the primary goal and an end in itself, gave way to a more sophisticated conception that encompasses both social and economic dimensions of development. In this new conception, people are the leading actors: 'the purpose of development is to widen the people's choices' (*Human Development Report 1993*: 3). Changes in Turkey's development plans clearly illustrate this dramatic transformation. Turkey's first national plan adopted in the early 1960s '... aimed to achieve an annual growth rate of 7 percent, to solve the unemployment problem and to reach a balance in external payments ... "in accordance with the principles of social justice" ' (Eastham 1964: 133). Although social justice was invoked as a guiding principle of national development, the meaning of social justice remained abstract. On the other hand, Turkey's Seventh Development Plan (1996) elaborated social dimensions of development in great detail:

...efforts shall be made to ensure a free and democratic environment, render prominence to individuals, realize a sustainable rapid development, raise the standards of living and improve income distribution, increase productive employment, accelerate industrialisation, leap forward in technology, raise the level of education in order to get a higher share from the world welfare and to provide education to all the individuals of the society commensurate with their abilities, assure cultural development, provide social security and basic health services for all and improve the quality of the health services, protect and improve the environment (21).

The conception of development in the post-World War II period has gone through a dramatic expansion from a limited notion of economic growth to the present understanding of sustainable human development. Although the economic conception remains intact, greater attention is now paid to redistributive, environmental, and social welfare concerns. Equally significant is the emergence of the people as the primary beneficiary and driving force of development.

3.3. GLOBALIZING VISIONS OF DEVELOPMENT

As the conception of development, conceived primarily as a property of the nation-state, has expanded, global society has been increasingly constructed as a unit of development. This aspect of globalization has escaped the attention of students of globalization. In a fundamental sense, globalization involves: (*a*) the construction of an 'imagined community' (Anderson 1991; Meyer, Drori, and Hwang, Chapter 1 and Conclusion) at the global level; (*b*) the structuration of global governance mechanisms, institutions, and organizations (Boli and Thomas 1999; Fligstein 2005; Drori, Chapter 4); and (*c*) the rationalization of knowledge around *loosely* integrated scientific and epistemic communities (Haas 1992; Drori et al. 2003; Drori and Meyer,

Chapter 2). These processes to a great extent recast many national issues into a global frame. Negotiated and constructed in global institutions and governance mechanisms are norms and rules of a new order. Transnational epistemic communities produce knowledge increasingly at the global level. In short, globalization produces an upward shift in the visions of development and many other issues previously embedded in national states to the world level.

The normative bases of the international development field during the heyday of state planning were the image of the world as divided into wealthy and poor countries, and the conception of the integrated political economy of embedded liberalism (Ruggie 1982). Growing inequalities would eventually lead to instability and conflicts (Tinbergen 1967; also Meyer 1980), and development of poor regions of the world would benefit both the poor and the rich—the mutual benefit assumption in development economics (Hirschman 1981). One way to control growing inequalities among nation-states was mobilization and integration of the Third World into the world economy through the empowered and interventionist state.

The vision of the partitioned world along the development continuum can be observed in the ways in which development indicators are organized and presented in development-related publications. One such publication is *World Development Report*, published annually by the World Bank since 1978. Various country-level indicators are reported, and some of these are aggregated to higher-level categories into which nation-states are grouped. In *World Development Report* published in 1980, for example, countries were divided into 'developing countries' (which are made up of 'middle-income countries' and 'low-income countries'), 'oil-exporting developing countries' or 'capital-surplus oil exporters', 'industrialized countries', 'centrally planned economies', and so on.[3] Although the conception of the integrated world economy had existed for a long time, data depicting the world itself as a measurable unit of development did not appear in the World Bank's account until 1991—at least for the general public.[4] World-level data depict and construct the world as an integrated unit, in a similar way the nation-state has been constructed in the postwar period (McNeely 1995).

What makes world data possible is standardization in 'the compilation and dissemination of statistics that monitor the degree of progress achieved by the national society' (Ramirez and Boli 1987: 155). States, as responsible for national development, collect data to account for progress in various domains. In doing so, they rely on the global definitions, methods, and standards formulated and promulgated by international organizations such as the UN and United Nations Education, Science and Culture Organization (UNESCO) (McNeely 1995). Further, as the expanding conception of development identifies new relevant social domains, states expand their

Table 3.1 Breakdown of development indicators by domains and aggregation levels reported in *Human Development Report 2000*

Issue domains	Nation	Country group	World	Row total
Economy	12	2	23	37
Gender	16	13	19	48
Health/Nutrition/Food	7	1	17	25
Human development	12	1	17	30
Demography	1	0	14	15
Development aid and finance	0	15	9	24
Education	5	0	9	14
Communication/Information/ Transportation	0	5	8	13
Energy	2	4	8	14
Environment	10	3	5	18
Personal distress/Crime	14	1	2	17
Poverty	15	1	2	18
Military	4	2	0	6
Politics	7	0	0	7
Work/Employment	4	10	0	14
Column total	109	58	133	300

Source: Human Development Report 2000.

data collection efforts to include those new domains under international guidelines. More national-level data become available over time for cross-national comparisons and for further aggregation to the world level.

Table 3.1 summarizes the breakdown of development-related indicators by issue domains and by highest aggregation levels—national, group of countries, and world—reported in *Human Development Report 2000*.[5] Three hundred indicators are reported on fifteen issue domains, which are rank-ordered based on the number of world-level indicators in Table 3.1. High on the list are economy, gender, health/nutrition/food, human development, development aid and finance, demography, and education. The level of standardization and rationalization of each domain is reflected in the total number of indicators regardless of aggregation levels. A simple correlation of the proportion of world-level indicators to the total number of indicators, and the total number of indicators in each domain shows that this indeed is the case. The correlation is high and significant (0.77 at $p < 0.001$). Comparable data-collection and reporting systems across countries render international comparison, and the compilation and aggregation of cross-national data possible.[6]

These highly standardized domains have been fundamental features in the broadly conceived notion of development. Gender equity (indicators on gender differences in various issues), access to education, to health care and basic services (number of doctors and nurses, and percentage immunized against TB and measles, etc.) are social dimensions of development. The emergence of world-level data indicates both the globalization of development beyond national borders and the construction of the world as an imagined community. These aggregated data in turn account for and measure progress at the world level.

At the top of the list is the economic domain, in which the world is portrayed as an integrated system of production (agriculture and services as percentage of GDP and total GDP), consumption (private and government consumptions), and exchange (imports of goods and services). Further, together with indictors on communication, information, and transportation, economic data forge a network image of the world as flows of capital (foreign direct investment), goods, services, and information (Internet hosts, telephone lines, cellular mobile subscribers, and televisions). Curiously, flows of people, either as workers or as tourists, are not yet part of this image of the world. At the bottom of the list are military and politics; indicators in these two domains describe political structures and processes of individual countries (such as political parties, voter turnout, means of selection to parliament, etc.), and military expenditures. In the absence of a world state in the mold of a national state, there are no equivalent political structures (such as a political party system or democratic representation) at the world level although the European Union is increasingly headed in this direction. Therefore, the absence of world-level indicators in these domains is not surprising.

World-level data, in addition to constructing a global entity, explicitly frame many issues as global problems requiring global solutions. For example, the spread of HIV/AIDS is a global, not a regional problem. Some regions where the spread is more explosive demand more focused attention, but it certainly affects all beyond national borders. Similarly, global warming, regardless of the scientific validity of its threat, is depicted as a global concern. In this way, lives of global citizens are fundamentally interconnected and embedded in a larger collectivity beyond national borders.

In economic or business-related fields, there has been an explosion of numbers about the world. In other areas of social life, we can easily observe the rise of world-level data, which assume common frames of references, standards, and preferences. Although national rakings of schools (such as universities and professional schools) have existed in many countries for quite some time, a global ranking of business schools, for instance, is now only one click away from anyone with access to the Internet (Hedmo, Sahlin-Anderson, and Wedlin 2005*a*, 2005*b*). In this ranking, business schools, regardless of national origins, are evaluated on a common set of metrics. Assumed in these metrics are: (*a*) business schools teach and operate in a more or less similar manner; (*b*) consumers—in this case potential MBA students—have more or less uniform preferences; and (*c*) schools, potential students, and employers are looking beyond national borders—that is, the field of management education stretches the entire globe. Another example is the comparison of international test scores. Various international rankings of countries based on student test scores assume common sets of educational materials taught in schools across the globe; more importantly, students as global citizens can learn the same materials and can be compared to one another (Ramirez et al. forthcoming). These universalistic assumptions of schools, students, and education help facilitate the transformation of the university into a modern organizational actor (Krücken and Meier, Chapter 10).

The emergence of world-level data indicates the construction of problems and issues explicitly at the global level. This occurs, however, without a similar upward shift in agentic capacities underlying state planning. In the absence of a global or world state, globalization creates an interesting situation. While global issues and problems abound, 'getting action' to address these problems is difficult (see White 1992 for the inherent difficulty in getting action in social organizations), particularly given the associational culture and acephalous state of the current world polity (Meyer et al. 1997). A call for a 'world development plan' (Tinbergen 1968) is yet to be materialized, for instance. The associational nature of world society produces a lot of debates, talks, treaties and agreements, and even organizations. This upward shift of visions of development without centralization of authority in a charismatic entity at the world level would likely generate a plethora of actors unhindered by a centralized control system in this new frontier.

3.4. THE SHIFTING LOCUS ON PLANNING

While the visions and rationality of development have shifted upward with globalization, planning authority and actorhood more generally have shifted downward to non-state entities who have been increasingly seen as legitimate, empowered actors. This downward shift has occurred in the long-term historical process of cultural devolution (Meyer and Jepperson 2000), and has given rise to a new governmentality (Foucault 1991; Burchell, Gordon, and Miller 1991; Barry, Osborne, and Rose 1996; Mitchell 1988, 1991) or a government at a distance (Rose 1996, 1999). In this section, I discuss the changing role of the state, the rise of organizational actorhood, and the increasing influence of consultancy in the era of declining state planning.

State planning for development was a global modernization project of the post-World War II era and was to achieve development as defined and financed by the international development field. This, however, has often been followed many unanticipated consequences: the rise of authoritarian regimes, violation of human and civil rights as well as extreme income inequality in many parts of the Third World, despite the progressive nature of national development plans. Decoupling between the collective aspiration and the day-to-day reality of national development was all too easy to observe. This has partially contributed to the decline of state planning since the mid-1970s. Figure 3.2 shows this decline as observed the annual frequency and cumulative distribution of plan terminations or expirations over time.

Although the state recedes to the background as a central locus of action and vision, this decline represents neither the end of development nor the death of planning. Much progressive agenda has become taken-for-granted. For example, basic education, a significant part of state planning, is now a routine reality of nation-states. The decline of state planning undermines neither the institutional importance of education nor the role of the state in education. The failures of state planning, moreover, have led to the elaboration in the global conception of development. The evolving conception of development has propelled the people or human individuals to the forefront of development as the main driving force.

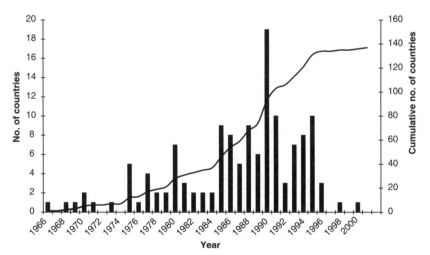

Figure 3.2 Frequency and cumulative distributions of last national development plan expirations

There certainly is doubt about the state as the primary agent for development, and the role of the state is being redefined especially with the growing importance of human development. Within government bureaucracy, planning—the sole responsibility of a charismatic unit such as a planning ministry or economic planning board—is now routinely performed in various state bodies and actors. In the meantime, the role of the state is being redefined to that of a super-stabilizer (Bauman 1998: 65), the 'basic' services provider (Meyer 1998), or as a rule maker (Fligstein 1996*a*, 1996*b*). The state provides stable (legal and regulatory) environments and services for its citizenry. In turn, free associations (democracy) and free exchanges (markets) among actors planning in their own interests would produce collective goods or outcomes. The state is to strengthen the institutional infrastructure that would facilitate the participation of the citizenry in the creation of collection goods through democratic means (Evans 2005).

While the role of the state is being redefined, the state as an organization has expanded dramatically in the past few decades (Kim et al. 2002). This expansion, accompanied by devolution of authority within the state, has not resulted in the growth of a modern Leviathan. Discourse on the new public finance management, which aims to 'reconstruct and rationalize public organizations as responsible, integrated, and empowered rational actors' paints the image of the reconstructed state (Burkitt and Whyman 1994; Painter 1994; Rhodes 1994; Meyer 1998: 10; Olson, Guthrie, and Humphery 1998). This reform is about unshackling public agencies from state control and constructing them as 'organizations' with clear boundaries, goals, resources and budgets, information systems, decision-making apparatus, and plans (Brunsson and Sahlin-Andersson 2000). Public agencies are disembedded from the state and transformed into rational actors who are evaluated on their ability to produce whatever services they purport to provide and are held accountable; the state is disaggregated and disembodied into various organizations separate from state bureaucracy and one another. The reform is transnational in scope, and driving this global reform movement is the highly professionalized epistemic community of accounting and management experts (Meyer 1998).

In the broader arena of the economy, organizations and individuals plan. The issue is the locus of planning or actorhood: 'In market economies there is planning and coordination—the planning occurs within firms, there is extensive coordination among firms. The issue is not whether there is planning, but rather the locus of planning' (Stiglitz 1994: 251). The assumption is that modern individuals and their voluntary associations have the capacity, resources, and information to plan.

At the organizational level, the rise of strategic planning and strategy signals the downward shift in the locus of planning. Since the mid-1960s, strategic planning has been an obsession of American corporations (Mintzberg 1994).

Strategic planning is a 'formalized procedure to produce articulated result, in the form of an integrated system of decision' carried out by planners detached from day-to-day organizational operation. A planner's job is to take future into consideration in the context of organizational goals and resource constraints, to produce an organizational strategic blueprint or a plan' (Mintzberg 1994: 31–2). Careful analyses and systematic forecasts, organizational actions, and strategies are deliberated and predetermined from the center, or by the Chief Executive Officer (CEO) as the chief planner (Mintzberg 1994). Strategic planning, consequently, would less likely allow for emergent strategies. On the other hand, emergent strategies imply that (some) strategies may be discovered only in the midst of action and that anybody can be a strategist or a planner. In other words, individuals who actually carry out their tasks, not the chief planner of the organization, know best what needs to be done and can flexibly respond to fast changing environments. This points to the growing importance of individual actors in organizational settings and parallels the downward shift in planning authority from the state to substate levels. The major criticism of central strategic planning has been that it is all about talk, but not about action, and it is an expensive operation that sometimes does not pay off. Central planning is too bureaucratic and hierarchical, and diminishes organizational flexibility; instead all members in the organization should be planners of their own action. Thus, the locus of planning devolves through the organizational chart from top to lower-level units. Luo (Chapter 9), in this context, documents the rise of human resources culture in employee training that emphasizes the empowerment of individuals within organizations. Likewise, scholarly interests have shifted from strategic planning to organizational strategy.

Data are collected from *Strategic Management Journal* presented in Figure 3.3 and *Long Range Planning* presented in Figure 3.4, and show changing discourse in the management field. In *Strategic Management Journal* first published in 1980, the number of articles containing either 'planning' or 'plan' in their titles has declined over time from nine articles in 1981 to two articles in 1999, while the number of article titles containing 'strategy' has steadily hovered around ten articles a year. In *Long Range Planning*, the shift in management discourse from strategic planning to strategy is even clearer. The number of articles on planning dropped significantly from the highest of forty-two in 1976 to seven in 1999, while the number of articles on strategy has increased from three in 1975 to twenty in 1997.

While strategic planning and, of late, strategy have been an integral part of for-profit corporations, the nonprofit sector in the United States has recently embraced these practices. Gammal et al. (2005) report that in a random sample of 200 nonprofit organizations in the San Francisco Bay Area,

Figure 3.3 *Strategic Management Journal*

46 percent have adopted a strategic plan. This is an astonishing figure given the median number of full-time equivalents (FTE) is 2.4, and more than half of nonprofits in the region have an annual budget of less than $200,000. Many nonprofit organizations do not have the financial means, staff capacity, or managerial knowledge to implement their plans. Nevertheless, they often adopt a strategic plan because their current (and/or future) funders require it as part of their financial support and/or because both nonprofits themselves and their constituents see it as a taken-for-granted feature of a legitimate organization (Hwang and Suarez 2005). In addition, in many cases, adoption of strategic plans involves consultants who provide much needed management expertise to nonprofits.

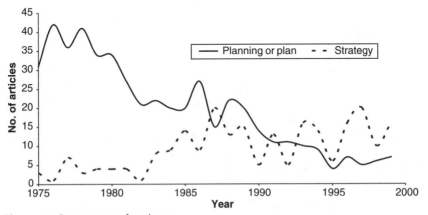

Figure 3.4 Long-range planning

While the locus of planning or actorhood shifts downward, organizations rely increasingly on outside consultancy for advice. Various organizational activities and functions—from information systems and market research to human resource planning and even strategic planning—have become legitimate domains of consulting firms, and the number of consulting firms has exploded over the years (Kipping 1999; Mckenna, Djelic, and Ainamo 2000). Even public sector 'organizations' make up a significant part of the consultancy clientele. The consulting industry is a global and highly professionalized industry, often requiring a specialized training (Kipping and Engwall 2002; Moon and Wotipka, Chapter 5). The worldwide expansion of management consulting industry coincides with the fall of state planning in the late 1970s and early 1980s.

The translation of the multidivisional form into the European context illustrates consultancy's role and the process of global diffusion of organizational models. Management consultancy has its origin in the peculiar history of American business of the 1930s (Kipping 1999) and developed as an unintended consequence of the Glass Steagall Act and other related legislations. It was required that 'listed companies hire independent auditors to file quarterly reports, that commercial and investment banking operate independently of each other, and that management consulting be separate from commercial and investment banking' (McKenna 1995; McKenna, Djelic, and Ainamo 2000). After its success and consolidation in the United States, American management consultancy went to Europe in the late 1950s and then became global in the 1980s. In the United States, the multidivisional form (Chandler 1962; Williamson 1975; Fligstein 1985, 1990; Djelic 1998), initially conceived at the Du Pont Company and General Motors in the 1920s, was disseminated and popularized with the great help from the burgeoning consulting industry (Kipping 1999). When American consultants entered the European market in the 1960s, they brought with them the multidivisional form (Kipping 1999: 209–10).[7] Faced with challenges of organizational reengineering and industrial renewal, European companies turned to 'the "know-how" and the aura of professionalism of US industry' represented in American consultants (Kipping 1999: 209). First, experiences in the US industry were seen as directly applicable to the European cases. Organizations—European or American—are *perceived* to be comparable units or entities (Strang and Meyer 1993; Meyer 1994; Meyer, Boli, and Thomas 1994), and experiences and knowledge from one context can be either directly or with slight modifications applied and transplanted to another context. Second, management consultants as carriers of management knowledge are highly scientized and professionalized, and thus seen as legitimate (Czarniawska-Joerges and Sévon 1996; Sahlin-Andersson and Engwall 2002).

From management, accounting, the environment, to education and others, there has been a worldwide expansion of loosely integrated and decentralized global epistemic communities of professionals and international nongovernmental organizations (INGOs). Transnational epistemic communities in various domains produce models and prescriptions for action and mobilization based on scientific knowledge of universal applicability. Jang (Chapter 7) shows the rising importance of transparency in accounting practice as transmitted by the Big 6 accounting firms worldwide. Mendel (Chapter 6) analyzes the role of the international standardization movement as an instance of global rationalization. More generally in management, the worldwide expansion of business schools facilitates the rapid spread of various management models (Moon and Wotipka, Chapter 5). A nascent business plan writing industry has emerged for high technology start-up companies to help pursue venture capital funding (Nguyen 2000). These are all but a few instances in which global rationalization provides actors with highly professionalized, scientized, and stylized prescriptions and advice. Across the globe, rationalized, universalistic models and standards are locally translated, interpreted, and implemented (Czarniawska and Sévon 1996, 2005; Amorim and Kipping 1999; Kipping 1999; McKenna, Djelic, and Ainamo 2000). With the growing salience of authoritative models and standards formulated by consultants and professional experts, the downward shift of planning and actorhood generates, in various areas of organizational life, a surprisingly high level of standardization and isomorphism among substate level actors, who adopt and practice similar models of action and organizing.

3.5. SUMMARY AND IMPLICATIONS

In this chapter, I have shown the rise and fall of state planning in the postwar period and argued that the decline of state planning has been accompanied by both the upward shift in the visions of development to the global level and the downward shift in the locus of planning or actorhood to non-state actors— individuals and organizations.

Failures to realize the promise of development have led to expansion and differentiation in the global conception of development in which a narrowly conceived notion of economic growth gave way to a more multifaceted conception of human development. In this enlarged vision, moreover, human individuals are the primary beneficiary and driving force of development. Increasingly, the world itself has emerged as an integrated collectivity and as a unit of development. The devolving locus of planning or actorhood redefines the role of the state and transforms substate level entities and organizations into legitimate actors. The state no longer serves as the primary agent for development on behalf of the nation, and human individuals are increasingly replacing the state as the primary engine of development. In the contemporary world, as Block and Evans (2005: 506) aptly put it, 'The driving force behind (economic) development has moved out of the state to the intersection of the state and civil society....' With accelerating globalization, development is no longer seen as an exclusive property of the nation-state, and civil society has become increasingly global.

The institutionalization of development means both the globalization of development and the rise of human individuals as the main agent of development. Institutionalization, in this context, implies deepening or intensification across different levels of social analysis: the frame of development goes upward while the driving actorhood of development goes downward. In the meantime, development continues to evolve as an ideal of the imagined community explicitly at the global level, and to provide actors with scripts for action. As Shanahan and Khagram (Chapter 8) demonstrate, even corporations, as part of their CR repertoire, pursue such social issues as poverty alleviation, which are distant from their profit motivation.

Despite its decline at the state level, planning, too, has undergone institutionalization in the similar sense of deepening and intensification across levels of social units. The emergent global (civil) society is an increasingly scientized one (Drori et al. 2003; Drori and Meyer, Chapter 2) in which uncertainties are rationalized into 'risks' (Beck 1992) and/or 'opportunities' (Meyer, Drori, and Hwang, Chapter 1). In this rationalized world, there is no alternative to planning or rational action; therefore, planning gains even more legitimacy. Mitchell (1988) appropriately quipped, 'No plan, no anything'. The diminishing authority of the national state as a charismatic planner combined with the absence of a global state opens up the world as a stage, and everyone plays the role of a planner.

NOTES

1. I would like to thank John W. Meyer, Mark Granovetter, Robert Freeland, Francisco O. Ramirez, Gili Drori, Yong Suk Jang, Woody Powell, and participants of the Stanford Comparative Workshop for their comments. The dissertation research from which this chapter derives was supported by the Littlefield Fellowship in International Political Economy, Institute of International Studies, Stanford University.

2. Colonial linkages were also important as both France and the United Kingdom carried out development planning in their colonial and other dependent territories (Bose 1997). In many countries, colonial plans became full-fledged national plans after independence. In the Colonial Development and Welfare Act of 1940, the British government established that development planning was necessary and eventually required colonial governments to publish development plans. Similarly, through development planning in colonies, France attempted to complement the metropole.

3. Notice both planning and development are used to map the world. Interestingly, in the following year's report (1981), 'nonmarket industrial economies' replaced 'centrally planned economies'. Also along the way, countries became 'economies'. That is 'low-income countries' became 'low-income economies', for example.

4. Of course, this does not mean that there had been no world-level data before 1991.

5. *Human Development Report* is an annual report published by the United Nations Development Programme since 1990.

6. According to the World Bank, aggregated data can be compiled 'only if the country data available for a given year account for at least two-thirds of the full group.... So long as that criterion is met, uncurrent reporters (and those not providing ample history) are, for years with missing data, assumed to behave like the sample of the group that does provide estimates' (*World Development Report 1991*: 272–3). Alternatively, high variation makes compilation of world-level data difficult.

7. McKinsey, in particular, played an important role in bringing about decentralization to Europe. According to Kipping (1999), 'In the U.K., 32 out of the 100 largest companies hired consultants to help overhaul their organization. In 22 of these cases, the service provider was McKinsey. The consultancy also decentralized several French and German companies' (210).

4

Governed by Governance: The New Prism for Organizational Change

Gili S. Drori[1]

Recurring disappointment with rates of growth and a growing frustration with the lack of effect after pouring aid and investment money into developing countries for several decades directed the attention of developmentalists to political conditions. By the mid-1990s it was clear that corruption, mismanagement, and capricious bureaucracies were standing in the way of modernization in developing countries. Thus, even before the much-publicized cases of corporate misconduct in the United States and Europe, corruption emerged as a worldwide concern, as did its curbing as a social policy subject to globalization. This concern has since been extended to the related issues of the rule of law, bureaucratic efficiency, and risks to foreign investment in nationalization schemes. And, with the extension of these related concerns, the term *governance* was coined to capture the overall movement for management reform.

Today, governance is a solid global field of action: governance-related activities are coordinated—and initiated—by a web of transnational organizations and national agencies. Currently, transnational organizations, from the World Bank and Transparency International to the World Trade Organization (WTO), propagate the advancement of transparency, accountability, and the rule of law in countries and markets worldwide. But what are the notions of governance that are advanced by the work of these transnational organizations? When did these notions consolidate into the global field of governance? And who are the social actors behind the institutionalization of governance as a global social concern? These questions are the heart of this chapter.

This chapter explores several dimensions of the global institutionalization of governance and adds an institutional perspective to the current scholarship on the issue. Specifically, the institutionalization and globalization of governance are described as an expression of rationalized social reform. The argument is that governance is a product of a world steeped in rationalization and the primacy of individual actorhood. This cultural atmosphere of rationalization and actorhood leads to the translation of 'management' into 'governance'.

4.1. GAUGING INSTITUTIONALIZATION EMPIRICALLY: A RESEARCH STRATEGY

The chapter has two goals: (*a*) to describe both the historical process and the current form of the institutionalization of governance and (*b*) to trace the world culture of rationalization and actorhood in the institutionalization of governance. Methodologically, the research relied on a two-pronged empirical approach: describing the organizational structuration of the field and mapping the discursive themes carried by the organizational actors.

Because the chapter approaches governance from action and discourse dimensions as well as from content and form dimensions, data from many sources were used. Organizational data came from the online version of the directory of the Union of International Association (UIA) in August 2004. From this now conventional source for organizational and transnational activism data (Diehl 1997; Boli and Thomas 1999; Beckfield 2003) came information on *all* organizations that identify themselves as dealing with governance and corruption.[2] The organizational histories were culled from dates of founding (to track the timing of the structuration) and declarations of goals and activities (to track discursive content).

Additional discursive information came from sources in the academic literature. Hints of the discourse of governance in these professional discussions were sought by counting the uses of the term *governance* in works in five academic disciplines: sociology (Sociological Abstracts), economics and business (EconLit), political science (PAIS), history (Historical Abstracts), and anthropology (AnthroPlus). To these academic sources I add a bibliometric count of terminology in the popular press, specifically the *New York Times*, seeking to see the echo of the discourse in 'lay' discussions. Because *governance* is the current term for the notion of appropriate administration and management (in the public and the private sectors), the primary key word used in searching for information was *governance*. For getting at possible earlier works on governance, several alternative key words were used for parallel searches, for example, *corruption, transparency, accountability, management, bureaucracy, stewardship, state, citizenship*, and *organization*.[3] In this way, Mauro Guillén's strategy for the study of globalization (2001)[4] was augmented by an open-ended approach to the discursive boundaries for the term *governance*.

Last, to trace intraorganizational changes that would enrich the tale of the evolution of the field of governance, the various constitutive documents drawn up by several organizations over time were used, supplemented with organizational narratives of their history and interviews with key figures in the organizations.

Data from both bibliometric and organizational sources were used for mapping and commenting on three dimensions of the institutionalization process: (*a*) the emergence of the field of governance in discourse and action, (*b*) the carriers (organizational and disciplinary) of this new theme, and (*c*) the themes and lines of logic that are bundled into this term and field. The structure of the chapter follows this three-part logic.

4.2. THE INSTITUTIONALIZATION OF GOVERNANCE

Today, the World Bank identifies corruption as 'the single greatest obstacle to economic and social development. [Corruption] undermines development by distorting the rule of law and weakening the institutional foundation on which economic growth depends.'[5] And today, anticorruption and progovernance initiatives are anchored in national and international law: from the OECD 1997 Convention to Combat Corruption to the 2002 American Sarbanes-Oxley Act. With the anti-corruption field growing in complexity (Bryane 2004), still these laws reflect only the most recent—even if also the most dramatic—transformation of the attitudes of global players toward governance and the causes of progress. The following section describes the process and timing of the institutionalization of governance, tracing watershed events and major activities.

4.2.1. Organizational Structuration

Transparency International (TI), the primary international organization working on anticorruption, originated in a 1990 meeting in Swaziland between World Bank officials and several African leaders.[6] Frustrated by the Bank's resistance to assisting these government leaders in establishing an anticorruption program, Peter Eigen, then the World Bank director for East Africa, retired from the Bank and founded TI in 1993. Starting in 1994, TI pushed the World Bank into starting a series of cooperative projects on governance and development issues organized by the Economic Development Institute.[7] The first workshop, which focused on governance and anticorruption, was held in Uganda that year. Finally, in 1996, when TI already had thirty-eight national chapters, the World Bank, under the presidency of James D. Wolfensohn, acknowledged anticorruption as an important matter for development. In what came to be called his 'cancer of corruption' speech before the World Bank's annual meeting in October 1996, Wolfensohn opened the floodgates of work on what later came to be called governance issues (Mallaby 2004: 176). To mark this new concern, in 1996 James Wolfensohn announced the creation of WBI's governance unit. And throughout the 1990s the World Bank was the center of activity on anticorruption initiatives, sponsoring national anticorruption and progovernance programs (Marquette 2003; Bryane 2004).

The mid-1990s were the high point of the institutionalization of governance as a global social concern. UIA data confirm that during the 1990s the number of governance-minded organizations doubled. In 1990, there were 126 international organizations whose main concern was either governance or corruption; by 2003, the number of these organizations climbed to 214, showing a dramatic structuration.

This structuration in the early 1990s was important confirmation for the institutionalization of governance as a global social concern. Nevertheless, the history of work on governance-related issues on a global scale is older. The oldest governance-minded organization is Crown Agents for Overseas Governments and Administration, founded in London in 1833.[8] By 1945, only nine such international organizations were formed, but the rate of founding has accelerated dramatically thereafter. In the 1990s alone, forty-seven governance-minded international organizations and seventeen corruption-minded international organizations, or 34 and 71 percent of their respective fields, were founded.[9] The most 'productive' years, in terms of founding of governance- and corruption-minded international organizations, are 1993 (fifteen organizations founded), 1994 and 1995 (eleven institutions founded each year), and 1992 (eight organizations founded). These data are offered in Figure 4.1 and Table 4.1.

Today, the global organizational field of governance, although small in size compared with the health and education fields (numbering about 3,000 and 3,500 international organizations listed with UIA, respectively), enjoys great diversity and strong overlapping ties in its network or among its affiliates. Among the active international and transnational organizations today are the International Corporate Governance Network (ICGN, founded in 1996 and registered in the United Kingdom), the International Council for Information Technology in Government Administration (ICA, founded in 1968 in the United Kingdom), the International Association of Official Statistics (IAOS, founded in 1985 and headquartered in the Netherlands), and the International Network of Progressive Governance (founded in 1992

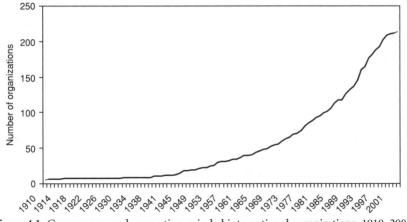

Figure 4.1 Governance- and corruption-minded international organizations, 1910–2004

and headquartered in the United Kingdom). For some of these international organizations, the matter of governance is a secondary concern; for example, the Pacific Islands Forum (founded in 1971 and headquartered in Fiji), which is concerned with all political and social issues that unite the nations of this region, also identifies governance among its concerns and classifies itself as a governance organization for UIA identification. For others, governance is central, but their sphere of operation is a specific region

Table 4.1 Founding of governance- and corruption-minded international organizations

Time	Number of foundings	
	Governance	Corruption
1833–1944	9	
1945–9	5	
1950–59	7	
1960–69	12	1
1970–79	24	0
1980–89	29	1
1990–99	47	17
2000–04[a]	5	5
Total with founding data	138	24
Total in data set	235	30

[a] Coded until August 2004 only.

only: for example, the Latin American Center for Local Government Training and Development (founded in 1983 and headquartered in Ecuador) is concerned primarily with the 'administrative and technical capacities of Latin American public officials and local governments'. Oddly enough, the International Association of Professional Bureaucrats (founded in 1968 in the US state of Texas) lists among its primary goals the 'improvement of bureaucracy through humor'. Overall, it seems, the global organizational field of governance is very varied in composition. Together, the governance- and corruption-minded international organizations form a dense network of international action.

The founding of international and transnational organizations focused on governance not only reflects the institutionalization of governance as a global social concern. The organizations are central to the process of the globalization of governance and its transference to other international and transnational players. In their role as 'teachers of norms' or 'norm exporters' (Finnemore 1996; Finnemore and Sikkink 1998), the organizations encourage governments and other local social institutions to comply with their standards. Indeed, they provide acceptable standards as models for governing entities that are seeking to reform. For example, the European Corporate Governance Institute compiles various governance codes of conduct from forty-six countries and four global sources.[10] In its work, the institute exemplifies the role of organizations in globalization. First, in making these documents available as scripts for proper governance measures, it encourages normative and mimetic modes of isomorphism in the field of governance (see Guler, Guillén, and MacPherson 2002). Second, in setting accountability and transparency as recommended features, the institute encourages organizations of various sorts to subject themselves to the same scrutiny that they now demand of public institutions (see Woods 1999).

Isomorphism is a clear feature in the field of governance, caused primarily by the culture of expertise and the 'teaching' role of international organizations. Describing the rapid replication of the World Bank's anticorruption initiatives from one country to another—beginning with a few pilot programs in East Africa, moving on to full-fledged plans in Latin America within 2–3 years, and reaching Eastern Europe by the mid-1990s—Michael Bryane writes:

Given that these programmes were run by the same organization and often the same individuals, it is highly probable that they were operating according to the same evolutionary rule—learn something, add to what you already know, apply and then go to the next project. Even the high degree of similarity in the evaluations of such country programmes suggests such rule following... (2004: 1078).

4.2.2. Discursive Institutionalization

Evidence in the academic literature makes it clear that governance is a new notion for the social sciences (and, by implication, for the policy world). The first mentions of the term *governance* appear in academic literature by the mid-1970s, but the term does not receive meaningful attention until the 1990s. The data in the literature also show that the process of institutionalizing governance in the literature is driven primarily by the disciplines of sociology and political science. Institutionalization has received backup force since the mid-1990s with the forceful adoption of the notion of governance by the discipline of economics.

The bibliometric analysis of references to the term *governance* reveals a clear trend of increase since 1970 in the use of the term *governance* in the social sciences. As displayed in Figure 4.2, only a few mentions of the term *governance* appear in social science literature circa 1970.[11] The term did not become standard until the early 1990s, common use of this term started only in 1995 and 1996, and the use of the term peaks in 2000 and 2001. Similar trend of increase in use of the term *governance* is evident in popular press: mentions of the term in the *New York Times* increased from 51 in 1970 to 218 in 2001, peaking in 1999. The notion of governance is, then, a relatively new form of thinking about management of organizations (public and private) that consolidated in the late 1990s.

Terms related to the current notion of governance, however, appeared in academic discussions prior to the 1990s. Specifically, the ideas expressed by

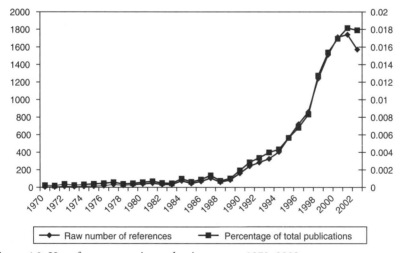

Figure 4.2 Use of *governance* in academic sources, 1970–2003

the terms *management* and *state* have been traditional concerns in the social sciences, and the terms have been used, even if at lower rates than today, since 1970 (which is the beginning of the coding period in this bibliometric analysis). The terms *accountability* and *transparency*, both of which are closely associated with the discourse of governance, cropped up in the mid-1990s. As evident in Figure 4.3, comparing between frequency of use of *governance* and alternative terms, the terms *management* and *state* are far more frequently used in the social sciences than *governance*.[12] *State* has been used over 12,000 times

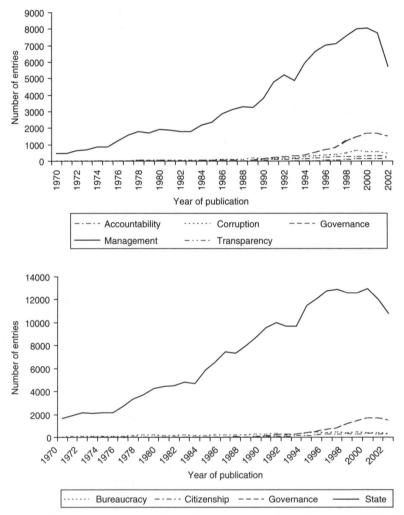

Figure 4.3 Use of *governance* and alternative terms in academic literature, 1970–2003

per year since 1995 in four disciplines; uses of the term *management* peaked in 1999 and 2000 at over 8,000 per year. These terms are constitutive terms for the social sciences, and their importance is evident in their number of uses.[13]

The novelty of the use of the term *governance* is a resurrection of a Greek classical term. The Greek verb *kubernân* (to steer a ship or a wagon) was used for the first time metaphorically by Plato to designate the governing of men, argues an etymological study of the term *governance*.[14] This original use gave birth to the Latin verb *gubernare*, which had the same significance and which, obliquely through its derivatives, is manifested in several of the Latin-based languages.[15] The French term *gouvernance* appears as early as the thirteenth century as an equivalent to *government*; since then it has been used specifically to mean certain territories in the north of France endowed with a unique administrative status. Used with a similar logic in a purely domestic context, the Portuguese *governança* connotes significance in politico-administrative and domestic spheres. In both French and Portuguese, the term became outmoded and used specifically in connection with the Old Regime. However, in English, as does the Spanish term *governanza*, the term *governance* means the action or manner of governing. Even the aforementioned etymological study acknowledges the very recent resurrection of the term to stand for the art or manner of governing, confirming that a new meaning was poured into an outmoded and legalistic term (Doornbos 2001: 92–3). The use of this term to (*a*) distinguish between the logic and the institutions of governing and (*b*) promote a new mode of management encouraged its reintroduction in other languages, most often as the literal English term.

What are the terms that the new term *governance* replaced? Clearly, sites of discourse (from professional disciplines to international organizations, as will be described in the following section on carriers) have recently adopted the term *governance* to describe their mission, even if their dedication to the issue is older than the recent history of the term. I reflect on this matter from two different viewpoints. First, through examining the frequency of terms in academic literature and news media, the term *governance* is compared with other synonym-like terms. It seems that the use of all terms increases, most probably because of the expansion of forums for academic publication. From this viewpoint, therefore, *governance* does not replace *stewardship, bureaucracy,* or other terms, even if it is clear that the pace of increase of use of *governance* during the 1990s was much greater than that of all other related terms. Second, from studying the historical change of particular governance-minded international organizations, it is clear that the emergence of the notion of governance required organizational adaptation. As an example of intraorganizational change in response to the institutionalization of governance, we look at the oldest organization in the field, namely, Crown Agents (see note 7). The trail of constitutive documents of this organization shows that it has adapted to the changing world. Specifically, the language used in the documents has changed from listing the organization's tasks of 'confer[ring] appointments', 'suspending or dismissing public servants', and 'administer[ing] the appointed oaths of all persons' to listing tasks regarding its own affairs: rights and responsibilities, hierarchical relations with British government offices, and private-sector incorporation. Governance thus changed from being a method of administration to being also an internal task for corporations and organizations. Overall, the term *governance* does not literally 'replace' other terms referring to administrative tasks, but rather it came to be more frequently used because, as is described in the following analysis, it has new meanings attached to it.

4.2.3. Institutionalization Process: Discursive and Organizational Structuration

The 1990s were the period of the institutionalization of the notion of governance and mobilization around it. This is evident both discursively and organizationally. From a discursive perspective, governance emerges in the 1990s as a new terminology, and thus viewpoint, for the social sciences and news media in the study and analysis of state, management, and policy. The term is intertwined with the terms *accountability* and *transparency*, thus explaining the current common use of all three terms as a discursive package.

The 1990s were also the era of major structuration of governance as a global organizational field. It is evident from the much-edited chronology of world-wide initiatives on governance issues (Appendix 4.A) that the wave of activity around governance issues during the 1990s included a wide variety of work. Legal, organizational, corporate and public, national and international initiatives and institutions were placed on the global agenda during this decade. The activity peaked with the widespread 'new public management' movement, which called for an aggressive reform of administrative systems in different countries and for a parallel launch of an international program for regulatory and administrative reform. These calls, broadcast loudly by OECD's Public Management Service (PUMA) program, are highlighted by the inclusion of good governance in the ambitious Millennium Development Goals (MDG) of the United Nations. Goal 8 of the MDG is to 'build a global partnership for development', with the first of its targets (number 12) '[developing] further an open, rule-based, predictable, nondiscriminatory trading and financial system. It includes a commitment to good governance, development and poverty reduction—both nationally and internationally.' The

MDG initiative aims to accomplish its goals by the year 2015 as a lever supporting the implementation of the related reforms in governance. Because of the newness of the term *governance* in its current meaning, the structuration of governance is a way to resolve the dichotomy between national or cultural sovereignty and a world commitment to development. It casts national and cultural inadequacies as administrative problems related to modernization, thus normalizing and transnationalizing them. And the parallel emerging emphasis on corporate governance has similarly changed the disciplines that analyze these problems of governance and expanded the range of disciplines and professions (Davis 2005), as well as organizational carriers, that address this wide range of issues that are now captured by the new term.

4.3. CARRIERS OF GOVERNANCE

The structuration and institutionalization of governance create a web of carriers for the idea of governance. Ideas and carriers are the yin and yang of an institutionalization and diffusion process: the institutionalization of ideas reifies the legitimacy of the carriers, while the carriers labor to reproduce, promote, and diffuse the ideas and thus establish their legitimacy. As explained by Sahlin-Andersson and Engwall (2002: 9–10), the term *carrier* implies not a passive role as propagator but involvement in the process of institutionalization and diffusion of ideas. Carriers encourage, support, transport, and transform ideas while raising them into the social conscience. As the following section demonstrates, the carriers of governance are clearly marked by certain organizational and disciplinary features.

4.3.1. Organizational Carriers

The international and transnational organizations that identify their core mission as governance and anticorruption issues have distinct features. First, they are overwhelmingly nongovernmental: only seven of the anticorruption-minded international organizations and only thirty-nine of the governance-minded international organization are distinctly intergovernmental international organizations. This may be a sign of the time of their founding, much in line with the notion of organizational imprinting. Considering that the founding of most of these organizations occurred during the 1990s, also the era of strong participation in policymaking by civil society and private-sector organizations,[16] these emerging governance organizations bring together multiple constituencies and regard multisector partnership as a constitutive principle. In this sense, the traditional demarcations between INGO and IGO are problematic for a new global organizational field such as governance.[17]

Second, these organizations are mostly headquartered in the developed world. As indicated in Table 4.2, most international and transnational organizations in this field are headquartered in OECD member nations. The fact that global social action comes primarily from the developed and affluent world is not unique to the field of governance.[18]

Third, most of the governance- and corruption-minded organizations are 'mega organizations', or associations of associations and networking organizations (Ahrne and Brunsson 2006). Such organizations, like the International City/County Management Association (ICMA; founded in 1914 and headquartered in Washington, DC), the International Corporate Governance Network (ICGN; founded in 1995 and headquartered in London), and the Global Corporate Governance Forum (GCGF; headquartered in Washington, DC) serve as centers for discussion and action for their members and many of them declare advocacy among their primary tasks. Many others are more clearly education or consultancy institutions; for example, the European School of Governance (founded in 1999 and located in Berlin) and European Corporate Governance Institute (ECGI; founded in 2002 and registered in Brussels). Others are arms of regional or communal organizations; for example, the Commonwealth Association for Corporate Governance (CACG; founded in 1998 and headquartered in Marlborough, New Zealand) is serving members of the British Commonwealth and the Urban Governance Initiative (TUGI; founded in 1998 and headquartered in Malaysia) serves urban municipalities in East Asia.

Table 4.2 Governance- and corruption-minded international organizations by location of headquarters

	Headquarters in OECD member countries	Headquarters in non-OECD member countries	More than one headquarters location	Location not specified	Total
Governance-minded organizations	148	35	18	44	235
Corruption-minded organizations	21	6	1	2	30
Total	169	41	19	46	265

4.3.2. Academic Carriers

From the bibliographical academic data, we learn that there are clear disciplinary variations in the use of the term *governance*. The general patterns of the distribution of the term hold across the disciplinary sources, as they do in the whole field of the social sciences: (*a*) the use of the term *governance* and related terms dramatically increased during the 1990s, (*b*) the term *governance* was not the most widely used term of this group, and (*c*) the terms *state* and *management* and sometimes even *corruption* were widely used before the focus of the 1990s on governance. But although the general patterns are the same, there are also dramatic differences among the social science disciplines in their use of *governance* and related terms.

Most dramatic is the difference in total number of references to *governance* and related terms across the social science disciplines. Whereas the number of references to *governance* in the economics field (EconLit) in the late 1990s is in the thousands, the number of references in sociology (SocAbs) and political science (PAIS) is in the hundreds; in history (HistAbs) it is in the tens, and in anthropology (AnthroPlus) the total number is negligible. The numbers are evident in Figure 4.4.[19] This disciplinary variation in use of the term *governance* clearly indicates who the champions of governance are, namely, the disciplines of economics, political science, and sociology. In particular, the institutionalization of governance as a social science notion is driven by political scientists: the term appeared first in political science writing[20] and was used most in the writing of this discipline.[21] The other disciplines that later adopted this idea are sociology[22] and economics.[23] The academic

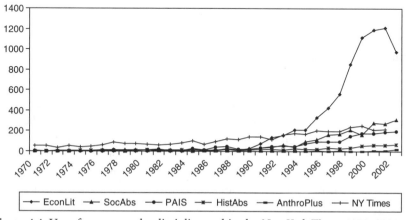

Figure 4.4 Use of *governance* by discipline and in the *New York Times*, 1970–2003

disciplines of history and anthropology, to which the notions of governance, administration, and effectiveness are intellectually marginal, appropriately hardly use the term *governance*.

Similar to the general trends, in each discipline the terms *state* and *management* are more commonly used, far surpassing *governance* even in the 1990s. And these terms, as well as *corruption*, were in use before the peaking of *governance* (and its dependent terms *accountability* and *transparency*) in the 1990s. The dramatic expansion in the use of the term *governance* in literature, academic and news media, revealed by the bibliographic data may be an expression of the general expansion of academic literature rather than the dominance of this specific notion. But, as presented in Appendix 4.B, when the number of uses of the term *governance* is standardized by total volume of work, the overall trend of expansion is maintained in all these discursive sites.

From these numbers, it seems that sociologists and political scientists, to whom administration and the state are core ideas—if not constitutive myths—have been instrumental in the process of institutionalizing the notion of governance. Once the notion was institutionalized, sometime in the mid- to late-1980s, the economists adopted it with a vengeance: to date, the 'top ten' most cited articles on governance are all from the discipline of economics. Through this process of transference across disciplinary lines, the notion of governance absorbs its different meanings and is infused by the logic of the different disciplines that use it. And the literature on governance, even if not anchored in bibliographic and disciplinary evidence, seems to indicate that the notion of governance has also permeated the work of engineers (especially development engineers) as well as management and business professionals.

4.3.3. Advocating Governance

On the field of global action, the notion of governance seems to be carried, much like other global social agenda, by developing countries and the non-governmental sector: few of the governance- and corruption-minded organizations are from the developing world or are IGOs. As mentioned earlier, this may be a sign of the time of their founding and of the era of the institutionalization of governance. With many of the organizations in this field being advocacy and education organizations, or set up as networking or 'mega organizations', it seems that the different constituencies are creating an integrated community of discourse. This networked field links one activists and scholars across disciplinary lines, administrative levels, and professional background. Networking organizations are specifically important for this role. And the cooperative connections with other organizations that are only marginally dedicated to the cause of governance reform spread the word outside the immediate network.

If there is any sense of agency in this global field of governance action, it would center on a few people and a few organizations, most notably Peter Eigen and TI. Eigen's career path has spanned both the small nongovernmental organization TI and the major international organization the World Bank; this bridge of personal connections has resulted in a strong alliance on the issue of governance and further established the emerging field of action and talk. This bridging translates into the term *governance* itself, which—as described in the following section—connects social or political logic and economic logic.

4.4. THEMES AND LOGIC: THE MEANING OF GOVERNANCE

Governance is convincingly a global field of action, with distinct and wide-reaching carriers. But beyond the process of expansion and the related role of social carriers, there remains the core meaning. Hence, in this section I ask: What is the meaning of governance that is conveyed though the organizational work and carried by the organizational and academic carriers? In answering this question, I explore the content of the current model of governance and comment on the meaning attributed to the term *governance*.

4.4.1. Searching for a Definition of Governance

The World Bank has a clear definition of governance, summarized in the following formula: $GI + AC = F (KI + LE + CA)$: successful governance improvement (GI) and anticorruption (AC) programs depend on the public availability of knowledge and information (KI) plus political leadership (LE) plus collective action (CA). To this formula, they add: '[T]hrough this integrative logic our program is able to respond to client-country demand for anticorruption assistance and to provide innovative, action-oriented, nonlending activities illustrating a new way of doing business in which the client is in the driver's seat.'[24] In this definition, as in all their other declarations, the World Bank pairs governance with anticorruption. This pairing is not trivial but very telling of the focus of the definition. It reflects not only the formulaic approach by the World Bank to matters of national development but also the infusion of the approach with econocentric and neoliberal tones, through the use of such terms as *client* and *demand*.

In these underlying developmentalist tones, the World Bank is not alone. Rather, most governance initiatives worldwide list the following among the features of good governance and use these terms synonymously with good governance: enhancing the transparency and accountability of administrative systems, curbing corruption, institutionalizing oversight of administrative operations, strengthening the rule of law, ensuring the sanctity of contracts and foreign investment, deepening democracy, empowering civil society, and establishing trust between civil service, corporate heads, and the public. A few mostly economic and financial organizations, like the World Bank and the International Monetary Fund (IMF), explicitly add to this list the liberalization markets and encouragement of competitiveness, which are among the themes of the liberal economic model summarized in the label *Washington Consensus* (Williamson 1993, 2000; Gore 2000). From this perspective, governance is a prerequisite for growth and development, misgovernance or bad governance is cited repeatedly as obstacles to prosperity (e.g. Delacroix and Ragin 1981; Bardhan 1997; Goldsmith 1999; World Bank 2002), and corruption specifically is defined as a global social problem (LaFree and Morris 2004). Indeed, there is a surprising international consensus on what constitutes corruption (LaPalombara 1994: 336) and unethical administration in general (Tanzi and Davoodi 1997) and what are their harmful consequences.

This developmentalist and neoliberal logic is clearly expressed by the currently active governance- and corruption-minded international organizations. They explicitly define their goals as aspiring to 'enhance the quality of local government through professional management',[25] to 'promote good standards in corporate governance and business practice [... and] facilitate the development of appropriate institutions in order to advance, teach, and disseminate such standards',[26] and to 'assist local governments in [...] strengthening capacities, promoting good governance principles, [and] enhancing tools available to urban administrators and decision makers'.[27] These organizations frequently use in their description of goals such terms as *capacity, efficiency, standards, management,* and *administration.* And if any target population is mentioned, they frequently name administrators and policymakers. Some twenty-six international governance organizations explicitly and exclusively apply this logic in their self-described scripts.

Some fifty-five other governance organizations apply a different logic and still consider their primary concern to be governance. For example, the Society for Participatory Research in Asia describes the purpose of its interventions as 'reforming governing institutions, local self-governance in rural and urban areas, environment and occupational health, citizenship and governance, civil society building, social development monitoring and citizen empowerment.'[28] The Society of Jurists of the French Commonwealth aspires to 'promote the legal systems of Commonwealth countries, where this is common law and law in French in general, defend the rule of law, democratic government, and fundamental human rights in Commonwealth countries, and develop exchanges among Commonwealth lawyers.'[29] International governance organizations in this group frequently use such terms as *participation, empowerment, equity and justice, self-determination, rights,* and *freedoms.* They frequently refer to desirable political arrangements as democratic, decentralized, involving civil society, safeguarding the rule of law, and ensuring the principles of sovereignty and emancipation. And they frequently refer to their target populations as weak, marginalized, and excluded, or specifically mention women or indigenous peoples.[30]

As mentioned earlier, the term *governance* has come to mean the art of governing, as distinct from the institution of government. But although this meaning is strongly connected with the spirit of reform and change of current governance, two lines of logic seem to be ruling this field, each pulling the term *governance* in a different discursive direction.

4.4.2. Extracting a Discursive Framework for Governance

The language used to describe organizations whose main concern is governance is indeed complex. Most interestingly, it projects two distinct clusters of terms, which convey two distinct lines of logic: (*a*) the logic of management, administration, and modern organization and (*b*) the logic of political participation and citizenship. A discursive tree (a relational and hierarchical sketch of relations within a discursive field) of both lines of logic of governance is presented in Figure 4.5.

The logic of management views governance primarily as a form of effective and efficient administration; it centers on rationalization and professionalization of supervision, control, capacity, competence, and organizational structure. As mentioned earlier, the discursive clues to this logic are such words as *efficiency, corruption,* and *capacity.* This logic calls for a new form of management that is uniquely rationalized, standardized, and open to scrutiny in the name of efficiency and disclosure. To solidify these calls, statements recall sometimes explicitly the recent management failures in such big corporations as Parmalat and Enron. To correct for failures, the framework assumes a level of professionalization that allows the standardization, implementation, and maintenance of this new mode of administration. At the heart of this logic is the economy, and the primary concern is with efficient progress.

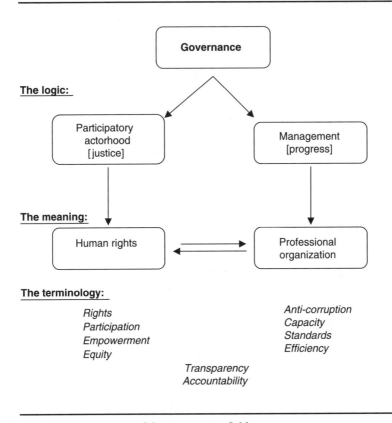

Figure 4.5 Discourse tree of the governance field

The logic of participatory actorhood, on the other hand, views governance in the framework of the social order; it focuses on review as the objective of administrative or governmental reforms and calls for greater participatory practices. It calls for the promotion of a new mode of managing public affairs founded on the participation of civil society at all levels (local, regional, national, and international); governance is the 'linking pin' between societal attributes and political governing (Kooiman 2003: 5). This is also evident in the for-profit sector: the language changed recently to celebrate the input of 'stakeholders' (and not exclusively shareholders) in guiding corporate decision-making. This logic therefore imagines a world of social agents participating and engaging in setting social agendas and shaping social affairs in a manner equivalent to Wilensky's image of the 'professionalization of everybody' (1964). At the heart of this logic is the social role of the individual: from this anti-hierarchical standpoint, the individual is obliged to get involved in public affairs through the process of review of management systems. In these terms, participation is both in the review of public and state agencies and in the overseeing of market entities.

What is left out, conceptually, of this discourse of governance between the logic of management and actorhood? Strikingly absent is the set of ideologies that are concerned with power relations and inequality. If power is invoked in any way, it is invoked in the emphasis on the appropriate process and hence comes under the canopy of empowerment.

Each logic reflects a unique content world, meaning of governance, and scheme for action and policy. And both are used to interpret issues, events, and programs. Their interpretations dramatize their unique perspectives by emphasizing unique sets of issues. For example, the notion of accountability is defined in management logic as an enforcement of fiscal and resource oversight through the adoption of strict accountability standards and tools; if stakeholders are involved, the issue is their coordination. From the perspective of participatory actorhood, on the other hand, accountability is seen as a regime of oversight through public review, possibly organized through review boards representing the multiplicity of stakeholders; the approach emphasizes the involvement of an empowered citizen in the process of policy-making and planning. The two approaches also differ in the focus of their attention: the individual human versus the organization, lay (or everyone) versus professional, state versus economy.

To some degree, the new twin terms that emerged with the resurrection of governance in the 1990s—*transparency* and *accountability*—are infused with both lines of logic, as is appropriate for a late globalization era discourse. Each of these commonly used terms is interpreted differently, setting a unique path for action and policy, without raising a doubt about the commensurability of the two lines of logic. In this way, international governance organizations as different as the World Bank, the Earth Council, and Freedom House all call for and work cooperatively on encouraging transparency and accountability, even if their interpretations of what such calls would entail are different. Furthermore, both lines of logic and the two paths for action they would entail exist in the same, even if loosely coupled, organization. The World Bank works on plans regarding 'corruption and human rights' and 'youth and corruption' in the hope of giving citizens a stake in social change, while also laboring on programs for 'corruption and aid', 'corruption and growth', and 'investment climate and e-governance tools' in the hope of setting up the proper administrative infrastructure for economic development. This is an instance of opposing lines of logic converging to naturally replace the state as the sole or primary administrative system. *Governance*, then, absorbed disparate lines of logic and meshed into a single linguistic term to allow networking among disparate social actors.

This intertwining (or commensurability) of the two lines of logic in practice is possible because the two lines of logic are not completely independent of each other. Rather, the two lines of logic co-constitute each other and both view governance as a means toward a goal (of either development or participatory citizenship). Governance is conceived as 'grander than administration, less business-like than management, and having political concerns handled discretely but firmly' (Doornbos 2001: 94), thus merging these different viewpoints into a single term. Most important, the two lines of logic draw from the twin pillars of Western modern thought—justice and progress (Meyer et al. 1987, 1997a, 1997b). In the late twentieth century, these lines of logic translate into a neoliberal developmentalist agenda, mixed with the notion of a participatory democracy, and hence reflect modern sensibilities and collective morality. The governance discourse of the 1990s was not as new as it might have appeared. Rather, as new institutional forms morph from changes and elaborations to existing institutions, each new institution emerges as a bricolage of existing notions (see Campbell 1997; Clemens 1993; see also Clemens and Cook 1999). In this way, the emerging discourse of governance builds on existing lines of logic and remolds existing terminology.

4.4.3. Considering Organizational Change

The descriptions of both discourse and structuration are limited by the nature of the coding basis: since the UIA data offer the viewpoint of 2004, the history of the field is retrospective, 'flattening' the change that organizations experience once the notion of governance emerges to alter their environment. For old and established organizations to redefine their mission in terms of the emerging discourse of governance requires organizational change. This change may come in the definition of the organization's mission as well as in its practices.

Crown Agents, the oldest organization among the currently active governance-minded international organizations listed in UIA 2004, is one organization that has adapted itself to the institutionalization of the governance discourse. Crown Agents had changed little in its activities, even when it became a private-sector agency in 1995. Still, now it relies extensively on the fashionable governance terminology. Crown Agents changed over the years in administrative ways. Founded in 1833 as a colonial civil agency of the British Crown, it underwent several inquiries into its activities, each followed by intraorganizational reforms to tighten its management and review procedures. Following major liquidity problems in 1973, the agency was incorporated in 1979 as a foundation; in 1995 the agency was privatized. Even if not in corporate terms, the recent 'age of governance' changed Crown Agents further. Crown Agents refers to governance on a routine basis in their brochures and documents, and they use governance as a part of their strategic plans for their clients as well as a prism for internal review. 'The concept appeared and we figured out that this is what we do and always have been', says a member of its executive team. Yet Crown Agents does not consider the organization's change as a hypocritical act, but as one of the executive team says, 'We did not engage in purposeful rebranding; PR is a task to describe our core tasks and so we did.' In its reformulation, Crown Agents explicitly surveys its environments: its agents report noticing mentions of *governance* in documents from their German counterpart agency, GTZ,[31] in World Bank formal and informal meetings, and in conversations with their clients. They therefore see the recasting of their ongoing work in governance as merely serving the current needs of their clients. And they do not regard themselves as 'moral entrepreneurs'; rather, they see their role as a private development agency today in terms of service to, and support of, local governors and governments, much as the organization viewed its responsibility and domain at the time of the British Empire.

Many additional organizations underwent a similar process of adaptation to the new dicourse. As mentioned earlier, the World Bank, which is now among the most vocal champions of governance reforms, began to address governance per se only after 1996. Not that the 'problems' went unnoticed before 1996; rather, World Bank documents prior to Wolfensohn's 'cancer of corruption' speech were peppered with references to problems of 'suboptimal procurements' and 'implicit taxes'. Still, it took the discursive shift of the mid-1990s for the bank to even see corruption as a block for development and to mobilize developmentalists to speak of governance needs (Mallaby 2004: 176), let alone to frame the idea of corruption in the more abstract notion of governance.

Much smaller and more peripheral organizations experienced similar transformation to the emerging discourse of governance. For example, FENU (Forum for Education NGOs), a network nongovernmental organization for education in Uganda and hence a 'minnow' of management consultancy worldwide, lists among its goals the advancement of the governance notions transparency and accountability and the encouragement of participatory policymaking among Ugandan education organizations and agencies (Murphy 2005). It too adjusted its language to align with the global discourse of appropriate policymaking, management of public systems, and empowerment of stakeholders.

4.4.4. The Narrative of Governance

Not only did the term *governance* emerge in the 1990s as the term for capturing the idea of organizational change, but governance also emerged as a notion to describe organizational reform. As a notion describing organizational change, it envelopes the two distinct lines of logic of actorhood and effective management. The two lines of logic are not coincidental; rather, each of them emerge from a theme of modern global culture—the themes of justice and progress, respectively. Therefore, in spite of the possible tension and competition between these lines of logic, they are commensurate within the notion of governance. It is the cultural environment of the turn of the twenty-first century that allows both lines of logic to coincide. Organizational realignment with the emerging discourse of governance is especially viable in an environment where management is increasingly seen as having universal, rationalized, and standardized features that bridge organizational particularities. Again structuration and newness allow for flexibility in a world rife with the contradictory pressures of globalization; decoupling is the natural result. Governance discourse is not, therefore, a fragmented discourse with tensions between the ideas of justice and progress; rather, it allows various different and decoupled concrete meanings to coexist in the same terminology because the notion and the term have acquired a general and religious-like meaning.

4.5. DISCUSSION

The 1990s were the period of institutionalization of the notion of governance and mobilization around this notion. Although both the notion of governance and the term itself are much older, they were recast at the end of the twentieth century into a new agenda for social change. This change is evident both discursively and organizationally. The institutionalization process is driven primarily by certain social carriers: most organizational work emerges from developing countries and greatest use of the term comes from the social science disciplines that are preoccupied with the state and with development.

A broad range of social movements operates at a global level and aims at governance reforms. The dominant vision attached to rationalized reform proposals is a neoliberal one, assuming transparent nation-states managed by accountable governments and operating in a world of open international markets. Also assumed is the role of highly rationalized firms and public agencies operating within and among these states with clear purposes, effective management, transparent accounting, and high standards of quality.

Although the primary goal of governance reforms is to mitigate the destabilizing effects of bad governance on markets and societies, it is the informal purpose that shapes the contours of world culture and the machinery of world polity. The assumptions of reforms set up the expectations (or models) of nation-statehood and of the organizational actors. In deciphering the discourse of governance and tracing the history of the field, I follow the historical institutionalization of the rationalized model of governance and nation-statehood. In the work on governance, I join other institutionalists in an investigation of the history of the world polity, its cultural content (or guiding discursive themes), and its central players.

The heterogeneity and multiplicity of the carriers of governance are frequently summarized in the catchphrase 'governance without government'. Although this phrase is intended to encourage stakeholders to involve themselves in the management and planning of social agendas rather than leaving all this work to state agencies, as tradition has it, it also reflects a salient feature of world society: that policy and planning are based on self-correcting and thus agentic principle, without the guidance or domination of a central source of power. Indeed, globalization occurs without a world state, and the postmodern language that accompanied globalization's latest period has also created the perception of leveling across social actors. Similarly, in bringing together various stakeholders, the current logic of governance blurs the demarcation between the private and public sectors. Indeed, the universalistic claims of governance make clear that the art of administration and management is equal across all sorts of organizations.

That 'governance without government' became the catch phrase at the start of the third millennium is no surprise: this phrase captures the nature of the new form of authority that is both global (canopy-like) and globalized (cross-national). This phrase is popular not because it captures the dream of stateless or government-less social order. Rather, the new global format of authority is more along the Tocquevillian description of American social organization: voluntary, formally organized, civil or associational looking, exercising mostly soft power if any law at all. World society is organized this way, without a world state or crowned global authorities (see Etzioni 2004: 172–7). This arrangement of diffused authority breeds organizations: specifically, this particular institutionalized form of governance encourages further constitution of formal organizations.

The features of this institutionalized form of governance reveal the deeply cultural roots of this emerging notion. The emerging notion of governance is rooted in the two main features of world society: actorhood and rationalization. First, with the establishment of the modern secular moral order that calls for agentic actorhood (the individual is expected to take responsibility for social

agendas through involvement in policymaking), governance became a culturally preferable way to manage private and public organizations. Supporting
this secular moral turn is a pervasive personification process, rooted in the
modern secularized version of moral order and in the broadening of the circle
of social entities (see Meyer, Drori, and Hwang, Chapter 1; Jepperson 2002*a*,
2002*b*; Boli, Elliot, and Bieri 2004: 391–2). In this new world, corporations,
universities, transnational social movement organizations, primary schools,
and hospitals alike are all legitimate social actors and organizations, and thus
they are bound to the requirement to govern and be governed effectively and
inclusively. The end of the twentieth century brought this moral and activist
tone, once reserved to the state and public sector, to the for-profit private
sector, as well and to the associational world of church groups and social clubs.
Reflecting Jacques Ellul's concern (1975) with the nature of the sacred, the
inherent morality of social responsibility and the inherent capacity for strategic and planned action by collective actors is an expression of modern secular
religiosity. Second, world society champions rationalization, viewing standardized and universalized formats as efficient and thus desired. Under pressures to rationalize, the management of administrative systems too takes a
universalized tone and adopts the model of governance.

In its turn toward actorhood and rationalization, the late twentieth century's
notion of governance replaced the former and dominant notion of state planning (see Hwang, Chapter 3). Most dramatically, although state planning
emphasized state action and conceived of the state as a bounded, rational, and
competitive entity, the logic of governance regards the relevant imagined community to be both global and local and, most importantly, transcending national
boundaries. Hence, if by the state planning logic problems of resource management called for state strategies, the current logic of governance acknowledges
such problems as transcending national borders and calls for multilevel coordination of action, or, in the language of the Millennium Development Goals, a
partnership. For example, the migration of 'knowledge workers', previously conceived as a problem of 'brain drain', is currently recast as a population flow
appropriate for the age of globalization and is thus 'brain circulation'. This recasting
of social problems also redefines who the social agents responsible for the solution
are: it further reinforces the transference of planning from the state to corporations
and civil society, transnational actors, and local groups. And although the logic of
state planning focused on evaluation and performance defined primarily as cost–
benefit analysis, the current logic of governance dramatizes accountability and
actorhood as integral parts of the 'triple bottom-line' evaluation.

These consequences, however, go beyond a change in the language. The
institutionalization of governance is starting to show its effects on the practice
of management of different organizations. Clearly, more organizations (of
various sorts and in different places worldwide) now rely on 'business artifacts'

(see Powell, Gammal, and Simard 2005: 14) for their administrative tasks: from drafting strategic and technology plans to composing periodic reports and setting standards for performance and evaluation. Numerous studies reveal the worldwide reaches of recent governance reforms of various sorts. Guler, Guillén, and MacPherson (2002) demonstrate the pervasive worldwide compliance with ISO 9000 standards (see also Mendel, Chapter 6). Others show the global dissemination of anticorruption measures (Mauro 1995), governmental mechanisms of transparency (Grigorescu 2003), initiatives to curb unofficial economic activity (Friedman et al. 2000), and recalibration of governmental agencies according to Weberian professional principles (Evans and Rauch 1999). These reforms are often accompanied by the rationalization of performance (the matching of goals, means, and outcomes and a focus on outcome measures, or 'dashboard tools') and the professionalization of workers (see Moon and Wotipka, Chapter 5; Luo, Chapter 9). All these ideas together make up the complex and ambitious notion of governance.

APPENDIX 4.A

CHRONOLOGY OF TRANSNATIONAL GOVERNANCE INITIATIVES

1. Founding and Action

1993	Founding of Transparency International
1997, October	World Bank charts its Policy Statement on Corruption and Good Governance.
1997, August	IMF charts its commitment to governance in the note The Role of IMF in Governance Issues.
1997	International Anti-Corruption Conference, The Lima Declaration
1997	Establishment of Group of States against Corruption (GRECO) to monitor European anticorruption convention
1998, April	International Monetary Fund charts the Declaration of Principles of the Code of Good Practices on Fiscal Transparency.
1998, August	Asian Development Bank charts its Policy against Corruption.
1999, October	The first Bribes Payers' Index, compiled by TI, is published.
2001, October	The first Global Corruption Report, composed by TI, is published.

2. International Conventions and Treaties

1990, November	Council of Europe, Convention on Laundering, Search, Seizure and Confiscation of the Proceeds from Crime

1993	The Commonwealth, Lusaka Statement of Government under the Law
1993	OECD Recommendation on Bribery in International Business Transactions
1996	Inter-American Convention against Corruption
1996, December	United Nations Declaration against Corruption and Bribery in International Commercial Transactions (UNGA Resolution 51/191, December 16), United Nations Resolution on Action against Corruption (UNGA Resolution 51/59, December 12), and United Nations International Code of Conduct for Public Officials (UNGA Resolution 51/59, December 12)
1997	OECD Convention on Combating Bribery of Foreign Public Officials in International Business Transactions
1997, December	United Nations International Co-operation against Corruption and Bribery in International Commercial Transactions (UNGA Resolution 52/87, December 12)
1998	Council of Europe, Criminal Law Convention on Corruption
1999	Council of Europe, Civil Law Convention on Corruption
2003, October	United Nations Convention against Corruption (UNGA Resolution 58/4, October 31)

APPENDIX 4.B

STANDARDIZING REFERENCES TO *GOVERNANCE* IN ACADEMIC LITERATURE, 1970–2003

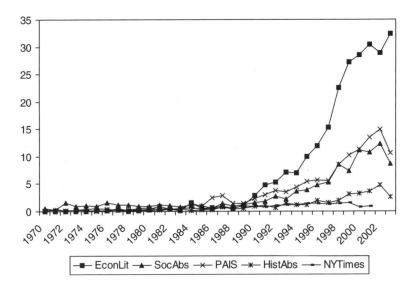

NOTES

1. I thank Emily Flynn, Eric Kramon, Vijaya Tripathi, Colin Beck, and Mark Bekheit for their diligent work in compiling the various data for this research. I thank Helena Buhr for her valuable advise on the strategy of content analysis. I thank Stuart Raine, Lynn Hale, and Stanley Adamson of Crown Agents for opening their organization before me. And I greatly thank Penny Hull for laboring to make this manuscript readable, even if I left some jargon in place. Earlier versions of this research were presented at workshops and conference panels in Saïd Business School, Cardiff Business School, the Scandinavian Consortium for Organizational Studies (Scancor), the Comparative Workshop at Stanford University, and the American Sociological Association. I thank the participants in these forums for their thoughtful comments.

2. Data on the founding of international governance- and corruption-minded organizations are drawn from the list of currently active organizations and thus draw a retrospective picture of the field. Boli and Thomas (1999: 22–4) report that the rates of dissolution of international organizations in the post-1945 era run between 1 and 3 percent annually and thus treat it as negligible, especially considering the much faster rate of founding events during this era.

3. Additional 'synonyms' are *public management, administration* (or *administrative reform* if *administration* is too big a category), *government reform* (assuming that *government* is too wide a net to cast).

4. In this work, Guillén traces the annual counts in the literature of the term *globalization* to demonstrate the newness of the phrase in academic circles.

5. See http://www1.worldbank.org/publicsector/anticorrupt/index.cfm (accessed October 4, 2004).

6. See http://www.transparency.org/about_ti/history-timeline.html (accessed October 4, 2004).

7. The World Bank's EDI, founded in 1955, merged into the World Bank Institute in 1999.

8. Crown Agents historically played a vital role in the creation and management of the British Empire. According to its charter, Crown Agents is an 'Emanation of the Crown'. Hence, while formally a not-for-profit agency and today also not a part of state bureaucracy, throughout its operation it was overseen by the Colonial Secretary and is now supervised by the Minister of Overseas Development. I use this venerable organization later in this work to exemplify intraorganizational change in response to the institutionalization of governance.

9. Percentages are calculated from totals of 138 and 24 international organizations with founding dates mentioned for governance and corruption fields, respectively.

10. http://www.ecgi.org/codes/all_codes.htm (accessed November 15, 2004).

11. Only five such mentions in 1970 and 1971, in four bibliographic sources.

12. And more frequently used yet is the term *organization*.

13. The high numbers for these terms are very possibly somewhat inflated because the coding mechanism does not discriminate in terms of content or use of the terms.

14. From http://europa.eu.int/comm/governance/docs/doc5_fr.pdf, White Paper for the European Commission's (EC) Europa project on governance in EU (accessed July 10, 2004).

15. French: *gouverner, gouvernment, gouvernance,* etc.; English: *govern, government, governance,* etc.; Portuguese: *governar, governo, governação, governança,* etc.; Italian: *governare, governo, governamento,* etc.

16. To the point that partnership is listed among the UN Millennium Development Goals.

17. For more on the distinction between IGOs and INGOs and their trends of constitution, see Boli and Thomas (1999: 28–30).

18. See various chapters in Boli and Thomas (1999).

19. The number of references to governance and related terms in anthropology is usually very small: most years the number was 0, since the early 1990s the numbers per year rose to 2 or 3, and in 2002 the number of uses seems to have exploded, with references to *governance, organization,* and *corruption* amounting to 18 each. The number of references to the term *bureaucracy* in anthropology peaked in 1989 at 21.

20. The first substantial number of references to governance was in 1977.

21. The standardized figure for this discipline shows that the term *governance* held a ratio of 13 percent in 2001.

22. In sociology, the first substantial mention of *governance* was in 1977 (11 mentions), but since 1970, higher numbers appeared in sociology than political science. Also, references to *governance,* as a share of the total publications, were at 8.3 percent in 2001.

23. In economics, and the first use of *governance* was only in 1979; the first substantial number of uses was in 1984 (25 uses). The references to *governance* as a share of the total disciplinary publications stood at 22 percent in 2001.

24. See http://www.worldbank.org/wbi/governance/about.html (accessed June 1, 2005).

25. Aims description from UIA, for the International City and County Management Association (founded in 1914 and headquartered in Washington, DC).

26. From the Commonwealth Association for Corporate Governance (founded in 1998 and registered in New Zealand).

27. From the Urban Governance Initiative (founded in 1998 and headquartered in Malaysia).

28. Founded in 1982 and headquartered in New Delhi, India.

29. Founded in 1996 and headquartered in Paris, France.

30. Only ten organizations combine language from both lines of logic. The text of goals from some seventy-four other governance organizations is unclassified. All other governance organizations do not include a description of their goals in UIA 2004.

31. The Deutsche Gesellschaft für Technische Zusammenarbeit (GTZ) is the German aid and development organization working mainly for the German Federal Government; see http://www.gtz.de/en/index.htm (accessed June 9, 2005).

Part II

Dimensions of Organizational Rationalization

5

The Worldwide Diffusion of Business Education, 1881–1999: Historical Trajectory and Mechanisms of Expansion

Hyeyoung Moon and Christine Min Wotipka

The universalistic and standardized organizational forms resulting from globalization as argued in this volume have without a doubt caused dramatic changes in the business arena. Businesses regardless of nationality have come to be viewed as similar—organizational actors that share universal and standardized characteristics. Challenges for businesses are expected to call for similar solutions, i.e. new managerial knowledge and skills, and to be carried out by rational actors. In order to meet the need for professional managers, we have witnessed, along with the massive expansion of higher education, a global explosion of professional management education throughout the twentieth century, across countries (Locke 1984, 1989; Engwall and Zamagni 1998)—from a handful of countries at the dawn of the twentieth century to more than 100 countries by the end of the same century. At the same time, the professional management education field has expanded within countries where it was already born. Right at the center of such global expansion of the professional management education field rests the globalization of Masters of Business Administration (MBAs) and business schools (B-Schools hereafter). They have become the most visible element in the professional management education field around the world, especially in the last three decades.

To provide evidence in support of these arguments, we sketch historical and cross-national trends in the expansion of the MBA and B-Schools. We then present results from an event history analysis of the adoption of B-Schools around the world over the past hundred years. In the end, we reveal how the B-School expanded gradually early on, and in the current period has exploded and gone global. Furthermore, we argue that the degree of its expansion in individual societies is heavily determined by a country's involvement in world society rather than functional need or demand for professional management education, particularly in the more recent period. We also demonstrate that the MBA has taken the dominant form of management education in the more recent period.

The literature on management education, which has developed extensively over the last two decades, portrays modern management education generally as the invention of the American education system (see Locke 1984, 1989; Daniel 1998; Baalen and Karsten 2000). It has evolved around two main themes: homogeneity and American management education influences across national contexts (see Engwall and Zamagni 1998; Amdam 1999) and areas of improvement needed in management education (see Segev, Raveh, and Farjoun 1999). We expand upon this work by beginning with a global and historical analysis of trends in the expansion of the MBA and B-Schools.

5.1. THE MBA AND B-SCHOOLS: GLOBAL PHENOMENA

Despite cross-national differences in higher education systems and local characteristics, countries have been increasingly accepting B-Schools and MBAs as the most legitimate forms of professional management education. Considering it was less than a century ago that B-Schools were an alien concept even in the United States, where B-Schools were born (Locke 1984), the current level of worldwide expansion of B-Schools is simply astonishing. One efficient way to trace the trajectory of the worldwide diffusion of B-Schools is to examine the timing of the creation of the first B-School in each country from 1881 to the present.[1] Figure 5.1 presents the cumulative number of countries that have established their first B-Schools, along with the hazard rate of the initial adoption of B-Schools. The diffusion of B-Schools was relatively slow up to the 1960s, with about forty countries having adopted B-Schools since the establishment of the first B-School in the United States. By the late 1990s, more than 100 countries worldwide have established B-Schools and this number is still on the rise (Crainer and Dearlove 1998; see also UIA 2000; UNESCO 2000).[2] The hazard rate—the probability that the initial adoption of B-Schools takes place at a given year given that a country has not adopted one before that time—clearly shows that the rate of initial adoption jumped around the 1960s, and that its upward trend continues into the 1990s. It implies that a country is highly likely to adopt B-Schools at the turn of the twenty-first century if it has not done so yet: a compelling piece of evidence for the global institutionalization of B-Schools.

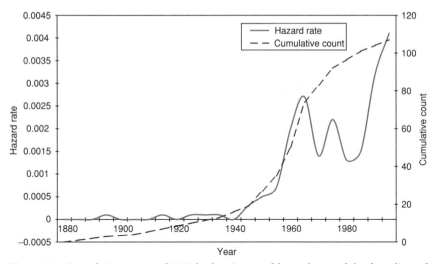

Figure 5.1 Cumulative count of initial adoptions and hazard rate of the founding of the first B-Schools, 1880–1999

As for the growth of the MBA, there is a likewise dramatic rise in the number of countries where the MBA is adopted—from approximately fifty countries in the late 1970s (Viola and Agrawal 1979) to more than a hundred by the end of the 1990s as presented in Table 5.1. Moreover, the number of educational institutions that offer the MBA has increased dramatically to around 1,600. As seen in Figure 5.2, the rapid global expansion of MBA programs in the last decade seems to be driven by the increase in the number of MBA programs in countries other than the United States. Finally, the proportion of students enrolled in business and administration at the tertiary level reached about 14 percent at the world level by 1990. This number is even higher than other traditional disciplines such as humanities, law, natural sciences, and engineering (UNESCO 2000; Drori and Moon 2001). Not only are countries contributing to the global spread of MBAs, but their students are similarly seeking out such degrees to become players in modern and international economic markets.

To further illustrate the global institutionalization of the MBA, we looked more qualitatively at the public discourse surrounding professional management education over time. First and foremost, the increasing visibility of the MBA as the primary form of professional management education is evidenced by professional management education organizations in many countries reorganizing and relabeling existing programs of the MBA-equivalent as the MBA. In addition, we find that the public discourse on professional

Table 5.1 Number of institutions offering the MBA by country, 1999

Country	No. of institutions	Country	No. of institutions
Antilles	1	Macedonia	2
Argentina	8	Madagascar	1
Armenia	1	Malawi	1
Australia	41	Malaysia	34
Austria	13	Malta	3
Bahamas	1	Mauritius	1
Bahrain	6	Mexico	9
Bangladesh	4	Monaco	3
Belgium	16	Morocco	2
Belize	1	Namibia	1
Benelux	1	Netherlands	39
Bermuda	1	New-Zealand	11
Bolivia	1	Nicaragua	4
Botswana	1	Nigeria	1
Brazil	5	Norway	3
Bulgaria	2	Oman	2
Canada	67	Pakistan	3
Caymen Islands	1	Panama	6
Chile	8	Papua-New Guinea	1
China	14	Paraguay	1
Colombia	2	Peru	2
Costa-Rica	11	Philippines	4
Croatia	2	Poland	10
Cuba	2	Portugal	8
Cyprus	4	Puer-Rico	3
Czecho	6	Qatar	1
Denmark	6	Romania	1
Ecuador	1	Russia	23
Egypt	4	Saudi Arabia	5
El-Salvador	1	Singapore	25
Estonia	3	Slovakia	2
Ethiopia	1	Slovenia	5
Fiji	2	South Africa	26
Finland	12	Spain	61
France	75	St-Kitts	1
Germany	37	Swaziland	1
Greece	7	Sweden	7
Guam	1	Switzerland	22
Hong-Kong	5	Syria	1
Hungary	8	Taiwan	5
Iceland	1	Tanzania	1
India	14	Thailand	8
Indonesia	3	Trinidad-Tobago	2
Ireland	8	Turkey	2
Israel	11	Uganda	2

(*continued*)

Table 5.1 *(Continued)*

Country	No. of institutions	Country	No. of institutions
Italy	23	Ukraine	3
Jamaica	3	Ulster	1
Japan	12	United Arab Emirates	5
Jordan	2	United Kingdom	271
Kazakhstan	2	Uruguay	2
Kenya	2	United States	490
South Korea	6	Virgin Islands	1
Kuwait	2	Venezuela	1
Latvia	2	Vietnam	1
Lebanon	3	Yemen (former Yemen AR)	1
Lesotho	1	Yugoslavia	1
Lithuania	1	Zambia	1
Luxembourg	2	Zimbabwe	1
Macau	4		
Total			**1620**

Source: WebInfoCo, 2000.

management education has taken up the MBA as the common platform since 1970 to the present, and this trend became particularly obvious since the 1980s. Increasing proportion of discourse related to professional management education in academic and popular publications universally treated the MBA as if the MBA were the only form of professional management education. What is more, the amount of the published discourse on the MBA has

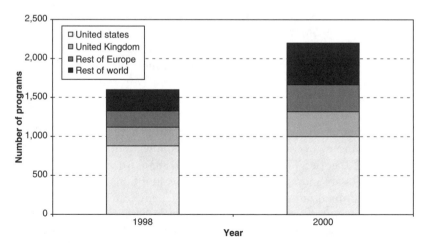

Figure 5.2 The increase in the number of MBA programs in the world, 1998–2000

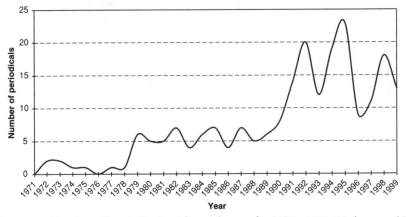

Figure 5.3 Number of periodicals with articles on the MBA, 1971–99 (among 217 periodicals with 'managment' in title)

increased during this time, with three major periods of growth as evidenced in Figure 5.3.

Lastly, the nature of the discourse on the MBA has changed, indicating that it has become widely accepted as the legitimate form of professional management education. By the 1990s, the proportion of neutral discourse increased, suggesting that the MBA became less contentious and more of a reality.

5.2. EXPLAINING THE GLOBALIZATION OF PROFESSIONAL MANAGEMENT EDUCATION

The indicators presented in the above section strongly support the notion that MBA and B-Schools are indeed global phenomena. We argue that the effect of institutionalization and the degree to which countries are embedded in globalization processes may explain the initial adoption of B-Schools across countries. Internal demands and intervening factors have traditionally shaped our understanding of the rise of B-Schools. Following the line of research in institutional theories (Tolbert and Zucker 1983), we argue that national characteristics are more consequential for the adoption of B-Schools earlier in the institutionalization process, while global environments become more crucial later (see Ramirez, Soysal, and Shanahan 1998). In other words, in the earlier stage of institutionalization, B-Schools are more likely to be adopted at countries faced with internal demands. Yet, as B-Schools become more widely accepted in world society, countries are more likely to establish them, even in the absence of internal demands, if they are closely connected to the world society. In this section, we provide a statistical analysis of first B-School founding from 1880 to 1999 using an event history analysis. Measures capturing the ideas and arguments elaborated below are presented in turn.

Drawing on the institutionalist literature on organizations (Tolbert and Zucker 1983; Powell and DiMaggio 1991; Scott 1995), we expect that as B-Schools become more widely accepted, and therefore, taken-for-granted, societies are more likely to adopt them regardless of internal demands (e.g. Olzak 1989; Strang 1991; Jang 2000; Ramirez 2001). Throughout the twentieth century, justification for management education has been offered to the extent that even the critics of B-Schools now take them for granted (Moon 2002). Positive discourses on B-Schools from practitioners of business education, businesspeople, and international actors generate normative pressures on societies yet to adopt them. In addition, to the extent that it is not clear how to increase efficiency in managing developing economies, societies deal with this uncertainty by mimicking those they perceive to be successful. Therefore, countries that attempt economic development and efficient management may adopt B-Schools since other societies with similar characteristics have adopted them. In sum, B-Schools become increasingly taken-for-granted over time, taking on institutional characteristics that make the establishment of B-Schools much more likely.

On the other hand, Strang and Meyer (1994) posit that perceived similarity among adopters and objects of adoption is crucial in diffusion processes. That is, diffusion is more likely when adopters are theorized and seen as similar and objects are perceived to be relevant to adopters in similar ways. Accordingly, diffusion of B-Schools is likely when adopting societies are conceived as similar and when B-Schools are expected to have a similar effect on the societies that adopt them. The former has occurred as result of the nation-state having emerged as the dominant form of organizing societies (Thomas et al. 1987; Strang and Meyer 1994; Meyer et al. 1997a, 1997b), accelerating diffusion of myriad forms, systems, and practices across societies. Accordingly, higher education systems are perceived as similar cross-nationally, and hence, increasingly organized in a similar format (e.g. UIA 2000; UNESCO 2000). This contagion effect refers to the positive relationship between previous occurrence and the likelihood of future occurrence of an event across similarly perceived actors (e.g. Olzak 1989; Strang 1991; Jang 2000). Therefore, the more nation-states and higher education systems have adopted B-Schools, the more likely others are to adopt them. We measure this effect using the cumulative number of initial adoptions of B-Schools at the nation-state level that have taken place for the previous twenty years around the world. This indicator represents the extent to which B-Schools are collectively seen as the right form of management education, thereby resulting in multiple adoptions in the world.

We argue further that the adoption of B-Schools is primarily determined by how deeply societies are embedded in globalization, and therefore, affected by world models and standards. Globalization pulls businesses into expanded markets that are supposed to pose an increasing level of uncertainties, and thereby, to increase the need to improve efficiency in terms of control and coordination. For one thing, globalization forces businesses to operate in the global market, where they are no longer protected by nation-states. In the global market, businesses are subject to universalized and generalized rules of management and compelled to assume a universal form: organizational actors (Brunsson and Sahlin-Andersson 2000; Meyer 2002). Accordingly, strategies and theories dealing with growing uncertainties and new efficiency requirements are constructed independent of national contexts (Drori, Jang, and Meyer 2000; Meyer 2002). This transformation is accompanied by the emergence of the global market and global society as perceived boundaries for economic, political, and social actions. In this context, businesses regardless of nationality are viewed as similar—organizational actors that share universal and standardized characteristics, and challenges for businesses are expected to call for similar solutions, i.e. new managerial knowledge and skills, and to be carried out by professional managers.[3] It is within this context of globalization that B-Schools—a place to produce professional managers who can run organizations—are institutionalized in global society.

Certainly, cross-national variation exists in the degree to which nation-states are involved in global society, and thus, in the extent to which globalization may affect them. Two channels of global involvement seem especially relevant in explaining the adoption of B-Schools: participation in the global market and polity. First, as national economies participate in the global market, business organizations are exposed to global models of management coupled with professionalization of management. As a consequence, nation-states are more likely to subscribe to standardized models of management and professional management education. A conventional measure of a country's participation in the global market is openness, which is calculated as a proportion of the sum of export and import in goods and services in Real GDP (log; World Bank 2000*a*, 2000*b*, 2000*c*). As this indicator is unavailable for the pre-World War II era, similar to the case of GDP per capita, we are able to test the effect of this indicator on the initial adoption rates of B-Schools only in the analysis that explores the effects of globalization for the later period.

As more and more international actors promote professional management education, a country's greater involvement in the world polity also positively influences their adoption of B-Schools. Hence, B-Schools as they become part of these world models and standards diffuse to societies that are more involved in global society than isolated ones. To capture this, we produce an index score employing three indicators. First, we measure participation in the world polity as the number of a country's memberships in INGOs (log). The INGOs are seen as important elements of the world polity in and by which global models and scripts are addressed, generated, and delivered (Boli and Thomas 1997, 1999; Frank, Hironaka, and Schofer 2000). The second indicator is the number of memberships a country has in IGOs (log). The IGOs have played important roles in promoting B-Schools as discussed earlier, along with other world models and rules (Finnemore 1996). Thus, the more a country is involved in INGOs and IGOs, the more embedded a country is in the world polity. Both measures were collected from UIA (2000). Finally, we use the number of diplomatic linkages that a nation-state has established to measure its connectedness to other nation-states. The data source is Singer and Small (1977).

In contrast to these external factors, much of the literature on management education attributes its expansion to increased demand from within societies, in particular, economic development (see Mosson 1965; Chandler 1977, 1990; Whitely, Thomas, and Marceau 1981). According to this line of argument, efficiency is the driving force of structural changes in the economy (see also Djelic 1998). As the economic and technological environment became bigger and more complex, there was an increasing demand for managing this environment more efficiently through corporations. The increasing size of enterprises caused by economic development made the issue of managing businesses more challenging, thereby driving demand for the people to run them with specific management knowledge and skills. We take such arguments into consideration in our analysis by employing an indicator of economic development that is widely used in historical analyses: iron and steel production per capita (log). Gross Domestic Product per capita (log) is used in the analyses that further investigate effects of globalization in the later period and is derived from the World Bank (2000*a*, 2000*b*, 2000*c*).

We also consider three intervening factors that affect the likelihood of B-School establishment, especially in the earlier periods. First, the expansion of education makes it more likely that increasing demands, perceived or real, for skills and knowledge for managing developing economy will be handled by education. In contemporary society, education has taken over functions of traditional institutions in socialization and allocation (Meyer 1977; Collins 1979). This explains why real or perceived requirements of developing economies result in the establishment of B-Schools.[4] Only within this context does the thesis that new managerial requirements due to economic development should be fulfilled through education, i.e. B-Schools, make sense. In our analysis, we use a measure that is an index[5] of two indicators—number of universities per capita (log) and tertiary educational enrollment as a proportion of the 20–24-year-old age group (log). IAU (2000) and UNESCO (1998–2000) provide the data, respectively. The former measures the expansion of institutions, while the latter that of participation within the system of higher education.

Second, drawing on Weber's conceptualization (1978) of authority and rationalization and on neoinstitutionalist theories in the similar vein (Brunsson and Sahlin-Andersson 2000; Meyer 2002), we argue that as businesses are arranged as organizational actors, the basis of authority of managers increasingly shifts from traditional sources to knowledge and skills. Thus, B-Schools expand as the locus of transferring knowledge and skills of general management to potential managers. Rationalization of business is constructed as an index of three indicators in our analysis: existence of stock exchanges, age of stock exchange system (dummy for stock exchanges older than 100 years), and number of domestic firms listed in the stock exchanges per capita (log) (Meridian Securities Markets, 1999).

Finally, in terms of intervening forces, following Stinchcombe's theory (1965) of imprinting and liability of newness, we expect that newer systems (i.e. countries and education systems) are more susceptible to adopting B-Schools than their older counterparts. Two systems seem especially relevant for the adoption of B-Schools: the higher education system and the nation-state. A higher education system is considered new if its first institution was created less than five years earlier (IAU 1959–2000), while a nation-state is considered as a new system during the five years after its independence. Data for these variables are derived from IAU (1959–2000) and CIA (2001), respectively.

5.2.1. Modeling the Hazard Rate of the First B-School Founding

Event history analysis allows us to analyze the transition rate (or hazard rate) of each country from not having a B-School to adopting B-Schools, in terms of both the timing of transition as well as conditions under which the transition takes place (see Tuma and Hannan 1984). The starting point of the analysis is 1880, one year prior to the first establishment of the modern form of B-School at Wharton in 1881. Countries (independent and with universities in place) remain in the risk set as long as they have not yet adopted a B-School.

Founding dates of the first B-Schools in each country were compiled from the *International Handbook of Universities* (1959–98) and *Commonwealth Universities Yearbook* (1918–2000). The first time when a B-School appeared in any of universities or colleges within a country was recorded as the timing of the initial adoption of B-Schools.[6]

As shown in Figure 5.1, there is a clear difference in transition rates between the periods before and after 1960. Such dramatic variance in transition rates between two periods calls for a modeling that allows the transition rate to vary across time. A piecewise exponential model with period-specific effects is ideal for this task (Blossfeld, Hamerle, and Mayer 1989). Based on the hazard rate of the first B-School founding, we split the time axis into two periods: 1880–1959 and 1960–1999.[7] The transition rate from origin state j (not having a B-School) to destination state k (founding a B-School) in the piecewise exponential model with period-specific effects is specified as

$$r_{jk}(t) = \exp\{\alpha_l^{(jk)} + A^{(jk)}\beta_l^{(jk)}\} \quad \text{if } t \in I_l$$

where

$$0 = \tau_1 < \tau_2 < \tau_3 < \cdots < \tau_m,$$

with $\tau_{m+1} = \infty$, one gets m time periods

$$I_l = \{t \mid \tau_l \leq t \leq \tau_{l+1}\} l = 1, \ldots, m$$

For each transition (j, k), $\alpha_l^{(jk)}$ is a constant coefficient associated with the lth time period. $A^{(jk)}$ is a row vector of covariates, and $\beta_l^{(jk)}$ is an associated vector of coefficients for the lth time period (Blossfeld and Rohwer 1995).

5.2.2. Results from the Analysis of National Founding Rates of B-Schools

Table 5.2 presents the results from the models that test the general institutionalization effects, the effects of embeddedness in the world polity and market, economic development and several intervening factors on the founding rates of the first B-Schools at the country level. Model 1 includes both time periods and a measure of participation in the world polity, which has a positive and significant effect on the initial adoption rates only in the post-1960 period. Given that the roles and influence of INGOs and IGOs have become much more enriched and pronounced since World War II (Meyer et al. 1997*a*, 1997*b*; Boli and Thomas 1997, 1999), the effect of participating in the world polity on the initial adoption rates is more evident in the post-1960 period than prior to this period. Thus, nation-states that are deeply involved in the world polity are much more likely to adopt B-Schools than those distant from the world polity.

The results also strongly support the notion that business rationalization has a positive impact on the initial adoption rates of B-Schools. This result for both time periods confirms the argument that as business is increasingly arranged as an organizational actor that is held accountable to rationalized standards and rules of management, B-Schools are more likely to be established.

The newness of systems appears to matter in both time periods. In both stages of the diffusion of B-Schools, there appears to have been a significant difference in the vulnerability to changes between newer and older systems. That is, changing institutional contexts legitimizing B-Schools have been more likely to penetrate into newly independent countries with budding higher education systems than their older counterparts imprinted with then-conventional institutional contexts that did not see B-Schools necessary.

The results for economic development suggest that it has a significant negative effect on the adoption rates in the post-1960 period but no effect for the earlier period. Thus the conventional rhetoric in the business education literature, which would predict a positive effect of economic development over time, is hardly supported. As for the remaining variables, the contagion effect is believed to lead to an increase in the initial adoption rates yet the results do not support this argument in the models presented here.[8] Educational expansion likewise fails to show any effect in either time period.

Next, we test the effect of participation in the world market, measured by economic openness on the adoption rates in Model 2. Constrained by the limited availability of data, we are able to examine this effect only for the post-1960 period. However, the significant and positive influence of participation in the world polity on B-School adoption rates only in the second period suggests that the effect of participation in the world market, if any, should exist in the same period as well. Indeed, we find this to be the case. Thus, countries that are deeply involved in the economic interactions with other countries are more likely to adopt B-Schools. As for the other possible predictors of adoption rates of B-Schools, we find that neither business rationalization nor economic development has a significant impact in this model while participation in the world polity and newness of systems continue to exert significant and positive influences.

Table 5.2 Maximum likelihood estimates of the first B-School founding rates (piecewise exponential model with period-specific effects, 1880–1959 and 1960–99)

Independent variables	Model 6		Model 7[a]
	1880–1959	1960–99	1960–99
Economic development	0.11	−0.15**	−0.16
	(0.07)	(0.05)	(0.17)
Educational expansion	0.24	−0.02	−0.06
	(0.19)	(0.12)	(0.20)
Rationalization of business	0.70**	0.43*	0.27
	(0.24)	(0.16)	(0.17)
Newness of system	0.65**	0.23**	0.31*
	(0.18)	(0.09)	(0.14)
Contagion effect	0.10	−0.01	0.00
	(0.06)	(0.01)	(0.01)
Participation in the world polity	0.10	0.66**	0.39*
	(0.26)	(0.22)	(0.19)
Participation in the world market			0.26+
			(0.14)
Period effect	−5.26**	−4.09**	−3.04**
	(0.70)	(0.59)	(1.16)
Log likelihood		−430.88	−246.54
No. of events	39	64	64

Note: Numbers in parentheses are standard errors. Number of spells = 4856. Number of countries = 140. +$p < 0.10$; *$p < 0.05$; ** $p < 0.01$ (two-tailed tests).
[a] Number of spells = 1257. Number of countries = 95. Maximum likelihood estimates are from exponential model. Here, GDP per capita (logged) is used to measure economic development.

Regarding the period effects in all models,[9] we find that the baseline adoption rates always increase from the first period to the second. That is, when all the independent variables are held constant, a nation-state is much more likely to adopt B-Schools in the post-1960 period than the pre-1960 period. This finding provides empirical evidence for the notion that B-Schools have become a much more taken-for-granted element in recent decades to the extent that the initial adoption rates increase at a faster pace when other factors are held constant.[10]

5.3. CONCLUSION

This chapter has provided a global perspective for a better understanding of the similarities and differences in the development of professional management education over time. We reveal the phenomenal extent of the globalization of

MBA programs and B-Schools despite cross-national differences in higher education systems and other national characteristics. The growth in the number of MBAs, programs, or institutions offering the MBA, and countries that have adopted the MBA and B-Schools, strongly support the global character of the MBA and B-Schools. Furthermore, the academic and popular discourse literature reveals the degree to which the MBA and B-Schools have become the most visible elements in the professional management education field around the world since the 1970s to the present. Despite calls for the need to reform some aspects of the MBA, it has nonetheless taken the dominant form of management education in the more recent period.

Our analysis of the adoption of B-Schools around the world over the past 100 years leads to several main findings. First, internal characteristics are consequential in the diffusion of B-Schools in the early phase of its institutionalization, while external factors are consequential in the later phase. In the earlier period, the initial adoption rates of B-Schools are strongly influenced by the degree to which businesses are rationalized as organizational actors. Once this organizational characteristic of the economy is taken into account, economic development alone fails to predict the adoption of B-Schools contrary to common accounts in the existing literature. In addition, the positive yet partially significant effect of educational expansion implies that as B-Schools take on a rule-like status (Meyer and Rowan 1977), B-Schools are established even in the absence of expanded higher education systems. That is, B-Schools may precede the expansion of higher education systems and coincides with its founding in some countries. Finally, newness of system, measured by the ages of higher education system and political independence, increases the initial adoption rates of B-Schools in the earlier period.

In the post-1960 period, our study shows strong evidence for the effects of globalization on the initial adoption rates of B-Schools. Nation-states that are more involved in the world polity as well as in the world market have shown stronger inclination to establish B-Schools regardless of their internal characteristics. This finding offers empirical support for the world polity thesis that countries are more likely to adopt similar models and rules of operation in general as they increasingly participate in the world market and in the world polity (Meyer 2002). It also suggests that a country's participation in noneconomic domains may promote the diffusion of world models of management as much as that in the economic domain.

Finally, we find strong support for general institutionalization effects. First, previous adoptions of B-Schools by other countries increase the likelihood of future adoptions, though only in the earlier stage of the diffusion of B-Schools. The more widely accepted B-Schools are at the world level, the less important becomes the actual number of previous adoptions. However, the institutionalization of B-Schools at the world level, indicated by period effects in a series of analyses, influences all the potential adopters to a similar extent regardless of their characteristics, increasing the likelihood of adoptions in the later period.

In conclusion, the MBA and B-Schools have achieved a rule-like status in global society as the primary program and institution of educating and producing professional managers needed to lead increasingly universalistic and standardized forms of business around the world. Despite criticisms and controversies, the MBA and B-Schools have diffused to a majority of countries worldwide, and it is extremely challenging to find a society that is immune to this trend. As more business organizations take on the form of rationality in various ways and more countries participate in global society noneconomically as well as economically, MBA programs and B-Schools will continue to spread to churn out 'modern' managers.

NOTES

1. This is to be consistent with the literature on the history of business education that treats the Wharton School as the first incidence of the modern B-School (e.g. Sass 1982).
2. We use the term 'B-Schools' not only literally but also figuratively to refer to different forms of management education. Cross-national variation in the higher education system yields paralleling variation in adopted forms of management education. For one thing, some are set within universities, while others are located outside universities. Inside universities, B-Schools sometimes take forms of independent school (mostly in cases of the United States and Britain), department, or faculty (e.g. in Germany). Outside the setting of university, they are often established as an independent college (e.g. Copenhagen), an education center or an institute (Engwall and Gunnarsson 1994; Engwall and Zamagni 1998).
3. There are ample examples of the rise of standardized and universalized models of management, in which similar logic of liberal market ideology is applied to businesses around the world. Examples include the increasing number of companies worldwide employing the international accounting rules (Jang 2001), and a global expansion of consulting industries that propagate global models of management (Sahlin-Andersson and Engwall 2002).
4. For example, England and France, despite economic development, were slow to adopt B-Schools, partly because their higher education systems were not as expansive as that of the United States in size or scope. Furthermore, the expansion of education system in terms of scope may lead to the establishment of B-Schools even in absence of economic development.
5. All the index variables are produced using principal component analysis.

6. Complementary data for the period prior to the first publication of the IHU and CUY come from the literature on business education history (Source: Engwall and Zamagni 1998).

7. We also explored different dividing points from 1955 to 1965, and results were generally consistent with those of chosen periods.

8. In models not containing the measures of embeddedness in the world polity, we do find this to be the case in the earlier period but not in the later period, which implies that previous adoptions of B-Schools in the world certainly encourage future adoptions, but mostly when the institutionalization of B-Schools is at its elementary stage. The noneffect of previous adoptions in the later period suggests that once B-Schools become taken-for-granted as the appropriate form of management education, the marginal effect of additional adoptions may turn insignificant.

9. As mentioned previously, a piecewise exponential model with period-specific effects allows its own baseline adoption rate for each time period, which is constant within time periods, but can vary across time periods. Period effects, then, are indicated by the baseline adoption rates while controlling for other independent variables.

10. We also tested the resistant effects of institutional characteristics peculiar to European and communist countries, as presented in the literature on the history of business education (Locke 1984, 1989; Engwall and Zamagni 1998). First, being a Western European country has a negative and significant effect on the initial adoption rates only in the pre-1960 period. This negative effect is consistent with what the literature suggests: European countries were slower to adopt B-Schools than other countries with similar characteristics, due to the persistence of traditional models of management and management education. Next, we found negative but insignificant effect of communist economy on the adoption rates in both periods. The insignificant effect may result from the small number of communist countries included in the analysis. Although not significant, the effect works in the direction as predicted in the literature. Still, this finding may imply that the communist effect may not exist above and beyond the effects of characteristics associated with communist societies that are already captured by other independent variables.

6

The Making and Expansion of International Management Standards: The Global Diffusion of ISO 9000 Quality Management Certificates

Peter Mendel[1]

The ISO 9000 series of international standards for quality management presents an ideal empirical focus for a study of the global diffusion of organizational reforms, as it possesses several distinctive features that illustrate the dynamics underlying the globalization of modern organization and management. It is one of the foremost exemplars of an organizational model rooted in global institutions and claiming an expressly international scope. This set of standards also rose to prominence through its role in European integration and incorporation into European Union trade directives. As an accreditation regime, described in more detail later, it constitutes a facet of global governance, providing an explicit mechanism of trust in international environments by certifying the status of organizational actors.

For the international standards-development sector, the ISO 9000 program is novel as well in that it offers a system of standardization for organizational actors—or 'soft' standards—as opposed to conventional product or technical requirements. This extension into managerial domains appears to have been extraordinarily successful: to date, ISO 9000 is the most popular set of standards ever published by the International Organization for Standardization (ISO), with over 560,000 active certificates in more than 150 countries since its introduction in 1987 (ISO 2003). The model has even been replicated with the subsequent ISO 14000 management accreditation for environmental issues (Delmas 2000; Mendel 2002).

This chapter describes the development of the ISO 9000 standards from the confluence of two globalizing movements—global managerial culture and international standardization—essentially producing a formal accreditation system that contrasts markedly from much of conventional quality management and typical managerial solutions and reforms generally touted as 'management innovation' or 'organizational improvement'.

The chapter then empirically examines the transnational diffusion of the ISO 9000 standards: Why have the ISO 9000 standards spread so rapidly throughout the world, and what factors predict their differential diffusion across societies? The results of these analyses demonstrate the power of the two globalizing movements above in encouraging worldwide adoption of ISO 9000 and how the incorporation of the standards into European Union trade regulations in 1992 provided a pivotal legitimating anchor for this formal organizational reform at the international level. The analyses further illuminates the role of national political cultures and styles of rationality as well as a country's position in the world polity in mediating the diffusion of organizational ideas and practices in a globalized environment.

6.1. A GLOBAL MODEL OF ORGANIZATION

6.1.1. The ISO 9000 Model and Certification Process

The ISO 9000 standards are composed of a series of five documents, two 'guidance standards' intended as interpretive references, and three 'contractual standards' from which an organization may choose to become certified (Lamprecht 1993: 4–7; Tamm-Hallstrom 1996: 68–9).[2] The most comprehensive quality assurance model, ISO 9001, specifies standards for twenty quality system elements covering a full range of an organization's operations, from management responsibility for quality and quality system principles to areas such as contract review, document control, control of nonconforming product, corrective action, internal audits, and training (Byrnes 1992; Hutchins 1993a: 76).

In addition to ISO 9000's breadth of coverage, the standards are extremely generic, as reflected in their brevity (ISO 9001 is only seven pages long). They are intended to apply to organizations in any type of product or service industry. For example, one of the twenty system elements, Contract Review, specifies that 'the supplier shall establish and maintain procedures for contract review and the coordination of these activities.' How to accomplish this is essentially up to the organization, except for the following broad guidelines: 'for each contract the supplier shall (*a*) ensure that customer requirements are properly defined; (*b*) discrepancies between the customer and supplier [i.e. the organization] are resolved; (*c*) supplier is capable of satisfying contractual requirements; and (*d*) proper records are maintained' (Hutchins 1993*a*: 75–6).

Lamprecht (1993: 42–4) describes how the broad ISO 9000 standards, such as the Contract Review element, can be applied to a variety of industries, including services such as restaurants, hotels, and software development.

Would the interpretation be the same for a hotel manager, a dentist, a hospital director, or a software company? Obviously not, and yet there are similarities. In a restaurant, the contract review is performed at the customer/waiter interface. Customers order from a catalogue (better known as a menu). Requirements differing from the 'tender' are resolved on the spot with the full confidence that the kitchen will be able to meet the modified contractual requirement … In the rare event that the kitchen (where paragraph 4.9 *Process Control* would take effect) cannot deliver what was promised by the waiter(ess), a nonconforming meal (paragraphs 4.13 *Control of Nonconforming Products* and 4.13.1 *Nonconformity Review and Disposition*) will be the end product. However, as is the case with some manufacturing industries, meal nonconformities can only be resolved after the product is delivered. Most restaurants will gladly apply corrective action (4.14) by either replacing or otherwise adjusting the order at no extra cost to the customer.

As for the requirement to keep quality records, records of all contract reviews are written on the ordering ticket which is probably retained (see 4.16) for no more than a few days at the most. Consequently, we see that service organizations can indeed bring relevance to most if not all of the twenty ISO 9001 paragraphs. [Underlines have been added to indicate terminology emblematic of ISO 9000.]

ISO 9000 registration rests on documentation of the organization's 'quality system', ultimately codified into a comprehensive 'quality manual' (Mullin 1992). This organization-specific document is usually quite brief—in most cases less than forty pages (Lamprecht 1991), and references other second-, third-, and fourth-tier documents listing more detailed procedures (from departmental procedures to work instructions and standard documentation forms). During initial certification and periodic 'surveillance' audits thereafter, the private third-party auditors (termed registrars or notifying bodies) focus on verifying that organizational operations conform to the documented procedures. Likewise, internal audits attempt to keep the quality system documentation and actual processes in alignment (Lamprecht 1993: 31–3).

Preparing and continually referring to such an overarching operational manual requires an organization to review, outline, and integrate procedures across varied departments according to the ISO-developed framework (Mullin 1992; Hutchins 1993*a*: 79). This systematization occurs predominantly at the conceptual level in extracting and codifying the essential elements of a quality system from a forest of current procedures (Rothery 1993: 16).

Where procedures have not been formalized and documented, the process acts to increase the rationalization of operations along a set of standard categories.

In this way, ISO 9000 certification represents a short-hand means of communicating internal systems to customers and other constituents as well as providing a common procedural language across organizations and subunits (Kagan 1992). For example, improving the transparency of work processes and communication between departments has been ranked among the highest benefits of ISO 9000 by adopters in the United States and Germany (Dun and Bradstreet 1996; Walgenbach 1997). To the wider external world, it sends a signal that an organization runs a 'tight ship' according to a rationally ordered and widely recognized model.

The commitment and investment to become and remain ISO 9000 certified is not trivial. A US survey of ISO 9000-certified companies (Dun and Bradstreet 1996) reported a mean time for an organization to achieve registration of approximately fifteen months, with average total combined costs (including internal expenses, preregistration consultants, and initial registration audit) of between $82,000 for smaller organizations (less than $11 million revenue) and $434,000 for the larger entities (over $1 billion revenue). While approximately 85 percent of companies are registered on their first attempt, losing certification, although relatively rare, may be more costly in terms of reputation than if an organization had never been ISO 9000 certified in the first place (Lamprecht 1993: 88).

6.1.2. Origins of the ISO 9000 System

Although now associated with the formation of the European Single Market, the ISO 9000 standards evolved from quality systems widely implemented by Western military procurers in the 1960s, such as the US Department of Defense's MIL-Q-9858A and subsequent NATO quality specifications. These standards, which became the template for many procurement requirements in industries such as health care, aerospace, and nuclear energy (Hutchins 1993a), rely heavily on second-party verification, i.e. periodic quality audits of suppliers performed by the customer. Such schemes became increasingly common in both the public and private sectors during the latter part of the twentieth century as many corporate customers tended toward deeper integration with more limited sets of suppliers (Rothery 1993).

As of the late 1970s, a number of national standardization bodies had produced similar national level standards for quality control systems, such as the British Standards Institute's BS 5750, an influential early model that included verification of compliance to the standards by third-party auditors. These national standards bodies in turn were active in the International Organization for Standardization, also known by the acronym ISO, which designates only one national standards development organization (SDO) per country to represent all national standardizing interests (e.g. corporate firms, the sciences, consumers, and government). This membership system also utilized by the other central pillars of the international standards community, such as the International Electrotechnical Congress (IEC) and the various regional standards organizations, has resulted in a relatively integrated structure (compared to other examples of international organization) of interlinked global, regional, and national sectors within the global voluntary standards movement, which rather quietly and mundanely has pursued the standardization of primarily technical areas (e.g. credit card thickness, automobile dashboard symbols, etc.) throughout the world (Loya and Boli 1999).

During the same decade, the ISO supported an initiative on conformity assessment aimed at producing an international plan to harmonize product certifications. By 1980, the involvement of individual and national members of the ISO with various quality verification systems as well as the international conformity assessment plan had generated enough interest to extend the ISO's efforts from technical into managerial issues through the development of an international series of quality management standards. In August of that year, standards representatives from forty countries, including the United States, Canada, several European countries, South Africa, and Australia, convened in Ottawa (Peach 2000*a*). The momentum of this first meeting continued in typical ISO fashion with the formation of a technical committee, TC 176, chartered to 'refine . . . all the most practical and generally applicable principles of quality systems' (Rothery 1993: 19) into a single global standard that could replace the burgeoning number of multiple, yet substantially similar, national and industry quality certifications (Hagigh 1992; Heller 1993).

After several years of gestation, the ISO 9000 series was first published in 1987. Standards professionals were quick to promote the quality management system in Europe, and in 1989 the European Union published a 'Global Approach to Conformity Assessment' that advised companies to adopt a certified quality management system based on ISO 9000. In 1992, the European Union issued trade directives mandating conformity assessment of both products and production processes for a limited set of 'regulated' product categories with particular health and safety issues (European Commission 1997), incorporating ISO 9000 certification as a means for organizations to comply with these requirements.

6.1.3. Management Standards as a Formal Organizational Reform

As described earlier, the ISO 9000 standards, unlike other quality initiatives, do not attempt to evaluate a finished product, a delivered service, an organization's operational effectiveness, or its competitive performance in providing customer value or meeting market requirements (Lamprecht 1991; Reimann and Hertz 1994). Hence, a company's certification of ISO 9000 standards is not a sign of product quality in the conventional sense that a firm's output is 'fit for its intended purpose'. In fact, an organization could make a product that nobody wants and still become certified (Levine 1992; Kochan 1993).

ISO 9000 registration merely assures, through third-party verification and internal audits, that an organization has a documented 'quality management system'—a written set of rules and procedures—in place to which it adheres (Hagigh 1992). To achieve and retain certification, organizations are evaluated for conformance according to the standards' 'model' (Lamprecht 1993: 24) or 'template' (Rothery 1993: 16) of a management system. In this respect, an ISO 9000 certificate represents a 'seal of approval' that a registrant is a minimally qualified 'quality' organization. In other words, the standards serve as an accreditation regime similar to those for educational or health institutions, but generally applicable to any type of organization: commercial, public, or otherwise.

In this sense, the ISO 9000 standards incorporate an underlying style of rationality—i.e. logic for 'rationalizing' or conceptualizing organizations as efficient and progressive social actors—that differs from organizational reform programs typically touted by management gurus and the organizational studies literature alike as 'management innovation' (Kimberly 1984; Barley and Kunda 1992; Abrahamson 1996a), including other incarnations of the conventional quality movement such as Total Quality Management (TQM) and Continuous Quality Improvement (Hackman and Wageman 1995; Strang 1997).

According to Weberian distinctions between formal and material rationality, theories and rhetorics on how organizations should act may emphasize how well an organization conforms to established practices and procedures (i.e. formal 'means compliance') or how well it transforms resources into desired outcomes (i.e. material 'means-ends comparisons'). These logics of propriety and instrumentality represent varying pressures and contrasting modes of accountability for organizational actors (Meyer and Scott 1983; see also March 1981 for a similar distinction between 'obligatory' and 'consequential' models of decision-making in organizations).

Organizational reforms based on material styles of rationality offer principles, techniques, and guidelines appealing to the self-interest of the organization to improve itself (analogous to the popular self-improvement literature for individuals). Reforms based on formal logics tend to be highly codified with contractual, even legalistic overtones, and are more specifically linked to a rational authority sponsoring the program. In religious terms, materialist reforms can be likened to 'born again' rituals, in which organizations demonstrate proper actorhood through displays of self-transformation. Formal reforms, on the other hand, are closer to a 'baptism', in which one is anointed into the community of actors by the direct agent of a higher authority.[3] As a result, although the spread of material-style reforms is aided by regulatory endorsement (cf. Davis and Greve 1997; Kelly and Dobbin 1998), formal reforms are especially dependent on governance structures as a source of their scope and legitimacy (Mendel 2001).

While both styles of rationality are endemic to modern systems,[4] patterns of authority that vary across national polities tend to privilege one or the other logic. Bendix (1956) was among the first theorists to explicitly associate differences in managerial ideologies with patterns of authority engendered in the relationship of the state to society. In broad terms, modern polities tend to invest sovereignty and action in the state or in civil society (Jepperson and Meyer 1991; Jepperson 1999). Modern systems of both varieties propound rational organization. However, in the first, authority for action resides in a separate and superior state apparatus that takes responsibility for calculating and planning collective endeavors. This pattern of authority is conducive to a formal style of rationality, in which social actors look to a concrete higher authority to rationally establish their roles and procedures for appropriate behavior. In liberal polities, the capacity and responsibility for reasoned action are devolved and diffused among members of civil society, and rational outcomes expected to naturally emerge through their interaction. In the United States, for instance, management experts and practitioners naturally refer to materialist-oriented reforms as 'management innovation' (Kimberly 1984). Formal programs are tolerated as bureaucracy, or worse regulation, to be severely limited, even when grudgingly recognized as necessary (cf. Dobbin and Sutton 1998; Dobbin 2000). In polities with statist traditions, such as France or Latin American countries, formal mechanisms are more de rigueur and do not carry such onerous connotations.

Thus, it is not surprising that prominent leaders of the quality movement in the United States considered the early acceptance of the ISO 9000 accreditation system in Europe as an overly 'bureaucratic' response to industrial quality concerns (Juran 1993; Stratton 1993). But despite these contrasting styles of reform and initial antagonisms, there has been a surprising degree of accommodation and mutualism as the ISO 9000 standards have proven their popularity in international markets. Although the ISO 9000 standards were not initially founded on TQM principles, neither do they explicitly contradict them (Lamprecht 1993: 24).[5] At present, both quality approaches share a substantial amount of support among professional consultants and associations in the quality field, such as the American Society for Quality (ASQ) in the United States, with many viewing ISO 9000 as a foundation for more advanced TQM practices (Spizizen 1992; Kochan 1993; Port 1993).

6.2. GLOBALIZATION AND THE SPREAD OF MODERN MANAGERIAL FORMS

The current phenomenon of globalization consists not simply of growth in economic exchange or interdependence, but more fundamentally in an increasingly elaborated and accepted depiction of the world as a whole community (Giddens 1990; Robertson 1992)—a so-called global village and marketplace—requiring rational and progressive development (Meyer et al. 1997). The construction of this global condition, both real and virtual, has generated a variety of movements to define universal guidelines, rights, and standards (Boli and Thomas 1999), as well as an organizational and regulative infrastructure to produce, monitor, and occasionally enforce them. International management standards, as the description of their origins and history earlier indicate, represent the intersection of two of these universal movements—the rise of global managerial culture and the expansion of international standardization.

While international trade has been 'globalized' for several centuries (Waters 1995), management as a general occupation and set of ideas did not begin to evolve into a distinct profession until the turn of the twentieth century (Shenhav 1995; Pedersen and Dobbin 1997). Even then, managerial elites tended to remain nationally or even locally segmented, and well past the end of World War II the spread of management ideas primarily occurred through instances of cross-border transfer (Cole 1989; Guillén 1994; Djelic 1998). Today, professionals and institutions at the international level—including cadres of management practitioners in multinational enterprises (MNEs) and consulting firms, many of whom have been trained in internationally recognized business schools and MBA programs—comprise a global field of managerial culture (Guillén 1998; Kipping 1999; McKenna, Djelic, and Ainamo 2000) having the power to produce and legitimate, as well as conduit, new managerial concepts and organizational forms the world over.

The regimes described earlier for promoting 'voluntary' standards have a slightly longer international legacy, dating from the interwar period (NRC 1995; Loya and Boli 1999). The unique form of social rationalization and coordination offered by these systems is especially suited to environments in which markets and hierarchies are weak or fragmented such as in the current global context (Meyer 1997; Brunsson 2000). Not surprisingly, organizations and governing bodies across a wide range of countries and industries have found standardization increasingly attractive.

Historically, the intersection of these two movements has been strongest in Europe, which has experienced the most pronounced degree of globalization over the past half-century (Tsoukalis 1993; Nugent 1994). The force of this 'Europeanization' and the tensions involved in integrating economic activity across multiple sovereign national states have led to a strong reliance on international standards-making bodies to harmonize rules and regulations at the European level (Fligstein and Mara-Drita 1993) and the emergence of Europe as a global node of standardization activities (Zuckerman 1997), including the development of the ISO 9000 standards. European globalization has been equally integral to the spread of the international management standards. The status of ISO 9000 as an international credential is both a great inducement to organizations to become certified and at the same time highly dependent as a formal reform on regulatory structures at the world level for its authority and legitimacy. Thus, the inclusion of the standards into European trade directives, even in a limited fashion, has served as a spring-board, facilitating its global scope and credibility, even in countries that might not normally be predisposed to formal managerial solutions.

6.2.1. Institutional Mechanisms of Diffusion

Many common arguments for the rise of the standards, including those asserted by standards producers themselves, center on the benefits to adopting organizations in terms of operational efficiency. In addition to potential process improvements, advocates of ISO 9000 and others argue that the emphasis on consistency comprises a basic aspect of perform-ance (ISO 1992*a*; NRC 1995), which may be especially important for firms utilizing process technologies such as chemical or steel production. Similarly, organizations in fields employing 'uncertain' or 'pre-paradigmatic' (Kimberly 1984: 99) technologies not amenable to precise measurement of outcomes—e.g. software development, mental health, education, and public administration—may rely extensively on procedurally oriented assessments (Meyer and Scott 1983; Wilson 1989).

In the face of skepticism over direct effects on productivity, still others point to ISO 9000 as an efficient collective solution that replaces a plethora of incommensurate or redundant national, industry, and customer requirements with a single international system (Hagigh 1992; Heller 1993). Thus, organizations confronting a multitude of separate standards and verifications would be expected to adopt most quickly. Unfortunately, case research suggests that the ISO model has augmented rather than reduced the number of costly audits by validating their use as a social control mechanism (Walgenbach 1996).

But regardless of the veracity of these benefits, the functions of an organizational form do not substitute as an explanation for its adoption (Scott 1992). While not completely unfounded, the above functional arguments lack sufficient attention to the underlying social processes of diffusion (Strang and Soule 1998). Collective agents and influential others help define salient issues and provide proper solutions (Meyer and Rowan 1977). What problems are most pressing, which methods are considered rational, how to identify criteria—even how to gauge 'uncertainty'? Organizations and other actors rely on general perceptions of appropriateness, adoptions by influential peers, and judgments by opinion leaders, such as management gurus, issue advocates, public officials, various media and the like, to answer these questions and lend support to organizational activities (Kimberly 1984; Barley, Meyer, and Gash 1988; Abrahamson 1996a). As a result, the spread of organizational solutions and models, including ISO 9000, is strongly conditioned by the institutional and cultural contexts in which organizations find themselves and by their locations and relationships with respect to other actors.

This study focuses on these fundamental institutional dynamics of diffusion on a global and national scale to understand why the ISO 9000 standards have spread so rapidly through the world and the factors that predict their differential diffusion across countries. The discussion to this point has identified four sets of institutional influences central to the diffusion of the ISO 9000 standards—European globalization, standardization regimes, global managerial culture, and position within the world polity.

These influences demonstrate a full range of institutional pressures to adopt new organizational forms and practices, from coercive (compulsion through regulatory or other mandates), normative (sense of obligation to follow 'best practice' and advice of experts), and cognitive (predisposition toward taken-for-granted assumptions) (DiMaggio and Powell 1983; Scott 2001). For example, European integration represents the most extensive case of globalization precisely because it incorporates a host of regulatory, professional, and cultural agents across economic, political, and social dimensions.

The four sets of institutional influences also display varying modes of diffusion, from relational ties in which forms are transferred through direct contacts among actors to broadcast modes of transmission that allow for easier access to models through common cultural links (e.g. newspapers, professional journals, television, and other media). Particularly under the latter, the more general and abstract a model, the more rapid and universal is its diffusion (Strang and Meyer 1993). With regard to ISO 9000, many observers, including the ISO Secretary-General, have attributed the popularity of the standards to their breadth and generic character (Lamprecht 1991; Byrnes 1992). These patterns are increasingly evident as the standards become institutionalized in managerial culture more broadly and spread to localized organizational sectors not normally associated with networks of international trade such as public utilities (Hutchins 1993*b*), training and education (Berthelot 1993; Elliot 1993; De La Salle University 1997), and hospitals (Quality Systems Update 1996). Similarly, interview and survey research on ISO 9000 have noted the nebulous nature of environmental pressures for its adoption. Managers report reasons for certification that include orders by higher level executives, competitors' certification, and perceived marketing and market entry advantages, but rarely mention direct customer or regulatory demands (Dun and Bradstreet 1996; Walgenbach 1997). These processes are described further for each set of influences in the following sections.

6.2.2. European Globalization

As discussed previously, the ISO 9000 standards owe much of their notoriety to the role of standardization in European integration and their specific inclusion in legal rules related to the formation of the Single Market in Europe. In 1989, the European Union published a 'Global Approach to Conformity Assessment' that advised companies to adopt a certified quality management system based on ISO 9000. In 1992, a series of European Union trade directives directly mandated conformity assessment of both products and production processes for a limited set of 'regulated' product categories with particular health and safety issues, including construction products, pressure vessels, medical devices, and telecommunications equipment among others (European Commission 1997). ISO 9000 registration for these categories is technically neither mandatory nor sufficient—there are alternate means to certify production processes, and it usually must be combined with product testing in order to obtain the necessary 'CE mark' product certification (Saunders 1992). However, because of the complexity of regulations and expense of alternatives, ISO 9000 certification is in practice a de facto requirement for regulated products in European Union member countries (Byrnes 1992).

These legal rules in turn have become marketing requirements for supplier organizations (Rothery 1993), which generate a pyramiding diffusion down the supply chain (Brokaw 1993). Moreover, markets tend to develop prestige hierarchies (Kimberly 1984) or status orders reflecting cost, revenue, and quality profiles of producers (Podolny 1993). ISO 9000 certification is frequently used as such a visible, although relatively blunt, marketing tool to distinguish among suppliers (Brokaw 1993).

Such general market-related processes have had strong effects. Soon after the introduction of ISO 9000, adoption appeared driven more by diffuse market and customer pressure than government regulation (Hagigh 1992), spreading rapidly outside of European regulated product sectors. For example, ISO 9000 certifications in the United States have grown at rates similar to Germany and other European countries, even though only a fraction, approximately 19 percent, of the $103 billion worth of American goods exported to Europe in 1992 fell into regulated categories (Kochan 1993). Clearly, the initially limited legal requirements have operated by 'authorization'—conforming to rules to gain legitimacy, as much as by 'imposition'—complying to avoid or induce sanctions (Scott 1991), and have translated into even stronger normative pressures for adoption as reflected in its perception as a 'method of demonstrating the kind of careful management' that can 'protect one from product liability or charges of negligence' in European courts (Rothery 1993: 4).

6.2.3. Standardization Regimes

Although Europe has evolved into a central node for standards-development activities, international standardization is composed of numerous national infrastructures linked in a variety of relationships to international bodies at the regional and world levels. The span and influence of the standardization sector within a country, and its participation in the wider global regime of standardization where the international management standards are broadly accepted, should amplify the diffusion of ISO 9000.

Traditional standards producers, however, are by no means the only professionals involved in disseminating the ISO 9000 standards. In many countries, standards organizations have been joined by quality professionals and associations in coordinating registration activities. For instance, in the United States, the Registrar Accreditation Board is jointly administered by the American National Standards Institute (ANSI) and the American Society for Quality (ASQ) (Peach 1992), while in Germany, the German Society for Certification of Quality Assurance Systems (DQS) was jointly founded by the German Standards Institute (DIN) and the German Association for Quality (DGQ) (Walgenbach 1996). At the European level, similar bodies primarily focus on professional coordination, for example, the European Organization for Quality Control (EOQC) and the European Organization for Testing and Certification (EOTC).

The demand for ISO 9000 certification itself has spawned additional professional services and occupations directly related to certification activities, such as registrars, notifying bodies, and registration consultants, which operate independently of the ISO itself. In a typically American approach, one consulting firm has established support groups for organizations in the United States and Europe undergoing certification (Industrial Engineering 1993*a*, 1993*b*).

In addition to the magnitude and penetration of standardization sectors, their composition reflects national political cultures and the 'mentalities' of political, economic, and technical elites that can decidedly shape and filter the diffusion of management ideas within countries (Maier 1970; Guillén 1994). One highly consequential dimension distinguishing national polities in this regard is the predominant pattern of authority—whether statist or liberal. As discussed earlier, statist patterns of authority are expected to encourage greater degrees of bureaucratization, including the use of codified procedures, rationalized central planning, and accreditation regimes such as ISO 9000 and, in terms of the standardization sector per se, would be reflected by a strong state role in standards-making activities (Mendel 2001), which varies considerably across countries (Loya and Boli 1999).

6.2.4. Global Managerial Culture

The rise of a global managerial culture provides powerful conduits for organizational reforms legitimated at the world level. While the appeal of ISO 9000 has been most intense in Europe, it clearly has also become a 'premier standard for optimal customer–supplier relationships' (Zaciewski 1993) in the world marketplace (Tattum 1992). As the prevalence of ISO 9000 has grown throughout global industries and regional economies, the standards have become a taken-for-granted element of organizational environments and an easily accessible solution for addressing quality issues, even in countries and local contexts that might not be predisposed toward formal managerial programs. The most prominent illustration of this has been ISO 9000's ability to largely overcome initial antagonism in the

United States, one of the major bastions of managerial logics based on material styles of rationality as well as the main exponent of modern professional management.

Indeed, the more sustained effect of a strong culture of professional management is to produce a secular demand for all types of management reforms. Modern managerial ideology is historically and deeply rooted in popular, professional, and legal definitions, spawned in mid-nineteenth-century America, of organizations as autonomous social entities with the capacity for independent agency (Creighton 1989; Roy 1997). For example, the modern organization accrued its current status of a legal personality or fictitious individual with the right to hold property and enter contracts (Coleman 1991: 4), the license to speak and be referred to in the first person (e.g. 'IBM denies charges of misleading customers') and even the ability to commit suicide (i.e. bankruptcy).

This assumption of organizational 'actorhood' exposes organizations to ever-increasing expectations to enact their standing as legitimate, efficient, and responsible social actors (Brunsson and Sahlin-Andersson 2000; Meyer and Jepperson 2000; Mendel 2001). These expectations create demand among organizations for programs of reform and improvement—a demand which management professionals, consulting firms, and the business media both spur and fulfill (Furusten 1995). Thus, although mainstream strategic consulting houses typically leave ISO certification services to more specialized auditing companies, the use of management consultancies in general may indicate a susceptibility to external managerial norms.

The presence of MNEs is an important source of such managerial and organizational ideologies, especially in societies without an indigenous base of professional management (Arias and Guillén 1998). Over time, multinational corporations have evolved from aggregations of relatively compartmentalized subsidiary operations into truly transnational enterprises of integrated strategic and technical operations (Bartlett and Ghoshal 1989). To the extent that the culture of a MNE cuts across national boundaries, it acts as a medium circulating management knowledge and philosophies across borders (Guillén 1998) and throughout the broader global fields in which it operates.

6.2.5. World Polity Position

Finally, organizations are much more likely to model the behavior of others considered to be either similar or more successful and advanced. For example, organizations tend to emulate others who are perceived to occupy equivalent role positions within a social system (Galaskiewicz and Burt 1991). Likewise, diffusion research has frequently emphasized the impact of initial adoption by 'opinion leaders' and 'high prestige' organizations (Kimberly 1984).

Similar processes of reference and comparison based on social roles occur among nation-states as well (Meyer et al. 1997). Countries tend to cluster into groupings based on geographical region and economic development, which form the basis of a rough status order within the world polity. Developed countries located in core positions tend to act as referent societies, supplying and demonstrating organizational models to peripheral nation-states (Guillén 1998). Countries whose economies have historically depended on large amounts of foreign trade are particularly open to ideas and practices from central powers.

One problem with using level of development—i.e. core versus peripheral economies—as a simple predictor for adoption of organizational models is that it poorly distinguishes among countries. Elites in both core and peripheral nation-states engage in emulation, the latter in order to catch up and the former to achieve or maintain supremacy (cf. Arias and Guillén 1998: 121–2). Authorities have mounted major national campaigns for ISO 9000 registration in developed countries ranging from the United Kingdom (NAO 1990; Dale and Oakland 1991) to Japan (Marquardt 1992). The European Union itself has encouraged adoption of the standards through a variety of programs, including subsidies to small and medium-sized enterprises (Walgenbach 1996). Similarly, in many developing countries, such as members of the Association of Southeast Asian Nations (ASEAN), the standards are at the heart of industry improvement efforts 'aided by promotional campaigns launched by government and business leaders' (Coeyman 1993).

However, conditions of perceived national crises or performance lags will heighten the mobilization within a country for the search and adoption of putatively effective archetypes. Core countries that once had been or are close to becoming world leaders are especially sensitive to declining economic competitiveness and geopolitical status, as opposed to other developed countries that have been disavowed of these ambitions (Djelic 1998). Such a desire to improve its long-waning standing as an industrial power was certainly the impetus for the United Kingdom's successful campaign for widespread adoption of the BSI's national quality certifications and, later, of the ISO 9000 international standards (DTI 1982; McWilliam 1997). In contrast, Germany, whose industrial reputation for quality was relatively well-regarded during the same period, never saw a national quality system gain much popularity, and industry and labor representatives—rejecting claims that 'Made in Germany' was no longer sufficient in the global economy—initially gave heated resistance to the acceptance of the ISO 9000 standards within the national quality and standards associations (Walgenbach 1996).

6.3. ANALYSIS OF THE GLOBAL SPREAD OF ISO 9000 STANDARDS

6.3.1. Comparative Trends in the Rise of ISO 9000

Figure 6.1a shows trends in the prevalence of active ISO 9000 certificates for the G-7 (core industrialized) countries based on data in the *ISO Survey* from 1992 to 1998 (ISO 1999*a*).[6] The United Kingdom was among the first countries to develop a national quality management system and to initiate the development of the ISO 9000 standards. Yet it still accounts for an unexpectedly large proportion of ISO 9000 certificates worldwide, and has maintained this predominance even after a slight leveling off after 1995. By 1998, the United States and Germany are still a distant second and third in number of certificates, followed by Italy and France.

The picture remains similar for the United Kingdom in terms of certificates normalized by size of economy in terms of GDP (Figure 6.1b). However, Italy now occupies the distant second position, and Canada moves to third highest in relative numbers of certificates by 1998. Next, Germany slightly edges out France, with the United States and Japan demonstrating the lowest levels of relative adoption among the most economically advanced countries.

The differences between actual and relative numbers of certificates are even more striking in regional trends. Although Western Europe (by far), Asia, and North America lead the world in sheer numbers of certificates (not presented), the normalized counts by geographic region in Figure 6.2 reveal Oceania— weighted heavily by Australia and New Zealand—to have the highest relative level of ISO 9000 adoptions, surpassing even Western Europe by a fairly substantial margin. This pattern of higher standards among British Common-wealth countries is explored further in the discussion of results. The fact that the relative level of certificates for North America—driven largely by the United States—languishes near the bottom of these trends, suggests a continuing American exceptionalism, even compared to other anglophonic countries.

6.3.2. The Dynamics of Global Diffusion in ISO 9000 Certificates

Next, we examine the dynamics of institutional influences affecting the rise of ISO 9000 across countries around the globe using time series regression analysis of national counts of ISO 9000 certificates from 1992 to 1998.[7] All statistical models presented below lag independent variables by one year in order to preserve causal inference[8] and adjust for serial autocorrelation between country observations from year to year.[9]

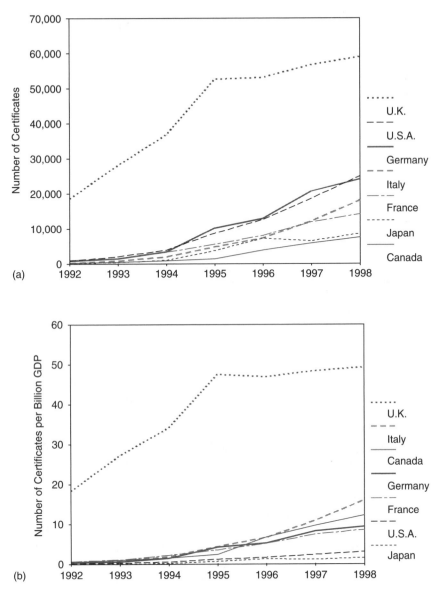

Figure 6.1 (a) ISO 9000 Certificates, G-7 Countries 1992–1998 (b) ISO 9000 Certificates per Billion GDP, G-7 countries 1992–1998
Source: The ISO Survey of ISO 9000 and ISO 14000 certificates (ISO 1999a).

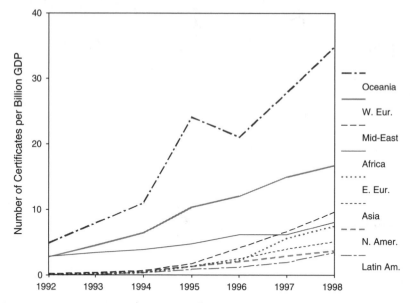

Figure 6.2   ISO 9000 Certificates per Billion GDP, by Region 1992–1998
Source: The ISO Survey of ISO 9000 and ISO 14000 Certificates (ISO 1999a).

The models in Table 6.1 systematically incorporate key indicators for each cluster of influences which were found to be significant in separate analyses, controlling for size of economy in terms of real GDP. See Mendel (2001) for methods used in calculating indicators from the data sources cited later. Based on χ^2 tests, the log-likelihood statistics indicate that each successive model represents a statistical improvement in fit ($p < 0.001$).

The first model begins with results for the influence of European globalization and standardization regimes. Exports in European Union regulated product is calculated as the proportion of a country's annual exports to the European Union that are composed of categories covered in European Union directives specifying ISO 9000 accreditation as part of import requirements for product safety (European Commission 1997, 1998, 2000; Feenstra, Lipsey, and Bowen 1997; Feenstra 2000). The presence of this variable has a strong positive effect on the level of ISO 9000 certificates, and in prior separate analyses, reduced the magnitude of a blunt dichotomous indicator for national membership in the European Union to nonsignificance. Thus, it appears that a large portion of the effect of the European Union can be accounted for by European integration processes related more specifically to ISO 9000, but also affecting non-European Union countries.

Table 6.1 Institutional influences on the global diffusion of ISO 9000 certificates, 1992–1998

Variable	Model 1	Model 2	Model 3	Model 4	Model 5
Constant	−14.459 **	−11.941 **	−4.237 #	−12.977 **	−29.171 **
	(1.233)	(1.533)	(2.182)	(1.587)	(2.102)
Control					
Real GDP (log)	0.559 **	0.501 **	0.108	0.411 **	0.765 **
	(0.062)	(0.066)	(0.097)	(0.067)	(0.077)
European globalization					
Exports in EU regulated product (proportion)	19.007 **	14.896 **	13.803 **	−1.314	−4.601
	(3.913)	(4.237)	(4.053)	(3.943)	(3.455)
Standardization regimes					
ISO participation (factor score)	0.161 *	0.140 *	0.105	0.129 *	0.126 **
	(0.063)	(0.064)	(0.064)	(0.061)	(0.048)
National SDO budget (log)	0.267 **	0.204 **	0.292 **	0.337 **	0.234 **
	(0.055)	(0.056)	(0.058)	(0.047)	(0.042)
ISO 9000 registrars (log)	0.987 **	0.942 **	0.843 **	0.574 **	0.390 **
	(0.070)	(0.073)	(0.068)	(0.066)	(0.060)
National SDO legal status		−0.110	0.005	0.002	−0.005
		(0.086)	(0.076)	(0.068)	(0.063)
National SDO legal status × First world country		0.311 **	0.170 *	0.311 **	0.196 **
		(0.084)	(0.080)	(0.060)	(0.056)
Global managerial culture					
Multinational enterprise presence (factor score)			1.363 **	0.709 **	0.488 **
			(0.209)	(0.132)	(0.154)
MBA programs, 1999 (log)			−0.059		
			(0.082)		
Global prevalence of ISO 9000 certificates (thsds)				0.009 **	−0.000
				(0.000)	(0.001)
World polity position					
Exports as percent of GDP (log)					0.605 **

(continued)

Table 6.1 (*Continued*)

Variable	Model 1	Model 2	Model 3	Model 4	Model 5
Trade network cohesion (log)					(0.103)
					0.992**
					(0.084)
Relative economic performance					2.473 #
					(1.412)
Number of countries	81	81	74	74	74
Number of observations	399	399	370	370	367
Log likelihood	−361.94	−352.92	−318.80	−300.74	−235.50
Autocorrelation (*rho*)	0.824	0.842	0.828	0.699	0.733

Notes: Standard errors reported in parentheses. Independent variables lagged one year.
Source: Coefficients from GLS time series regression models.
# $p < 0.10$; * $p < 0.05$; ** $p < 0.01$ (one-tailed tests).

The remaining indicators in Model 1 reflect the international linkage and magnitude of national standardization sectors. Linkage to international standardization, measured by a factor score index of three variables related to participation in the ISO—years membership in ISO adjusting for spells of suspension or withdrawal, category of ISO membership, and representation on the ISO Council (ISO 1997; ISO 1999*b*)—is positively associated with adoption of the standards, while holding constant the size of the national standardization sector—indicated by annual budget of the national standards body (ISO 1988*a*, 1991*a*, 1996*a*, 2000*a*),[10] and the span of professionals and consultants specific to ISO 9000—in terms of extent of ISO 9000 registration services within a country (ISO 1992*c*, 1993*c*, 1995*c*, 1999*c*). By themselves, such large and active bases of standards professionals, either specific to ISO 9000 or more generally, have positive and strongly significant effects in all models ($p < 0.01$). This may help explain the observation of higher levels of ISO 9000 adoption in Anglophonic countries, since they tend to have slightly larger national standards sectors.[11]

Model 2 additionally examines the composition of standardization sectors in terms of degree of state involvement. Legal status characterizes the legal relationship of the national standards body to the state, here coded into a four-category ordinal variable ranging from *private* (incorporated under usual laws for private organizations) to *quasi-private* (incorporated under laws for private organizations, but officially recognized or sponsored by the state), *quasi-government* (incorporated under specific public laws or legislative action, such as an independent board or commission), and *government* (a governmental department or office) (ISO 1988*a*, 1991*a*, 1996*a*, 2000*a*).

Contrary to expectations, legal status indicating a close relationship with the state was negatively associated with levels of ISO 9000 certificates. However, interacting legal status with a dichotomous variable for first world countries at the core of the world political economy (as indicated by inclusion in the World Bank's 'high income' (2000*b*) category) reveals an overall positive effect for developed societies ($0.311 - 0.110 = 0.201$). In prior separate analyses that did not include the variable for European globalization, the base effect for legal status was also statistically significant and a similar pattern was found using other indicators of state involvement in standardization— the proportion of the national standards body's budget provided by the state, and the proportion of standards issued by the national standards body that are considered mandatory by government regulation. Clearly, an important difference exists in the impact of national institutional configurations between core and developing countries.

Model 3 considers the role of global managerial culture in the diffusion of ISO 9000 certificates. The presence of MNEs, measured by a factor score index of three variables related to the activities of MNEs within a country—number of foreign subsidiaries (Reed Reference Electronic Publishing 1994, 1998), total stock of foreign direct investment (World Bank 1999 and United Nations 1994–9, cited in Guler, Guillén, and MacPherson 2002), and gross flow of foreign direct investment (World Bank 2000a), has a highly significant effect in the expected direction.

The effect for number of MBA programs within a country, which was positive in separate prior analyses, was not confirmed in this fuller model. This indicator of the expanse of modern, rationalized management as a distinct profession, both in terms of demand for credentialing—by MNEs or indigenous firms—as well as supply of trained administrators, unfortunately was only available for one time point near the end of the observation period (Merlin Falcon Limited 1999). An indicator that varies over time may better reflect the role of professionalized management education in proliferating global managerial culture.

Model 4 removes the indicator for MBA programs and tests the effects of the global prevalence of ISO 9000 on levels of certificates within countries. Prevalence is generally associated with the taken-for-grantedness of a form within a relevant organizational field (Hannan and Freeman 1977; Scott 2001). It is measured here for ISO 9000 as the annual aggregate number of active certificates in the world to reflect the pervasiveness of the standards in global managerial culture over time. The parameter for this indicator is positive and significant, but the coefficient for exports in European Union regulated product becomes nonsignificant with its inclusion. It appears that the impact of European Union regulatory processes is substantially intertwined with the pervasiveness of the ISO 9000 standards as a general norm.[12]

The findings in the last model suggest a substantial role as well for dynamics related to comparative position in the world polity. General economic openness and interaction with the international economic environment, as indicated by exports per GDP (World Bank 2000a), is a strong predictor of standards certificates.

Similarly, organizations in countries that have direct, complementary trade may be more likely to learn and copy organizational forms and innovations from each other, what Guler, Guillén, and MacPherson (2002) term 'institutional mimicry'. Such levels of ISO 9000 adoption in countries that represent direct trading partners of a country, as measured by a 'trade network cohesion' indicator (a sum of trade with other countries weighted by the number of ISO certificates in those countries), have a strong positive effect.

Worsening economic performance relative to a country's referent economic strata[13] also proves a stimulus to adoption of these globally legitimated standards, albeit at a weaker level of significance ($p < 0.10$).

With the addition of these three final indicators, however, the coefficients for global prevalence now cease to be significant. Stepwise insertion of each variable separately revealed this result to be due to the trade network cohesion indicator. This is not entirely surprising, since, in effect, the network cohesion variable acts as a more refined prevalence measure, weighting levels of certificates in other nations by those most salient to the international environment of the focal country.

6.3.3. Summary of Results

The findings of the time series analyses provide compelling evidence of institutional influences on the cross-national spread of the ISO 9000 standards as well as important insights into global diffusion processes. Standardization sectors, which represent a relatively integrated regime compared to other examples of international organization, are shown to have the power not only to project organizational models at the global level but also to disseminate them within national settings. Similarly apparent is the role of global managerial culture in stimulating demand for organizational reforms and affording conduits for the circulation of solutions legitimated at the world level. The intersection of these two movements in the embodiment of international management standards suggests their capacity to diffuse specific organizational forms, such as ISO 9000, even in local contexts that otherwise might not be predisposed to such formal managerial solutions.

At the same time, the results substantiate the impact of national contexts in mediating the diffusion of organizational ideas and practices. National institutional configurations visibly influence the diffusion of the ISO 9000 standards, with notable differences in effects between core and peripheral countries. In developed countries, statist construction of standardization sectors appears to benefit formal organizational reforms such as ISO 9000 as predicted. But this outcome is reversed or nonexistent outside the core of the modern nation-state system.

Together, these findings suggest that our usual institutional typologies generated from developed countries may not be directly applicable to non-Western or less modernized polities. It may be that state institutional structures in developing countries are more a reflection of externally imposed regimes than of broader cultural orientations. Or perhaps, cultural and institutional norms represent weaker filters for globally legitimated models compared to core countries, especially if economic sectors are less integrated into civic society within developing nations. State-centered standardization in less developed countries may also indicate state domination of economic sectors as opposed to state involvement. In these cases, statist authorities may strongly encourage adoption of ISO 9000 if endorsed by government functionaries, but otherwise inhibit the spread of the standards or reforms more generally.

A major theme of investigation has been the fundamental contribution of European integration to globalization processes at the world level. The effects of the European Union and its elaborated networks of political, cultural, and economic activity are evident both explicitly as an instance of evolving transnational society and indirectly through various other instruments of globalization, such as the production of international regulatory and normative frameworks, the incorporation of standardization regimes, and the proliferation of particular organizational and managerial forms, such as the ISO 9000 standards.

The analyses further illustrate the multifaceted influence of this prevalence and related institutionalization processes. First, the impact of European Union regulation appears associated with broader authorization of the standards as much as with imposition of a narrow set of trade requirements. Moreover, effects of prevalence were conspicuous whether measured by global, regional, or more refined country-network indicators, suggesting the multiplicity of levels on which such general institutionalization operates. Thus, it would not be surprising to find analogous processes in motion within global industry channels.

The strong results for national position in the world economic system and the more refined measure of prevalence in other countries additionally allude to national contexts as enduring units of reference, despite the increasing internationalization of corporations and other organizations. This most likely stems not only from the response of individual organizations to global pressures but also of political, economic, and technical elites within countries who continue to define progress according to nationally delineated criteria for development that endure in world society (Meyer 2000).

6.4. CONCLUSION

6.4.1. The Cultural Foundations of Global Organizational Reforms

Several distinctive features of the ISO 9000 international standards potently illustrate the dynamics underlying the globalization of modern organization and management. This organizational reform is expressly international in scope and has attained far-reaching popularity throughout more than 150 countries. Yet even more exceptionally, these quality management standards, which rose to prominence through their use in European integration, reflect a formal style of rationality that contrasts markedly from organizational reforms typically touted in the United States and elsewhere as management 'innovation'. How did a reform of such a 'bureaucratic' nature gain widespread acceptance, even in the United States, the bastion of management thinking rooted in material styles of rationality? Moreover, how does its worldwide diffusion reconcile with the typical imagery of globalization as forcing the dissemination of American models of organization and management throughout other societies?

As this chapter has demonstrated, these seeming anomalies are readily understandable by attending to the cultural underpinnings of globalization and modern managerial ideology.

Contemporary professional management at its core rests on a conception of the organization as a peculiarly modern social actor. Thus, the spread of modern managerial ideologies contains not only specific organizational models, but the underlying cultural blueprint and rationale for creating organizations and imbuing them with the capacity for independent agency. Where this assumption of organizational actorhood lands and takes hold, the outcome is a constant hunger for all types of discourse and reforms to rationalize and improve the organization as a social actor, especially universal paradigms and programs legitimated at the global level.

This global managerial cultural in turn is situated within a wider world society which provides both a foundation and context. Indeed, the international scene is awash with a pluralist mix of globalizing movements, rarely synchronized and regularly in tension with one another. For example, efforts to structure national economies along standard lines of development frequently conflict with attempts to encourage various forms of social and political progress.

But when globalizing trends intersect, they can produce astonishingly rapid and extensive acceptance of cultural models. The ISO 9000 standards represent such a meeting of global managerial culture with international standardization, a worldwide regime promoting 'voluntary', consensual standards-making as a unique form of social coordination. Historically, the juncture between these two movements has been strongest through European integration, which has relied on international standards bodies to achieve the most pronounced degree of regional globalization over the past half-century. Consequently, Europe has emerged as a global node of standardization activities, including the development and recognition of the ISO 9000 standards.

In addition to promulgating the underlying impetus for organizational reform and specific reform packages, these broad social movements have supported the formation of tangible transnational institutions. With such an expansion in both real and virtual terms, world society has a growing capacity to create, as well as conduit, organizational models. As a result, modern managerial culture is increasingly characterized by the global diffusion of managerial ideas and practices, in contrast to earlier instances of cross-border transfer from one societal context to another.

Moreover, these global infrastructures provide a platform for formal organizational reforms, which are highly dependent on concrete governance bodies to codify rules and define the level and range of their authority. Thus, the inclusion of the ISO 9000 standards in European Union trade directives, albeit in a limited fashion, has served as a springboard, facilitating their global scope and credibility. Once available as a global model, the usefulness of the standards both internally in mobilizing and structuring efforts around quality and externally in relations with other organizations the world over, becomes attractive to organizations even in countries, such as the United States, that normally would not be predisposed to formal managerial solutions.

6.4.2. Implications for Comparative Organizational and Management Research

This study points to the necessity of taking into account the substance and cultural content of organizational models in understanding their diffusion (see also Strang and Soule 1998). For example, the abstract nature and style of rationality embodied in ISO 9000, in addition to its expressly 'international' status and implication of being a 'quality organization', have proved to be influential factors shaping the diffusion of the standards.

The study also emphasizes the need to truly consider the constitutive elements of institutional contexts at the global and national levels and their interplay in order to explain the worldwide diffusion of modern organizational forms. This study has attested to the influence of global managerial culture in disseminating the basic rationale and desire for organizational reforms, while also ascertaining the role of other global movements and institutions in carrying these models.

From the analysis, it was clear that the relatively integrated international standardization regime has the power to project models at the global level as well as disseminate them within national settings. In this way, international standards bodies constitute an extensive yet mundane and, to now, rather silent force of social rationalization across the globe. The development of international management standards indicates the expansion of this movement outside of purely technical areas and into socially salient domains. Mandated revisions to each standards series also provide built-in 'boosts' and revitalization to standardization efforts (Daniels 2000). Their visibility will undoubtedly continue to escalate as they become integral to international trade and coordinating regimes such as the European Union.

This reliance on standardization for regional integration has helped Europe to emerge as a central node for standards-making activities. But what makes the European Union the most advanced instance of globalization is the strong transnational vision at its core of Europe as a whole and celebrated community (Swedberg 1994). Thus, the European Union encompasses a burgeoning network of institutions stretching beyond economic to a host of other spheres, from social welfare to security and defense. Whether other regional coordinating regimes, such as the North American Free Trade Association (NAFTA) or the ASEAN, will also develop an elaborated communal imagery is not obvious. However, results from the analysis show that European globalization, as a proverbial '800-pound gorilla' on the world stage, can produce significant effects in countries outside of Europe with respect to such important processes as the flow of organizational and managerial models.

Findings from the cross-national examination of ISO 9000 certificates also illustrated the enduring influence of national contexts and their linkage to international movements in mediating the diffusion of global forms. The interpenetration of national polities by elements of world society facilitates the spread of globally legitimated organizational models. For example, national participation in the ISO was shown to significantly increase the number of quality certificates within a country, even while controlling for the size of standardization sectors and professional communities at the national level.

The differences in effects of national institutional structures on diffusion of the standards between societies at the core of the world polity and those connected farther along its periphery are clearly an important area for future research. The flow of modern organization and management in less developed countries has been a particularly neglected process. Yet understanding these mechanisms can help shed light on change within these societies and yield a fuller picture of the nature and consequences of globalization.

Finally, the transnational diffusion of the ISO 9000 standards illustrates the panorama of international forces and institutions propagating modern management and organization. A variety of globalizing movements vie to spread modernity, sometimes in concert, but frequently in tension. This study demonstrated the ability of ISO 9000 to largely reach accommodation with

materialist strains within managerial culture, which serves to generally increase the susceptibility of organizations to reform activities. At the same
time, the analysis has substantiated how the diffusion of the standards has
been as or more dependent on movements for international standardization
and European integration, which play out amidst a wider context of referen-
cing and copying conditioned by positions within the world polity. In spreading the most virulent forms of organizational actorhood, management
professionals, and related promulgators of modern managerial logics may
be among the new 'missionaries' of the twenty-first century (Kostera 1995).
But their church has become increasingly international over the past half-
century, and, as illustrated by the ISO 9000 standards, continues to
both incorporate and contribute to elements of an already expanding global
society.

NOTES

1. The author would like to thank John Meyer, W. Richard Scott, and Francisco
   Ramirez for extensive comments on earlier versions of this work, as well as Mauro
   Guillén and Isin Guler for generously sharing indicators from their cross-national
   analysis of ISO 9000 certificates.
2. ISO 9000 certificates may be issued for an entire organization or to specific
   subunits as defined by the applicant. Many large organizations prefer to certify
   subunits in order to ease the burden of registration and protect against the loss of
   certification in one area from affecting other divisions.
3. Both methods are potentially powerful, even with jaded or sophisticated participants. A charismatic 'revival' can sway the seasoned sinner or disaffected parish-
   ioner, and an officious certification can attain the force of a social fact, regardless of
   the individual disbeliefs of communants. While the use here of religious imagery is
   metaphorical, the oft-noted strains of evangelical spirit in American management,
   both figurative and literal (Ackers 1997; Babson 1920), are not surprising from this
   perspective (see also Kostera 1995).
4. Weber's classic definition of rational-legal bureaucracy contains the features of
   seniority, a formal criterion, and meritocracy, a material criterion. Similarly, Scott
   (1992) observes that some organizations may find themselves in environments that
   evaluate on both means compliance and means–ends comparisons (i.e. facing both
   strong 'institutional' and 'technical' pressures). However, as the ISO 9000 standards suggest, it does appear difficult to fully accommodate both styles of rationality
   into a specific reform package.
5. In fact, the 'guidance standards' included in the ISO 9000 series specifically address
   conventional quality concepts such as customer satisfaction and continuous qual-

ity improvement at length (Kochan 1993; Tamm-Hallstrom 1996), although the contractual standards upon which actual certification is based do not evaluate either the choice of quality techniques employed by an organization or their effectiveness in terms of quality outcomes.

6. Unfortunately, comprehensive data on ISO 9000 certificates across countries do not exist before 1992. Tracking of national counts of ISO 9000 certificates was initiated by in-house consultants at Mobil Europe, Ltd. in 1993 apparently after the inclusion of the standards in EU trade directives in 1992 and their subsequent rise in popularity (Mobil Europe 1995). As is frequently the case, the measurement of a social phenomenon is not completely disconnected from the process that generates it. However, the analysis attempts to specifically incorporate the effects of European integration through other indicators, as described later in the multivariate models. The ISO eventually assumed the tracking of certificates in 1998 through a series of periodic surveys, which is the source of the data in this study (ISO 1999a). The January 1993 data point reported in the ISO data is used as a measure for 1992, while the September data point is used for 1993. In 1994, figures are only reported for June and after 1995, for December. Zero values were imputed for cases without any certificates listed in prior years, given the *ISO Survey*'s methodology and lack of missing data after a country's first year of reported certificates.

7. The time series regression models are based on feasible generalized least squares (GLS) methods (see Greene 1997), which take the general form:

$$y_{i,t} = x_{i,t}\beta + \varepsilon_{i,t}$$

where $i = 1, \ldots, m$ and m is the number of panels, and $t = 1, \ldots, T_i$ and T_i is the number of observations for panel i.

8. Such a one period lag is a common parameterization in time series regression models and appears a reasonable assumption given the processes underlying the diffusion of the standards and the typical length of time necessary for an organization to become registered to ISO 9000.

9. The models implemented in these analyses correct for a common 'first order', period-to-period autocorrelation for all panels, which is realistic when the individual correlations are nearly equal and the time series are short. This permits the use of 'non-balanced' panels (i.e. unequal numbers of observations per country case), providing additional information in estimating the autocorrelation parameter and thus more reasonable estimates of regression coefficients (Stata Corporation 2000: 366). It should be noted that although the models in these analyses allow for 'non-balanced' panels, all panels are continuous.

    The models also adjust for heteroskedasticity, i.e. unequal variance of error terms across panels over time. Estimations of all models were computed with the Stata v.6.0 statistical software application (Stata Corporation 1999). In addition, nine variables are transformed using a natural logarithmic function to correct for skewness, as noted in the table of results.

10. Since, as mentioned previously, the ISO recognizes only one standards development organization (SDO) per country which is obligated to represent all parties with interests in standardization, the scale of the national standards body is a reasonable indication of the overall extent of professional standards activity within a country, regardless of the composition of the standards sector or the SDO itself.

11. Dichotomous indicators for nation-states affiliated with the British Commonwealth, as well as for core Commonwealth countries (the United Kingdom, Canada, Australia, and New Zealand), were both strongly related to ISO 9000 certificates ($p < 0.01$) when entered separately in models controlling for real GDP.

12. The positive effect for this global indicator was also replicated in prior separate analyses for measures of prevalence that vary by geographic region (e.g. Asia, Latin America, Western Europe, etc.).

13. Computed as a country's average annual change in GDP over the previous three-year period subtracted from that of its referent economic strata (either the G-7 countries, other countries categorized by the World Bank as 'high income' economies, countries classified as 'middle income', or those as 'low income' (World Bank 2000b)). The measure is constructed so that higher values indicate worsening relative economic performance.

7

Transparent Accounting as a World Societal Rule[1]

Yong Suk Jang

A worldwide movement of theorization and professionalization of management has spread a variety of modern organizational systems, including personal training, decision-making, accounting, organizational behavior, and strategy. This movement advocates expanded notions of organizational 'rationality', denigrating older forms of organization. In this chapter, I examine and explain this movement, focusing on the area of accounting. The core theme is the elaboration of an accountability model for global governance in general and of modern corporate accounting in particular. The main explanatory story is that of globalization. The world is being together through a globalized package of notions about organizational rationality (e.g. international standards on management and accounting), common concepts of legitimate actorhood, and dissolving barriers to political and economic internationalization. These trends both encourage and are fed by expanded models of transparency and accountability. Communities, states, and business actors are reconstructed and affected by this new emerging system of control.

Accountability involves social relations in which actors are required to provide explanations for their actions. In its simplest sense, accountability can be seen as a relationship invoking 'the giving and demanding of reasons for conduct' (Roberts and Scapens 1985), and 'the ongoing demand for and provision of explanations, justification, and excuses' (Kirk and Mouritsen 1996). Accountability also has a more specific modern connotation associated with the putatively objective and scientific techniques of corporate accounting (Sinclair 1995).

Corporate accounting can be defined as the collection, processing, and reporting of financial data about an organization. As an economic and social activity, it involves the handling of data regarding flows of resources in-and-out of an organization, resources controlled by the organization (i.e. assets), and claims against the resources (i.e. debt) (Short 1993). Transparency through accounting—emphasizing better measurement and greater disclosure—is a vision of many advocates for 'management by accounting'. Corporate account-ability and transparency, by comprehensively quantifying all relevant corpor-ate information, are claimed to represent the modern rational concepts and practices. The efficacy of such quantification and calculation is believed to be proven in many other scientific and professional domains, which tends to be exaggerated due to the general prestige accorded to the objectivity of numbers (Porter 1995; McSweeney 1996).

In this sense, the expansion of the model of accountability is a cultural and institutional process (Hopwood and Miller 1994; Carruthers 1995), not only or principally a technical one (Elliott and Jacobson 1994; Gray, Meek, and Roberts 1995). While the conventional views on accounting emphasize accounting work expands to maintain better control over increasing technical complexity, and reflects the functional differentiation of modern organiza-tions (Blau and Schoenherr 1971), this chapter highlights the symbolic and ritualistic properties of accounting practices and their growing cultural he-gemony and institutionalized legitimacy in making activities visible in eco-nomic terms (Mezias 1995). Reinforced and structured by various academic literatures and professional actors including business schools, professional accountants, consulting firms, and international accounting bodies, the ab-stract ideas of accountability provide a rational and universalistic set of models on which to constitute and evaluate modern actors. The symbolic and ritualistic power of accounting is apparent through the history of its development (Carruthers and Espeland 1991). Today, this broad cultural movement expands with aspects of modern globalization as its core elements (Meyer 1986).

In the age of globalization the heightening of liberal market ideologies throughout the world economy orients organizations to wider social envir-onments that produce and diffuse all sorts of standards and norms on organizational rationality. Organizations increasingly conform to these ra-tional standards. The model of expansive accountability is one of the most important market standards that generates a perceived need for organiza-tional conformity. As a result, we observe the global expansion of accounting activities and the worldwide development of the transparency model. The evidence is clear. Accounting work and accounting professionals have become increasingly necessary and prevalent in organizations across the world. Mod-ern nation-states have come to provide more complete social and economic accounts of the national polity (e.g. GDP, life expectancy, school enrollment, endangered species, welfare expenditures, etc.). An increasing number of governmental policies and public services are framed and justified with the logic of cost–benefit analysis and evaluation. Similarly, individuals become more adept at providing more accounts and opinions to demonstrate how their activities are rationally selected for their intended purposes.

However, there are also noticeable patterns of variability in the worldwide expansion of accounting. In some nation-states, accounting and the transparency model have expanded more rapidly. For example, elaborate accounting activities, rather than simple reports to government bureaucracies or other authorities, are observed more often in liberal market societies than statist or community-oriented societies. Properties of firms and their environments also create much variation in the expansion and development of corporate accounting. Influenced by internal factors and external environments, such as size, performance, governance structure, financial structure, auditor, industry, and market characters, firms may produce and process more or less accounting information. This chapter, therefore, addresses both the general global expansion of contemporary accounting and how it varies in different nation-states.

This chapter proceeds as follows. In the next section, I describe accounting as a global practice and investigate a wide range of dimensions related to the worldwide expansion of accounting activities in recent periods: (*a*) the internationalization of the accounting profession; (*b*) the growth of international auditing firms; (*c*) the movement toward transparency in corporate accounting; and (*d*) the rise of business discourse on accountability. In the following section, I also consider accounting as an institutional practice and explore the relations between cultural and institutional environments and the development of accounting. Drawing on the world culture perspective, I emphasize the role of international organizations as carriers of cultural norms and guidelines regarding the notions of accountability and transparency.

Finally, I present an empirical analysis to explain how and why accounting activities expand and vary across organizations and societies. The analyses include a diverse array of environmental factors and pressures (industrial, national, and international as well as organizational) affecting variation in the financial accounting disclosures of firms.

In examining my main research question, the global expansion and variation in accounting, particular organizational and industry characteristics, certainly play a significant role. However, important macro conditions must be taken into account. Attributes of national structures and orientations provide the context in which firms select and implement various organizational practices and strategies, including corporate accounting and information disclosure. Overall, this chapter formulates a broad macro-level research agenda on the global expansion and variation of accounting, employing a comparative statistical approach. I emphasize the rise of accounting and the spread of the accountability model as a worldwide and cultural phenomenon that reconstructs modern social actors.

7.1. THE EXPANSION OF MODERN ACCOUNTING AS A GLOBAL PRACTICE

The world economy has become integrated more than ever before. Under-lying the current trends of economic globalization has been the penetration of liberal market ideologies—including the phenomena of moneterization, standardization, and commercialization—that rationally structure and trans-parently present an ever-increasing range of social and economic activities (Meyer 1986). For many national and international elites, liberal market principles have become largely taken-for-granted as means for bringing modernity, rationality, and progress to society.

The diffusion of these liberal principles has involved a number of global processes. First, there has been a considerable rise of abstraction and gener-alization at the world level (Scott and Meyer 1994). This rise has embodied general principles and universalistic claims. For instance, management and organization can be discussed as proper rationalized forms in both general and abstract terms that can be applied in any time and place. General accounts make use of transnational and universalistic languages that are applicable across societies. Therefore, many organizational structures and processes become isomorphic and more predictable worldwide (Meyer and Rowan 1977; DiMaggio and Powell 1983). Likewise, accounting and book-keeping rationalize business activities by reducing assets and equities to numerical abstractions and by expressing total results of operations as profit and loss in universalistic mathematical languages (Chatfield 1977).

There has been also rise of standardization at the world level. The uni-versally acceptable social meanings of actors and activities have been standardized into various comparable categories (e.g. managers, workers, management, labor, etc.). These standardized categories are reduced to monetary prices in modern societies. This often happens through routinely simulating markets even where real markets do not exist. In universities, for instance, courses can be reduced to credit units that can also be reduced to prices, regardless of the disciplines to which the courses belong. Therefore, modern liberal market principles often imply the causal integration of means–ends chains that include activities and actors with market monetary values. The means are usually technical development and expansion of exchange. In the most general sense, the ends entail progress (e.g. profit) and justice (e.g. various employment benefits). The elaboration of these chains requires greater specifications of entities and categories (Thomas et al. 1987).

Finally, globalization also involves the rational principles of depersonalization. By substituting an abstract concept of capital for the notion of private ownership; for example, the separation of firms from the owners and the growth of large corporations have been facilitated.

The above-mentioned global processes make a variety of counts and accounts more possible by transforming organizations to more autonomous actors that orient to bigger and more complex environments, and by delegitimating the traditional controls of local communities and the states over organizational activities (Meyer 1986). Corporate actors in multiple and global environments are expected to provide universalistic stories with abstract principles of accounting to explain their activities regardless of their industry or country.

Accounting becomes a powerful mode of thought and code of conduct in the modern world, closely associated with a natural extension of rational management. The expansion of accounting as a rational modern principle has a worldwide character. We now observe increasingly sovereign (organizational) actors that are able to provide expansive rational accounts even in Continental Europe or Asia where the roles and protections of the state have been emphasized. Accounting work and organizational transparency have increased in general over time, and particularly faster in societies where they experience rapid globalization (e.g. in Europe).

Several indicators presented below show this worldwide expansion of accounting activities in recent periods. Most of all, the accounting professionals have been continually increasing. Although as early as 1926, the *Daily Express*, a British newspaper, argued that there were too many accountants in business in the United Kingdom, the accounting profession has been steadily expanding in the world as well as in the United Kingdom. This worldwide trend has continued after World War II, with accountants attaining prominent positions in general management. Today, accountants outnumber other professionals in top management (Allott 2000). The expansion of this profession has continued even in more recent periods. The number of certified public accountants per million population across countries tracked by the International Federation of Accountants (IFAC) has increased from 553 in 1988 to 776 in 1995.[2]

In Figure 7.1, I compare the average number of accountants in different regions. While regional differences exist in the size of the accounting profession, the average number of accountants has increased in all areas of the world from 1988 to 1995. The worldwide expansion of the accounting profession is also observed in the increase in number of national accountancy bodies and individual accountants affiliated with the IFAC. In 1977, the IFAC consisted of sixty-three accounting organizations and professional accountants from

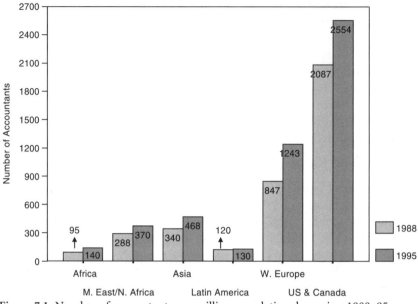

Figure 7.1 Number of accountants per million population, by region 1988–95

Source: The International Federation of Accountants.
Number of countries = 77.

fifty-one countries. In 2000, the IFAC included 153 national accountancy bodies from 113 countries as member organizations and more than 2 million accountants worldwide as individual members.

This continued growth, despite the earlier functional concerns on oversupply of accountants, reflects the ritual element in accounting work and professionals. Many conventional accounting services and procedures are quite established and seen as necessary elements regardless of the conditions facing particular organizations. Budgetary control systems and cash-flow forecasts are credible rituals that accounting professionals are expected to produce. Accounting and auditing processes are only legitimized when professionally conducted and create organizational reality where financial statements are perceived to be credible (Perks 1993). This ritualistic character of accounting work along with its functionality contributes to the rapid expansion of the accounting profession in the modern period.

The internationalization of accounting services is another indicator of the expansion of accounting. Until the 1970s, the roles of accountants and accounting firms were mainly defined by each national government and operated almost entirely within the boundaries of national economy. With the growth of international business and the expansion of international financial markets from the early 1980s, however, the large accounting firms became operators in a world, rather than simply national, market and started following clients as they moved around the globe. The domination of US and British multinationals in the world market gave an advantage to the large Anglo-American accounting firms where many of the large multinationals were already regular clients. Combined with the domination of New York and London as financial centers, this international expansion of large accounting firms facilitated the concentration of accounting services. As a result, a few accounting firms known as the Big Six (and the Big Five after a merger) became the dominant players in a world market with the increasing demand for global accounting services.

In recent years, there has been a rapid internationalization of the top accounting firms in terms of the numbers of offices located in different countries, revenues generated from abroad, and partners and professionals employed overseas. Table 7.1 shows that in 1992 the top six accounting firms earned more than 50 percent of their gross revenue from their overseas operations. These firms also have tremendously increased their offices and partners in different countries.

From 1982 to 1994, the total number of offices of the major six inter-national accounting firms increased worldwide by 59 percent and the number of partners enlarged by 67 percent. The expansion of accounting firms was even faster in Europe where they experienced rapid economic and political globalization. The number of partners in Europe increased by 96 percent and offices by 153 percent in 12 years. The number of offices in Asia increased to 639 from 425, a 50 percent increase in 12 years, while partners increased by 119 percent. The average number of partners per office increased from 4.8 in 1982 to 6.9 in 1994. In North America partners increased by 38 percent and offices by 3 percent. In other regions, offices increased by 32 percent and partners by 64 percent. The twelve-year trends are summarized in Table 7.2.

Table 7.1 Gross revenue ($mil.) of Big Six accounting firms, 1992

Firms	Worldwide	United States	Foreign	% Foreign
KPMG Peat Marwick	6150	1800	4350	71
Ernst & Young	5701	2281	3420	60
Arthur Anderson & Co.	5577	2680	2897	52
Coopers & Lybrand	5300	1557	3743	71
Deloitte & Touche	4800	1955	2845	59
Price Waterhouse	3761	1367	2394	64

Source: *US Industrial Outlook* (1994: 51–2).

Table 7.2 Total number of offices and partners of Big Six accounting firms, 1982–94

Region	Offices			Partners		
	Number of offices		% Growth	Number of partners		% Growth
	1982	1994	(1982–94)	1982	1994	(1982–94)
Europe	811	2051	153	5507	10814	96
Asia/Pacific	425	639	50	2019	4425	119
North America	1042	1068	3	8939	12356	38
Other regions	527	696	32	1626	2678	64
World total	2805	4454	59	18091	30230	67

Source: *International Accounting and Auditing Trends*, 4th edition (1995).

As discussed earlier, the number of accountants has increased greatly and the activities of accounting firms have expanded globally. In addition, corporate accounting activities have increased and their accounting transparency has improved over time. This trend can be observed even within a relatively short period.

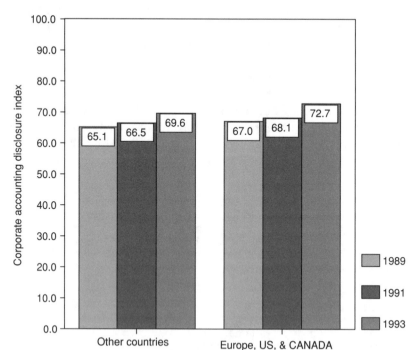

Figure 7.2 The expansion of corporate accounting transparency (by regions), 1989–93

Figure 7.2, from research conducted by The Center for Financial Analysis and Research (CIFAR), summarizes data from 1,000 industrial companies in forty-one countries over a four-year period (1989–93). From 1989 to 1993, the Accounting Information Disclosure Index increased from an average of 66.0 to 71.1. In addition, as is clear from Figure 7.2, corporate accounting transparency increased more quickly in Western nations (European countries, the United States, and Canada), which experienced rapid rates of economic and political globalization.

Another way to explore the expansion of accounting is to examine the management discourse (e.g. journal and trade articles) on accountability. Here, I examine the American Business Index, a database that covers 1,611 business periodicals worldwide on advertising, marketing, economics, human resources, finance, taxation, and computer-related subjects.

I performed title searches for the years from 1974 to 2000 to identify articles that having the word 'accountability' in the title. Figure 7.3 shows that the total number of articles on 'accountability' increased dramatically over time. In 1974, there were only six articles addressing accountability in the

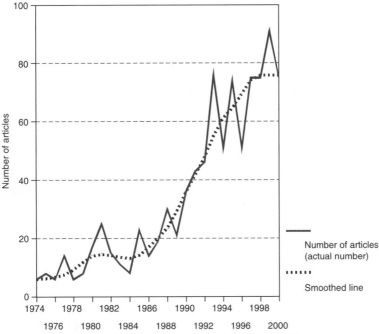

Figure 7.3 The number of articles with accountability in the title, 1974–2000

Source: American Business Index (periodical database).

title, while in 1999 the number jumped to ninety-one. The number of articles on 'accountability' in the 1990s increased even more rapidly compared to earlier periods. This trend reflects the general increase in prevalence of accountability concerns in business discourse, especially after the 1990s.

7.2. ACCOUNTING AS AN INSTITUTIONAL PRACTICE

Conventional views on accounting emphasize that the methods of accounting transfer qualities as inputs to quantities as outputs, which helps people to produce rational and technical decisions. With accounting information people in business are able to devise and demonstrate profitable actions. The process of accounting measures events, records transaction, evaluates organizational outcomes, reduces uncertainty, and most of all rationalizes decision-making. It shares the assumptions of economic and rational choice approaches that efficiency and means-ends logics are crucial tools to explain human and organizational behaviors. Accounting work expands to maintain better control over increasing technical complexity, and reflects the functional differentiation of modern organizations (Blau and Schoenherr 1971). The rational aspect of accounting is exemplified in Weber's explanation (1968) of its role of in the rationalization of capitalist societies. He believed that rational calculation is especially facilitated by the system of double-entry bookkeeping, which allows a highly technical examination of the profitability of each step or process within different departments of an enterprise.

In contrast, institutional theorists argue that formal organizations try to incorporate structural and policy elements defined by prevailing concepts of what is rational (Meyer and Rowan 1977). The primary reason organizations adopt these rationalized elements is to maintain appearances as proper and rational social actors. To the extent that organizations incorporate such practices and procedures, they increase their legitimacy and survival prospects, regardless of their actual efficiencies or productive outcomes.

From an institutional perspective, accounting is seen as one of the ways in which organizations come to incorporate rational conceptions of ways of organizing. Quite apart from its possible usefulness and efficacy, the myth of accountants and the accounting system have become part of the taken-for-granted means to accomplish organizational ends. We easily observe the symbolic and ritualistic properties of accounting practices and their growing cultural hegemony and institutionalized legitimacy in making activities visible in economic terms. For example, an important role of accounting is rationalizing and justifying decisions that have already been made rather than enabling those decisions in the first place (Gambling 1977; Brunsson 1989). Information accounting is part of 'social language' by which corporations present what they do, why they do it, and how they might do it better (March 1987). Though the role of accounting in decision-making is ambiguous, it has acquired a certain ideological and cultural dominance as a symbol of economic rationality, not only within a certain nation-state or region, but throughout the world over time as economic, political, and cultural globalization has been rapidly in progress.

Institutional arguments, thus, stress the importance of the wider environment as a determinant of the expansion of accounting work. The environment is considered as a supplier of cultural guidelines and recipes for organizing (Meyer and Rowan 1977; DiMaggio and Powell 1983). The contrast between institutional approaches and rational arguments begins in the models of what guides the efforts to increase the accountability of firms. In contrast to the emphasis on organizational rationality and managerial efficiency in managerial economics, institutional theory stresses the firm's compliance with the requirements of the institutional environment as expressed in generally accepted accounting principles, professional guidelines, and legal requirements (Mezias 1995). Institutional perspective, therefore, emphasizes the organizational embeddedness in broader social context (Granovetter 1985). Accounting systems are embedded in many areas of economic and social life and are not considered as neutral technical devices that report and document economic activities of organizations. The accounting practices of an organization are oftentimes determined by local and global conditions such as the level of economic and political globalization of a country where the organization is operating. Accounting practices also are always linked to other managerial practices of organizations in complex ways.

In the next section, I provide specific hypotheses for how aspects of environmental factors determine the degree of accounting information disclosure of corporate actors, in contrast to the accepted view that this derives necessarily from technical work processes (Meyer 1986; Hopwood and Miller 1994).

7.2.1. Organizational Environments and Corporate Accounting

The major source of pressure for increased accounting disclosure consists of the investment communities that use and desire financial information. A firm is viewed as a 'nexus of contracts', and the parties involved in the firm believe accounting information is a rational means of monitoring contracts and making effective evaluation and investment decisions (Gray, Meek, and Roberts 1995). In this context, accounting has highly taken-for-granted and ritualistic significance for justifying activities of organizations to third parties such as stockholders, regulators, and communities (Carruthers and Espeland 1991). The provision of objective financial analyses may help legitimate the plans of the organization in the eyes of outsiders, although it does not confer direct technical support to the activities. Firms may disclose larger amounts of accounting information to investors not with the intention of providing improved technical analyses, but in order to display their rationality and maintain legitimate appearances.

This symbolic significance has been magnified as a shareholder-oriented conception of corporate control has acquired greater importance than in the past, and especially as institutional investors, such as banks, insurance companies, and investment companies, have become increasingly influential in controlling the firm's equity (Useem 1993). These institutional investors themselves are social actors who expect investee companies to enact appropriate models of organizations. As the notion of shareholder value has evolved and been applied to corporate decision-making, corporate accountability and the organizational model of transparency have become integral parts of cultural repertoires and strategies of organizational actions (Swidler 1985). This leads to the following hypothesis:

Hypothesis 1: Firms with a greater proportion of outside shareholders and less closely held by insiders are more likely to disclose accounting information.

A number of large accounting and consulting firms have emerged during the past several decades. The professionals, such as accountants and consultants, are the carriers of rational managerial culture in modern world, and they are expected to provide objective analyses of corporations. There is evidence that these professionals offer substantial knowledge and information and are expected to resolve impending problems the client companies confront. In addition, independent of their actual technical capacity and functional contribution, these professionals are hired in order to maintain external legitimacy and reduce uncertainty. They deliver various sorts of rationalized and standardized recipes including business models, industry norms, strategies, and guidelines, and the client firms accept them as effective solutions (Sahlin-Andersson and Engwall 2002).

Under the limited liability system, it is highly rationalized belief that the external audit and accounting process would provide an independent check on the quality of accounting information while also limiting the effects of moral hazard problems to which companies may be susceptible (Whittington 1993). As carriers of modern management knowledge, accounting firms play an important role in persuading their clients to disclose additional items in financial statements and to maintain transparency and reliability. In particular, compared to small accounting firms, big international accounting firms can maintain independence from clients' pressures for limited disclosure and to push their clients to disclose more accounting information (DeAngelo 1981; Schipper 1981; Watts and Zimmerman 1986; Chow and Wong-Boren 1987). Corporations choose large international auditors, if affordable, despite their tendency toward greater disclosure, because the choice of a 'good' external auditor can serve as a signal to the market about the quality of disclosed information and firm value (Bar-Yosef and Livnat 1984; Datar, Feltham, and Hughes 1991). From the previous discussion, I offer the following hypothesis:

Hypothesis 2: Companies that hire big international accounting firms disclose information to a greater extent.

Accounting work absorbs uncertainty by extraction and abstraction of information, which reduces the number of possible interpretations and judgments (Carruthers and Espeland 1991; March and Simon 1993). Organizations with less rationalized structures of formal rules in uncertain environments, therefore, are more likely to increase the involvement of accounting work. On the other hand, one can imagine other companies or industries in which the division of labor and bureaucratic structure are completely and authoritatively delineated. In such relatively closed systems, accounting work, beyond book-keeping and record-keeping, is not always as useful in reducing uncertainty as in more liberalized and less bureaucratized companies or industries. For example, we may expect less accounting in government bureaus and state-owned companies (e.g. utilities, transportation, etc.) than companies in the private economy (Meyer 1986). Accounting control systems are usually employed because straightforward command-and-compliance authority is lacking (Scott 1991).

Accounting arises to count not the visible and clear, but the invisible and vague. Companies handle the demands and uncertainties of environments with gathering, processing, and disseminating information. Thus, we may expect to find companies generating more accounting work when their markets are multiple and less stable, when the final products have unstable specifications, and when the technology of production is changing rapidly (Stinchcombe 1990). For example, MNCs need to disclose additional accounting information due to the diverse geographic spread of their operations and investors in multiple and rapidly changing markets. The significant impact of MNCs on a nation-state's social, economic, and ecological environments has also resulted in the enactment of many new statutes and laws in recent years requiring additional disclosures. Firms operating in many countries need to satisfy the requirements and requests from different legal and professional environments as well as various market situations in different countries.

For similar reason, corporations in stable industries, like electricity production (Stinchcombe 1990), are expected to disclose less information. On the other hand, one can imagine that companies with final products having fluctuating specifications or services of an intangible or invisible quality (e.g. recreation, service, software, apparel, retailers, publishing, cosmetics, health care, etc.) disclose more accounting information, which helps reduce uncertainty and detect market reactions promptly through gathering, processing, and disclosing news and information.

Accounting systems tend to stabilize organizations by establishing standard repertories over time. However, organizations in unstable and changing environments need information that is flexible and often redundant enough to cope with unexpected developments. Hedberg and Jonsson (1978) employ the notion of 'organized anarchies' as a way of understanding how accounting systems can provide a basis for the rationalization of behavior rather than as an input into decisions. Accounting systems can stimulate organizational curiosity, facilitate new decision processes, and increase the ability to handle variation and change in environments. From the previous discussion, I posit the following hypotheses:

Hypothesis 3.1: Firms that operate actively in foreign countries are more likely to disclose accounting information as a means of dealing with various requests from multiple environments.

Hypothesis 3.2: Firms that have hard and stable products are less likely to disclose accounting information than those with soft or 'invisible' (less stable) products or services.

Hypotheses 1–3 relate to the aspect that the rise of the modern organization is naturally associated with the expansion of accounting work as an element of rationalization. Accounting, a major tool for communicating business information, however, has developed differentially in application and content from country to country as it has adapted to local purposes and diversity in national polity contexts. For example, in some countries accounting information is mainly used to communicate with investors, but in others it is adapted to convey information to banks or tax authorities. Macro-level economic, political, and cultural globalization of a country is also an important predictor for accounting transparency of firms operating in the country. In the following section, I hypothesize how these macro social and national characteristics affect the degree of transparency in modern corporate accounting.

7.2.2. Globalization and Corporate Accounting

As the world economy has become integrated and international business and trade have accelerated, global discourses and activities regarding transparency and accountability of corporate actors have also increased. Economic and political globalization of a country and its exposure to world society, therefore, are important macro-level factors explaining how accounting expansion varies among firms in different countries.

First, the amount of economic ties with other countries reflects the realistic intensity of international economic connections and pressures. If a country is more open to the global economy, it is more likely to possess legal and institutional instruments for increasing the accountability of firms in the country in order to satisfy modern international standards requiring transparent economic activities. Second, the amount of political and organizational contacts of a country within world society—namely, embeddedness in the world polity—reflects the institutional and cultural intensity of international norms and pressures. This cultural and institutional embeddedness can be indicated by organizational linkages (e.g. the number of memberships of a country in IGOs). If a country has more organizational linkages to the world, the country is more likely, to observe the norms and discourses disseminated by world society (Meyer et al. 1997*a*, 1997*b*). It is important to understand the roles of international actors providing guidelines and recipes with respect to accounting. Many IGOs and professional associations have made efforts to set up international accounting standards and to increase corporate transparency throughout the world. Most notable are the United Nations (UN), the Organization for Economic Cooperation and Development (OECD), the International Accounting Standards Committee (IASC), and the International Federation of Accountants (IFAC).

These two factors identify potential sources of pressures on countries to rationalize and modernize local business laws and practices and to increase the transparency and accountability of firms operating within their borders. From the earlier discussion on globalization and the expansion of accounting, I posit the following hypothesis:

Hypothesis 4: Firms in countries that are economically and politically embedded in global society are likely to increase accounting transparency more than firms in less globalized countries.

7.2.3. National Polity Contexts and Corporate Accounting

The modern national polity embodied in the nation-state provides guidelines and legitimacy to the rational structures and practices of a society, including those of formal organizations. The fact that the modern national polity varies in form leads to variations in social rationalization and formal organizing. For instance, liberal polity styles (e.g. the United States or the United Kingdom) promote the construction of legitimate individual actors with sovereignty and rationality, while advocating less explicit legal and social controls. Statist polities (e.g. France) in contrast emphasize the state as a model and locus of rationality and employ formal rules as a primary control mechanism (Jepperson 2002b).[3]

As with the structure of formal organizations, the development of accounting has also been strongly affected by the nature of the national polity. Certain polities prefer spelling out clear and specific rules and hierarchies as opposed to producing the abstract accounting of exchange values. For example, Germanic societies have been traditionally constructed not on liberal ideas of free individuals and firms engaging in contractual relations, but on substantive notions of the modern community as made up of fixed occupational parts (Meyer 1986). Rules clearly define the rights and obligations of given occupational groups, which are organized according to modern aims. In such a system, priority goes to the formulation of rules and procedures that constitute the relations among groups in organizations, not to the accounting of abstract exchange values. Similarly, Latin nations, such as Portugal, Spain, Greece, and Italy, have progressed less in accounting work, retaining their social traditions of a belief in bureaucratic rules and norms. Therefore, there are negative trade-offs between elaborated formal rules and hierarchies and the growth of accounting work.

Hofstede (1980, 1991) has derived useful indicators measuring national polity styles that govern the way people in organizations in different countries manage authority, relationships, and uncertainty and that shape the accounting systems of societies. He presents several distinct dimensions, which reflect cultural orientations related to contrasting methods of organizing: (a) individualism versus collectivism, (b) large versus small power distance, and (c) strong versus weak uncertainty avoidance.

In a society with strong uncertainty avoidance, people prefer to create security and avoid risk. They also tend to accomplish these through formalization mechanisms, such as laws, rules, and planning to guide behavior, not through the accounting work of abstract values and the discretion of accounting professionals. With similar reasoning, we expect less accounting work in a large power distance society. Large power distance is related to a higher degree of inequality and centralization of authority. In a high power distance society, people tend to accept ascribed roles and positions that need no further justification. In decision-making procedures, subordinate consultation and participation are not highly important. Formal procedures and positions by rules are respected more than justification based on discussion and evaluation through data.

This power dimension is directly related in a negative direction with the dimension of individualism. Usually collectivist societies show large power distances (Hofstede 1980). In an individualist society, employer–employee relationships tend to be calculative and loosely built around business relations, whereas in a collectivist society they tend to be morally based and more tightly constructed by cultural norms. For instance, in Japan hierarchical relationships are established through collective values and beliefs built on greater trust of those in authority and on greater interdependence (Hickson and Pugh 1995). Therefore, we expect less accounting work in a collectivist society due to the tightly coupled relations of members based on norms and rules. By comparison, an individualist society is more concerned with the provision of information to investors, shareholders, and workers.

Overall, we expect less accounting work in societies where their national polities emphasize prescriptive legal regulations, norms, rules, direct controls, and collective values built into organizational formal procedures. In this approach, therefore, information disclosure has less to do with the technical accounting capacities of individual organizations, but more to do with principles of societal organizing and the institutional contexts of polities. From the previous discussion, I offer the following hypothesis:

Hypothesis 5: Firms in liberal individualist societies disclose more accounting information than those in collectivist societies.

7.2.4. Managerial and Legal Rationalization and Corporate Accounting

Elaborating the earlier discussion, I also argue that the heightening of liberal market ideologies throughout the world reduces the role of direct state or community powers to control organizations. The expansion of liberal and individualist principles guides organizations to wider social environment in which a variety of operating standards and managing principles are found. In the modern period, management is seen as an increasingly standardized and universal activity in a globalized world. It is assumed that general management knowledge and standards are sufficiently abstract and scientific to be applied to organizations existing in diverse parts of the world. The explosion of all sorts of standards of organizational rationality are produced and diffused by professions in both local and global environments (e.g. consultants, accountants, scientists, associations, etc.). We observe a dramatic increase worldwide of organizational conformity to rational standards and the sense that organizations should be proactive and effective 'actors' in these complex environments. The social meanings of organizational actors and activities are also standardized into various comparable categories reflecting the generally increasing standardization of management. In many instances, these categories are further reduced to monetary prices that should be accounted for in proper ways. Therefore, accounting becomes a powerful mode of thought in the modern world, closely associated with the extension of rational management and standards.

For example, ISO 9000 is a set of international standards and guidelines that serve as a basis for establishing standardized quality management systems in both manufacturing and service firms (Guler, Guillén, and Macpherson 2002). Obtaining an ISO 9000 certificate sends a signal that an organization has been documented according to a rationally ordered and widely accepted general model of managerial standards (Mendel 2001, Chapter 6). We expect that in a society where larger numbers of organizations conform to the norms and models of rational managerial standards, organizations will be more likely to provide accounts for their activities that express their capacity as proactive and effective actors.

A neoliberal market environment and related legal institutions are also important preconditions for expanded accountability. For example, liberal individualist systems—more so than other polities—protect market environments, promote managerial rationality, and facilitate transparent economic transactions. The legal systems of these countries belonging to common-law traditions based on the British Company Act are more likely to emphasize shareholder rights compared to those of countries with civil law traditions, derivative of Roman statutory codes. Shareholder rights include various protection mechanisms such as the one-share-one-vote rule, the protection of minority shareholders against expropriation of managers (anti-director rights), etc. (La Porta, Lopez-de-Silanes, and Shleifer 1998). These rights and protections allow shareholders better access to corporate information and push companies to provide more highly detailed accounts of their activities. I, therefore, argue that firms in societies proactively conforming to such liberal norms of managerial and legal rationalization will be more likely to increase accounting transparency, which leads to the following hypothesis:

Hypothesis 6: In societies conforming to norms of managerial and legal rationalization, firms are more likely to increase accounting transparency.

7.3. DATA, VARIABLES, AND RESEARCH DESIGN

The empirical analyses of this chapter explore how the global expansion of contemporary accounting varies among firms located in different industries and societies. I investigate how and why this expansion in corporate accounting transparency varies in different societies through the examination of cross-national data on accounting information disclosure.

The Center for Financial Analysis and Research and the Global Business Reference Center (GBRC) have assembled an Accounting Information Disclosure Index (AIDI), which is composed of eighty-five accounting information items. These measures were compiled from the annual reports of approximately 1,000 industrial companies in 41 countries at three time points (1989, 1991, 1993; CIFAR 1995). In this chapter, I use this AIDI as a dependent variable and report results from the empirical analyses that test the previous hypotheses on corporate accounting transparency for 653 companies in 25 countries in 1993.[4]

The disclosure items of AIDI are divided into seven broad subgroups: General Information, Income Statement, Balance Sheet, Funds Flow Statement, Accounting Policies, Stockholder's Information, and Supplementary Information.[5] A dichotomous procedure was used to calculate each subgroup reporting index whereby each is scored 'one' if it is disclosed and 'zero' if it is not disclosed.[6] Within each group, therefore, a percentage representing the availability of items in the annual report of the firm was computed. The average of the sum of percentages of all seven categories was calculated to produce the AIDI for each company.[7]

I investigate how an organizational practice, accounting activity, is influenced by social and institutional contexts as well as organizational conditions. The research design requires the simultaneous consideration of effects across the organization and societal (nation-state) levels. The independent variables, therefore, need to be calculated at each of these levels.

To test the impact of external financial markets (i.e. outside shareholders) on the expansion of organizational accounting disclosure (Hypothesis 1), I employed the percentage of shares that are closely held. The influence of international auditors can be captured by a dummy variable to indicate whether or not big six international auditing firms are hired (Hypothesis 2).

To test hypotheses regarding multiple and less stable environments (Hypotheses 3.1 and 3.2), I use the percentage of foreign sales to total sales as a measure of the extent of a company's activities in multiple markets and environments. I also include a dummy variable (called stable and hard product industry) to indicate to which industry a company belongs in order to capture the characteristics of markets and products in different industries. If a company belongs to the automotive, metal, machinery equipment, coal, transportation, or utility industry, I consider it as a company in a stable and hard product market. These firm-level variables were obtained from machine-readable data files (e.g. Disclosure Inc. 1996).

The national-level independent variables were collected from various sources that include the *World Development Report* (computer file), 1978–96 (World Bank 1996), Hofstede's Indexes (Hofstede 1980), and La Porta's shareholder right measures (La Porta Lopez-de-Silanes, and Shleifer 1998). These independent variables testing Hypotheses 4, 5, and 6 are as follows.

To measure economic and political globalization of a country (Hypothesis 4), I constructed two factor variables.[8] Economic globalization factor scores were calculated with national trade openness in 1990 (total imports and exports divided by GDP) and foreign direct investment in 1990. A political and institutional globalization factor was constructed with the measures of nation-state participation in international organizations (number of IGO memberships and NGO memberships, respectively), and the total number of international treaties signed by a country from 1981 to 1985.

To test the effect of a national polity context (Hypothesis 5), the collectivist society (as a mirror image of liberal individualist society) factor was constructed with national polity measures such as Individualism/Collectivism, Large/Small Power Distance, and Strong/Weak Uncertainty Avoidance from Hofstede's studies.[9] These indexes are frequently used in the international management literature. The Individualism/Collectivism Index captures the extent to which a society values goals and interest of individuals more than those of groups. The Power Distance Index measures the extent to which a society accepts and tolerates power differences, centralization, and tight controls. The Uncertainty Avoidance Index captures the extent to which a society establishes formalization mechanisms such as laws, rules, and planning to guide behavior.

A managerial and legal rationalization factor is composed of two indicators (Hypothesis 6).[10] One indicator is the number of ISO 9000 certificates at the national level to capture the degree to which a country conforms to the norms of international management standardization. In addition, to capture the degree to which a country provides liberal and rational legal supports, I employ the shareholder right index from La Porta, Lopez-de-Silanes, and Shleifer's study. This index measures how strongly the national legal system favors and protects liberal markets and minority shareholders against managers or dominant shareholders in corporate decision-making and voting processes.[11] With this managerial and legal rationalization factor, I test if firms are more likely to increase accounting transparency in societies proactively conforming to the liberal norms of managerial standardization and legal rationalization.

I also include the total number of employees (logged) as a company-level control variable to measure organizational size. Gross national product per capita in 1993 as a country-level control variable is included to capture the level of national economic development of countries in which the firms are operating.

As a research design, I employ multivariate analyses that examine both organizational and environmental (e.g. industry and nation-state) level effects on organizational accounting transparency. The basic model for the empirical analyses is

$$Y_{ij} = \alpha_0 + \beta X_{ij} + \gamma Z_j + \varepsilon_{ij}$$

where the subscript i is for company and j is for nation-state. Y_{ij} is the dependent variable, AIDI, of a company in 1993. X is a row vector of micro-level (organizational level) independent variables, and Z is a row vector of macro-level (nation-state level) covariates. α_0 is an intercept, β is a vector of coefficients associated with organizational level covariates, and γ is a vector of coefficients associated with nation-state level covaraites. The ε_{ij} are independent random disturbances.

7.4. RESULTS AND DISCUSSION

In this section, I report the results from the empirical analyses to test the hypotheses on corporate accounting transparency of 653 companies in 25 countries in 1993. In Model 1, I included only the variables that measure company characteristics without including indicators measuring societal differences. Model 1 shows that the results support all the hypotheses with regard to the relationship between organizational characteristics and accounting transparency. All models (1–6) also consistently indicate that, while controlling for country-level variables, the results still support the Hypotheses 1, 2, 3.1, and 3.2.

The control variable at the organizational level, organizational size measured by the number of employees, shows positive and significant effects on corporate accounting transparency. Firm size is a comprehensive variable of magnitude and differentiation which can act as a proxy for several corporate characteristics such as competitive advantage and information production costs. Collecting and disseminating information is a costly practice, and larger firms can afford such an expense. Moreover, managers in smaller firms may perceive information as proprietary and believe that disclosure of that information may result in the entrance of competitors into the market, thus endangering opportunities for profits. Thus, smaller firms may feel that more disclosure of their activities leads to competitive disadvantage with respect to other firms in the same industry (Firth 1979). Also, larger firms are more likely to distribute their securities via diverse networks of exchange that require extensive information disclosures. As a result, accounting work and corporate disclosure expand to maintain better control over the increasing financial and technical requirements placed on companies, and reflect the expansion and differentiation of organizations. In contrast to positive effects of organizational size, the control variable at the nation-state level, the degree of national economic development measured by GNP per capita, is not a significant factor predicting organizational accounting transparency.

Hypotheses 1, 2, 3.1, and 3.2 test the general effects of broadly defined 'organizational openness' to multiple environments. As predicted in Hypothesis 1, a company's financial openness to the public is an important predictor of the company's accounting transparency. The effect of a variable measuring corporate governance demonstrates that if a company is held more by the public and less by insiders, the company is more likely to disclose accounting information. Professional and technical influences from global accounting firms matter too. As stated in Hypothesis 2, companies hiring big international accounting firms are more likely to disclose accounting information than companies working with small domestic accounting firms.

The results also support Hypotheses 3.1 and 3.2. The proportion of foreign sales over total sales was used as a proxy for measuring a company's transnational activities, i.e. a company level globalization measure. Companies that operate actively in other countries are more likely to disclose accounting information than companies that are less active in foreign countries. As predicted by Hypothesis 3.2, companies in stable and hard product industries are less likely to disclose information. Companies with fluctuating specifications for final products or services often of an intangible quality (e.g. recreation, service, software, apparel, retailers, publishing, cosmetics, health care, etc.) disclose more accounting information, as these companies confront relatively more uncertain outcomes and unclear market reactions. Gathering, processing, and disclosing news and information help these organizations to reduce uncertainty and detect mark reactions. Multiple and uncertain environments thus require companies to be more transparent and accountable. In sum, if a company exhibits greater openness to financial, professional, global, and multiple environments, the company is more likely to disclose corporate accounting information.

In Models 2–6, I entered the remaining country-level variables to examine how national characteristics affect the degree to which companies disclose accounting information (Hypotheses 4, 5, and 6). As mentioned earlier, the level of national economic development measured by GNP per capita is not a significant factor in any models. In contrast, the political and institutional as well as economic globalization of a country exerts positive and significant effects on corporate accounting transparency. If a country is more open to the

Table 7.3 Factors affecting corporate accounting transparency[1]

Concepts		Indicators	Model 1	Model 2	Model 3	Model 4	Model 5	Model 6
Organizational Characteristics	Organizational size (control variable)	• Number of employees (logged)	0.575***	.656***	0.665***	0.661***	0.488**	0.507**
			(0.234)	(.240)	(0.236)	(0.234)	(0.225)	(0.221)
	Corporate governance (H1)	• Closely held shares (%)	−0.091***	−0.092***	−0.110***	−0.071***	−0.036***	−0.051***
			(0.011)	(0.011)	(0.011)	(0.011)	(0.011)	(0.012)
	Accounting firm (H2)	• Big six accounting firms (Dummy)	6.197***	6.190***	5.928***	4.902***	5.137***	4.551***
			(1.280)	(1.279)	(1.235)	(1.267)	(1.199)	(1.170)
	Open to the Global Market (H3-1)	• Foreign sale/total sale	0.107***	0.106***	0.085***	0.095***	0.107***	0.084***
			(.010)	(0.010)	(0.010)	(0.010)	(0.010)	(0.010)
	Industry & market characteristics (H3-2)	• Stable & hard product Industry[2] (Dummy)	−2.606***	−2.554***	−2.722***	−2.253***	−2.149***	−2.220***
			(0.606)	(0.606)	(0.584)	(0.593)	(0.568)	
Nation-State Characteristics	Economic development (control variable)	• GNP per capita (1993)/100		−0.0007	−0.001	−0.005	0.002	0.007
				(0.005)	(0.005)	(0.005)	(0.005)	(0.005)
	Economic linkage to World Society[3] (H4)	• Trade openness 1990 • Foreign direct investment 1990		2.311***	2.311***	1.941***		
				(0.344)	(0.344)			(0.326)

(continued)

Table 7.3 (Continued)

Concepts	Indicators	Model 1	Model 2	Model 3	Model 4	Model 5	Model 6
Political and institutional linkage to world society[3] (H4)	• IGO memberships 1992 • NGO memberships 1992 • National treaty signings 1981–85				1.274*** (0.381)		1.163*** (0.357)
Collectivist polity (as a mirror image of liberal individualist polity)[3] (H5)	• Collectivist/individualist index • Uncertain avoidance index • Power distance index					−1.874*** (0.321)	−0.742** (0.357)
Managerial and legal rationalization[3] (H6)	• Number of ISO9000 Certificates • Shareholder right index						3.023*** (0.309)	2.656*** (0.311)
	Constant		64.961 (2.704)	65.869 (2.767)	65.676 (2.723)	65.851 (2.699)	64.309 (2.589)	64.454 (2.544)
	R^2		0.334	0.336	0.387	0.370	0.422	0.468
	Number of cases		653	653	653	653	653	653

(1) ** Significant at the 0.05 level. *** Significant at the 0.01 level.
(2) Coded as 1 if the company belongs to the automotive, metal, machinery equipment, coal, transportation, or utility industry.
(3) Factor score measure combining listed variables.

global economy, it is more likely to possess legal and institutional instruments for increasing the accountability of firms in the country in order to satisfy modern international standards requiring transparent economic activities. In addition, a country has more organizational linkages to the world, participating in international organizations and treaty formations, the country is more like to observe the norms and discourses disseminated by world society (Meyer et al. 1997*a*, 1997*b*). It is crucial to understand the roles of international actors providing guidelines to nation-states and organizations with respect to accounting. Many international organizations and professional associations have made efforts to set up international accounting standards and to increase corporate transparency throughout the world. More globalized countries tend to be under greater potential pressures to rationalize and modernize local business laws and practices and to increase the transparency of firms operating within their borders. The results support Hypothesis 4.

To test Hypothesis 5, I included a factor variable measuring collectivist national polity style (as a mirror image of liberal individual national polity). The results also support the hypothesis. Firms in liberal individualist societies disclose accounting information more than those in collectivist societies. Liberal individualist countries (e.g. the United States or the United Kingdom) promote the construction of legitimate individual actors with sovereignty and rationality (Jepperson 2002*b*) and are more concerned with the provision of information to those sovereign actors including investors, shareholders, and workers. By comparison, we may expect less accounting work in a collectivist society due to the tightly coupled relations of members based on rules. In such a system, priority goes to the formulation of bureaucratic rules and procedures that constitute the relations among groups and actors in organizations, not to the evaluation of abstract values and the discretion of participants. In this system, people tend to accept roles and positions and request no further elaborate justification. In decision-making procedures, subordinate consultation and participation are not highly important. Formal procedures and positions by rules are respected more than justification based on discussion and evaluation through data. In this aspect, there are negative trade-offs between elaborated formal rules and hierarchies and the growth of accounting work.

As expected in Hypothesis 6, companies in countries supporting rational managerial standards and liberal legal and market principles are more likely to disclose corporate accounting information. In a society, for instance, where larger numbers of organizations conform to the norms and models of rational managerial standards (e.g. ISO 9000), organizations will be more likely to provide accounts for their activities that express their capacity as proactive and effective actors.

A neoliberal market environment and related legal institutions are also important preconditions for expanded accountability. Liberal systems—more so than other polities—protect market environments, promote managerial rationality, and facilitate transparent economic transactions. The legal systems of these countries are more likely to emphasize shareholder rights and protection mechanisms to encourage companies to disclose more highly detailed accounts of their activities.

In sum, I argue that the degree of national and organizational openness and the affinity for different societal polity styles are crucial factors for predicting the extent of corporate accounting transparency displayed by different organizations in various societies, while controlling for the effects of organizational size and national economic development.

Organizations present rational accounts and justifications for their actions to social environments that demand increasing rationality and justification of organizational activities. Although organizational accounting is produced in universal and standardized terms, it is shaped and modified by particular conditions under which it interacts with social environments. The roles of global and local contexts need to be considered in order to better understand the expansion of modern accounting. This chapter highlights how social and institutional environments as well as functional and technical elements of organizations affect the degree to which organizations disclose such corporate accounting information. Viewing organizations as open systems embedded in local and global environments, I argued that the varying degree of openness of organizations determines the extent to which they are accountable and transparent.

7.5. CONCLUSION

Organizations are supposed to be intentional and rational (Thompson 1967). The behavior of organizations is expected to be governed by rational procedures that can be accounted for through methods of reasoned argumentation. This chapter has focused empirical attention on the global expansion of modern accounting as a process of expanded organizational rationality. I document the global isomorphic increase of organizational conformity to the norm of expansive accountability, emphasizing how these models of accountability and transparency flow as rules and practices from wider collective levels (at the levels of nation-states and world society) as well as from sources at a micro individual level. I also address how accounting varies in different social and organizational contexts. I highlight the aspects of organizational openness to broader social environments and of national economic and political globalization to world society as crucial explanatory factors for variation in the accounting transparency of organizations across countries.

The widespread acceptance of liberal market ideas along with globalization poses new uncertainties for social actors and requires more effective information processing and disseminating to enhance decision-making. Models of modern accountability have diffused globally in recent periods, and at an even higher rate in Western nations (European countries, the United States, and Canada), which have experienced rapid rates of economic and political globalization.

The development of accounting and the spread of the model of accountability and transparency, therefore, have a worldwide and universal character. Regardless of the social and economic conditions of different societies, modern social actors are continuously involved in providing accounts to others and to themselves about who they are and what they are doing. In other words, individuals and organizations incorporate measures and procedures that institutionalize the notions of accountability and transparency into their routines (see also Drori, Chapter 4). The most prominent examples are similar efforts across the globe to produce standardized formats for corporate annual reports to shareholders.

Stressing these global dimensions and ceremonial aspects of accounting, I examined how national and organizational environments determine the degree to which organizations disclose financial accounting information. The technical and functional requirements of organizations are important factors to explain the development of accounting transparency. I also focus attention on the aspects of broader social environments as crucial predictors of variation in accounting transparency in different societies. In particular, economic, political, and cultural globalization and the openness of organizations and nation-states to these processes produce elaborated organizational accounting and increased transparency of corporate financial information.

The model of accountability has triumphed at both the global and national governance levels, which is especially evident with respect to corporate accounting. Much of the literature on globalization views this triumph as a technical achievement brought about by economic processes. Following a broader sociological perspective, I view the expansion of accounting as an institutional process reflecting world models of organizational rationality. This chapter examines worldwide trends and analyzes cross-national variations in the triumph of the accountability model.

NOTES

1. An earlier version of this chapter appeared as 'The Expansion of Modern Accounting as a Global and Institutional Practice.' *International Journal of Comparative Sociology* 46, no. 4 (2005): pp. 287–326.
2. The IFAC is an organization of national professional accountancy organizations that represent accountants employed in public practice, business and industry, the public sector, and education as well as some specialized groups that interact frequently with the profession.
3. The term national polity is used here in a broad sense. By national polity I mean the system of national rules bestowing societal authority in search of collective ends and establishing collective regulation and intervention in formally organized and rationalized social contexts (Thomas et al. 1987). It includes not only state actions but also various forms of social movements, collective discourse, and the rationalized activities of publicly chartered private bodies including the sciences, professions, and business organizations (Jepperson and Meyer 1991).
4. The sample size in the analyses reduced to 653 due to the availability of relevant indicators for the independent variables yielding consistent cases throughout the models. Different combinations of indicators with larger sample size produce substantively similar results to those presented here. The twenty-five countries in which the sample companies operate are Australia, Austria, Belgium, Brazil, Canada, Chile, Denmark, Finland, France, Germany, Ireland, Italy, Japan, the Netherlands, New Zealand, Norway, Portugal, Singapore, South Korea, Spain, Sweden, Switzerland, Turkey, United Kingdom, and the United States.
5. The detailed items in subgroups are available from the author.
6. The Sub-Group Disclosure Index (SGDI) was calculated as follows:

$$\text{SGDI}(\%) = \frac{\sum_{i=1}^{m} d_i}{m} \times 100$$

Where $d = 1$ if the item d_i is disclosed
0 if the item d_i is not disclose
$m = $ the total number of items in the subgroup.
7. The AIDI is a measure of the relative level of disclosure by a company:

$$\text{AIDI}(\%) = \frac{\sum_{sg=1}^{n} \text{SGDI}(\%)}{n}$$

In the equation, n denotes the total number of subgroups. For the AIDI, n equals 7, since we have seven broad subcategories.

8. Two factor measures were constructed with exploratory factor analyses. The extraction of the primary factor accounted for 93 percent of the variance of economic globalization variables and 80 percent of the variance of political and institutional globalization variables.
9. The factor measure was constructed with an exploratory factor analysis. The primary factor extracted with the indicators accounted for 65 percent of the variance of collectivist society variables.
10. The factor measure was constructed with an exploratory factor analysis. The primary factor extracted with the indicators accounted for 64 percent of the variance of managerial and legal rationalization variables.
11. This index was formed by adding 1 when (1) the country allows shareholders to mail their proxy vote to the firm, (2) share holders are not required to deposit their shares prior to the general shareholders' meeting, (3) cumulative voting or proportional representation of minorities in the board of directors is allowed, (4) the minimum percentage of share capital that entitles a shareholder to call for an extraordinary shareholders' meeting is less than or equal to 10 percent, or (6) shareholders have preemptive rights that can be waived only by a shareholders' vote. The index, therefore, ranges from zero (less rationalized legal supports for liberal markets and shareholders) to six (more rationalized legal supports for liberal markets and shareholders) (La Porta, Lopez-de-Silanes, and Shleifer 1998).

8

Dynamics of Corporate Responsibility

Suzanne Shanahan and Sanjeev Khagram[1]

State retrenchment and scandals of corporate governance are just two of the more recent concerns that have fueled an almost thirty-year international debate over business–society relations. Is profit maximization the sole obligation of business or should private enterprise play a broader role in society? Should business be expected to more directly address pressing economic, social, and environmental issues? By 2000, public opinion, at least, was becoming increasingly clear: two in three individuals surveyed across twenty-three countries and six continents expected companies to play a significant part in the collective pursuit of societal goals (Environics 2000). And while 'global corporations did not wake up one day and decide to become socially responsible citizens' (Oliviero and Simmons 2002), and despite lingering diffidence, many firms have responded actively.

Today, talk of corporate responsibility—good, bad, and ambivalent—is everywhere. Over the past decade, in particular, CR has been the ever-increasing subject of popular discourse, state policy debate, firm strategizing, international standards, and social mobilization (Shamir 2004). Green labels, triple bottom line reporting, and socially responsible investing (SRI) were important first early markers of a (re-)emergent form of business society relations and critical expressions of something now increasingly known as 'corporate responsibility' (CR).[2] A growing industry of trade and social scientific research on the virtue and vice of CR has paralleled the rise of this pubic debate.

All this 'talk' has not been, however, idle chatter. In 1997, the Global Reporting Initiative (GRI) was established to support, develop, and disseminate Sustainability Reporting Guidelines around the world. In 1999, the United Nations launched the Global Compact—a voluntary consortium of companies, UN agencies and civil society organizations dedicated to the protection of human rights, labor, and the environment—that now includes the participation of almost 2,000 firms across the globe. In 2000, the World Bank launched a Corporate Governance and Corporate Social Responsibility Initiative to promote CR through dialog and education worldwide. And in 2008 the

International Organization for Standardization (ISO) will launch ISO 26000—a new set of voluntary guidelines centering on socially responsibility.

States, too, are increasingly involved. In Great Britain, for example, the government recently published *Business and Society-Developing Corporate Social Responsibility in the UK* highlighting exemplars of CR. The government simultaneously launched a website to provide a forum for discussion among stakeholders and strong examples of specific CR policies. And in 2002 the European Union published a white paper, *Promoting a European Framework for Corporate Social Responsibility*, marking a shift away from a purely voluntary framework toward a more legislative or regulatory structure for European business practice. These global, regional, and national initiatives are supported by a profusion of advocacy and technical NGOs and INGOs that lobby, support, promote, and facilitate firm and industry-level changes. The African Institute for Corporate Responsibility, US Organization Business for Social Responsibility, Corporate Social Responsibility Europe, and Instituto Ethos in Brazil are just four examples.

Firm behavior is also changing. As of 2003, 50 percent of the Global 100 published social and/or environmental reports. In South Africa, virtually all firms listed on the Johannesburg Stock Exchange (JSE) publish some triple bottom line or sustainability report. And in Brazil more than 50 percent do as well. Today 90 percent of Global 500 firms report that CR is significantly more important than it was five years ago (Environics 2000). Indeed one would be hard pressed to find a major corporation that did not have some policy (if not an entire unit complete with staff) to address CR concerns. Even Duke University has an environmental policy, one just approved by their trustees in the spring of 2005. Socially responsible investing is also on the rise reaching over $2 trillion in the United States.

At the level of research and analysis there are an increasing number of business schools worldwide that offer classes and special programs on CR. The Nottingham Centre for Corporate Social Responsibility offers an entire MA in CR. Then there is Boston College's Center for Corporate Citizenship and the recent *Journal of Corporate Citizenship* both dedicated to detailed research in the field. And in summer 2005, the First Southern Africa Corporate Responsibility Symposium was held to promote interdisciplinary discussion of CR. This paper too is perhaps but one more element in the growth of the CR discourse.

This flurry of activities, however, obscures four inter-related facts about transcontinental CR dynamics. First, such activity in no way implies an incontrovertible triumph of CR. While it often appears that 'everyone is doing it', or saying they are, CR is neither the ubiquitous nor hegemonic model of business society relations. If 50 percent of the Global 100 are publishing social and environmental balance sheets it still means that 50 percent are not. If 4 percent of the US firms in the Global 500 are participating in the Global Compact (GC), 96 percent are not. Kraft's decision to buy only sustainably produced coffee beans makes news, their earlier nondecision does not. Corporate responsbility has not only engendered palpable change it has yielded ambivalence, trepidation and importantly, active dissent. For many industries, CR is perhaps not even on their active agenda. A 2004 assessment of banking in Asia makes no note of CR whatsoever (*Bangkok Post* January 6, 2004). The decision of Equator Banks to halt further elaboration of CR and the G8's 2003 decision to eschew all discussion of CR after it was to be a centerpiece of discussion reflect some of the common unease with CR. The January 2005 *Economist* details how the value and virtue of CR are still the subject of often trenchant disagreement. Within segments of the business community, Milton Friedman's insistence that business is about making money and money alone still prevails (Friedman 1962). From this 'CR is bad capitalism' perspective (see Blowfield and Frynas 2005: 505), CR is a thoroughly misguided enterprise (Henderson 2002).[3] 'The proper business of business is business. No apology required' (Crook 2005: 22). Clearly Exxon Mobil agrees. In spring 2003, chief executive Lee Raymond almost bragged to shareholders, 'We won't jump on the bandwagon just because others may have a different view. We don't invest to make social statements at the expense of shareholder return' (www.telegraph.co.uk June 13, 2003). Indeed, the debate between advocates and opponents of CR often exists within single firm (Stopford and Strange 1991).

Second, where consensus on the principle of CR exists, precisely what it should *be* in practice differs widely across firms, sectors, NGOs, and geographic regions. Should the priorities of CR be issues of corporate governance, worker health and safety, or the environment? Should CR be purely voluntary or can states and international institutions act in a non-command-and-control regulatory capacity? 'To complicate matters further, the vocabulary of business-society debates is being expanded to include new terms such as corporate accountability, social responsible investment and sustainable development...' (Blowfield and Frynas 2005: 501). Nor are these words simply synonyms for CR. Indeed, they are 'aimed as replacing, redefining or complementing the CR concept' (Blowfield and Frynas 2005: 501).

Third and related, the litany of new practices, standards, and organizations that support CR do not imply logical or organizational coherence to this principle. Historically, CR has developed in an uneven and often disconnected way as a response to a crisis within a particular firm as with Union Carbide and Dow Chemicals, to rehabilitate the reputation of a particular sector as with mining or as part of a new vision of state market relations following political transition as in India or South Africa. Sometimes these initiatives are proactive, sometimes preemptive, and sometimes reactive or even resistant. Some have drawn from common ideas in the business community, worked with similar NGOs and international organizations and some have developed much more isolation as if invented anew. The development then of CR as is reflected clearly in the vast geographical, sectoral, and firm-level variations in the philosophy, policy, and practice of CR. It is the terminology of CR, itself, that often signals and enables these idiosyncratic and often unrelated behaviors to be understood as a coherent set. Thus, while there is an analytic temptation to depict CR as a singular phenomenon CR dynamics are more accurately described as many different things to many different people (WBCSD 2000; Jackson 2003). The terminology of CR connotes many meanings and many institutional forms. Like children's rights, effective schools, or clean water—CR is often cast as an unspecified social 'good' or 'goods'. So while nine out of ten companies may remark on its importance, they may well not be able to fully articulate precisely how or why. But in contrast to other accounts (see Blowfield and Fyrnas 2005), we understand the conceptual imprecision of CR to be one of its central virtues. Indeed, the ability of CR to function as a highly variegated marker of the archetypical 'good' corporation' has played no small role in the 'success' of these diverse initiatives (Sethi 2003). This implicit diversity makes CR far easier to effectuate in some form, however token.

Finally, these points together lead us to assert there while there is a clear (but highly varied and decentered) CR movement, there are also counter-movements and even nonmovements. As both an idea and a set of practices CR remains in many places highly contested. Corporate responsibility is itself a paradox. As a concept CR is the tenuous union of a left-progressive support for human rights, the environment, etc. with a right neoliberal market logic. This structuration in form means that while there appears to be ever-increasing interest in CR, not only is the 'movement' amorphous in character but is the continual site of contestation. Thus, we observe an eclectic set of geographically disparate initiatives to reconceive and reconstitute business society relations each with different historical origins, objectives, expectations, social networks, and organizational forms. These diverse initiatives have multiple axes of interaction, overlap, and exchange, of course, but as of yet, perhaps less than expected. The coherence we attribute to this activity then is more analytical than empirical (Blowfield and Frynas 2005). Indeed, the authoritative language of CR as promulgated by international organizations, professionals and academics appropriates, tames, coalesces and lends singular meaning to a sometimes fragmentary and contested set of activities.

To understand the dynamics of CR, we look to its sites of unequivocal triumph but as well as sites of its hesitance and absence. Here, we will argue that contestation and ambiguity (conceptually and strategically) are constitutive features of CR necessarily affecting the historical and geographical variegated patterns of its emergence and spread. Thus understanding the dynamics of CR requires their disaggregation. In this chapter, then, our objective is straightforward: to provide an analytical framework to describe the rapidly changing, contested transnational social field of CR. Toward this end, we situate the current literature on CR found almost exclusively in the literatures on business ethics and management—in a broader framework of theories of transnational social change. We then provide a synthetic overview of the tradition and terrain of CR before turning to two schematic sectoral case studies—mining in South Africa and banking in Brazil. Through this set of empirical materials we aim to illustrate why an explanation of the emergence and dynamics of CR requires an interactive multilevel approach. And finally, we conclude with a speculative discussion about the conditions under which CR might ultimately represent a constitutive change in the very nature of business–society relations.

8.1. THEORIZING THE 'A-THEORETICAL': LITERATURE ON CORPORATE RESPONSIBILITY

Fragmentary US academic discussions of CR first emerged in the 1950s. Then the 'dangers' of social responsibility were center stage (Levitt 1958). But it was not until the 1970s that CR was prominently featured and then most significantly in the organizational management literature (Carroll 1979, 1999; Margolis and Walsh 2003; Matten, Crane, and Chapple 2003). At this time the focus was on understanding what it was and how it might affect firm profits. It is Carroll's typology of firm responsibilities first developed in the 1970s that is still the dominant conceptualization of CR. Carroll (1999) notes four sets of responsibilities: economic (maximize value), legal (abide by law), ethical (do what is right, fair, and just), and philanthropic (help finance the general well-being of society). And until the recasting of these responsibilities in terms of the duties of citizenship (that provide parallel rights of citizenship) this model retained a significant element of paternalism indicative of the management literature (Matten and Crane 2003).

    Current discussions of CR—be they couched in the language of corporate responsibility or otherwise—tend increasingly to emphasize the collaborative relations between firms and stakeholders (Handy 2003; Kanter 2003; Prahalad and Hammond 2003; Smith 2003). Today, the dominant sentiment underlying discussions is not fear but either a mix of reluctant acquiescence and cautious enthusiasm (see 2003 special issue of *Harvard Business Review* on corporate responsibility) or a sanguine cynicism (see 2004 special issue of *International Affairs* on corporate responsibility and development).[4]

In a near exhaustive review of this literature (nearly 600 articles), we found that almost two-thirds of all work since the 1970s has concerned itself with the evaluation of the financial impacts—short or long term of CR. The logical assumption underlying this work is straightforward; the primary objective of business is profit or shareholder maximization. Thus, understanding CR is about detailing economic effects. According to Margolis and Walsh's study 2003, between 1972 and 2002 there were 109 empirical studies of CR and financial performance. More than half of these were published between 1993 and 2002 revealing the escalating interest in this relationship. Half of these studies found a positive relationship between CR and financial performance variously defined and the other half found either no relationship or reported mixed findings (272).

But we estimate that less than 2 percent of this rapidly growing body of work directly examines *why* firms adopt CR or *what* drives CR. Even less examine *why* CR takes form in particular policies or institutional arrangements.[5] Still less draw upon social science insights to understand CR. And even less again situate these processes in the context of the tropical world (for an exception recent issue of *International Affairs*). The larger project from which this chapter is derived seeks to begin to fill these gaps.

So, where does the current literature on CR leave us if our central question is simply, *why?* As an eclectic bundle of ideas, institutions, and activities, there are perhaps three basic but very divergent, competing ways to explicate CR in the current literature. Each perspective provides a different set of arguments about where, when, and why we are apt to see CR practices. We provide a simplified schematic overview (and perhaps necessarily a caricature) of their logic.

First, there is a narrowly materialist, firm-level perspective where CR is about self-interest (Porter and Kramer 2003; see also above discussion). Corporate responsibility either directly or indirectly contributes to firm value. Here lies the literature that makes the economic case for CR—why it is good for firms and indeed why it is good for countries (Swift and Zadek 2002). So, for example, corporate philanthropy can be 'truly strategic' and can improve 'a company's long term business prospects' (Porter and Kramer 2003: 27–8). A perhaps more benevolent form of this argument depicts CR as a development opportunity—to provide jobs, goods, and services to the poor (Grayson 2004; Prahalad 2004; Blowfield and Frynas 2005). Within this framework there would be at least three central propositions about the type of firms most apt to develop CR.

Proposition one:
Large, profitable firms will be more likely to develop CR-related policies.
Here we would expect that Global 500 companies—Walmart, Toyota, and Banco Brasil—would be more apt to consider CR because the marginal cost would be less.

Proposition two:
Firms that rely on brand loyalty will be more likely to develop CR-related policies.
Here we would expect Nike to be quicker to respond to allegations of sweatshop labor than Provident Mutual.

Proposition three:
Companies that find themselves in a credibility deficit will be more likely to develop CR-related policies.
Here we would expect new environmental policies following disaster like at Exxon Valdez.

The second perspective attributes the rise of CR not to changes within firms but to the needs and demands of national societies. Within this framework firm size and firm product are not critical. Rather, it is the national context of the firm that is most critical. Here the rise of CR can be attributed largely to either state or market failures (or limitations)—both often symptomatic of neoliberal economic reform associated with globalization. Some variants of this perspective highlight the contested character of CR and in doing so attend to its institutional context. This model is one of social mobilization where CR is a response to the demands of civil society and NGOs that through both direct and indirect collective action leverage both states and companies (Baron 1999; Oliviero and Simmons 2002; Shamir 2004; Crook 2005). Here the institutional context business is critical to policy change. Where there are strong civil society organizations and the state is responsive to these organizations are most apt to more aggressively pursue CR.

This perspective offers hypotheses about how either the nature of the state, market, or civil society will make CR more likely. Three propositions are central.

Proposition one:
Firms may take on a greater social role as states retrench social or developmental policies (state failure argument).
So one might expect countries in which neoliberal market-oriented policies have become hegemonic to exhibit increased CR.

Proposition two:
Firms may take on a greater social role under national conditions of declining prosperity (market failure argument).
From this account, firms do what markets should under ideal conditions. They may, for example, act as a redistributive mechanism.

Proposition three:
Firms may take on greater social role in societies where there are strong civil society organizations.
From this view, CR of firms should be more salient in countries like India than Indonesia.

Certainly changes in the organization and role of the state and fluctuations in the market are part of the explanation. But like firm-level explanations they seem to miss part of the empirical picture. At least some of this picture is further revealed when one examines not just the institutional context of firms but the broader global institutional context.

The powerfully ideational view associated with world polity theory (Meyer et al. 1997*a*, 1997*b*) where CR is a triumphant universalized notion of the new corporation constitutes a third perspective. Corporate responsibility is an idea whose time to be global has come. The core proposition of this perspective would be that corporations, like nation-states and indeed individuals, are embedded in a dense network of international institutions that shape their perceptions, preferences, and policies. Whether researchers argue that inter-national institutions affect the interests and incentives facing national actors (more realist versions)[6] or that international institutions actually constitute actors' identities and interests (more phenomenological versions),[7] the result is often the same. Both perspectives identify dramatic structural isomorphism across societies once characterized by profound diversity.[8] The scope of this policy convergence is extensive (Beckfield 2003), spanning legislation securing the rights of women (Berkovitch 1999) and immigrants (Soysal 1994) as well as family planning (Barrett and Frank 1999), welfare (Strang and Chang 1993), education (Bradley and Ramirez 1996), environmental (Frank, Schofer, and Hironaka 2000), science policies (Drori, Meyer, Ramirez, and Schofer 2003), and thus CR as well. Two core propositions derive from this perspective.

Proposition one:
CR is a coherent, dramatic, explicitly global movement that is universally and abstractly conceptualized and organized.
Here CR is part of a larger world culture that supports a set of universal norms, values and organizational practices.

Proposition two:
CR has a worldwide scope that penetrates into even the remotest (geographically and politically) societies.
From this view, CR is elaborated in the places like the UN Council for Sustainable Development and Corporate Social Responsibility Europe and then diffuses to Thailand and Malawi as a new set of best practices and indeed as a new ideal typical form of corporation.

Here we argue that each of these perspectives has considerable merit. Indeed, each captures at least *part* of the picture—but only *part*. As the empirical illustration later reveals, this diverse set of practices captured by the moniker CR eschews the easy, singular explanation. In of themselves, as single accounts, none of these three adequately explains the empirical scope of the origins and diffusion of CR movements. Corporate responsibility does not emerge first or foremost in large profitable firms. It does not consistently emerge to remediate either state or market failures. Nor does it appear the predominantly the work of local, national, or international activists. And it does not always appear as part of a new understanding of the 'good corporation' (Sethi 2003) disseminated in a top–down or core–periphery fashion. State-level or firm-level variations in CR practice are not just localized expressions of universal norms.

Our contribution then is both empirical and conceptual. Current explanatory frameworks are not capable of fully capturing the dynamics of CR precisely because they conceive of CR as unitary and examine CR from the perspective of a single level of analysis. Accordingly firm behaviors are conceptually distinct from the discourse that supports them, networks of NGO's that prod them, or states that regulate them.

8.2. THE TRANSNATIONAL STRUCTURATION OF CORPORATE RESPONSIBILITY

To both better understand the increasing interest in and activity around CR and to reconcile (or perhaps combine) these alternative models we adopt the conceptual architecture of transnational structuration and transnational social fields.[9] Transnational structuration implies a multilevel, interactive set of social processes that cross borders though they may not be global or worldwide. Transnationalism highlights the clear embeddedness of the phenomenon (like CR) in 'local' settings—be they states, sectors, or firms—and how they are both made palpable and translated by the filter of local culture. Second, we understand social fields to be sets of interlocking networks of actors, ideas and institutions. In the case of CR this includes international organizations, states, NGOs, business associations, firms, activists, and managers as well as the ideas, interests, and institutions they represent (Khagram 2004: 210–15).

Here the notion of a contested transnational structuration provides a conceptual and methodological point of departure to understand CR as part of a broad set of cultural, political, and economic processes variously operating at different levels and in different social spheres. This structuration of transnational fields approach leads us to a multilevel research strategy where we look not only at societal level changes—globalization, the changing authority of the state, sector-level changes—shifting market conditions, profitability and competition, or firm-level changes—brand identity, consumer support, profitability, and competition but the interaction between changes at each of these levels.

Take the following example. The most straightforward model of CR is perhaps stakeholder management where firms are accountable to communities and shareholders. We understand this model to have emerged from two different transcontinental discourses. The first is a set of cultural scripts legitimating equity, social justice, human rights, and environmental sustainability (world polity theory). The second is a set of cognitive models advocating the replacement of strong state regulation with more decentralized participatory regulatory forms (market theories). Corporate responsibility emerges first in *local* contexts (firms, sectors, or countries) where these scripts have prior cultural resonance and where they are congruent with existing cultural frameworks. Thus we see strong support for CR in Brazil where traditional Catholic ideas and institutions have historically advocated the clear embedding of corporations within communities. The success of these local variants of CR facilitates the diffusion of this form via social learning through transnational, cross-sectoral professional networks that valorize the perceived success stories and that reinforce this professional network.

For CR to become a more dominant model of business–state–civil society relations—a model less subject to fluctuating economies or shifting policy agendas—there must first be a growth and deepening of transnational, cross-sectoral professional networks across sectors constructing rationalized cultural and structural systems legitimating CR and delegitimating its challengers. Corporate responsibility the oxymoron must be replaced with CR the obvious way. This shift would then generate change in powerful leading field organizations (states, intergovernmental organizations, leading firms, leading business associations, and leading educational institutions) as well as a set of novel organizational arrangements. This can then offer state actors (some of which may well be part of those professional networks) a broader set of cognitive and practical tools to enact statehood effectively and thus legitimate themselves. And to the extent that their legitimacy increases, CR will be further institutionalized. But it can also offer firm or market actors a broader set of cognitive and practical tools—if you will—for firms to enact 'businesshood' effectively, for business schools to enact 'research and teaching' effectively, *for* accountants to enact 'auditing' effectively, and so on to legitimate themselves.

Here we begin to see that the conceptualization of CR as a facet of the contested transnational field of CR might potentially offer a new set of explanations. It might help us to understand why you get CR in some small firms and not others, why you get great enthusiasm for CR in some sectors and disdain in others, or why you get much European interest in CR but much less North American interest? And it might also help us to understand under what circumstances long-standing historical CR initiatives are reinforced and indeed help create regional or world models for CR and under what circumstances CR initiatives appear more impervious to exogenous trends.

What then does CR actually look like and how might we ever begin to explain it? In Section 8.3, we provide a broad sketch of the transcontinental, cross-sectoral, inter- and intra-firm dynamics of CR. We do so neither to refute anyone of these three perspectives nor to reject any single proposition but rather to suggest they may not be completely capturing the emergent but highly contested and eclectic cluster of CR initiatives. Instead we tentatively offer a new theoretical framework as another frame to explicate this still unfolding, and often unexpected and unlikely social dynamic.

8.3. THE CONTEMPORARY TERRAIN OF CORPORATE RESPONSIBILITY

General Patterns and Dynamic: A Transcontinental, Cross Sectoral, Inter Firm View. Quite certainly there has been a palpable surge in CR practices across the continents and sectors. But neither the underlying logic nor language is wholly new or given. Broader debates over business–society relations (and indeed the business–state–society relations) are perhaps endemic to discussions of capitalism generally and state–market relations more specifically. A most dramatic historical example of societal mobilization to hold private enterprise accountable was, of course, the late eighteenth century mobilization to prohibit British companies and shipowners from participating in the slave trade (Oliviero and Simmons 2002). This London based effort was the first step toward the increasingly transcontinental eradication of slavery. And while the specific terminology of CR today may have Anglo-Saxon origins (Blowfield and Frynas 2005), the notion that business has social obligations to the wider society can be found historically in a variety of Asian and African societies as well (Turner and Trompenaars 1993).

More recent, historical examples include state and civil society debates in India following independence. Many sought alternative models to conceive and govern business–state–society relations. At a 1965 national seminar in Delhi, 'Social Responsibility of Business', the logic is clear. 'An enterprise is a corporate citizen. Like a citizen it is esteemed and judged by its actions in relation to the community of which it is a member, as well as by its economic performance.' Indeed, it is possible to understand the contemporary drive for CR as part of both a broader historical transition from a paternalistic relationship between business and society characteristic of various forms of corporate philanthropy to a more collaborative one as well as the reinvention and rearticulation of transnational efforts of the 1970s to promote corporate accountability (Carroll 1999; Matten, Crane, and Chapple 2003).

Transnational efforts during the 1970s to foster an environment of CR met with limited success. And by the early 1990s few of these initiatives remained: the OECD Declaration on International Investment and Multinational Enterprise, the ILO Tripartite Declaration of Principles Concerning Multinational Enterprises and Social Policy, and the Sullivan Principles. The attempt to produce a United Nations Code of Conduct for Transnational Corporations was thwarted. Most individual company corporate codes of conduct were adopted in the 1970s by US firms, and focused predominantly on occupational health or safety issues and bribery. The components of CR were parsed. Labor codes tended to be concentrated in consumer goods sectors, whereas environmental codes tend to be found in firms in the primary sector: oil, mining, and forestry.

But by the 1990s the terrain of CR was quickly shifting. In 2003, nearly half of the world's top companies (the Global 100) published an environmental, social, or sustainability report. In the mid-1990s this figure was less than 20 percent. In 2002, 40 percent of reporting companies included independent assurance of their reports up from 18 percent in 2000. Nearly a quarter of top global firms produced integrated social and environmental reports, another quarter or so produced only environmental reports, and nearly one-third have stakeholder engagement processes. It is estimated that 70 percent of top Japanese companies provide annual reporting on sustainability-related issues as do 69 percent of businesses in Europe, and 18 percent of those headquartered in the United States. Leading transnational electronics, auto, and mining firms tend to report at a very high level whereas others, such as financial services, were less likely to do so. In contrast, of the 100 reporting companies in Canada as of 2003, nearly one-fifth were in the financial sector (this represented an increase from four to nineteen firms in just two years) or utilities. In Brazil, the banking sector now even produces a sector 'social balance sheet'.

Socially responsible investing also increased during this same time. In 1997, assets in SRI screened funds equaled $529 billion in the United States. This figure rose to nearly $1.5 trillion in 1999, over $2 trillion in 2001, and nearly 2.15 trillion in 2003. This means SRI assets as a percentage of total assets under professional management most likely doubled during this period. From 1995 to 2003, social investing assets have grown 40 percent faster than all professionally managed investment assets in the United States. Between 2001 and 2003, social-screened portfolios grew 7 percent while all professionally managed portfolios combined fell 4 percent.

The first European ethical investment fund was launched in the United Kingdom in 1984. By 2001, at least sixty funds existed in that country. In 1997, total SRI assets were calculated at £22.7 billion. This figure grew to £52.2 billion in 1999 and £224.5 billion in 2001. The total assets that were social screened had increased from £11.1 billion in 1999 to £14.4 billion by 2001. But the share of ethical funds relative to the total investment in markets remains very low: ranging from close to 0 percent in Germany to 1.35 percent in the United Kingdom. And only an estimated $2.5 billion of socially responsible investment was under professional management all across Asia as of 2001. Prominent SRI indices have been established over the last few years, including the FTS4Good Index in London and the Dow Jones Sustainability Index in New York.

The pattern continues: a recent World Bank survey of 107 transnational corporations in the extractive, agribusiness, and manufacturing sectors found that more than one-third had withdrawn from a country and nearly one-half chose countries of investment or operation, based on CR concerns. Over 80 percent of respondents reported analyzing partner companies' CR performance and 50 percent actually chose particular partners over others because of CR concerns.

The current transnational field of CR is made even more vivid through an analysis of the firm level, regional, and sectoral distribution of current global initiatives. Multistakeholder initiatives—where multiple groups across sectors play an active role in the design and potentially implementation of codes of conduct and standards through a variety of reporting, auditing, monitoring, verification, and certification arrangement—have proliferated widely (Khagram and Saleem 2005). Among the best known are GC, GRI, Accountability 1000, Social Accountability 8000, Fair Labor Association, Global Union Framework Agreements, Ethical Trading Initiative, Forest Stewardship Council, Marine Stewardship Council, and ISO 14001. Figure 8.1 outlines the scope of CR policies through an examination of participation in three of these international multi-stakeholder initiatives: the GRI, the GC and ISO (ISO 9000 series or ISO 14001 series).

Concretely, the first two pie charts in Figure 8.1 depict the geographic distribution of those Global 500 companies that participate in either the GRI or the GC. So, for example 3 percent of all Global 500 companies that

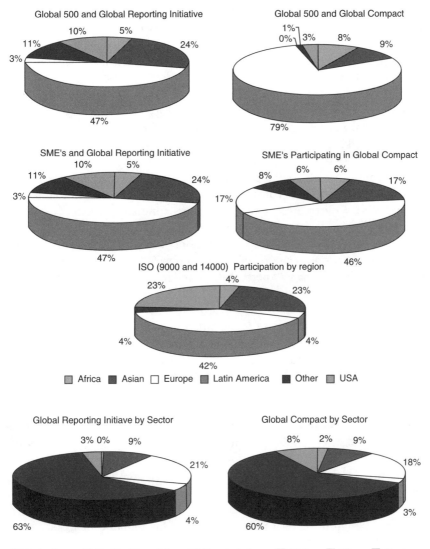

Figure 8.1 Regional and sectoral distribution of participation in international CSR initiatives

participate in the GRI are US-based companies and 79 percent of all companies that have signed onto the GC are based in Europe. The second two pie charts in Figure 8.1 array a similar geographical distribution of those small/medium size firms that participate in either the GRI or the GC. And the fifth chart outlines participation in the ISO 9000 and 14000 series in the same way. The last two pie charts try to provide a different perspective on GRI and GC by parsing participation by firm sector. So, we see for example, that 9 percent of the firms participating in either the GRI or the GC are in the banking and/or financial sector.

Figure 8.1 illuminates three general points. First, CR is a *transcontinental* phenomenon but with varied geographical and sectoral participation; thus it is not worldwide or global. When examining either Global 500 or small/medium-sized enterprises (SMEs), Europe has the most significant participation in both the GRI and Global Compact GC. Noting the first four pie charts, Europe constitutes almost 50 percent of the total participation in each case. American participation is consistently only about one-quarter of that level.

The seeming overrepresentation of Europe is measured when considering the national origins of most Global 500 companies together with the fact that such companies themselves account for 25 percent of GC participants. Fifty percent of the European companies in the Global 500 participate in the GC (a figure markedly less than 79 percent displayed in the relevant pie chart). And only about 4 percent of the US-based Global 500 have signed on. This same figure is 25 percent in Latin America. Note also that in the case of SME participation, Asia, Africa, and Latin America perform far better. And when considering ISO 9000 and ISO 14001 certification, Asia is significantly represented garnering 27 and 34 percent of the total certificates respectively. In 2002, China and Japan held first and second place in terms of total number of ISO 9000 certifications.

Indeed, taken as a set what these figures reveal is that the critical geographic centers of these dynamics may well lay outside the advanced economies of the North and West. Certainly, the more narrow focus on large, transnational firms (e.g. those in the Global 500) reveals a strong European presence among GC participants. Some 47 percent of all European companies in the Global 500 have signed onto the GC. Though, it is important to note that only 4 percent of similar US companies have signed on. And with dramatically less representation in the Global 500, 50 percent of the Indian Global 500 and 65 percent of the Brazilian Global 500 participate in the GC.

Second, we expose the very different levels of participation across sectors at the bottom of Figure 8.1. These levels do, in no way correspond with their relative sectoral contribution to world GDP. The case of mining is instructive: while mining constitutes about 4 percent of all participants, it constitutes less than one-tenth of 1 percent of world GDP. Similarly, the fact that more than 30 percent of all mining firms in the Global 500 participate in the GC and 50 percent participate in the GRI reveals comparatively strong levels of support within this sector for CR activities. In contrast, only 15 percent of the participants of the Global 500 participants in the GC are drawn from the banking sector. And finally is the variation (by region and sectors) between the different types of initiatives. That is, while here we cast these different multistakeholder initiatives as single cluster of CR activity, the participants clearly vary across these initiatives. Quite clearly, ISO certifications have the largest non-European/non-American representation. But the relative proportion of GRI participants in Asia, Africa, and Latin America is also markedly larger than GC participation.

The character of this geographic variation if further evidenced in Table 8.1 where the participation of four emerging economies (Brazil, India, South Africa, and Thailand) in the GC and the GRI are compared to both economies of similar GDP/capita and economies of similar national GDP. The table simply arrays the number of small or medium firms and the number of Global 500 firms from each of these countries that participate. In the case of the GRI it is the total number of firms of any size participating. The table also provides data on GDP/capita and total GDP to provide information on the size and general well-being of the economy. This table reinforces the simple but critical point, that it would be a mistake to view CR as a Northern or Western, elite global model of business–society relations. Brazil, India, South Africa, and Thailand alike fair relatively well when compared to Northern countries with a similar GDP. Indeed, in certain cases they do considerably better. Both Brazil and Thailand have more SMEs participating in the GC than does Germany. And both South Africa and Thailand's exceeds that of the Netherlands. Corporate responsibility is not a policy of purely wealthy economies.

The implication we derive from this heuristic review is that the patterning of CR may well not be as core driven as extant models of global change might imply. These patterns are further complicated by the obvious regional, national, and industry level variations detailed in Figure 8.1 and Table 8.1. This variation is further dramatized by firm-level comparisons of CR policy and mission as self-described on company websites in 2004. Consider for example, the statements from the largest oil/energy or mining companies in Brazil, India, South Africa, and Thailand.[10]

The resilience of a philanthropic model, wherein the firm funds cause it to be identified as worthy, remains prevalent in India.

Bharat Petroleum continues its endeavors in meeting social obligations to the under privileged sections of the society through development of roads, schools, clinics and vocational training centres in rural areas. Cataract camps for villagers, vocational classes to make the rural women self-reliant, development of rural women and children, providing sanitation and drinking water in the villages, are just a few of the many contributions made by Bharat Petroleum to meet its social responsibilities (www.bharatpetroleum.com, February 1, 2005).

Table 8.1. International standard participation in emerging markets compared

Country	GDP/ Capita	#SMEs in Global Compact	#Global 500 Companies in Compact	#GRI Participants	Country	GDP	#SMEs in Global Compact	#Global 500 Companies in Compact	#GRI Participants
India	$2,900	9	2	5	India	$3,033,000,000,000	9	2	5
Honduras	$2,600	0	0	0	Germany	$2,271,000,000,000	5	12	28
Georgia	$2,500	0	0	0	United Kingdom	$1,666,000,000,000	17	15	68
Nicaragua	$2,300	0	0	0	France	$1,661,000,000,000	139	23	28
Serbia and Montenegro	$2,200	0	0	0	Italy	$1,550,000,000,000	16	6	14
Thailand	$7,400	4	0	3	Thailand	$477,500,000,000	4	0	3
Romania	$7,000	1	0	0	Netherlands	$461,400,000,000	1	1	25
Turkey	$6,700	31	0	0	Turkey	$458,200,000,000	31	0	0
Bosnia and Herzegovina	$6,100	0	0	0	Poland	$427,100,000,000	3	0	1
Mexico	$9,000	0	0	3	Belgium	$299,100,000,000	2	1	4
Brazil	$7,600	53	1	6	Brazil	$1,375,000,000,000	53	1	6
Romania	$7,000	1	0	0	Germany	$2,271,000,000,000	5	12	28
Turkey	$6,700	31	0	0	United Kingdom	$1,666,000,000,000	17	15	68
Bosnia and Herzegovina	$6,100	0	0	0	France	$1,661,000,000,000	139	23	28
Mexico	$9,000	0	0	3	Italy	$1,550,000,000,000	16	6	14
South Africa	$10,700	3	0	26	South Africa	$456,700,000,000	3	0	26
Croatia	$10,600	0	0	2	Netherlands	$461,400,000,000	1	1	25
Latvia	$10,200	7	0	0	Turkey	$458,200,000,000	31	0	0
Poland	$11,100	3	0	1	Poland	$427,100,000,000	3	0	1
Lithuania	$11,400	1	0	0	Belgium	$299,100,000,000	2	1	4

But there is variation even among large, global oil companies in India. India Oil, which was the first company to sign onto the GC defines its obligations to the community in terms of significantly more than resources in its threefold mission statement:

To develop techno-economically viable and environment-friendly products for the benefit of the people. To encourage progressive indigenous manufacture of products and materials so as to substitute imports. To ensure safety in operations and highest standards of environment protection in its manufacturing plants and townships by taking suitable and effective measures (www.iocl.com February 1, 2005).

The Brazilian firm Petrobras adopts a similar approach:

Petrobras is a company committed to Sustainable Development. When it interacts with the environment and uses its natural resources, the company is aware that it should render accounts to society on the impact of its operations on the biosphere, and contribute towards a better quality of life for the population. Accordingly, the company has enormous socio-environmental responsibility and invests in programs that not only defend environmental preservation but also encourage the development of ecological awareness within the communities.

Some policy visions are profoundly vague and invoke a general set of long-accepted social goals. This lack of specificity is clear in the language of PTT in Thailand.

Social safety and environment, public and community are of great concern of PTT. We also value the treasure of natural resources and aim at conservation for the benefit of our next generation. Furthermore, we also promote efficient energy utilization to achieve sustainable development.

And yet, when compared to the responsibility statement of the US-based retail firm, Walmart, that of PTT appears detailed. Walmart simply states, 'We're committed to the communities we serve. We live here too, and we believe good, works' (www.walmartstores.com February 1, 2005). And while not much more detailed, at least Exxon fully embraces the rhetoric of CR: 'We believe that good corporate responsibility means helping to meet the world's growing demand for energy in an economically, environmentally and socially responsible manner' (www.exxon.com February 1, 2005). Thus, while an explicit, public rejection of CR is hard to imagine, companies quite clearly differ on the extent to which CR is core to their espoused mission or actual implementation efforts. Moreover, they quite selectively support and/ or neglect particular dimensions of CR.

We found one of the most explicit notions of CR in mining companies of South Africa. We see here a clear articulation of cooperative, mutually reinforcing business–society relations. (In Section 8.4, we will attribute this clarity to a combination of South African postapartheid politics and shifts in industry strategies.) Note also that we see in this very small sample of South African mining firms a more explicit organizational structure for CR: they have direct links from their web homepage to their CR policy. To put this in perspective: only 10 percent of firms provide such direct access in a stratified sample of more than 25 percent of the current Global 500. AngloGold makes clear both a form of engagement and specific initiatives:

AngloGold is committed to fulfilling its obligations and duties as a responsible corporate citizen, ensuring that its behaviour reflects a genuine concern for its stakeholders, including shareholders, employees, their families and the communities and environments in which we live and work. AngloGold aims to operate workplaces that are safe and healthy, to ensure that the environments in which we work remain ecologically sound and sustainable, and to ensure that the communities in which we operate derive real social and economic benefits from our presence.

AngloGold's areas of focus in the field of corporate responsibility encompasses ethics and good governance, occupational health and safety, including HIV/Aids, labour practices, environmental matters and community relationships.

Harmony Gold Mining has a similarly explicit mission, but here the links and references to both the particular influences in the South African national context and international convention are unmistakable.

Harmony has gone beyond just mining by giving back to our communities and caring for our environment. We understand the different sustainability challenges facing us and have designed our strategies and operative systems in such a way that we maintain compliance as we achieve our targets. Harmony's inclusion as a member of the JSE's Socially responsible Investment Index (SRI), which was launched on 19 May 2004, has made us proud. Everyone within Harmony is committed to sustainable development. This commitment is illustrated by the board's decision renaming the Safety, Health, and Environmental Audit committee the Sustainable Development Committee (SDC) of the board.... By providing you with our Sustainability report, we trust that our progress in achieving best practice in nonfinancial risk management is demonstrated. We believe that we have gone beyond compliance and aim to become one of the leaders in sustainable development...We have decided to use a more common language and set of indicators that can be applied by stakeholders in discussing our performance. We have also taken cognizance of the recommendations made by the independent auditors involved in the JSE SRI process. The Global Reporting Initiative's Guidelines (GRI) proved to be a useful tool in enabling us to measure and benchmark our performance both against our own targets and those of our competitors. This will be our first attempt at applying the GRI guidelines.

If this rhetoric is to be taken on face value, for Hamony Gold, CR is both an idea that increasingly organizes both their goals and the manner in which they achieve these goals.

8.4. TWO CASES OF CR: BANKING IN BRAZIL AND MINING IN SOUTH AFRICA

Case studies of banking in Brazil and mining in South Africa provide key insight into the global rise of CR. Both tell the story of contestation. But if one were to inductively generate a set of arguments about CR based on these cases, one is apt to generate two fairly different if not contradictory explanations. Not only does CR emerge from a confluence of different dynamics, CR is itself differentially framed and enacted in each of these country-sector examples.

The CR dynamic of South African mining is a reactive one about avoiding state intervention and rebuilding reputation. It is about social mobilization, direct action, and political opportunities. In each case the role of individual actors, NGOs, firms, the sector, the state, and global organizations played very different roles. Given the historical role of mining in Apartheid South Africa, and the lead mining has taken in proactively renegotiating business–society relations in post-Apartheid South Africa more broadly, issues of Black Economic Empowerment (BEE) and environmental sustainability are core elements of CR. But while BEE is also prominent in the South African banking sector, the latter does not pay attention to environmental stewardship issues. Not surprisingly, South African banks do poorly on CR and sustainability indices.

In contrast, the CR dynamic of Brazilian banking is a proactive one about reputation maintenance and stakeholder engagement. It is about individual action and sector-driven change. With banks taking the lead, issues of governance, accountability, philanthropy, cross-sectoral partnerships, and socially responsible lending have been the core of Brazil's CR repertoire. Historically, the banking sector has played a critical role in the development of CR across Brazil. And the industrywide promotion of social balance sheets is increasingly a transnational model of accountability (Nadas May 8, 2002). Three factors account for this importance.

The first and perhaps most important factor is the nature of the industry and its transnational character. Banking is by definition a multinational industry with clear global standards for foreign capital, etc. Moreover, with 175 banks operating in Brazil (and 93 in Sao Paulo alone), it is the clear financial center of Latin America. Adherence to exogenous standards and norms is then necessarily measure of Brazilian success. The transnational or multinational character of banking also means that it is the more likely object of transnational social mobilization and contestation. Brazilian civil society organizations and NGOs have clear and long-term external partners making their scrutiny and demands more consequential.

The second factor is the unusual significance of banking to the daily life of many Brazilians. Periodic financial crises and the pursuant rise in interest rates, escalation of inflation and currency devaluations have been routine in the past several decades. Banks' role as a buffer against these fluctuations has been unavoidable. And third and related, the banks have close ties to the public sector. Indeed, two of the largest five Brazilian banks are state owned.

Against this backdrop, banking was one of the first industries in Brazil to consider its role as a corporate citizen (ABAMEC April 9, 2002). In contrast to other industries that have only recently but aggressively begun to consider CR (Mello 1999; Oliviero and Simmons 2003) issues of responsibility and have been central to banking since the past three decades. In the early 1970s, The Association for Analysts of Brazilian Banks and Capital Markets (ABAMEC) was founded to respond to a clear crisis in Brazilian capital markets over run by speculation. Its objective was to raise professional and ethical standards and increase transparency through the provision of industrywide education. Today ABAMEC supports the broader proliferation of CR by actively promoting codes of ethics and multistakeholder partnerships.

The initiative of ABAMEC is supported by the banking's key trade association the Brazilian Federation of Banks (FEBRABAN). This organization was founded in 1966 but still a critical industry association with more than 90 percent of Brazilian banks participating. In 2004, the first three of FEBRABAN's core values were: (*a*) to value people; (*b*) to promote ethical, moral, and legal values; and (*c*) to stimulate the practice of citizenship and social responsibility. It also published the industrywide social balance sheet. Corporate responsibility in banking is also supported today by broader business associations including the Ethos Institute—a consortium of business leaders representing 25 percent of Brazil's current GDP founded in 1998. Ethos provides support for firm-based efforts through the production of support materials and management tools. They also conduct research on CR dynamics in Brazil and actively promote the GC initiative. Both the cultural influence of Catholicism as a set of ethical and moral values about community and philanthropy and the social dynamics attendant to recent democratization and marketization are important enablers of the CR in Brazil.

But across this common landscape we identify three different models of CR based on ownership structure and the underlying set of priorities these structures represent. First are firms owned by shareholders. Here CR is closely aligned to business strategy. Accountable to shareholders (and often foreign shareholders) means CR is more directly tied logically to financial success. Bank of Boston's attempt to almost double their customer base in 2002, for example, was facilitated by the social investment program, *Projecto 21*. Realizing the untapped potential of the ABC barrios in Sao Paulo Bank of Boston reached out to the community by providing a lifetime of education for twenty-one black children in the area. In doing so, the banks community efforts are simultaneously a way to promote the institution and expand banking services.

At ABN Real (the product of a 1998 merger) the motto 'Bank of Value' (ABN Real December 18, 2002) has a dual meaning—both capital and moral values. A balance between financial, social, and environmental welfare is key. A separate division of the bank promotes this vision through micro credit programs for the working poor, environmental certification for their clients, promoting and supporting volunteerism throughout Brazil, providing educational assistance for employees, and promoting diversity in the workplace. At ABN Real financial success is linked to the overall well-being of Brazilian society: 'The bank will not do well unless the country does well . . . We can't do well in a society that goes bad . . .' (Fabio Barbosa, President, December 18, 2002). These objectives and the policies that support them have a measurable impact on Brazilian society. But they are quite clearly strategically motivated.

Within the second model (family-owned firms), CR is an opportunity to reflect on highly personalized family values and priorities. Founding visions are much more influential on the form CR takes. The case of Bradesco—a leading family-owned bank in Brazil is instructive. The biography of Aquiar—the firm's founder—is the core of their CR mission. Aquiar came from as poor rural community in the state of Sao Paulo and this personal connection to the Brazilian underclass prompted him to establish Fundacao Brandesco. The primary objective of this foundation is social investment in education and today is the largest private donor to Brazilian education. For the foundation, 'Sustainability is the enabling of people to have the ability to assert their citizenship and see the limits of their environment so they can change it' (Bradesco Foundation September 19, 2002).

The priorities of Unibanco could not be more different yet here too the bank emphasizes social investment and reflect the founding vision. At Unibanco, CR has taken the form of investment in Brazilian high culture (funding museums, literary magazines, and the national cinema) and supporting the environment (funding small water clean up projects, reforestation initiatives, etc.) More recently, they have moved to provide a more comprehensive program of social responsibility with a five-part plan to promote culture, ecology, education, health, and volunteer work. Interestingly, CR activities at Unibanco that extend beyond social investment are strictly seen in terms of a business strategy. So, for example, Unibanco was the very first brokerage firm in the world to offer environmental reports to its analysts. But their principal objective in doing so was to garner new clients. What is most striking, however, is despite the profit motive, it is only when CR is integrated with business strategy that Unibanco moves away from the paternalism of philanthropy to more of a multistakeholder form.

State-owned firms in Brazil represent the third ownership structure. As state institutions their CR strategies reflect a different set of priorities. The objectives here ostensibly reflect national level needs and goals. Corporate responsibility then takes the form of national infrastructural investments and efforts aimed at stabilizing the economy. Banco do Brasil provides an example of state-owned firm. Corporate responsibility here was originally about social investments in the areas of poverty and illiteracy but also in response to broader trends and initiatives in the industry they too have begun to focus on issues of transparency and corporate governance.

The BNDES, a state-owned economic research and financial lending institution, epitomizes this form. It also reflects the statist development strategy prevalent during the 1950s, 1960s, and 1970s in Brazil. For BNDES, poor education and inequality plague the Brazilian economy and inhibit development. Thus the eradication of gross inequality and the provision of quality education have been the historical centerpiece of their CR mission. This vision broadened considerably in the 1990s as BNDES began providing financial and credit ratings that considered social responsibility. They have also begun to explicitly link corporate accountability and government accountability (BNDES September 23, 2002).

The importance of ownership type in Brazilian banking reveals an explanation of CR that turns alternatively upon a charismatic and a structural dynamics. The values and background of individuals together with the dynamics of transnational politics and industry concerns generate a particular conceptualization of business–society relations. It is an understanding of CR not made intelligible by one factor alone. The case of CR in South African mining firms offers a very different account of CR dynamics but one where structures and agents again play interconnected and interactive roles.

When asked why the JSE would boldly launch a sustainability index to rate and rank their companies, Nickie Newton King, the lead attorney for JSE explained that '[i]t is the right thing to do and it is something *I can do. It was just in me*'. 'Corporate South Africa', she continued, has a sustainable vision, Newton King understood her own push for this index as but a one initiative supporting an emergent understanding of how financial markets *should* work in South Africa and in the world more broadly. She went on to explain, 'I don't throw rocks. But *this* I can do' (King October 28, 2004).

The JSE index was not purely a product of individual initiative. This index represented yet another manifestation of the more than decade long mobilization of individuals, NGOs, labor, and the state to transform post-Apartheid economy and society. It also reinforced the twin imperatives of global reintegration of South Africa and South African industry. Modeled but moving beyond similar indices in Europe, the JSE socially responsible investing index was the first of its kind on the developing world. Not only would a new South African state be particularly attendant to frontier global norms and standards so too would South African firms be looking for external financing and support. Thus, the JSE index also reflects the important interrelated dynamics driving CR in South Africa.

These multiple, transnationally interacting drivers are further illuminated through the case of mining in South Africa. Here we see two dynamics: the role of external concerns for CR in general and the sustainability of mining in particular and the South African state and civil society's concerns for racial equality (Fig 2005; Lund-Thomsen 2005). Together these dynamics illustrate how the contested transnational structuration of CR is particularistically adapted to national-sectoral settings.

South Africa's unparalleled mineral and metal resources mean that the mining industry both historically and today plays an unusually important role in society. Mining was critical to both South Africa's economic modernization and its political development throughout the twentieth century. While mining only constituted about 12 percent of GDP between 1950 and 1990 (Hamann 2004) the industry employed a massive labor force and represented a disproportionate share of exports. This prominent role necessarily implicated the mining industry in the political oppression of colonial and apartheid governments. Indeed, the 2003 report of the Truth and Reconciliation Commission attributes the design and vision of apartheid not to the state but the mining industry itself (TRC 2003: 150). Moreover, it is clear that many mining companies 'knowingly propped up the apartheid state and made huge profits by doing so'.[11] It is within this context that some mining companies have long been involved in CR-like activities. Philanthropic efforts were historically an important tool to assuage the worst excesses of the apartheid regime, to help quell the social upheaval in the townships and to fend off the international sanctions campaign of the 1980s.

But the constitutional mandate in South Africa to 'heal the divisions of the past and establish a society based on democratic values, social justice and fundamental human rights'[12] means that new CR initiatives contrast both with the discretionary paternalism of classical philanthropy and the voluntarism of most contemporary notions of CR. The Mine Health and Safety Act of 1996, the Labor Relations Act of 1997, and the Employment Equity Act of

1998 together changed the contours of employment law and workplace standards in South Africa. Basic health and safety standards, policies of nondiscrimination, and fair labor practice became the norms. The National Environmental Management Act of 1998 further changed the context of South African mining by mandating environmentally sustainable practices and promoting industrywide multistakeholder initiatives.

This law was followed by the 2002 Mineral and Petroleum Resources Development Act which vested all mining rights with the state and required mining companies to reapply for mining permits. Permit preference was given to enterprises with significant Black ownership and that could demonstrate due diligence in social and environmental matters. And finally, the Black Economic Empowerment Act (BEE) promoting Black employment and ownership across industries was passed in 2003. Each of these state initiatives shaped the context within which South African mines operate dictating not only a clear commitment to a set of general principles of CR but also specific commitments to the environment and the eradication of historical racial inequalities.

The mining industry in South Africa has become a leader in CR. High-impact industries score better than either low- or medium-impact firms in terms of not just social and environmental sustainability but also in terms of CR and economic sustainability. As one prominent Black mining industry leader said, 'we have no choice, I tell my external counterparts that if there is no BEE, there is no CSR, and there is no mining industry in South Africa.'[13] This fact signals both the critical importance of the state in shaping CR but also how entering CR through one domestic requirement of an industry— BEE, for example—is often linked to other external ones such as the commitment to environmental sustainability, potentially leading to complex transnationally structured combinations of CR.

There are, to be sure, diverse skeptics and critics of CR in the South African mining industry.[14] Left elements of the labor movement still wonder whether the growing discourse of South African CR will deliver much concrete change for the health and safety of workers. Mid-level mine managers worry that the CR initiatives generated by headquarters are out of line with their daily needs and objectives. And community representatives still agitate for state sanctions (or even nationalization) for mining houses that are proactively empowering the blacks. Each constituency has different perceptions of CR—its objectives, potential, and effects. This is how CR is contested at the local and national levels. But this is also how CR is contested transnationally as these very arguments are offered in testimony to the global multistakeholder Mineral, Mining and Sustainable Development Initiative or the World Bank's Extractive Industry Review or the Mining CEO meetings at the World Business Council on Sustainable Development.

In sum, what these two cases reveal is that CR is not likely to emerge from a single set of factors but from different sets of transnationally interacting drivers. Even in the cases of mining in South Africa and banking in Brazil the ambivalence of CR is clear. Elsewhere, the future of CR is perhaps even murkier. A dramatic shift, for example, to a serious CR commitment in the Chinese manufacturing sector or even in much US manufacturing in the short term is probably quite low. More importantly, why these two manufacturing sectors currently eschew CR or what might make them embrace CR are due perhaps to two very different confluences of factors.

8.5. TRAJECTORIES OF SOCIAL CHANGE: PROSPECTS FOR CORPORATE RESPONSIBILITY

Understanding CR as shaped by contested transnational structuration enables us to link an analysis of postregulatory public policy that consists of novel and emergent forms of governance (voluntary standards, learning fora, transparency regimes, performance management frameworks, etc.) to an evolving set of firm policies and practices. Within the transnational field of CR each of these models is operative and represents competing discourses and organizational forms. Rhetorically, there are good (modern) firms and bad (classical) firms but in practice there is much more structuration, much more variation in form. Moreover, and as we have detailed, even where a shared corporate vision exists there is much disagreement about the best strategy to attain this goal.

Within the field of CR, within competing transnational, cross-sectoral professional networks of states agents, activists, managers, and citizens there are divergent arguments about how to promote responsible behaviors. Some advocate voluntary forms of social responsibility. Others advocate accountability regimes. Still others prefer the hegemonic model of the past and present—state regulation of the command-and-control form. The only difference between the ostensibly progressive advocates of state regulation (like CorpWatch) and their conservative counterparts (like Exxon) is the level of this intervention should take—they fully agree that CR whether voluntarily enacted or socially (rather than governmentally) induced is not only wrong, but worth challenging.

We might nonetheless conclude by suggesting that the emergent social field of CR represents, in fact, a dominant set of transnational state–market–society organizational dynamics. We could take, as the literature on CR so often does, an eclectic set of practices, as evidence of a coherent (or almost coherent) whole. Yes, it is increasingly difficult to imagine a firm that flaunts its socially 'irresponsible' behavior. Yes, it is increasingly difficult to find communities of executives, activist, scholars, or citizens anywhere who understand 'irresponsibility' to be a social good. (But of course, they never really did—responsibility was just defined differently.) And yes, it is increasingly difficulty to find a firm that does not adopt at least some token policies of social responsibility addressing a fairly standardized if not quite scripted set of issues from poverty to workers rights to environmental respect. From these observations we might assert the emergence of a new worldwide normative corporate organizational form—the socially responsible firm. And indeed, we anticipate that, under certain conditions, this might one day be the case.[15]

But today, we do not see this coherence. And to prematurely ascribe such coherence, as many analysts and activists increasingly do, we eschew an important intellectual opportunity to understand how and why organizational forms and the ideas and values that undergird them actually gain coherence. So, for us, while there is lots of talk of CR we do not yet live in a world where the good corporation and the good corporation alone dominates. Corporate responsibility is still as much of a question as it is a corporate form. And local variations are not just benign permutations of universally held ideals. Indeed, we have tried to illustrate that in the contemporary period the very meaning of CR lies in its daily practice, its daily variations, its constant ambiguities, and recurrent debates. Take the example of corporate policies to redress inequality. That the phenomenon social scientists call poverty is inextricably linked to different historical experiences in Sao Paulo and Johannesburg *is* highly significant for whatever CR is or will become in Brazil and South Africa. To analytically parse poverty in Brazil from the chronic instability of its currency on international markets or poverty in South Africa from a history of racial inequality would be obviously inane. These differences are important because if you happen to be 'poor' in Brazil your daily-lived experience is very different than were you to be 'poor' in South Africa.[16] And it is this lived experience from which collective identity and collective action are derived and thus where the local understandings and local policies of CR are necessarily and differentially rooted. Perhaps it is then why CR develops first in banking in Brazil and in mining in South Africa. It is perhaps also why a philanthropic model of CR dominates in Brazil and why a socially responsible investment model of CR dominates in South Africa.

If we offer a theory of social practice and change that is so abstract, alien, or unintelligible to those who actually participate in it than perhaps our *theory* is incomplete (Martin 2003). In this context (and indeed in these contexts) CR is neither *just* 'doing well by doing good' nor *just* an international (UN or

World Bank) vision of market–society relations in a post-welfare/developmental state world. Part of the story must also be Aquiar whose Catholic childhood as part of the Brazilian underclass led him to understand a human being's personal (moral) commitments in a particular way—a way that Bradesco's profitability, international activists, and the UN each supported, redirected and altered in very different ways. To extract Aquiar's experience—his narrative as an agent of change in the Brazilian landscape—and attribute his CR mission to purely firm, state, or global structures may well miss an element of the explanation. This relationship—between Aquiar, Bradesco, Instituto Ethos, Brazil, etc.—is, we argue, the essence of transnational structuration. Necessarily then we have offered less of a cogent theory to explain CR and instead we present a framework of transnationalism to make the lived experience of CR intelligible—intelligible today, next week, next year, and next century.

NOTES

1. This chapter is equally conceived and jointly written. We acknowledge generous support provided by the Hauser Center for Non-Profit Organizations and David Rockefeller Center for Latin American Studies. We also express special thanks to Christin Hokenstad and Ralph Hamann for research assistance.
2. See Blowfield and Frynas (2005). We employ the specific terminology of CR (in lieu of say CSR) as a general umbrella term to capture a variety of approaches to business–society relations. These include more voluntary forms of business responsibility as well as accountability models. Corporate responsibility itself is an open-ended and essentially contested concept (see Baron 1999). Here we inductively derive a working notion of CR as a highly variegated and often contentious set of practices that are associated with the rights and responsibilities of firms. We define CR as a set of practices (including discourses as practices) to highlight its conceptual ambiguity.
3. There is too, of course, considerable skepticism on the part of many groups in civil society who see this inherent contradiction and the resulting irony (or perversion) of firms providing social goods. See, for example, CorpWatch or Matten, Crane and Chapple (2003).
4. See Newell's 'Citizenship, Accountability and Community: The Limits of the CSR Agenda' (2005) for a much more sanguine view of CR and its potential.
5. For some important exceptions see: Baron (2001); Jones (1999); Swanson (1999).
6. See Finnemore and Sikkink (1998).
7. See Meyer, et al. (1997*a*, 1997*b*).
8. See Beckfield (2003) for a discussion of power relations and inequality inherent in transnational social relations.

9. While the concept of transnational social fields has been employed to understand an array of contemporary it is perhaps most widely deployed in recent analyses of migration (see Nina Glick-Schiller and Georges E. Fouron. 1999. 'Terrains of Blood and Nation: Haitian Transnational Social Fields.' *Ethnic and Racial Studies* 22: 340–66. See also Khagram (2004) for an application of transnational field notion to the dynamics of development.

10. See also, Maignan and Ralston (2002) for an examination of corporate websites in Europe and the United States and how they represent different conceptualizations and operationalizations of CR.

11. Nelville Gabrielle in *Business Day* November 12, 2002: 2.

12. 1996 Republic of South Africa Constitution, Act No. 108, p. 3.

13. Vincent Maphai, BHP Billiton, January 2005.

14. See Fig (2005) and Lund-Thomsen for two fairly sanguine discussions of CR in South Africa.

15. Of course, we would not expect this normative convergence around an ideal model of the corporation would lead to standardization in CR policy or form. Local variations in style and strategy would necessarily continue.

16. See Scott (1991).

9

The Spread of a 'Human Resources' Culture: Institutional Individualism and the Rise of Personal Development Training

Xiaowei Luo

In an era of increasing globalization, human resources have been considered as the ultimate competitive advantage for corporations (Pfeffer 1994), fostering the rapid spread of a new model of human resources training centered on personal development (Monahan, Meyer, and Scott 1994). Actual and perceived globalization has played an important part in the rise and diffusion of this new 'human resources' culture. First, globalized production is deemed capable of diminishing regional advantages in material resources, therefore positioning human resources as the only sustainable competitive advantage (Barney 1997). Second, with economic globalization and the rise of the world society (Meyer et al. 1997a, 1997b), notions of proper statehood and individual agency spread worldwide, facilitating the rapid diffusion of business and management models such as the 'human resources' culture.

Increasingly, human resources training has been elevated from a 'cost function' to a 'profit center' (Bassi, Gallagher, and Schroer 1996) for organizations. Even more importantly, the dominant philosophy underlying human resource training has shifted from fitting individuals to specific job tasks toward encouraging personal development. This new model of human resources training has demonstrated the following key characteristics: (*a*) training is about developing individuals to be active social and organizational participants so that they can contribute to the overall success of organizations; (*b*) the content of training is much broader than specific job-related skills, encompassing a wide range of knowledge and skills for professional and personal growth; (*c*) employees from the top to the bottom of organizations are all seen as in need of continuous learning; and (*d*) organizations make a network of training courses and programs accessible and encourage (but not require) employees to engage in continuous development (Monahan, Meyer, and Scott 1994; Noe 2005).

While the idea of training employees for their particular job tasks is century old, this new approach to training is fundamentally different and has been driven by completely different notions of the individual and the organization. In this chapter, I present the historical rise of the new model of human resources training, and argue that it has largely been shaped by institutional cultures promoting individualism and corporate citizenship. Under an organizational model where individuals are expected to play an enlarged and empowered role and organizations are expected to shoulder a broad range of social responsibilities, organizations tend to follow the logic of appropriateness and provide expanded and continuous training, and in particular personal development-oriented training. In addition, I propose that the global spread of the institutional culture around individual agency in particular has fueled the diffusion of the new model of human resources training around the world, and present some empirical evidence. In the worldwide diffusion of this new model, the globalized consulting industry and international organizations are important carriers of the changed notions about individuals and human resources training. Finally, if institutional individualism is the driving force behind the new model, countries that vary along such a dimension should exhibit differences in the influence of the new model. I discuss national variation in organizations' adoption of the new model of human resources training. The demonstrated link between institutional individualism and commitment to the new model of human resource training suggests that as institutional individualism characterizes more and more countries with increasing globalization, the new model of human resource training will become even more widespread and influential.

9.1. THE HISTORICAL RISE OF THE NEW MODEL OF HUMAN RESOURCES TRAINING

A historical survey of training in organizations in the United States reveals how much these practices have changed over time. For a long time after industrialization in the latter half of the nineteenth century, formal training programs were not considered necessary. Technical skills were acquired through the apprenticeship tradition and vocational education. Further specialization and the rise of scientific management at the beginning of the twentieth century for the first time initiated formal training within organizations in the form of specific technical skill instruction (Miller 1987). However, during the 1910s, only a few big companies invested in formal training for some entry-level workers. For example, less than 10 percent of the workers in Ford actually participated in these training programs, as most of the jobs were considered simple enough to be learned on the job (Li 1928). At the founding of the Personnel Research Federation, the federation president said (1921), 'the only purpose of a training program should be to teach the exact knowledge and methods which the employee will use on his particular job or the job just ahead of him' (Sweet 1938: 109).

The emergency demands for production during World War I stimulated the expansion of specific-technical training. During the interwar years, training for supervisors on how to handle workers became increasingly important. Between 1940 and 1945, again confronted with emergency production during World War II, the US government set up the 'Training Within Industry' program, providing both intensive specific-technical training and human relations training to boost morale. In 1945, Kurt Lewin initiated the Training Laboratory in Group Development. Several years later, the Human Relations Research Group was founded at University of California in Los Angeles. Throughout the 1950s and 1960s, these two centers became the engine for 'sensitivity training', a quintessential program of human relations skills training. Training of managers became an accepted practice within organizations during this period.

The post-World War II period witnessed rapid adoption of formal training programs. In a 1962 Department of Labor (DOL) survey of 9,600 establishments, about 20 percent sponsored or provided some type of formal training. In the 1998 survey of employer-provided training conducted by the Bureau of Labor Statistics (Frazis et al. 1998), 92.5 percent of organizations provided formal training.

Moreover, in this period there was an emergence of what I call 'personal development training', defined as programs aimed at improving cognitive and behavioral skills in dealing with oneself and others. Such training is intended to develop personal potential and is thus not immediately related to the technical aspects of one's job tasks (Luo 2002). Personal development training was first given to executives and managers as part of executive/management development programs. Since the 1970s, there has been a sharp increase in the kinds of personal development training offered, with employees from more levels included (Eurich 1985). The 1989 Training Survey reported that more money was spent on building interpersonal skills than technical skills (*Training*, 1989 Industry Report). In a 1997 survey of 315 corporations conducted by the Conference Board, 92 percent regarded leadership development, one type of personal development training, as among the most important types of training, whereas only 80 percent of them regarded technical skills as one of the most important (Hackett 1997).[1] Monahan, Meyer, and Scott (1994) describe the spread of personal development training programs based on their survey and interviews with more than 100 organizations in Northern California. Training programs became more elaborate; they incorporated, in addition to technical training for workers and human relations training for supervisors and managers, a widening array of developmental, personal growth, and self-management courses. Courses of this nature include office professionalism, time management, individual contributor programs, intrapreneuring, transacting with people, applying intelligence in the workplace, career management, and structured problem solving. Courses are also offered on health and personal well-being, including safe diets, exercise, mental health, injury prevention, holiday health, stress, and nutrition (Monahan, Meyer, and Scott 1994: 261–2).

To further examine changes in training practices, I conducted a content analysis of training articles from *Personnel Journal*, one of the oldest among the major journals in personnel field and one of the most frequently read journals for training practitioners. The journal is oriented toward practitioners, and reflects and encourages training practice. Selecting all the training-related articles in the even-numbered years from *Personnel Journal* between 1928 and 1996 (published monthly),[2] I coded the types of training described. A total of 639 articles were obtained. I present the over-time trends in the percentages of articles in the following training categories: (*a*) specific-technical; (*b*) general-technical; (*c*) human relations; and (*d*) personal development (Figure 9.1).[3] There is a sharp decline in the proportion of articles on specific-technical and human relations training over time and a rapid increase in articles on personal development training. When specific-technical and general-technical training are combined into the category of technical training, there is still a decline in the focus on such training and the emphasis on personal development training still exceeds that on technical training in recent decades. This confirms a shifting focus in human resources training over time and the rise of the personal development model of training.

What has driven the rise of the new model of human resources training? Instrumental explanations, such as the human capital and technology-based perspectives (Becker 1962; Kochan and Osterman 1991; Katz and Keefe 1993; MacDuffie and Kochan 1995; Cappelli et al. 1997), tend to focus on the increasingly complicated nature of work and the resultant need for skills in organizations. While this process is certainly going on, I propose that the perceived need for certain types of training (such as personal development training) is not only technically shaped but also constructed by the shared understandings about the individual and the organization. Building on an institutional framework (Meyer and Rowan 1977; Scott 1995), I propose that

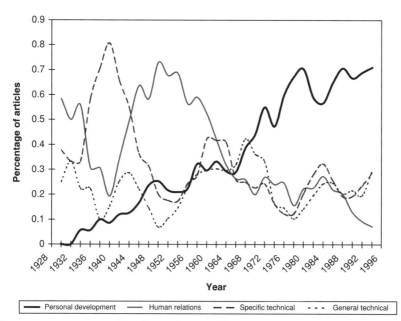

Figure 9.1 Percentages of articles on four types of training, *Personnel Journal*, 1928–96

changes in both an individuals' organizational role and an organizations' societal role drove the diffusion of training *and* especially the shift in the focus of training. These changes were reflected in the evolution of the dominant organizational models promoted by management experts and practiced by organizations. Research has documented how these organizational models spread across national boundaries (e.g. Guillén 1994). Globalization has shaped the recent organizational models by shaping the perception of organizational problems and solutions to such problems. Furthermore, globalization has facilitated the worldwide diffusion of such models. As an important aspect of organizational behavior and an enactment of the relationship between individual employees and the organization, training has been powerfully shaped by these fundamental organizational models over time.

Based on previous organization theories (Perrow 1986; Barley and Kunda 1992; Guillén 1994; Scott 1998), I abstract two core historical changes in organizational models: (*a*) individuals play an increasingly enlarged role in organizations and (*b*) organizations take on broader social roles over time. These changes have been brought out by broad societal changes. For example, the increasing educational level of individuals, growing knowledge about engineering, human psychology, and management science, globalization, institutionalized notion of actorhood (Frank, Meyer, and Miyahara 1995), as well as industrialization and post-industrialization with increasingly complex and changeable technologies all played a part in shaping expectations about the role of individuals in an organization. Meanwhile, with globalized production and consumption, organizations have increasingly invoked a citizen's role under the pressure of the civil society, state, and collaborative efforts across national boundaries through waves of labor movements, social movements, and state intervention in constructing social responsibilities for organizations. Today's organizations are required or expected to demonstrate commitment to environmental protection (including environment in developing countries), community well-being, amelioration of social problems such as poverty and discrimination, and employee development. Rankings of socially responsible corporations publicize the 'good' as well as the 'bad' guys, affecting support from important stakeholders.

As employees are increasingly perceived as empowered players, organizations are more likely to view investment in individuals through training as worthwhile and to develop individuals to be well-rounded contributing members. At the beginning of the twentieth century, the prevailing picture of average workers presented them as adjuncts of machines, coarse, unclean, unreliable, and prone to drunkenness (Commons et al. 1921). As such, workers were expected to follow exact procedures for simplified job tasks, with training focusing almost exclusively on specific-technical skills. In the first handbook for training, Greene (1937) laid down two principles for organized training: (*a*) technical skill deficiencies or business situations must be known in advance and training is devised to meet them *specifically* and (*b*) the results of training should be *immediate* and in some cases can be measured in economic returns.

As workers came to be viewed as human beings with affect and morale (Mayo 1945; McGregor 1960; Bernard 1968), the prevailing logic became 'the happier workers were more productive'. As a result, human relations training for supervisors, such as how to handle grievances, became valued. Further, as individuals were thought of as thinking and choosing actors, embodying professional expertise and capable of rational and creative behavior (Meyer 1992; Pfeffer 1994), solutions to organizational problems were likely to be regarded as located in individuals. Thus, training for such personal development objectives as creative thinking and leadership became perceived as useful tools.

In addition to this evolving understanding of individual roles and agency, the increasingly broad social responsibilities expected of organizations also facilitate the provision of personal development training. When the goal of an organization was exclusively technical improvement and profit maximization, nontechnical training was likely to be considered irrelevant by organizations.

However, when the 'citizenship role' of organizations was emphasized, organizations were more likely to expand the judgment of value beyond direct contributions to technical goals or economic bottom line. The logic of appropriateness (i.e. appropriate for its citizen identity) became a more salient guiding framework when providing training. Given that personal development training is a type of general-skill training believed to enhance employees' future employability, organizations were likely to perceive such training as fulfilling their responsibilities for employee development and career security, and therefore provide such training. Similarly, employees had more opportunities to claim organizational resources to develop their personal potential.

The growing importance of management gurus and management consulting industry since the 1970s also played an important role in the spread of personal development training. These experts helped internal management interpret problems (such as changes in technology and market competition) and formulate solutions. They helped push a variety of movements such as organizational reengineering, quality circle, total quality management, quality of work life, and learning organization. Despite their faddish nature, these movements strengthened and enlarged individuals' (including workers) and organizations' roles, often manifested in the broadening content of personal development training. This influence on training was both indirect through changes in organizational cultures and direct through the involvement of management consultants in the design and delivery of personal development training programs.

In recent decades, the American Society of Training and Development (founded in 1944), among other professional organizations, actively spreads success models through publications, conferences, train-the-trainer sessions, and consulting services. It periodically conducts benchmarking exercises of human resource and training practices for what it considers to be high-performance organizations, and recommends other organizations to benchmark their own. Personal development training programs, as a marker of the success models, have spread across boundaries of industry and resources.

9.2. GLOBAL SPREAD OF THE NEW MODEL OF HUMAN RESOURCES TRAINING

The rapid growth in human resources training has been described as a 'silent explosion' toward the end of the twentieth century. It is estimated that engagement in adult education or training activities has grown such that more than half of the entire adult population of some countries was active over the course of a calendar year in the 1990s (Belanger and Tuijnman 1997). Adult education and human resource development are now part of the official positions of the United Nations Educational, Scientific and Cultural Organization (UNESCO 1995) and the Organisation for Economic Co-operation and Development (OECD 1996).

Both academic and policy discussions have identified the knowledge-intensive economy, globalization, technological change, and increasing educational levels as the driving forces behind the training expansion (Carnevale, Gainer, and Villet 1990; Ferman et al. 1990; Cappelli et al. 1997). I propose that expanded training results from the diagnosis of these challenges based on a changed understanding of the individual's role. Common to analysts in many countries, and also shared with international organizations, such as the OECD (1996), the International Labour Organization (ILO 1996), the European Commission (EC 1993), and the World Bank (Belanger and Tuijnman 1997: 7), this understanding can be expressed as follows: 'If we are to survive, develop and compete, the most critical resource is our people's talent and energy' (Belanger and Tuijnman 1997: 7). The diagnosis enacts the increasingly institutionalized notion of empowered actorhood. Without a presumed enlarged organizational role for individuals, such a diagnosis would have been meaningless.

Frank, Meyer, and Miyahara (1995) note that history has seen '[t]he rise and legitimation of models of society in which the individual is seen as a central constitutive element: the sovereign source of public life ... and the source of problems in these areas; the proper beneficiary of political, economic, social, and cultural life; and the primordial or grounding element of all of social structure' (360). Indeed, what they call 'institutionalized individualism' has spread worldwide with globalization. Jepperson (2002*b*) documents how European integration has lessened the distance between political systems based alternatively on corporate orders and direct individual participation. For example, Sweden, traditionally built upon corporate elements, has increasingly become an individual-based liberal society since the 1960s. Inglehart and Baker (2000) also note the value shift in similar directions around the world in the modern period.

Figure 9.2 presents the degree of institutionalized individualism in the EU countries (see the measurement of this concept later). While the EU countries still vary in the individual's role, in the majority of these countries individuals are expected to play an enlarged and empowered role. As I have argued earlier, this changed institutional logic about the individual's role largely shifted the philosophy underlying human resources training.

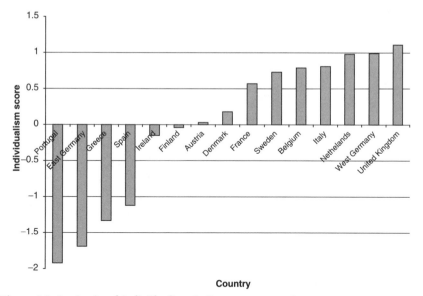

Figure 9.2 Institutional individualism in European countries

I describe later instances of training expansion in various countries. Governments have been encouraging more training within industry to meet social and economic policy objectives through legislation, training tax and government-sponsored training organizations and programs. For example, in the United Kingdom, the Industrial Training Act was passed in 1964, leading to the establishment of many Industrial Training Boards that have pressed for more training in firms in various industries. In France, training tax started to be levied on firms with more than ten employees in 1971. Initially the tax rate was 0.8 percent of the total wage bill; it rose to 1.2 percent in 1988 and 1.4 percent in 1994.[4] The Singapore government set up the Skills Development Fund in 1979 with a levy on firms' expenses on employee wages in order to induce more training investment by firms (Yuen and Yeo 1995). In 1990, Australia adopted a similar training tax, called the Training Guarantee. All enterprises with a payroll greater than A$200,000 must spend 1.5 percent of their payroll on training (Shelton 1995). In New Zealand, the government passed the Industry Training Act in 1992 to partially fund and stimulate training (Geare and Stablein 1995). The Swedish government stepped up expenditures on training programs. Approximately 0.46 percent of GDP in Sweden was spent on government-sponsored training in 1990. Although the US government spent only 0.09 percent of GDP in sponsoring training programs in the same year, it exerted its impact mostly by promoting various

discourses such as 'lifelong learning' and 'employability' to encourage training in the decentralized system.

In 1993, nearly 60 percent of enterprises employing ten or more people in
Europe offered some form of employee training, with more than three
quarters of all enterprises providing training in Denmark, Germany, the
United Kingdom, and Ireland (EC 1994).

The form of 'corporate university' as a centralized training function for
organizations has spread to Europe through international consultants and the
activities of American multinational firms. The now popular label of 'university'
for training function suggests the legitimacy of this function within organizations. There are now some 1,600 corporate universities in America, four times as
many as a decade ago. The practice is also increasingly popular in Europe. For
example, 'Anglian Water has a University of Water; Unipart, a British car-parts
company, has a place that likes to be known as the "U" ' (*The Economist* 1999: 78).

In addition to giving rise to more training in general, the global spread of the
notion of empowered actorhood has also led organizations in many countries
to engage increasingly in personal development training. International training organizations, American consultants, and multinational firms have played
an important role in spreading conjointly the notion of empowered individuals and personal development training. For example, the International Federation of Training and Development Organizations, founded in 1973 at the
initiative of the American Training and Development Society, currently has
more than fifty members all over the world. Its conferences and publications
advocate for more employee training, many of which specifically promote
personal development training and employability enhancement. The organization also provides 'train-the-trainer' sessions to guide training professionals
about the logistics and content of employee training. In recent years, the Asian
Productivity Organization has provided multicountry training courses,
seminars, and study missions that reflect a growing emphasis on personal
development. For instance, the *1996 Annual Report of Asian Productivity
Organization* includes seminars on 'Managing Organizational Change',
'Organizational Effectiveness', and 'Quality of Working Life'.

Here are examples of how organizations in various countries have broadened training content from a focus on job-specific skills to include training
of general skills and development of personal potential.

In Canada, the Bank of Montreal opened its Institute of Learning in 1994,
complementing existing training centers in Montreal and Calgary. The goal of
this Institute is to 'provide a forum for creativity and a source of innovative ideas
that can be disseminated across the organization' (http: //www.magmacom.
com/~mdwyer/CanPost.htm, n.p.). The bank is also restructuring its overall
training efforts so that the focus of training will be shifted 'to give them

[employees] responsibilities for their own learning' (n.p). The Canada Trust Management Institute has also emphasized courses that impart in employees how to deal with change and foster teamwork, according to its Assistance Vice President, Laurie Main (n.p. the same as earlier).

According to a study of management development by the National Board of Employment, Education and Training (NBEET) in Australia, the areas of greatest managerial deficiency were identified as 'entrepreneurship, developing subordinates, bias to action, creativity and vision' (NBEET 1990: 13). More organizations have started to engage in training in these areas. Nevertheless, currently, only 10 percent of the time is allocated for such training, whereas about 40 percent of the time is allocated for management training in functional areas (23).

Germany has been known for its strength in apprentice training. However, its curriculum for apprentice training came under attack in the 1980s. The reformists came to agreement in 1987 and formally proposed for a general emphasis in such training programs.

For most European countries, more firms offer training courses, which are conducted in classrooms away from work settings, than they offer training in work situation (EC 1994). Although the training content can be very diverse, classroom training is very likely to train more general skills than on-the-job training.

In Hong Kong, a study describes the history of employee training there as follows: 'whereas technical training has been taken care of for some time, supervisory and management training and development did not get off the ground until the 1980s' (Poon 1995: 107). A large-scale survey identified five serious management and supervisory problems: (*a*) poor communication; (*b*) insufficient knowledge of management techniques; (*c*) high turnover rate; (*d*) lack of motivation; and (*e*) poor caliber (Committee on Management and Supervisory Training of the Hong Kong Training Council 1980). As a result, the Hong Kong Management Development Centre (MDC) was established in 1984 to tackle these problems.

Employee training in China has focused on technical skills and political consciousness since the Communist government took over in 1949. The ideal employee (worker as well as manager) was to be an expert in his or her technical field and politically loyal. Since the economic reform and the 'Open Door' policy in the 1980s, desired competencies of individuals have incorporated attributes associated with strong actorhood, and American models have begun to influence employee training practices. For example, in the performance appraisal of the Xiamen Arts and Crafts Co., 'initiative' was listed as a factor of evaluation for both managers and nonmanagerial staff, in addition to 'discipline, coordination, responsiveness, and responsibility';

'innovation' was listed for managers (but not for nonmanagerial staff); 'judgment, expression, and negotiation' were listed for both (Liao 1991).

The history of management education and training in China is most indicative of the substantive changes detailed previously. After 1949, management education was modeled after the Soviet Union. During the Cultural Revolution between 1966 and 1976, it was totaly abolished. Since 1978, it has been resumed. Until 1991, there had been nine key universities that offered MBA programs. In recent years, Western management concepts, such as the 'Total Quality Circle' and 'Management by Objective', are widely discussed. In conducting executive training programs, China has also received help from European Economic Community (EEC) countries, Japan, Canada, the United States, and Hong Kong, as well as from professional associations and international consulting firms. Hundreds of management books and scores of management journals or magazines have been published in China since 1985 (Nyaw 1995).

The Asia Pacific Management Institute is one of the channels through which American training models affect employee training in China. Established in 1997, it is a joint venture of the American Management Association, CIMIC Group and East China University of Science and Technology. It promotes the ideas that 'today good management has no longer a nationality', and 'forward-thinking corporations should draw on a common fund of management knowledge' (from its 1998 Catalog of Seminars, n.p.). In 1997, it ran 40 programs attended by nearly 1,200 executives from foreign and Chinese companies. Many of these programs focus on the 'soft side' of management such as time management, project management, teamwork, leadership, communications, presentation, and negotiation.

In Thailand, big companies have started to hire prestigious American consultants to build their management training including personal development programs. For example, Siam Cement, one of Thailand's premier corporations, has utilized faculty from American business programs, such as UC-Berkeley Business School, Northwestern's Kellogg, and the Wharton School of Business, to conduct management development programs in Thailand (Lawler and Atmiyanandana 1995).

9.3. CROSS-NATIONAL VARIATION IN THE NEW MODEL OF HUMAN RESOURCES TRAINING

While the world has in general become more likely to develop and train human resources and to develop them in a particular way (i.e. through personal development training), countries still differ in the extent they have adopted this new model. If, indeed, the globalized notion of enlarged role for individuals is driving the diffusion of the new model of human resources training, we would expect that the new model is likely to take a stronger hold in countries where institutional cultures particularly embrace enlarged roles for individuals.

Nation-states have historically differed in how they organize authority and society (Jepperson and Meyer 1991; Jepperson 2002*b*). Such national scripts contain fundamental *expectations* of an individual's role: whether an individual should be an empowered well-rounded participant, or an individual is primarily supposed to conform and carry out duties. These expectations are shared by the state, employers or organizations, and individuals alike, and are reflected and reinforced through concrete social arrangements. In countries characterized with strong institutionalized individualism (Frank, Meyer, and Miyahara 1995), where individuals are expected to play an empowered role, organizations tend to be more decentralized with shorter hierarchy and less bureaucratic control. Evidence on national differences in organizational structure supports such a linkage (Brossard and Maurice 1974; Hofstede 1980; Laurent 1983).

In countries characterized with strong institutionalized individualism, individuals are considered to be the proper beneficiaries of social policies and arrangements. Thus, seeking personal fulfillment is not only culturally appropriate but also encouraged. Cross-national studies report that people in individualistic cultures are more likely to desire self-fulfillment and to give priority to their personal goals rather than collective goals (Triandis 1995). Therefore, people within such cultures tend to view this new model of training as legitimately instrumental to achieving personal goals and hence desire training more. Furthermore, since individuals rather than groups are considered as legitimate and important participants in all arenas of social life, individuals are expected to be highly committed and capable of contributing to the public agenda. Frank, Meyer, and Miyahara (1995) find strong association between countries with strong institutionalized individualism and the development of psychology, a discipline with individuals as the focus of study.

Given that individuals are expected to play an empowered and enlarged role by state authorities and employers alike and that comparatively they *are* given such a role, massive and continuous development and training of human resources are likely to be regarded as desirable. In contrast, in countries characterized with low institutional individualism, individuals are less likely to be driven by their personal goals, or to be expected as the locus of decision-making and source of rational action. Hence, people are less likely to desire this new model of training as the skills learned cannot be fully utilized (see the example of German auto plants in MacDuffie and Kochan 1995).

With regard to the content of training, an institutional culture of strong individualism should particularly encourage personal development and de-emphasize job-specific training. Given that individuals are expected to be empowered and well-rounded contributors, they value initiative and creativity, and strive to tap into their full personal potential. Studies of entrepreneurship find that people in individualistic countries tend to value creativity more than those in collectivist countries (e.g. Tiessen 1997). Therefore, people in individualistic countries are more likely to prefer the kind of training that will enable them to play the empowered and enlarged role, i.e. personal development training.

In contrast, people in countries with low institutional individualism are more concerned with fulfilling requirements and duties from the collective. Chan et al. (1996) suggest that collectivist cultures tend to be more 'tight' than individualistic cultures in that there are more rules and stronger expectations for individuals to follow group rules. Bond and Smith (1996) show that there is stronger emphasis on norms and conformity in collectivist cultures. As a result, people can be expected to desire improved fit and functional competence in their organizations, and hence are more likely to prefer job-specific training.

Moreover, since job mobility is much higher in individualistic cultures than collectivist cultures (Triandis 1995), employees in individualistic countries tend to perceive less gain from firm-specific occupational training, while people in collectivist countries perceive less gain from general development training.

Empirical studies of cross-national differences in training have emphasized the cost of training provision as the major reason for differences in training practices (Lynch 1994). I propose instead that the national institutional culture can shed light on the varying adoption of the new model of human resources training. For example, recent studies find the well-known apprenticeship training in Germany (a country low on institutional individualism) produced excellent functional specialists rather than multiskilled generalists (MacDuffie and Kochan 1995). Studies also report a lack of personal development training such as communication and general cognitive skills in German firms (Berg 1994; MacDuffie and Kochan 1995). South Korean business groups emphasize loyalty, dedication, and fitting employees into firms' specific corporate cultures. While they have incorporated American training goals and content, they still exhibit marks of their collectivist national culture. For example, the motto of the Daewoo Group is 'creativity, challenge, and *self-sacrifice*' (Koch, Nam, and Steers 1995: 228; emphasis added by the author). While one of its training objectives is 'to foster adaptability to meet changes' (Daewoo Corporation 1991), only management training is meant to pursue such a goal. The strong internal hierarchy leads to huge differences between management training and the training of industrial workers. The latter is primarily concerned with 'improving job-related skills and correcting attitudes towards the company' (Koch, Nam, and Steers 1995: 231).

I conducted a cross-national analysis of the impact of national institutional individualism on human resources training using data from *Eurobarometer 44.0: Cancer, Education Issues, and the Single European Currency, October–November 1995* (Reif and Marlier 1998). I consider people's attitudes toward this new model of human resources training as reflecting such training practices in those countries. Eurobarometer is a long-standing high-quality public opinion survey conducted on behalf of the EC in all member states of European Union since 1973. This particular survey is so far the most detailed cross-national survey on training attitudes. In this analysis, institutional individualism of a country is measured by a factor score created out of democratic institutions, Hofstede's individualism index, welfare expenditure as percentage of GDP, membership in international psychological associations, and total number of psychology publications,[5] following prior research (Hofstede 1980; Frank, Meyer, and Miyahara 1995).

The results show that people's attitudes toward this new model of training (called 'continuous training' or 'lifelong learning' in this survey) are significantly affected by the institutional culture of their country over and above the influence of their personal attributes, and that institutional individualism provides better explanation for national variation in training attitudes than socioeconomic conditions and training and education levels of the country. Specifically, people from countries with high institutional individualism (the United Kingdom, Ireland, France, Norway, Portugal, Spain, Belgium, and Italy) desire continuous training more than those from countries with low individualism (Austria, Denmark, Finland, East Germany, West Germany, Greece, Luxemburg, and Sweden). Furthermore, to the extent people desire such training, those from countries with strong individualism tend to focus on personal development while those from countries with low individualism tend to emphasize job-specific training.

While revealing how nation-states differ in people's commitment to the new model of human resource training, the cross-national analysis suggests that institutional individualism plays an important role in producing both desire for continuous training and preference for personal development training. Given the rise of the institutional individualism around the world in the midst of increasing globalization, we expect that the new model of human resource training will take an even stronger hold across countries.

In conclusion, this chapter presents the historical rise of a new model in organizational training practices focused on the continuous development of personal potential of human resources. This new model has largely been shaped by notions regarding individual empowerment and organizational citizenship, which have in turn been driven by the increasing globalization. With such ideas spreading around the globe under the influence of economic globalization, American management models, international organizations, and consultants, the new model of human resources training has also diffused cross-nationally. Given that nation-states still vary in their domestic institutional cultures, countries characterized by strong institutional individualism are generally more amenable to the influence of the personal development model of training. An important prediction from this study is that as organizations around the globe become more penetrated by the notion of individual empowerment over time, this new model of human resources training will become part and parcel of the organizing principles of organizations.

NOTES

1. Respondents of this survey are allowed to consider more than one type of training to be the most important.
2. Data collection stopped in 1996 because since 1997 the journal has changed its name to *Workforce*. In order not to introduce any bias, I examined articles with the same journal name.
3. Specific-technical training emphasizes skills that are immediately related to the technical aspects of specific job tasks. Examples are specific new equipment training and product knowledge. General-technical training focuses on technical knowledge or skills that are useful across a wide range of job categories such as PC application, finance, and quality control. Human relations training emphasizes how people can get along with one another such as employee morale, grievance handling, and labor relation. Personal development training aims at improving one's cognitive and behavioral skills in dealing with self and others. Some examples are communication skills, time management, leadership, and creativity training. While human relations training emphasizes cooperation for the sake of cooperation and good employee morale (Guillén 1994), personal development training emphasizes how one can attain productive work through strategically dealing with self and others (Eurich 1985).
4. If a firm is not able to document training expenses greater than 1.4 percent of its wage bill, it must pay the difference between actual training expenditures and 1.4 percent of the wage bill.
5. Based on prior studies, I collected ten indicators of the individual's role in national political and cultural institutions. I conducted an exploratory factor analysis of all these indicators. Five of the ten indicators load above 0.70 onto the first extracted factor, and therefore I use these five indicators and construct a factor score to measure institutionalized individualism.

10

Turning the University into an Organizational Actor

Georg Krücken and Frank Meier

Universities worldwide have gone through a variety of changes over the last half-century. From the offspring of institutes for learning and teaching in higher education in the late 1960s to the current emphasis on e-learning, methodological and systematic approaches to academic teaching have more and more replaced the belief in the natural teaching abilities of university professors. Educating university students has come to be seen as something that can be taught like physics or languages, and the individual style and aura of the professor gives way to a more sober and rationalized image of academic teachers. Likewise, the societal conception of academic research has undergone profound transformations. Academic research is no longer seen as a natural source of wealth and progress, which unidirectionally and in a quasi-evolutionary way leads to technological development and commercial applications. Instead, rational societal planning, deliberate innovation policies, and active networking of individual researchers are now seen as essential for connecting academic research to its socioeconomic environments.

Both global trends have attracted much scholarly and political debate, highlighting the nature and the risks and benefits related to the rationalizing of teaching and research. In this chapter, we want to discuss a third general trend in higher education, which is closely related to the first two. 'Turning the university into an organizational actor', as we label this process, is here conceptualized as one of the many facets of the overall tendency toward organizational actorhood in the current era of globalization. By the term 'organizational actor' we try to evoke the image of an integrated, goal-oriented entity that is deliberately choosing its own actions and that can thus be held responsible for what it does. Organizational actorhood, then, is closely tied to institutional management and leadership. The 'organizational turn' in higher education is by no means a trivial process as universities traditionally were not conceived as important decision-making entities in their own rights. Caught between the academic profession and the state, there was not much legitimate space for institutional management. We suppose that this is going to change due to globalization processes, which, on the one hand, speed up observation and imitation processes and, on the other hand, foster the transformation of universities into organizational actors, which are able to act strategically and position themselves with regard to their competitors.

Mutual observation and imitation processes already took place among different national *systems* in the nineteenth and, especially, at the beginning of the twentieth century. However, a global horizon for comparison and competition among *individual* universities has only recently been established by global rankings, the proliferation of transnational degrees like MBAs, and the perception of a global market for higher education. Processes of observation and imitation foster the rapid diffusion of a generalized script for organizational actorhood, which cross-cut national and organizational boundaries.

Imitation is often connected to the active construction of a trendsetter whose allegedly superior practices are seen as worth taking into account. In our case the reference to the United States is obvious. Many contemporary trends discussed in this chapter can be traced back to American universities and early discussions on academic leadership and institutional management in the United States. Likewise, the United States is an important point of reference within international organizations, which actively promote the essentials of what it means to be a modern university organization. It is quite ironic, though, that in the 1960s, when concepts of higher education management began to diffuse on a global scale, American scholars and practitioners began to doubt the strength of leadership in American universities (see Section 1). Therefore, although American universities have effectively served as role models in the construction of universities as organizational actors, such models may have little to do with organizational realities. Indeed, the American university as the embodiment of central features of organizational actorhood is best understood as a powerful myth in current higher education discourse worldwide.

The diffusion of a globalized model of the university is not only driven by construction and observation processes *within* the sector of higher education. Nowadays, firms, hospitals, public administration agencies, and universities are conceptualized first and foremost as *organizations*, having typical *organizational* problems and being in need for efficient *organizational* solutions.[1] The number of organizations that may be selected as a role model therefore expands rapidly (Meyer 1994: 43–5; see also Strang and Meyer 1993). And exactly in this sense, universities are turned into 'real organizations',[2] to which solutions from other contexts may be successfully applied. Though it is typically claimed that these solutions should be cautiously adapted to universities and their peculiarities, the idea that the university is more or less an organization like any other stands in striking contrast to earlier, prevailing ideas about the university. Just over forty years ago, for example, Millett (1962: 4) matter of factly argued: 'I believe that ideas drawn from business and public administration have only very limited applicability to colleges and universities'. Through the successful diffusion of a generalized concept of 'the organization', whose abstract principles flow across different contexts, universities enact contemporary scripts about what it requires to be a modern organization.

Our foray into the new world of universities' organizational actorhood will start by briefly referring to traditional concepts in comparative and organizational research, which stress the role of national university systems and the uniqueness of universities as a specific type of organization (Section 1). Against this backdrop the shape of what we see as an emerging organizational model of the university becomes clearer, in which hitherto unquestioned boundaries between national systems and types of organizations are becoming blurred. Based on contemporary higher education research and discourse, we will discuss four main elements of the new, globalizing university model (Section 2): organizational accountability, mainly through the establishment of evaluation procedures; the tendency toward defining 'own' organizational goals through mission statements, in which the organizational self is created and openly displayed to others; the ongoing elaboration and expansion of formal technical structures around these goals; and the transformation of university management into a profession. These elements weaken traditional forms of control and solidarities central to universities. At the end of our chapter we will briefly discuss the consequences of the diffusion of the new, globalizing model of university actorhood. As it is re-embedded within specific national and organizational contexts, we strongly suggest that there will be heterogeneous outcomes (Section 3).

10.1. UNIVERSITY GOVERNANCE: THE DOMINANCE OF NATIONAL MODELS AND ORGANIZATIONAL SPECIFICITIES IN HIGHER EDUCATION RESEARCH

From their very beginning universities incorporated many aspects of what nowadays are seen as strong indicators for processes of globalization (Altbach 2004)—an international body of members, both students and professors; a common language, Latin; and the ideal of universal knowledge. The university, in fact, seems to be *the* inherently globalized institution. But universities displayed a strong local orientation ever since, and not only in the high period of the nation-state did universities mainly evolve in national settings, shaped by culturally different taken-for-granted assumptions of what it means to be a university. Therefore, historians and sociologists typically speak of the dominance of national models in the field of higher education.[3]

With the foundation of the University of Bologna in 1088, universities are undoubtedly among the oldest formal organizations.[4] However, as university organizations traditionally relied on internal control by the professoriate and external control by the state, the organizational level was of minor importance. In this respect, universities were seen as 'specific organizations' (Musselin 2004*a*).

In recent years, the traditional forms of university governance are under pressure. There is a considerable loss of confidence in the capacities for self-governance of the academic community. At the same time, strong state regulation has become subject to a fundamental ideological critique, in higher education as in other domains. Thus, on a worldwide scale, one can witness a common trend in university systems based on very different national traditions. Universities are being transformed, with a new emphasis on the organizational level as an important and independent level of decision-making. Strong institutional management is now considered a key component of university governance (Braun and Merrien 1999; Rhoades and Sporn 2002).

In this process, two hitherto unquestioned features of the universities are challenged: the uniqueness of the national university system and the uniqueness of the university as a specific type of organization. As this contradicts decades of research on universities in the social sciences, we will briefly remind our readers of some of that research in order to highlight the conceptual changes involved in the new model of university governance.

International comparative research on higher education has shown clearly how national university systems differed in their forms of governance. Especially Burton Clark's seminal work (1983), which locates national systems within a triangle of market, state authority, and academic oligarchy, made these differences obvious. Four countries seemed to be of particular importance when it comes to delineating distinct and influential, not to say archetypical, university systems: Germany, France, Great Britain, and the United States. We will briefly discuss each of them.[5]

According to this conceptual framework, the traditional German model was an example of a system based on strong state authority and an equally strong academic oligarchy. There was hardly any room and legitimacy for the organization as an independent decision-making actor. Of course, in universities collegial bodies produced collective decisions. Due to formal restrictions and the practice of mutual noninterference,[6] the university was nevertheless conceptualized as a community of professors. The German full professor, traditionally, was an autonomous 'prince' who could legitimately refuse attempts at 'top down' governance within the organization. This picture gradually changed with the advent of the 'group university' in the 1970s, which implied the inclusion of hitherto marginal actors (students, academic and nonacademic staff) into collective decision-making processes. However, critical observers noted a tendency toward nondecisions and immobility (Schimank 2001). The 'university as an organizational actor', in other words, was still to come.

The French model was even further away from a model in which intra-university governance was fostered.[7] In a comparison between the German and the French system, Musselin (1999) has shown that in the French case there was hardly any organizational backbone within universities. Correspondingly, university professors did not identify with their organization, and the state focused on disciplinary, but not on organizational boundaries when it came to regulating universities. As Musselin sums up: 'Nowhere was a university considered as an entity' (1999: 45).

Even in university systems in which the state had a much weaker position vis-à-vis universities, the university was typically not conceived as an organizational actor in itself. This was the case in Great Britain, where faculty guilds dominated and collective decision-making was emphasized. As this system 'has placed strong authority at the bottom' (Clark 1983: 128), universities were subject only to a limited degree of centralized administrative power and accountability.

At first glance, the United States seemed to be very different, as the situation here was dominated by the market as the key form of governance. As Clark (1983) points out, this market orientation stood in sharp contrast to the European approach. Indeed, this difference had been noted as early as 1905 when Henry S. Pritchett observed that 'the American university has tended more and more to conform in its administration to the methods of the business corporation' (Pritchett 1905: 294) and that, moreover, the American university leader 'possesses an autocratic power which would not for a moment be tolerated in an European institution' (Pritchett 1905: 295). In Pritchett's view, the American university had 'the compactness and the directness of responsibility which the business corporation carries with it' (Pritchett 1905: 295).

It is not by accident that in such an environment, already in the 1960s there was rather extensive theorizing about the organizational characteristics of universities[8] and the role of leadership in university governance, both from practitioners and social scientists (see Millett 1962; Blau 1973). This kind of theorizing was literally absent in the European context of that time. Along with this literature came what Rourke and Brooks in 1966 called the 'Managerial Revolution in Higher Education',[9] i.e. a broad trend toward rationalization in American universities: 'From now on the government of these institutions will reflect a much more conscious effort to plan the course of their development, to relate means to ends, and to seek to obtain a maximum return from the university's resources' (Rourke and Brooks 1966: vii).

A closer look, however, shows that these theoretical reflections were hardly an indication of a full-fledged model of organizational actorhood then in operation in the United States. On the contrary, the community character of universities was stressed in much of the academic writing of that time (Goodman 1962; Millett 1962; see also Musselin 2004*a*). Lazarsfeld and Sieber (1964: 13) even diagnosed an 'academic power vacuum' and 'a dangerously low level of organizational development' at American universities. Also George Keller complained: 'Yet, one of the most significant developments in postwar academic life has been the progressive breakdown of governance and leadership' (Keller 1986: 27). Generally, there was a broad consensus among sociologists of that time that universities had to be seen as governed by the professoriate exercising professional control in the absence of levels of strong internal governance.[10] In addition, organizational researchers in the United States characterized educational organizations as 'loosely coupled systems' (Weick 1976). In a similar vein, Cohen, March, and Olsen (1972) and Cohen and March (1974) pointed to 'garbage can' decision-making processes and labeled universities 'organized anarchies'. These scholarly descriptions found their counterpart among practitioners. An allegedly powerful university president like Kerr depicted himself as a 'mediator' between different forces beyond his control (Kerr 2001: 27–9).[11] He went on to compare the university—which he labeled 'multiversity' in order to express what he saw as a loss of unity—to a 'pluralistic society with multiple cultures' and to the United Nations (see also Soo and Carson 2004).

To sum up, even American universities, with their stronger historical reliance on market-based mechanisms nonetheless were hardly seen as an exception to the rule that universities are unique organizations in large part because they were internally fragmented and centralized power was limited. In this, universities were said to strongly differ from the integrated and tightly coupled entities usually depicted in American organizational research, in particular in research on industrial firms (Chandler 1977; Perrow 2002). German, French, and British universities with their traditional reliance on state authority and/or academic oligarchy were even further away from a model, in which the organization is understood as an autonomous decision-maker.

10.2. THE NEW UNIVERSITY: FOUR ELEMENTS OF GLOBAL ORGANIZATIONAL ACTORHOOD

The picture painted so far might be overdrawn, and the heterogeneity *within* national systems has not been touched at all.[12] This backdrop, however, suffices to throw into relief the current, global transformation of universities. Following our analysis, four main and highly interrelated elements of the new, globalizing model of what it means to be a modern university can be distinguished. These four features document the transformation of universities into organizational actors.

10.2.1. Accountability

Accountability is the first central feature. The proliferation of quality assurance practices like evaluation (Brennan and Shah 2000; Geuna and Martin 2003) and accreditation (Schwarz and Westerheijden 2004) is the most salient indicator of the overall trend toward accountability. Transnational organizations like the OECD (1999), the World Bank (1994), the International Association of Universities[13] or the European University Association (2004) strongly advocate the idea of quality assurance and accountability. The so-called 'Message from Salamanca', for example, signed by more than 300 representatives of European universities and university associations, stated:

Progress requires that European universities be empowered to act in line with the guiding principle of autonomy with accountability. [...] Thus, universities must be able to shape their strategies, choose their priorities in teaching and research, allocate their resources, profile their curricula and set their criteria for the acceptance of professors and students (EUA 2001: 7).

In a similar vein, the World Declaration on Higher Education insisted that:

Higher education institutions must be given autonomy to manage their internal affairs, but with this autonomy must come clear and transparent accountability to the government, parliament, students and the wider society (World Conference on Higher Education 1998, Article 13b).

The growing importance of evaluations and accreditations is accompanied by the creation of specialized organizations and associations.[14] In submitting academic work to standardized techniques of counting and accounting, a broader societal trend toward what Power (1997) has called the 'audit society' seems to be reflected. In an audit society, in principle, all activities must be subject to scrutiny if they are to be regarded as legitimate.[15] Of course, from the advent of the research university, at the latest, the idea of organized skepticism and collective criticism has been at the heart of academic culture. But this is quite remote from today's 'audit university'. On the one hand, traditionally, the output of universities (i.e. knowledge and educated people) was seen as distinct from the output of other organizations, and though it could and should be subject to scrutiny, the formal measurement of knowledge and education seemed to create insurmountable problems. These problems are not solved yet, nevertheless formal measurements, e.g. based on bibliometric data, are rapidly diffusing into academia. As Weingart (2004: 119) puts it:

[O]ne can now witness internationally a dramatic shift from the well founded scepticism to an uncritical embrace of bibliometric numbers. This change of mind is not limited to policy makers and administrators but has taken hold of deans, department chairmen, university presidents and officials in funding agencies and research councils as well, i.e., of representatives of the scientific community that were most strongly opposed to external evaluation of research by any means.

On the other hand, the attribution of responsibility, which traditionally has been much more individualized, is now transformed into an organizational account. This implies that the university as an *organization* has—to use a formulation of Trow's (1996: 310)—'to explain, to justify, to answer questions' about its decisions, including its omissions and nondecisions. Blame can be attributed, and positive or negative sanctions can be enforced. In sum, outputs are seen as both measurable and as consequences of the organizational decisions of universities.

This overall trend toward organizational accountability is accompanied by three other developments, which indicate the transformation of universities into organizational actors.

10.2.2. The Definition of Goals

Universities must increasingly define their 'own' legitimate goals—as opposed to centrally imposed tasks or assigned societal functions. Nowadays one can easily get information on the 'missions' and 'visions' of higher education institutions from all over the world on their homepages. Though this mainly holds true for universities in OECD countries, one can also find sophisticated mission statements in developing countries. The web presentation of the University of Botswana, for example, can easily match with universities in European and North American countries. Even the key words used to describe the organizational self ('center of excellence', 'national and international orientation', 'public accountability', 'quality management', 'life long learning', 'interdisciplinarity', 'focus on innovation and entrepreneurship') do not differ much from those of the most prestigious higher education institutions in the developed world.[16] Many universities even place what they refer to as 'strategies' on their internet homepages, a decision which at first glance seems odd, since mission statements typically go hand in hand with references to increased global competition in higher education. Why should a university provide its competitors with documents on strategy, if they really guide the organization's decisions?

The answer to this question is twofold. In many cases, mission statements are deliberately designed in order to trigger organizational change by providing new opportunities for actors who might take such statements seriously and mobilize around them. But mission statements and 'strategies' are often also simply organizational window dressing, only loosely coupled to day-to-day decision-making. Insofar as this is the case, universities here provide an excellent example of what Meyer and Rowan (1977) have called the loose coupling between the formal structure and the activity structure of an organization, and one might also be reminded of Goffman's classical distinction between the frontstage and the backstage of an actor's behavior when reflecting upon such ostentatious display of strategies, mission statements, and the like. In the presentation of the organizational self the ingredients of such 'frontstage' statements are not randomly selected. Universities enact globally institutionalized scripts of what a higher education organization is expected to be.[17]

The very idea that a university is in need of a mission statement is based on generally available concepts in organizational management (here: 'management by objectives' or MBO), which aim at strengthening the link between the organization and its individual members in a way that goes far beyond traditions of professional and/or state control in higher education.

Several universities transform traditional and standard accounts of the activities that anchor the general institutional identity of a university (like 'research and teaching') into their 'own' and explicit mission. This might not add any information concerning the central activities of a particular university because conducting research and teaching is what a university is supposed to do. Nevertheless, this transformation confirms the idea that the university is an autonomous entity that deliberately chooses its own destiny and that is thus responsible for what it does. In some countries, missions statements assume additional tasks. In the United Kingdom, they serve as a benchmark for evaluation processes used to determine public funding (Mackay, Scott, and Smith 1995), and in Germany, mission statements are of major importance to the accreditation of private universities (Wissenschaftsrat 2004). In short, mission statements may be understood as part of the overall trend toward transforming universities into accountable decision-makers.

10.2.3. The Elaboration of Formal Structures

An additional element of the new, empowered university is the ongoing elaboration, expansion, and differentiation of a fine-grained formal organizational structure, which is centered on explicit organizational goals. Historically, universities expanded in large part through processes of internal differentiation. In this, 'higher education is a differentiating society par excellence' (Clark 1997: 24). These differentiation processes, however, were mainly due to the ongoing creating of academic disciplines and sub-disciplines, especially in the nineteenth century (see Stichweh 1984; Ben-David 1991). In contrast, more recently, one can observe strong differentiation processes in formal organizational structures. A contemporary university has offices for a variety of tasks, which previously were not regarded as part of the organization's responsibility. Very much like the actorhood of the modern nation-state, which depends on a broad, yet standardized set of ministries (Meyer et al. 1997*a*, 1997*b*), the modern university is equipped with offices and organizational subdivisions for international affairs, personnel development, controlling, gender issues, organizational development, and psychological counselling.

A good example of the trend toward the differentiation of the university's formal structures is the institutionalization of technology transfer offices. Begun around 1980, the establishment of such offices has been hailed as 'a watershed in the history of technology transfer in the universities in the United States and Europe' (Gibbons et al. 1994: 87). The direct transfer of knowledge and technology between academic researchers and industry has a long history. But with the creation of transfer offices what was previously regarded as an activity of the individual researcher, carried out in addition to his or her main tasks of teaching and research, is now an institutional mission of the university itself. Informal and personal ties between academic researchers and industry are now explicitly complemented by formal, organized links, while the responsibility for technology transfer shifted from the individual to the organization.

The institutionalization of transfer offices is embedded in a broader *rationalization discourse* on how to effectively utilize scientific knowledge, which began in the 1950s. Step by step, what was seen as an unpredictable evolutionary development, became viewed as a process following rules, which could be analyzed and actively shaped.[18] Transfer offices, furthermore, are embedded in a variety of other activities that are supposed to enhance the university's agency with respect to economic activities, a development that led higher education scholars to introduce new labels like 'the entrepreneurial university' (Clark 1998) or 'the enterprise university' (Marginson and Considine 2000). Technology transfer as an organized activity is sometimes contested on normative grounds, but the potential and actual revenues that technology transfer activities are supposed to generate for universities are usually taken for granted. Yet empirical research shows rather disenchanting results. A survey from the United Kingdom suggests that only a small number of universities are realizing considerable net income from the commercialization of intellectual property rights (Charles and Conway 2001). Despite the fact that American universities are usually seen as trendsetters in the technology transfer process, sharing their expertise with European and Asian universities through organizations like the Association of University Technology Managers (AUTM), links between transfer offices and university revenues in the United States are ambiguous at best (Siegel, Waldman, and Link 2003). More generally, an OECD (2002: 196) report concludes: 'It is unclear whether the returns from inventions that are licensed from the public sector justify the costs of patenting by PROs [Public Research Organizations]'.

What is clear, however, is the rise of *managerial agency* in these processes. In addition to organizational accountability, the definition of organization goals, and the creation of formal organizational structures around these goals, a fourth element of 'the university as an organizational actor' becomes obvious: the proliferation of management functions and the rise of management professionals.

10.2.4. The Rise of the Management Profession

With the development and diffusion of the management model the demands on the organization and its members increase. This tendency can be observed with regard to the academic profession: professors are nowadays more and more involved in a variety of rationalized administrative tasks beyond teaching and research, including personnel management, accounting, and quality control. More importantly, since it is assumed that only a professionalized staff will have the ability to successfully achieve stated management goals, professional management of the university is established in parallel with the formal statement of university goals. Whole new categories of professionals and related academic management positions are created. As Rhoades and Sporn (2002) have shown most convincingly for the United States, beginning in the 1970s a whole new set of managerial professions came into being, especially in the areas of quality control, entrepreneurial activities, and students' services. Such new managerial activities are far from being 'peripheral' to the 'central' activities of teaching and research. Rather, 'the "periphery" has become the center' (p. 24). Notably, between the 1970s and 1990s, the number of full-time managerial professionals 'doubl[ed] in size as the proportion of academics who are part-time double[d]' (26).

One indicator of this trend toward the professionalized management of universities is the emergence of specialized journals on higher education management like the *Journal of Higher Education Policy and Management*, *Tertiary Education and Management*, *Higher Education Management and Policy*, or *Planning for Higher Education*. Another—perhaps even more important—indicator is the establishment of academic programs and courses on higher education management.[19] Currently one can apply to courses in higher education management, for example, in Pittsburgh (the United States), Bath (the United Kingdom), Speyer (Germany), Armidale (Australia), or Bangkok (Thailand).

Nevertheless, if in the United States higher education administration is an established and well-developed academic field with a large number of academic programs, as Altbach and Engberg (2000: 15) observe, the degree of management professionalization varies profoundly across national systems. Many observers point to the fact that the professional training of higher education leaders is often poor, especially in developing and transitional countries (Teferra and Altbach 2004: 31). This complaint reveals the global diffusion and taken-for-grantedness of the idea itself. While it is hardly surprising that higher education management in many countries does not meet global standards, it is striking to see that global standards are applied to universities worldwide in spite of diverging conditions and traditions.[20] This of course provides strong evidence for the assumption that globalized concepts of the university are advocated beyond instrumental justification.

Examples of transnational activities in the area of higher education management are manifold. In 1969, the OECD set up a Programme on Institutional Management in Higher Education (IMHE). As early as 1964, the International Association of University Presidents (IAUP) was founded with the aim to 'support university Presidents, Rectors, Vice-Chancellors, and university leaders in general, in their strategic efforts to enhance the qualitative development of their institutions' (IAUP 2002: 4). In 1983, the Institute for University Management and Leadership (IGLU) was established in order to 'contribute to the training or professional development for university executives in Latin America and the Caribbean'.[21] And the Association of African Universities (AAU 2003: 12) is involved with 'training in higher education leadership and management'.

These examples indicate that, obviously, chairs, courses, and journals are not enough when it comes to advising universities about how to become empowered organizations. Numerous actors like supranational organizations, state authorities, expert commissions, evaluation and accreditation agencies offer their help. Thus, every university can know how to be or how to become a modern—i.e. accountable, goal-oriented, differentiated, and professional-ized—organizational actor.

10.3. WITHER NATIONAL AND ORGANIZATIONAL CHARACTERISTICS?

Undoubtedly, there is tremendous organizational growth within and around universities, both through internal differentiation as well as externally through the creation of organizations that accompany universities on their way to achieving full organizational actorhood. Though most observers and actors stress the expected gains in terms of rationality, critics point to the 'personnel, time, capital and opportunity costs' (Rhoades and Sporn 2002: 26) of the new management model.[22] But more generally, what consequences does the new, globalizing university model have?

Institutional patterns that diffuse globally, across national boundaries, do not lead to homogeneous outcomes.[23] The relationship between globally diffusing expectations, values, and structures on the one hand, and those expectations, values, and structures which are deeply embedded in the specific context of any national university system on the other, is a permanent source of conflicts and attracts criticism from both sides. While those opposing a global model typically criticize the imperialism of the 'sender' by invoking a distinct, worthy national heritage, those in favor criticize the resistance of the 'receiver' by emphasizing the benefits of a modern, rational university organ-ization, which follows universal rules.

Since the diffusion of models across national boundaries is open to inter-pretation and deviation, the assumed 'culture clash' between global and national university models is not necessarily the end of the story. As Badie (2000) has shown in his analysis of the worldwide diffusion of the Western model of the state, the universalization of its dominant principles remains incomplete ('universalisation manquée') because of creative deviation ('dévi-ance créatice') on the 'receiver'-side. Given the long history of universities, which were shaped by different national systems it can be assumed that there is a lot of creative deviation in the transformation of universities into organizational actors. Rather than the straightforward diffusion of a single model (or its rejection) we suppose that globalized features of universities as organizational actors are actively constructed in a variety of national settings, hence leading to very different realities.

In practice, adoption of a global model is more complex than a simple 'choice' between the new, global model and the former national one. Complete universalization typically fails, as elements of global and national models merge and give way to creative deviation from a given path. In this, we see a major, yet rather unexplored source of institutional innovation. Historically, the invention of the American research university is a good example (Geiger 1986). It came into being through the diffusion of the 'von Humboldt' ideal of the German university, which was the dominant global role model in the nineteenth century. This model was adapted and contextualized in a national setting, which was shaped by traditions very different from the German ones, i.e. the English college tradition and the strong American emphasis on the social embeddedness of higher education institutions. The related 'culture clash' resulted in what nowadays seems to be the dominant global role model.

But not only national contexts shape global diffusion processes. Universities are prime examples of organizations which routinely adapt to external expectations without necessarily transforming them directly into organizational change. The spread of global models of modern actorhood will certainly generate a great deal of loose coupling, ritual adaptation, and symbolic politics at the level of the individual institution. The pace and depth of organizational adaptation, however, will vary considerably. History matters, also for organizations. We assume that universities, which also in their past showed a high degree of openness toward their social environments will incorporate new institutional elements easier than those whose institutional history was mainly defined by concern with purity and a sense of elitism.[24] Former technical institutes and universities founded in an era of mass education, for example, will differ strongly from the proverbial 'ivory tower'. Taking the long history of universities into account as well as the specificities of particular national settings, it is obvious that enacting the common script of 'turning the university into an organizational actor' will produce very heterogeneous outcomes.

NOTES

1. With regard to expectations directed at universities as organizations it is worthwhile noting that the new management model has been heavily fueled by debates on organizations which only remotely resemble universities. Here one has to

think in particular of the debate on New Public Management (NPM), which took off in New Zealand (not a country being known for being a model country in higher education discourse either). Nowadays, in many OECD countries NPM lends the theoretical underpinnings to administrative reform. Under this label, very different organizations typically embedded in the public sector are advised to implement organizational structures and procedures, which mostly derive from business firms.

2. This term is borrowed from Brunsson and Sahlin-Andersson (2000). In their instructive paper the authors describe a trend of organizational reforms in the public sector aiming at introducing properties like identity, hierarchy, and rationality. Through this, public sector organizations become more akin to the organizations traditionally described in organizational theory.

3. See, for example, Clark (1983, 1995) and Rothblatt and Wittrock (1993).

4. Kerr (2001: 115) once estimated that more than 80 percent of the organizations over 500 years old are universities.

5. The national traditions of university governance reflect underlying polities that shape more general political structures. For a typology of European polities, see Jepperson (2002b).

6. For an early account on this, see Plessner (1924: 420).

7. For a comprehensive account of the history and sociology of French universities see Musselin (2004b). Here, also more recent developments are discussed. With the introduction of contracts between the ministry and individual universities in 1989, each university 'now develops its own policy, defines its own project, with the institution's actors collectively determining its particular directions and priorities' (Musselin 2004b: 89).

8. Though Gross in 1968 lamented that: 'Universities are usually not viewed as formal organizations' (Gross 1968: 518). But see the edited volumes by Baldridge (1971) or Perkins (1973) only a few years later.

9. Clark Kerr noted: 'The managerial revolution has been going on also in the university' (Kerr 2001: 22).

10. See Parsons and Platt (1973) for the theoretically most ambitious statement on this structural feature of what they called 'the American university'.

11. A few years later Kerr complained: 'I wish I had not used the word "mediator" ' (Kerr 2001: 107) because the term suggested a weaker position than he had intended. Kerr's ideal university president is an active figure, an 'initiator' and a 'gladiator' but still he is far from being in control of the diverging forces that are shaping the university.

12. In a current research project on technology transfer between universities and industry funded by the German Research Council (DFG Grant KR 2001) we try to explore the idea that national university systems are composed of a variety of different university types which cross-cut national boundaries. In the United States and Germany we identified three distinct types. Preliminary results show that the variation between these types is greater than the variation between the

two national systems, hence challenging the commonly held assumption that the national context is the strongest predictor when it comes to explaining variances in technology transfer.

13. http://www.unesco.org/iaup/p_statements/af_statement.html (June 1, 2005).

14. Following Hedmo, Sahlin-Andersson, and Wedlin (2005*a*, 2005*b*) this tendency seems to be most advanced in the field of management education.

15. Power himself (1997: 98–104) uses the British Research Assessment Exercise (RAE) as an example from the field of higher education.

16. See http://www.ub.bw/ (May 30, 2005).

17. Here one might also be reminded of Michel Foucault's analyses of the constitution of *individual* actors (see especially Foucault 1990: vol. 1). The related paradox that in becoming an actor one has to actively submit to standardizing societal forces reminds of the underlying concept of the constitution of actors— individuals, organizations, and nation-states—in neoinstitutional theory (see Meyer and Jepperson 2000). The similarities and differences between Foucauldian and neoinstitutional thinking, however, have not been much explored to date. But, for one attempt see Krücken (2002: 248–53).

18. Our own research has shown striking similarities between the United States and Germany, despite nationally specific historical traditions. See Krücken, Meier, and Müller (2005).

19. Note that there are obviously two complementary developments taking place: with the management of education comes the education of management (Moon and Wotipka, Chapter 5). While on the one hand the sphere of higher education is increasingly filled with professional managers, these managers are increasingly educated by specialized higher education programs. In the course of advanced modernity, science, the most important rationalizing force gets rationalized itself.

20. The advocacy of global standards is not limited to the question of management training. The Task Force on Higher Education and Society, which was established by the World Bank and UNESCO, for example, states:

Traditions of governance vary from country to country and by type of institution, but the Task Force has suggested a set of basic principles that promote good governance across a wide variety of situations. Unfortunately these principles are frequently not observed, especially in developing countries, and especially where traditions of higher education are still not firmly established (Task Force 2000: 68).

For a critical stance on the imposition of globalized higher education models in newly industrializing countries and developing countries see Kempner and Jurema (2002).

21. See http://www.oui-iohe.qc.ca/Iglu/en-index_centres.htm (March 31, 2005).

22. Ironically, the remedy discussed by Rhoades and Sporn (2002), i.e. encouraging universities 'to improve their accounting practices' (26) is part of the very logic that lead to the spiraling costs in higher education, and surely the formal control of control mechanisms can be subject to further control. Here, a process unfolds that can be perpetuated *ad infinitum*.

23. This expectation is consistent with much of the evidence presented in international comparisons of higher education reforms (Goedegebuure et al. 1992; Felt and Glanz 2003; Huisman and Currie 2004).

24. The 'ivory tower' image of the university strongly resembles White's concept of *arena markets*, which are defined as formalized settings with rigid external boundaries, in which the logic of purity seems to be dominant (White 1992: 51–4). The general trend of transforming universities into organizational actors competing directly with each other is a striking example of what White labels *production market*, i.e. a market structure based on mutual observation and 'the variation among producers in terms of quality' (White 1992: 43).

Conclusion

John W. Meyer, Gili S. Drori, and Hokyu Hwang

The studies in this book examine the worldwide expansion of organization in the contemporary period. They document its scope, describe its features, and analyze its causes in a globalizing world. The chapters in Part I of the book delineate the scripts of expanded organization, which spread around the world, and trace their sources. In Part II, we show the impact of these recipes on national societies and their organizations, as they incorporate and embody them. Together, the chapters describe a world of more organizations and more elaborate organizations. They show how this pervasive system penetrates and transforms all sorts of social domains everywhere, over and above variations in issues, locales, and resources. The transformed world simultaneously empowers and constrains people, groups, and societies. There is vastly more rationalization, though perhaps not more rationality, and there is vastly more authority, though perhaps not coordinated centralization.

In this concluding chapter, we sum up in three ways. First, we stress a few general theoretical points reinforced by our studies. This book is a product of and a contribution to sociological institutionalism. Thus, we review our theoretical contributions to address institutional theory's core concerns in the study of world society. Second, we discuss the overall meaning and impact of the global rush to organizing. Who and what gains, and who loses? Is the globalized organizational system a dominating central scheme, or a system of ever-expanding but highly controlled rationalization? Third, our book is the product of many researchers and much research effort. On completing it, we reflect on directions for future research in the global macro-sociology of organizations. We take up these three issues in turn.

C.1. THEORETICAL EMPHASES

The arguments about globalization and organization, made throughout the various contributions to this book, address the core theoretical concerns of sociological neoinstitutionalism and its application to the study of world society.

C.1.1. Institutionalization and Organization

Modern society is riddled with arrogant claims about the fundamental reality of its social entities, and the rock-bottom reality of their interdependencies (whether these are seen in more functional terms or rather as a set of power and exchange relations). A world of real actors (with rather masculine properties) replaces myth and culture, which recede in to the background. Nowhere is this view more dominant and rampant than in the field of organizations—which is explicitly built on such realist assumptions. In both research and practice, the idea is that heroic and masculine actors, confronting real problems, build organizations from the ground up.

Our studies, on the other hand, portray organizations as creatures of institutional and cultural environments. These environments, in the modern period, tend to be global in scope. Great social movements carry one organizational reform or another, demand the organizational structuring of this or that new domain, and/or support the penetration of extant organization down into new levels of social structure. Thus, the modern legal system, regulating the rights and duties with all the forces we have described, reaches down into the formerly private worlds of intimate sexuality or childrearing, for example, on a worldwide scale. In the background, there is scientistic support, much emphasis on human rights, and rationalistic discussion of the social processes involved. The organizations of socialization and social control created to manage various situations have much training and management. Organizations are accounted in modern ways, and acquire ISO certificates. Knowledge systems expand and rationalize new uncertainties and social frontiers. So the problems of sexual relations or childrearing appear in many different departments as part of research and instruction in universities all over the world.

In this way, cultural materials accumulate and are institutionalized at the global level over time—as evident in the expansion of activities and talk, in policies and services, and in the consolidation of particular models or scripts, and create the environments in which societies rationalize. Consequently, organizations expand, and individuals are both empowered and disciplined on a global scale.

C.1.2. Institutional Embeddedness in Wider Environment

Modern organizational analysis attends to environmental and institutional factors much more than previous generations did. This represents a major advance over previous lines of thought. But there is great intellectual conservatism in analyses of where the new environmental and institutional factors come from. Researchers in this book question and challenge the notion that organizations are simply created on the ground by powerful or intelligent men, independent of environmental cultural materials. In many organizational analyses and in the literature, unfortunately, the powerful or intelligent men frequently reappear as a privileged causal factor. It is often supposed that powerful and deeply interested actors—now operating at a global level—produce institutional change.

Our studies cast a good deal of doubt on this imagery and provide a much-needed corrective to the conventional, interests-based views. The impetus for modern expanded and globalized organization arises from the changed rules of the game in a rapidly globalizing world and the analyses of that world by reflective (and often professionalized) analysts, not simply from the interests of powerful actors. Thus the causal factors to which our analyses call attention—the expansive rise of individualism and human rights, the extraordinary expansion of science, and waves of social rationalization—are seen as cultural and institutional in origin and character. Further, these causal factors themselves are interpretations of the world rather than rationalistic and purposive actions in it. Therefore, they cannot simply be analyzed as the products of powerful actors of the modern world.

C.1.3. Diffusion, Translation, and Editing

Organizational models, once institutionalized, flow into practice throughout the world. Diffusion brings organizational scripts (in their various forms as practices, structures, or discourses) into local settings with impressive effectiveness and occurs with modification to these scripts in light of variations in local conditions and linkages to the centers of world mobilization. All the organizing materials studied in this book—standards, accounting, management, training, and so on—can be readily found, at least as talk, in practically every society of the world. In the furthest village, one might find someone who vaguely knows what an MBA is. Our studies show that universal notions of organization emphasizing broad new themes like governance and human resource management flow very widely and that universalistic claims are particularly amenable to global diffusion.

We also trace the paths of diffusion and the role of organizational carriers (such as INGOs and various European Union and United Nations agencies) and professional agents (accountants, consultants, and other experts, for example). Finally, we show the importance of temporal dimensions of diffusion: endogenous factors are important in the early phase of diffusion whereas exogenous factors take precedence in the later phase, as in regards to business schools.

C.1.4. Institutional Change, Isomorphism, and Decoupling at the Local Level

In the face of institutionalization (of scripts and their carriers), social actors adapt to the changes and conform to the new wave. Adaptive changes by social actors one by one bolster further the field and intensify pressures on other social actors. Institutional change can take the form of drift in what actors take for granted in the world around them, but often there is contestation over local interpretation. And even in the absence of contestation, there is always much uncertainty, and consequently, organizations rely on experts such as professionals and consultants. Under the pressures of great global institutional changes, local adaptation takes on much legitimacy—far beyond what may be practical or possible in local settings. Thus, ceremonial or discursive commitment to institutional forms without too much adaptation in practice is pervasive and even inevitable. Therefore, structuration may take the form of symbolic gesturing or gratuitous compliance with external standards and may result in loosely connected structures and action.

Local factors do not simply dissolve in the face of external influences, however, and national polity characteristics—such as liberal, corporatist, and statist polity types—leave lasting imprints on local institutional structures and interact with the external influences to produce systematic variations. Further, sector-specific (e.g. economic impact) features, mediated by organizational factors influence the diffusion of practices, as shown in corporate accounting and CR practices. In short, the complex interaction between global scripts, on the one hand, and national, sectoral and organizational factors, on the other hand, produces a varied landscape in which isomorphism and decoupling are common place.

Although systematic variations produced in the course of institutionalization deserve careful analysis, however, it is important not to lose sight of the overall institutional process. Even social actors that only symbolically conform or adapt to new institutional standards play a role in reinforcing the value and legitimacy of those standards. As more and more participants subscribe, symbolically or otherwise, to a new institution, the pressures and exigencies of that new institution mount and multiply for both symbolic compliers and those who have not yet subscribed. Grizzled old entrepreneurs or ancient family firms, for instance, begin to hire the new managerialized MBAs—even if they do not believe in their value. Too many institutionalized pressures—from consultants, banks, investment advisors, and others—begin to pile up, and the game is no longer worth the candle.

Overall, our combined findings show that a modern form of organization—heavily laden with the themes of rationalization and actorhood, and mediated by professionalization—is sweeping around the world. Globalization extends cultural meanings and structural forms worldwide and serves as the motor of this organizational revolution. The timing of the process is difficult to identify, since current logics and structures have their roots in Western cultural forms. The intensifying global awareness since the middle of the twentieth century and the hyper-globalization of the 1990s in particular, however, have rapidly expedited and extended the rate and reach of formal organization. In the next section, we discuss the impact of the whole process on world society.

C.2. THE IMPACT OF EXPANDED AND GLOBALIZED ORGANIZATION AND ITS IDEOLOGIES

We have analyzed the penchant for the formal organization in terms very different from the views that trace social changes through specific developments of social complexity or through networks and chains of interdependence. This book is not about the evolution of more complex organizational structures in the lives and work of people playing the parts of ordinary 'men', with their feet firmly on the ground. Rather, our studies are about people playing the roles of small gods as they carry universal visions of rationality and empowered human actorhood in a very lawful, increasingly global world. Thus, in discussing the impact of the broad organizing movement in the world over recent decades, we must consider the impact of the *cultural* changes involved, not only their effects through organizational structure.

The broad social movement that sweeps around the globe has as much in common with traditional religious movements as it does with the mundane practicalities of day-to-day business. Like traditional religious movements, it is not the practical people, but the modern-day incarnations of priesthoods—professors, scientists, consulting gurus, and theorists—and their scientized homilies that carry the movement on. Waves of reform and revival emanating from the movement circulate doctrines of human rights and empowerment, principles of the natural environment, and rationalized models of action and coordination. These doctrines, principles, and models, it is understood, can integrate people and nature in effective and tranquil society—and increasingly on a global scale. Thus we observe their spread and penetration into various social spheres around the world. The specific components of the general organizing movement spread, however, more to those groups and places best linked to the priesthoods that preach the new gospels than to those social locations where they might be needed.

Reading down from this great movement, our studies show the penetration of various liturgies of rationality around the world: accounting reforms, a standards movement, managerialism and managerial education, personnel training around principles of empowered actorhood, managed and coordinated university systems, and generalized principles of expansive CR. Others have studied the spread of specific functional components of organizing: modern organizational information and data systems, safety and personnel arrangements, marketing and feedback reforms, R & D strategies, and so on. Modern organizing principles have also traversed into new frontiers—health management, rationalized schooling reforms, recreational arrangements for children and adults, diet and exercise packages, environmental protection and management, the more and less licit production of sexual satisfaction, or the acquisition of a hundred different skills.

We now turn to the meanings and consequences of this broad social movement and its specific instantiations, and focus principally on questions about the redistribution of advantages and liabilities produced by global hyper-organization. Who are the beneficiaries, and who are the disinherited of the new regime? A number of clear answers are put forward in the literature, but these answers are not consistent with each other. Accounts of globalization presented in this book confront the issue of social authority in an increasingly global world and thereby challenge the current understandings and interpretations of globalization and its core mechanisms and implications.

C.2.1. Winners and Losers I: Structures of Rationalization

It is not usually obvious which persons and groups benefit from episodes of rationalization. But it is often clear, almost as a matter of tautology, which social structures benefit, and which others are undercut. The taming of a social domain by formal organization weakens older forms of authority and solidarity in that domain. Primordial or corporate forms of authority decline under the pressures of the new rules. Traditional forms of the family and ownership arrangements, the state and local community elites, and ethnic and communal groups lose standing as they transition into more rationalized organizational forms.

Modern families have become associations of individuals that benefit these individuals rather than corporate bodies that preserve property and status at the expense of these individuals. The modern state has become less corporate and has far fewer independent purposes of its own apart from those of its individual members and their associations. The state is to be organized to serve the people, not processions honoring God, the dynasty, or a racial or historical tradition. Similarly, communal elites lose authority to organizational structures. Even ethnic groups restructure themselves as organized interest groups: Native American nations, like many other traditional societies, are recast as community organizations, with a governing board and governance procedures. More rationalized structures replace the authority of traditional professionals in medicine, law, religion, or schooling; the professions have become skill-based, certification-requiring, and standard-generating associations.

It is not so clear, however, how the great social changes spurred by the rise of the formal organization affect the distribution of power and advantage in the contemporary world. By becoming a modern teacher, the old schoolmaster or professor loses the capacity to exercise arbitrary authority over the student—students are now proper persons and organizational members, and beating or humiliating them, for instance, is generally frowned upon. But becoming a teacher or professor in the modern vein has its own advantages— in the capacity to organize and coordinate activity. The modern formalization of the social role protects teachers through elaborate organizational forms and supports. Thus, the modern teacher acquires new resources and gains many social supports as she trades arbitrary or traditional authority for rationalized organization. Exactly the same points can be made about other declining forms of traditional corporate authority. Traditional ethnic, tribal, or communal elites certainly lose symbolic status and authority, but they (or their replacements) may gain a great deal in the capacity to act in the new regime. Traditional state bureaucrats, similarly, lose standing to exercise rather arbitrary powers, but may gain resources and action capacity. Traditional business owners lose the arbitrary authority to hire and fire at will, but may gain greatly in the capacity to effectively coordinate action as organizational managers. Thus, it is easy to say that some structures gain and others lose in the broad changes toward organizational rationalization. It is not at all clear, however, what interests are being served.

C.2.2. Winners and Losers II: the Schooled

The global shift to rationalized organization does give advantages to some people and groups, although not in an interest-driven manner. The great beneficiaries in the world's stratification systems are the schooled people—but of course, vastly more people are now schooled. Causality runs several ways, which we do not need to disentangle here. (*a*) Most generally, the rise of modern and globalized models of society increases both organizing on a world scale and education of various sorts at many levels (Meyer 1977). (*b*) The modern global expansion of schooling clearly increases the likelihood that more domains and activities will become organized (Stinchcombe 1965; Drori et al. 2003). (*c*) Conversely, the modern wave of organizational expansion creates and further increases the demand for schooled personnel to play the expanded roles under construction (Moon and Wotipka, Chapter 5; Luo, Chapter 9). The extraordinary expansion and globalization of education at every level from preschool through doctoral and postdoctoral study has received less attention than it deserves. At the mass education level, universal enrollment is not far off and is a clearly an achievable goal for world society. At the university level, global enrollments grew from far lower than 1 percent of a cohort in 1900 to around 20 percent in 2000 (Schofer and Meyer 2005). The great bulk of the expansion occurred in the period since 1960: exactly the time frame for the organizational revolution(s) that we study.

To students of the world's stratification systems, the educational revolution is so obvious as to be taken-for-granted; education is no longer a cultural frill of some distinct status or occupational groups and has become the central component of social stratification for whole societies worldwide (see, e.g. Grusky, ed. 2001). Everywhere education serves as the legitimate route to individual success. This is in part because traditional roles are now seen to require much more education than in the past. More importantly, the expansion of the formal organization facilitates the creation of and demand for new roles and the perception and expectation that these new roles require more education. In American society, for instance, the schooled professions have long since replaced farmers and workers as the dominant occupational groupings. But changes in the same direction characterize every society in the modern world (Meyer et al. 1997*a*, 1997*b*).

Although it is clear that educated roles replace uneducated ones, it is not so clear what this does to the distribution of power and privilege in contemporary society. The demand for the schooled role-player certainly changes the character of the role, but not necessarily the scale of social relations; so the toothless peasants of an older world are now schooled citizens, many with university degrees.

C.2.3. Winners and Losers III: the Leviathan?

Faced with the hyper-organization of the modern world, a standard response is to decry the putative global rise of centralized power and the weakening status of the local and the personal. In this context, globalized and globalizing 'anti-globalization' movements arise. Ironically, however, encouraging communities worldwide to take an organized response, these critical perspectives themselves are among the driving forces behind the global organizational expansion. Indeed, the anti-globalization movement has generated a rapid expansion in global organizational structure in the 'third sector' or civil society in general (e.g. Boli and Thomas 1999). The fears driving this movement are generally economic in character. Coordinated economic organization on a global scale, often symbolized by the World Bank and the WTO; and the increase in the number of MNCs, threaten ordinary local social life, and exposes it to extraordinary 'risks' (Beck 1992). In the peripheries of the world, the fears may be more political and cultural, and the evil centralizers may be the West, American imperialism, or the CIA. In either case, the basis of the fears is the perception that the increased organization of the world is really at the hands of central and centralizing power.

It is certainly true that the organizational revolution we study links together activities and communication on an increasingly global scale. Commodities have properties and prices on a world scale. Health issues and disease rates are organized and managed globally. Schooling data on enrolment and achievement are routinely compared and exchanged in increasingly standardized formats. While these signal the rise of the global as a social horizon and recast society on a global scale, it is much less clear whether this now global, enormously expanded system of organization and communication is centralizing power in the hands of a Leviathan or a global equivalent of the national-state. The organizational links that bring local activity in line with rules established more universally, also bind global organizational centers to the similar rules that embody multiple conceptions of rights and obligations.

Simple examples can illustrate the point. Consider the paradoxical position of giant, global corporations. To protect themselves, large corporations can influence the legal environments that regulate them. They have the capacity to impose standardizing rules and principles on their subordinates and those outsiders they control. At the same time, they are vulnerably exposed to the movements that celebrate the rights of workers and/or consumers, or to the regulators who are concerned with the natural environment or community. On environmental matters, it is much easier for the wider world to control or influence a large mining concern in a corner of the world than a host of small 'fly-by-night' operators. Modern organizing, in other words, is likely to bring to bear a wide variety of rules and pressures that simultaneously incorporate (or 'structurate') multiple concerns in any given situation. A variety of pressures—from elaborate human rights and environmental norms to simple technical concerns with product quality—converge in the complex modern formal organization. Organizing, in this modern vein, is likely to integrate and coordinate disparate and at-times contradictory interests, concerns, and pressures in explicably structured and at least partially accountable ways.

If this is true in the long-run process of balancing disparate and contradictory interests and pressures, such as those about the short-run profit bottom line against those about long-run environmental impacts, it is also true about the balancing of local versus 'central' concerns. Organization gives 'centers' the capacity to control locals in light of standardized principles, but it also gives locals the capacity and standing with which to confront the 'centers'. In other words, globalization empowers and mobilizes the locals: locals 'discover' their human, community, cultural, environmental, political, and economic rights under the rules of modern organizing. These rules are built and legitimated on the expanded principles of human rights and capacities, after all. In the modern globalizing process, an enormous amount of such 'glocalization' (Robertson 1994) occurs.

We can see the impact of globalization on mobilization if we look at the extraordinary expansion of international nongovernmental organizations (Boli, and Thomas 1999). Many of these are what Jackie Smith (Smith, Chatfield, and Pagnucco 1997) calls 'social movement organizations', and constitute broad 'anti-globalization' efforts that are in essence globalizing movements opposed to the naked domination of economic globalization. It is striking how easy it has been for these forces to assemble themselves—*as organizations*—on a global scale. Starting from close to nothing, they have been able to block a renowned multilateral investment treaty, to force the world trading system to retreat in disorder in battles in Seattle, Genoa, and elsewhere, and to assemble their own global agenda in great conferences. Their successes are implausible *by their own accounts* of the dominance of great economic organizations, but reveal the nature of modern institutional globalization and its implications for organization.

From the point of view of the authors of this book, globalization constructs organized actors of all sorts—not just economic (or imperial). It structures the polluting destroyers of the ozone layer, and the scientists and environment organizations that protect this layer. It structures economic organizations that attempt industrial serfdom in the world's peripheries, but also a variety of CR initiatives that expose, resist, and sanction this activity. It speeds the sending of diseases to the exposed populations of impoverished countries, and also organizes a huge worldwide movement about the right to health.

The glocalized locals of the modern world, despite and because of the organization of that world, have more standing than most theories would propose. But they are not, of course, the old locals; the locals of the modern world become relatively standardized variants of locals everywhere else. They become glocalized, and gain a great deal of authority as a result. They have rights and standing because they are schooled and standardized. Their rights, furthermore, must be the standard set of rights, and must be demanded in organizationally correct forms and fora. Locals do not have the rights to kill their female children, and subject neighboring tribes to slavery; and cannibalism and human sacrifice are out. The cultural practice of female circumcision is on its way to be defined as trampling over the human (and specifically medical) rights of women. The rights to pollute streams and destroy endangered species as well as the rights to produce and sell inappropriate drugs are also in retreat. In essence, locals legitimately keep, as optional cultural matters, only those 'traditions' that have been appropriately edited, tamed, and (re-)invented for modern, global sensibilities—such as clothing, food, arts and crafts, and linguistic materials.

Thus, the balances between the standardizing and totalizing forces of globalized organization, and the individualizing and empowering forces of the same structures, are almost always unclear, difficult to assess, and are matters of normative contention. Both sides are the expressions of the dialectic relations between globalization, organization, and the empowerment of actors. On the one hand, globalization universalizes scripts of action and structure, and imposes a homogenizing umbrella of themes and carriers on a worldwide span of locales and contexts. On the other hand, great variation exists in these scripted forms, as 'glocalization' requires a meshing of the global and the local. In addition, the universal picture of a world of empowered and rationalized organizations, while encouraging homogeneity of forms, also encourages the fragmentation of legitimacy and empowered actorhood. The universalism of particularism (Robertson) or the totalizing and individualizing (Foucault) tendencies of globalization are obvious in the proliferation of the modern organizational form. Further, the carriers of the materials of globalized organization are constituted and authorized by the themes that they carry: governance presumes a system to be governed. Hence the theme and its carriers coevolve to render the whole system (including both carriers and organizations) governable. In this way, social units, actors, and hence organizations are entrapped by the same processes through which actors are simultaneously subordinated to and empowered by the wider structures.

C.2.4. The Rationality (and Irrationality) of Organizational Rationalization

The modern globalized world most clearly does not produce a Leviathan. Indeed, if there were more legitimated world centralization, we argue throughout this book, much of the expanded organizing of the present world would be less likely to occur. A world state of some strength and authority would obviate the drumbeat of efforts to make heroic empowered actors out of subordinated units like states, corporations, and NGOs. A world state could construct simpler bureaucracies, professional associations, as well as principles of private ownership and control. And a world state would develop and consolidate hierarchical command-and-control relations among its bureaucracies rather than encourage multisectoral partnerships. Thus, the contemporary global world is very far from a polity with a nicely rational modern sovereign at its core. Instead, people everywhere are creating substitutes out of the laws of science and rationality and a jury-rigged legal and moral celebration of rock-bottom human rights. This, we argue here, creates the modern world of expanded organization—of organizations legitimated and controlled by scripts of actorhood.

Global society is a rationalized world, but not exactly what one could call a rational one. Rationality requires a clear unitary actor and some boundaries around the actor. It requires that the actor have the capacity to set goals, make decisions, command technology, and implement decisions in action. The rise of a world of multiple and overlapping actors who possess (or pretend to have, or are socially assigned) these qualities is a world of inconsistent rationalities. These are reinforced by the penetration of competing and incomensurable principles of human empowerment, scientized nature, and intrinsic laws of rationality. Thus none of the features of simple rationality are in place, either at the level of the overall system or in the organized subunit actors as they actually exist. This point is most obvious at the level of the global system. Even if they were intensely (and naively) rational, the sum of multiple and overlapping actors does not make one big coherent rational actor. One may subscribe to doctrines about invisible hands and the way they produce satisfying outcomes, without further arguing that the resultant system makes up a rational actor. There is, in reality, no actor there; and without a purposive actor, rationality is difficult or impossible to define or sustain.

At the subunit (or organizational) level, this point is striking, if less obvious. If the modern expanded organization derives its sovereignty, purposes, control system, technology, and resources from standardized and standardizing rules in its environments, in what sense is it a real actor, and in what exact sense can it be said to be rational? The chapters of this book, over and over, raise these questions. Luo (Chapter 9) shows the institutionalized modern inconsistency between the organization that is built on notions of empowered participants and the studied and instructed autonomy of these participants. The result is a world of organizations spending money to train their people, in effect, to be able to, and want to, get better jobs elsewhere. Mendel (Chapter 6) shows organizations following standardized scripts for standardization, in good part independent of the actual activities and outcomes being standardized. Jang (Chapter 7) shows organizations adopting accounting principles that utterly expose them to their competitors.

This point is even more striking when we add other overlapping organizational structures to the mix. The modern organization is really a matrix structure that incorporates all sorts of inconsistent principles of authority (e.g. human resources, or environmental, standards versus the requirements of production). Most of these competing principles are themselves organized, and so organizational systems in the modern world overlap, rather than being bounded from one another. For instance, enormous numbers of employees are professionalized and belong to professional and other associations with principles in potential conflict with their focal organizations. Indeed, modern organizations are so enmeshed with external organizations in their environments that it is difficult, if not unthinkable, to sustain consistent loyalties to their focal sovereign structures.

If everything around and interpenetrated with a given organization are also organizations, rational actorhood may be as much an implausible dream than a reality. The analogy with Tocqueville's argument about traditional American society comes close to this imagery. Social control works to maintain order in America because 'the American individual' is a controlled role rather than a truly autonomous individual. Exactly in this way, the modern organization as actor is in no real sense an autonomous, rational, or purposive actor. Actorhood is itself a standardizing script, which expands and diffuses with rationalization at its wheel.

C.3. RESEARCH AGENDAS

The faith in organization is endemic in the contemporary world; organizations are believed to be where it is 'really at'. Our arguments are radically at odds with this view. We see contemporary organizations as instances of highly controlled wider scripts. The critics often see organizations as demonic; we see them as tamed conformists who anxiously incorporate each external pressure via therapists or consultants and internal role differentiation. The proponents see organizational development and elaboration as rational solutions to the widest array of problems; we see much organizational reform as the elaboration of modern rituals of rationality, and as serving a function more akin to religion than to technical development.

The faith in organization, anchored in the modern social sciences, leads to some distorted emphases in research in these fields. This may especially be true of work produced in settings that directly attempt to produce and promote rational organization as curative and ameliorative—like business schools. One problem is the intense research concentration on successful organizations in successful contexts. Case studies pile up of organizations for which things have, perhaps by accident, gone well. There is enormous hero worship, and lionization of the successful and the dramatic. Since success is often random and varies arbitrarily over time, this encourages all sorts of fashion-like movements in the field—TQM and MBO come to mind (see Mendel, Chapter 6).

All this is clearly part of the modern lionization of organizations as hard-wired and very real entities. Everything in our own work, of course, suggests that this is a modern cultural conceit. Thus, it should be analyzed as such, with impacts of its own. The pretense that we can solve problems by 'organizing' is endemic in the modern world, and produces all sorts of consequences, as we discuss above. Here we note some research strategies that may help give perspective on organization as cultural script and enactment, and suggest some research design ideas that pick up this theme. We propose first, looking at organization as it exists in the imagination, far from actual or possible realities. Then, second, we propose comparative studies of factors affecting the rise and fall of organizational models as ideologies. Third, we propose studies of the consequences of the institutionalization of organization as culture in the modern system.

C.3.1. Focus on the Periphery

In view of the ceremonial importance of organization in the modern system, it might be wise to look at the periphery as well as the core, at the margins as well as the center of the system, and at the dim failures as well as the bright successes. What does organizational elaboration look like in faraway Third World regions whose social sectors or arenas can barely find a foothold? Or even in the imagination of modern people in discouraging and adverse settings, as they dream of what structures might fix things. What are the properties, in such contexts, of the imagined good organization or good state or effective firm? As academics, we know that everywhere in the world, other academics have in mind the truly 'good university' as a city on the hill in their imaginations. In the contemporary world, this should be true in every social domain. If we want to understand the cultural mythology of organization, in short, we may try research designs that look for imagined organization in the absence of much real organizational structure at all.

Further, studies looking at the peripheries of modern organizing can show the effects of all the fashions and scripts as cultural materials, far from the possibilities of serious enactment. What does it do to very weak peripheral states to try to organize in the fashionable modern way? What does it do to very limited and weak economic structures—say sweatshop textile producers in the far periphery—to try to envision themselves as modern organizations? What does it do to organizations working with populations far from the schooled and tamed 'personnel' of the core societies—say mining organizations at the edge of coercive forms—to try to talk the modern language of standards, quality, accountability, human resources, and management?

C.3.2. Focus on Ideologies of Organizing

If organization is often derivative on the rise and change in exogenous cultural models, more research on the character of these models, and the factors that affect their rise and fall, is called for. Our studies here trace some of the changes over relatively long periods, and offer causal analyses (e.g. Luo, Chapter 9 or Shanahan and Khagram, Chapter 8). More work of this kind is needed, with comparisons across societies, time periods, and social sectors.

Further, comparisons across varying sources of organizational models are important. Professional groups differ and change over time. So do the sorts of consulting bodies, associations, and governmental and non-governmental organizations that prescribe proper expansions in organizational practice. For instance, the dominance of the United States in world society over the last half-century has greatly influenced the sorts of organizational models and reforms that have been fashionable (Djelic 1998). The rise of Japan in the 1970s and 1980s similarly generated and diffused some very distinctive organizational reforms—ending only with Japanese failures of the early 1990s.

In this book, we have offered general arguments about how the conditions of modern globalization in the absence of a centralized world state have created a huge wave of expanded organizational models, and have fashioned their substantive character. One can readily imagine comparative studies that put these arguments in context, showing how under different conditions, differing organizational models become ideologically and perhaps practically prominent. Comparisons across countries, sectors, and time periods can take advantage of a wealth of variation.

C.3.3. Consequences of the Dream of Organization

In this book, we have focused on the macro-social factors affecting the modern expansion of ideologies and models of organization, and on the effects of these models on the extraordinary expansion of organization in the contemporary world. It is useful to think about research designs that might explore what the effects of all this cultural material might be.

Naturally, dominant mentalities celebrate organizations, and imagine organizations have consequential effects because they are very real—functional and powerful structures that change everything in reality. There is an endless competitive search for new models that might be more efficient or effective than old ones, and an endless series of claims about just such matters of effectiveness. Each year, as we have stressed, new elements of organization-as-religion appear, with wonderful success stories, and the celebrations of various heroes (and occasionally villains, and even more occasionally fools).

It is useful to step aside from all this, and to speculate on the basis of the assumption that modern organizational expansion, as real management of function and power, accomplishes little, and makes little difference in comparison to plausible alternatives. Let us for the moment forget organizations themselves, entirely, and concentrate on thinking about studies of the effects of organization—not as reality—but as dominant models. If we think in this way, about organization as a sort of religious system, a variety of interesting and possibly testable consequences of the modern binge of organization come to light.

The imposition of the myth of organization on a domain previously structured in more traditional ways is likely to:

(a) Increase financial flows, and thus the apparent income or domestic product at hand. A world of friendship replaced by professionalized friendship (e.g. the therapies, the consultants, and so on) is a world of expanded financial wealth. This is true even if no functional change occurs at all.

(b) Increase the importance of education and meritocracy. Even if nothing changes in substance, organized sectors and societies face problems of legitimate assignment of persons to roles, and the legitimization of role-performances themselves. Certificates are needed that explain how role-differentiation (vertical and horizontal) is justified. Note that this consequence is likely even if nothing actual changes in effective performance. The enormous expansion of education in the modern world is closely linked to the explosion of social rationalization that our book analyzes.

(c) Increase aggressive universalism. A world dominated by myths of standard rationalized organization is one in which advice and assessment can go worldwide. For instance, a school tied closely to particularistic local society is difficult for a foreigner to understand and evaluate—everything is implicit, standards variable, function unknown. But as the school becomes a formal organization—a standardized and professionalized modern school—the opaqueness disappears, and standard recipes can be administered. Any skilled consultant can be an expert on the school within minutes—perhaps even at long distance. The universalism involved also enables a host of new forms of data and measures (see Hwang, Chapter 3). Standard measures can be created that are applicable anywhere, and they 'should', for efficiency, be applied anywhere. Formerly invisible role performances are rendered visible, and visible to the universal audience (including professional analysts).

(d) Increase aggressive individualism and self-expression. As we have stressed, the dialectics of the organizational revolutions increase both social control over individuals (and other actors), but also greatly expand the grounds of empowerment of these same actors. The modern organization entraps the individual, but its elaboration and differentiation supply the individual with more and more legitimate grounds for resistance, autonomy, and creative self-elaboration. Individuals can play their expanded selves in many directions. For instance, they can claim medical or psychological properties (stress, for instance, or an expanded list of 'special' abilities) against their organizations. Or expanded religious and cultural tastes. Or expanded claims deriving from other legitimated organizational roles. Or they can demand that those around them conform to the same constraining standards: a professor or boss or even military commander is now supposed to try to conform to considerable modern standards of interpersonal politeness.

(e) Expand aggressive organizing. The modern organizational revolutions feed on their own expansion. Each new differentiated structure, once articulated as organization, provides perspectives and grounds for further differentiated structures to arise. The rationalization of one social function drives the rationalization—in balancing, in resistance, or in conformity—of adjacent social functions.

Naturally, this all reaches the limits produced by the dialectic processes we have stressed. Organizational differentiation feeds on itself, but runs up against the expanding constraint, noted above, of modern individualisms and their celebration of the autonomy of the choices and tastes of persons. One can think of this, following Luhmann, as a kind of balance between differentiation and de-differentiation. But it is, of course, not really a balance—on both sides, it reflects the rapid contemporary expansion of something beyond established modernity. One can call it postmodernity. Or hyper-rationalization, combined with hyper-individualism.

BIBLIOGRAPHY

Abbott, K. W. and Snidal, D. (1998). 'Why States Act Through Formal International Organizations?', *Journal of Conflict Resolution*, 42(1): 3–32.

Abrahamson, E. (1991). 'Management Fads and Fashion: The Diffusion and Rejection of Innovations', *Academy of Management Review*, 16: 586–612.

—— (1996a). 'Management Fashion', *Academy of Management Review*, 21: 254–85.

—— (1996b). 'Technical and Aesetic Fashion', in B. Czarniawska and G. Sevon (eds.), *Translating Organizational Change*. Berlin: deGruyter, pp. 117–38.

—— (1997). 'The Emergence and Prevalence of Employee-Management Rhetorics: The Effects of Long Waves, Labor Unions and Turnover, 1875 to 1992', *Academy of Management Journal*, June 40(3): 491–533.

Ackers, P. (1997). 'Born again? The ethics and efficacy of the conversion experience in contemporary management development', *Journal of Management Studies*, 34(5): 677–701.

Ahrne, G. and Brunsson, N. (2006). 'Organizing the world', in Marie-Laure Djelic and Kerstin Sahlin-Andersson (eds.), *Transnational Governance: Institutional Dynamics of Regulation*. Cambridge: Cambridge University Press, pp. 74–94.

Aldrich, H. (2005). 'Entrepreneurship', in N. J. Smelser and R. Swedberg (eds.), *The Handbook of Economic Sociology*. Princeton, NJ: Princeton University Press, pp. 451–77.

Allott, A. (2000). 'Management Accounting Change' *Management Accounting*, 55 (July/August): 54–55.

Almond, G. A. and Powell, G. B. Jr. (2000). *Comparative Politics Today*, 7th edn. New York: HarperCollins.

Altbach, P. G. (2004). 'Globalization and the University. Myths and Realities in an Unequal World', *Tertiary Education and Management*, 10: 3–25.

—— and Engberg, D. (2000). *Higher Education. A Worldwide Inventory of Centers and Programs*. Chestnut Hill: Boston College Center for International Higher Education.

Alvarez, J. L., Mazza, C., and Pederson, J. S. (eds.) (2005). 'The Role of the Mass Media in the Consumption of Management', *Scandinavian Journal of Management*, 21(2).

Amdam, R. P. (1999). 'Towards Homogenization of European Management Education? The Scandinavian Case', Paper presented at SCANCOR Workshop in Stanford, 13 September.

Amorim, C. and Kipping, M. (1999). 'Selling Consultancy Services: The Portuguese Case in Historical and Comparative Perspective', *Business and Economic History*, 28: 45–56.

Anderson, B. (1991). *Imagined Communities: Reflections on the Origin and Spread of Nationalism*, 2nd edn. London and New York: Verso.

Aneesh, A. (2005). *Virtual Migration: The Programming of Globalization*. Duke University Press.

Anheier, H. K. and Cunningham, K. (2001). 'Internationalization of the Nonprofit Sector', in J. S. Ott. (ed.), *Understanding Nonprofit Organizations: Governance, Leadership, and Management.* Boulder, CO: Westview Press, pp. 382–90.

Appadurai, A. (1996). *Modernity at Large: Cultural Dimensions of Globalization.* Minneapolis, MN: University of Minnesota Press.

Arias, M. E. and Guillén, M. (1998). 'The Transfer of Organizational Techniques Across Borders: Combining Neo-Institutional and Comparative Perspectives', in J. L. Alvarez (ed.), *Diffusion and Consumption of Business Knowledge.* New York: St. Martin's Press, pp. 110–37.

Arndt, H. W. (1987). *Economic Development: The History of an Idea.* Chicago, IL: University of Chicago Press.

Arnett, J. J. (2002). 'The Psychology of Globalization', *American Psychologist,* 57(10): 774–83.

Aronowitz, S. (1988). *Science as Power: Discourse and Ideology in Modern Society.* Minneapolis, MN: University of Minnesota Press.

—— (2001). *The Knowledge Factory: Dismantling the Corporate University and Creating True Higher Learning.* Beacon.

Arrighi, G. and Drangel, J. (1986). 'The Stratification of the World-Economy: An Exploration of the Semiperipheral Zone', *Review,* X: 9–74.

Association of African Universities (AAU) (2003). *AAU Strategic Plan 2003–2010.* Accra: AAU.

Association of Universities of the British Commonwealth (1918–2000). *Commonwealth Universities Yearbook.* London: Author.

Axford, B. and Huggins, R. (2000). *New Media and Politics.* London: Sage.

Baalen, P. V. and Luchien, K. (2000). 'Legitimizing Academic Management Education: Diffusion and Shaping of an Educational Field', Paper presented for CEMP Workshop (The Content of Management Education in Europe), Paris, May 5–6.

Babson, R. W. (1920). *Religion and Business.* New York: The Macmillan Company.

Badie, B. (2000). *The Imported State. The Westernization of Political Order.* Stanford, CA: Stanford University Press.

Baldridge, J. V. (ed.) (1971). *Academic Governance. Research on Institutional Politics and Decision Making.* Berkeley, CA: McCutchan.

Bandy, J. and Smith, J. (eds.) (2004). *Coalitions Across Borders: Transnational Protest in a Neoliberal Era.* Lanham, MD: Rowman & Littlefield.

Bardhan, P. (1997). 'Corruption and Development: A Review of Issues', *Journal of Economic Literature,* 35:1320–46.

Barley, S. R. (1992). 'The New Crafts', Working paper, National Center for the Educational Quality of the Workforce, University of Pennsylvania.

Barley, S. and Kunda, G. (1992). 'Design and Devotion: Surges of Rational and Normative Ideologies of Control in Managerial Discourse', *Administrative Science Quarterly,* 37: 363–99.

—— Meyer, G., and Gash, D. (1988). 'Cultures of Culture: Academics, Practitioners, and the Pragmatics of Normative Control', *Administrative Science Quarterly,* 33: 24–57.

Barnett, M. and Finnemore, M. (2004). *Rules for the World: International Organizations in Global Politics.* Ithaca, NY: Cornell University Press.

Barney, J. B. (1997). *Gaining and Sustaining Competitive Advantage.* New York and Amsterdam: Addison-Wesley.

Barnes, B. (1985). *About Science.* Oxford: Basil Blackwell.

Baron, D. P. (1991). 'Private Politics, Corporate Responsibility and Integrated Strategy', *Journal of Economics and Management Strategy,* 12: 31–66.

—— (1999), 'Private Politics, Corporate Social Responsobility and Integrated Strategy', *Journal of Economics and Management Strategy,* 12: 31–66.

Barr, A. and Fafchamps, M. et al. (2003). Non-Governmental Organizations in Uganda (Draft report). Oxford, UK: Center for the Study of African Economies, Dept. of Economics, Oxford University.

Barrett, D. and Frank, D. J. (1999). 'Population Control for National Development: From World Discourse to National Policies', in J. Boli and G. M. Thomas (eds.), *Constructing World Culture: International Nongovernmental Organizations Since 1875.* Stanford, CA: Stanford University Press, pp. 198–221.

Barro, R. J. (1991). 'Economic Growth in a Cross Section of Countries', *Quarterly Journal of Economics,* 106: 407–43.

Barry, A., Osborne, T., and Rose, N. (eds.) (1996). *Foucault and Political Reason: Liberalism, Neo-Liberalism and Rationalities of Government.* Chicago, IL: University of Chicago Press.

Bartlett, C. and Ghoshal, S. (1989). *Managing Across Borders: The Transnational Solution.* Boston: Harvard University Press.

Bartoli, H. (2000). *Rethinking Development: Putting an End to Poverty.* Paris: UNESCO.

Bar-Yosef, S. and Livnat, J. (1984). 'Auditor Selection: An Incentive Signaling Approach', *Accounting and Business Research,* 14 (56): 301–09.

Bassi, L. J., Gallagher, A. L., and Schroer, E. (1996). *The ASTD Training Data Book.* American Society for Training and Development.

Baudenbacher, C. (2003). 'Globalization of the Judiciary', *Texas International Law Journal,* 38(3): 397–404.

Bauman, Z. (1998). *Globalization: The Human Consequences.* New York: Columbia University Press.

—— (1998). *Globalization: The Human Consequences.* New York: Columbia University Press.

Bazelon, E. (2005). 'Sentencing by the Numbers', *New York Times Magazine,* Sunday, 2 January 2005: 18–9.

Beck, U. (1992). *Risk Society, Towards a New Modernity,* Trans. Mark Ritter. London: Sage.

—— (2000). *What Is Globalization?* Cambridge, UK: Polity Press.

Becker, G. 'Investment in Human Captial: A Theoretical Analysis', *Journal of Political Economy,* 70 (supplement): 5, pt.2.

Beckfield, J. (2003). 'Inequality in the World Polity: The Structure of International Organization', *American Sociological Review,* 68: 401–20.

Belanger, P. and Tuijnman, A. (1997). 'The "Silent Explosion" of Adult Learning', in P. Belanger and A. Tuijnman (eds.), *New Patterns of Adult Learning: A Six-Country Comparative Study*. Pergamon and UNESCO Institute for Education.

Benavot, A. (1992). 'Curricular content, eductional expansion, and economic growth', *Comparative Education Review*, 36: 150–74.

Ben-David, J. (1990). *Scientific Growth*. Berkeley, CA: University of California Press.

—— (1991). *Scientific Growth. Essays on the Social Organization and Ethos of Science*. Berkeley, CA: University of California Press.

Bendix, R. (1956). *Work and Authority in Industry*. Berkeley, CA: University of California Press.

Berg, P. B. (1994). 'Strategic Adjustments in Training: A Comparative Analysis of the US and German Automobile Industries', in L. Lynch (ed.), *Training and the Private Sector: International Comparisons*. Chicago, IL: University of Chicago Press.

Berkovitch, N. (1999). *From Motherhood to Citizenship*. Baltimore: Johns Hopkins University Press.

Berle, A. and Means, G. (1932). *The Modern Corporation and Private Property*. New York: Harcourt, Brace and World.

Bernard, C. (1968). *The Functions of the Executive*. Cambridge, MA: Harvard University Press.

Bertelson, J. (2000). 'Three Concepts of Globalization', *International Sociology*, 15(2): 180–96.

Berthelot, R. (1993). 'Making the Most of ISO 9000', *Training and Development*, 47(2): 9.

Berthoud, G. (1992). 'Market', in W. Sachs (ed.), *The Development Dictionary*. London: Zed Books, pp. 70–87.

Bhagwati, J. (2002). 'Coping with Antiglobalization', *Foreign Affairs*, 81(1): 2–7.

Blau, P. M. (1955). *The Dynamics of Bureaucracy*. Chicago, IL: University of Chicago Press.

—— (1970). 'A Formal Theory of Differentiation in Organizations', *American Sociological Review*, 35: 201–18.

—— (1973). *The Organization of Academic Work*. New York: Wiley.

—— and Schoenherr, R. A. (1971). *The Structure of Organizations*. New York: Basic Books.

Block, F. and Evans, P. (2005). 'The State and the Economy', in N. J. Smelser and R. Swedberg (eds.), *The Handbook of Economic Sociology*, 2nd edn. Princeton, NJ: Princeton University Press, pp. 505–26.

Blossfeld, H. P., Hamerle, A., and Mayer, K. U. (1989). *Event History Analysis*. New Jersey: Lawrence Erlbaum.

—— and Rohwer, G. (1995). *Techniques of Event History Modeling*. New Jersey: Lawrence Erlbaum.

Blowfield, M. and Frynas, J. G. (2005). 'Setting New Agendas: Critical Perspectives on Corporate Responsibility in the Developing World', *International Affairs*, 81: 499–513.

Boli, J., Elliot, M. A., and Bieri, F. (2004). 'Globalization', in G. Ritzer (ed.), *Handbook of Social Problems: A Comparative International Perspective*. Thousand Oaks, CA: Sage, pp. 389–415.

—— and Thomas, G. M. (1997). 'World Culture in the World Polity', *American Sociological Review*, 62(2): 171–90.

—— (1999). *Constructing World Culture: International Non-Governmental Organizations Since 1875*. Stanford, CA: Stanford University Press.

Bond, R. and Smith, P. B. (1996). 'Culture and Conformity: A Meta-analysis of Studies Using Asch's (1952b, 1956) Line Judgment Task', *Psychological Bulletin*, 119: 111–37.

Bose, S. (1997). 'Instruments and Idioms of Colonial and National Development: India's Historical Experience in Comparative Perspective', in Cooper and Packard (eds.), *International Development and the Social Sciences*. Berkeley, CA: University of California Press, pp. 45–63.

Bowker, G. C. and Star, S. L. (1999). *Sorting Things Out: Classification and Its Consequences*. Cambridge, MA: MIT Press.

Boyle, E. H. *Female Genital Cutting: Cultural Conflict in the Global Community*. Baltimore, MD: Johns Hopkins University Press.

Boyle, E. H., McMorris, B. J., and Gomez, M. (2002). 'Local Conformity to International Norms: The Case of Female Genital Cutting', *International Sociology*, 17(1): 5–34.

Bradley, K. and Ramirez, F. O. (1996). 'World Polity and Gender Polity: Women's Share of Higher Education, 1965–1985', *Research in Sociology of Education and Socialization*, 11: 63–91.

Braun, D. and Merrien, F.-X. (1999). *Towards a New Model of Governance for Universities? A Comparative View*. London: Jessica Kingsley.

Brennan, J. and Shah, T. (2000). *Managing Quality in Higher Education: An International Perspective on Institutional Assessment and Change*. Maidenhead: Open University Press.

Brokaw, L. (1993). 'ISO 9000: Making the Grade', *INC*, 15(6): 98–9.

Brossard, M. and Maurice, M. (1974). 'Existe-t-il un modele universel des structures d'organisation?' *Sociologie du Travail*, 4: 402–26.

Bruner, E. M. (2002). 'The Masai and the Lion King: Authenticity, Nationalism, and Globalization in African Tourism', *American Ethnologist*, 28(4): 881–908.

Brunsson, N. (1985). *The Irrational Organization: Irrationality as a Basis for Organizational Action and Change*. Chichester: Wiley.

—— (1989). *The Organization of Hypocrisy: Talk, Decisions, and Actions in Organizations*. Chichester: Wiley.

—— (2000). 'Standardization as a Social Form', in N. Brunsson and B. Jacobsson (eds.), *A World of Standards*. Oxford: Oxford University Press, pp. 52–70.

—— and Jacobsson, B. (eds.) (2000). *A World of Standards*. New York: Oxford University Press.

—— and Olsen, J. P. (1998). *Organizing Organizations*. Copenhagen: Copenhagen Business School Press.

Brunsson, N. and Sahlin-Andersson, K. (2000). 'Constructing Organizations: The Case of Public Sector Reform', *Organizational Studies*, 21: 721–46.

Bryane, M. (2004). 'Explaining Organizational Change in International Development: The Role of Complexity in Anti-Corruption Work'. *Journal of International Development*, 16: 1067–88.

Burawory, M. (1979). *Manufacturing Consent: Changes in the Labor Process under Monopoly Capitalism*. Chicago, IL: University of Chicago Press.

—— (1985). *The Politics of Production*. London: Verso.

Burchell, G., Gordon, C., and Miller, P. (eds.) (1991). *The Foucault Effect: Studies in Governmentality*. Chicago, IL: University of Chicago Press.

Burkitt, B. and Whyman, P. (1994). 'Public Sector Reform in Sweden: Competition or Participation', *Political Quarterly*, 65: 275–84.

Burns, T. and Stalker, G. M. (1961). *The Management of Innovation*. Tavistock.

Byrnes, D. (1992). 'Exploring the World of ISO 9000', *Quality*, 31(10): 19–31.

Campbell, J. L. (1997). 'Mechanisms of Evolutionary Change in Economic Governance: Interaction, Interpretation and Bricolage', in L. Magnusson and J. Ottosson (eds.), *Evolutionary Economic and Path Dependence*. Cheltenham, UK: Edward Elgar, pp. 10–32.

Cappelli, P., Bassi, L., Katz, H., Knoke, D., Osterman, P., and Useem, M. (1997). *Change at Work*. New York: Oxford University Press.

Carnevale, A., Gainer, L. J., and Villet, J. (1990). *Training in America: the Organization and Strategic Role of Training*. San Francisco: Jossey-Bass.

Carroll, A. B. (1979). 'A Three Dimensional Model of Corporate Social Performance', *Academy of Management Review*, 4: 497–505.

—— (1999). 'Corporate Responsibility—Evolution of a Definitional Construct', *Business and Society Review*, 38: 268–95.

Carroll, G. and Hannan, M. (1999). *The Demography of Corporations and Industries*. Princeton, NJ: Princeton University Press.

Carroll, T. F. (1992). *Intermediary NGOs: The Supporting Link in Grassroot Development*, West Hartford, CT: Kumarian Press.

Carruthers, B. G. (1995). 'Accounting, Ambiguity, and the New Institutionalism', *Accounting, Organization, and Society*, 20 (4): 313–28.

—— and Espeland, W. N. (1991). 'Accounting for Rationality: Double-Entry Bookkeeping and the Rhetoric of Economic Rationality', *American Journal of Sociology*, 97 (1): 31–69.

Castells, M. (1996–1998). *The Information Age: Economy, Society, and Culture*. Oxford: Blackwell.

Central Intelligence Agency (2001). *The World Factbook*. http://www.cia.gov/cia/publications/factbook/

Chabbott, C. (1998). 'Defining Development: The Making of the International Development Field, 1945–1990', in J. Boli and G. M. Thomas (eds.), *Constructing World Culture: International NGOs since 1875*. Stanford, CA: Stanford University Press, pp. 222–48.

Chan, D. K., Gerfand, M. J., Triandis, H. C., and Tzeng, O. (1996). 'Tightness-Looseness Revisted: Some Preliminary Analyses in Japan and the United States', *International Journal of Psychology*, 31: 1–12.

Chandler, A. D. Jr. (1962). *Strategy and Structure*. Cambridge, MA: MIT Press.

—— (1977). *The Visible Hand: The Managerial Revolution in American Business*. Cambridge, MA: Belknap Press of Harvard University Press.

—— (1990). *Scale and Scope: The Dynamics of Industrial Capitalism*. Cambridge, MA: Belknap Press of Harvard University Press.

—— and Mazlich, B. (eds.) (2005). *Leviathans: Multinational Corporations and the New Global Economy*. Cambridge, UK: Cambridge University Press.

Chang, H.-J. and Rowthorn, R. (eds.) (1995). *The Role of the State in Economic Change*. Oxford: Clarendon Press.

Charles, D. and Conway, C. (2001). *Higher Education-Business Interaction Survey*. Newcastle upon Tyne: Centre for Urban and Regional Development Studies.

Chase-Dunn, C. K. (1998). *Global Formation: Structures of the World Economy*. Lanham, MD: Rowan and Littlefield.

Chatfield, M. (1977). *A History of Accounting Thought*. Huntington, NY: Krieger.

Chaves, M. (2004). *Congregations in America*. Cambridge, MA: Harvard University Press.

Chow, C. W. and Wong-Boren, A. (1987). 'Voluntary Financial Disclosure by Mexican Corporations', *The Accounting Review*, 62 (July): 533–41.

CIFAR (1995). *International Accounting and Auditing Trends*, 4th edn. Princeton, NJ: Center for International Financial Analysis & Research Publications.

Clark, B. R. (1983). *The Higher Education System. Academic Organization in Cross-National Perspective*. Berkeley, CA: University of California Press.

—— (1995). *Places of Inquiry. Research and Advanced Education in Modern Universities*. Berkeley, CA: University of California Press.

—— (1997). 'Diversification of Higher Education: Viability and Change', in V. L. Meek, L. Goedegebuure, O. Kivinen, and R. Rinne (eds.), *The Mockers and the Mocked. Comparative Perspectives on Differentiation, Convergence and Diversity in Higher Education*. Surrey: Pergamon Press.

—— (1998). *Creating Entrepreneurial Universities. Organizational Pathways of Transformation*. Surrey: Pergamon Press.

Clemens, E. (1993). 'Organizational Repertoires and Institutional Change: Women's Groups and the Transformation of US Politics, 1890–1920', *American Journal of Sociology*, 98: 755–98.

—— and Cook, J. (1999). 'Politics and Institutionalism: Explaining Durability and Change', *Annual Review of Sociology*, 25:441–66.

Coeyman, M. (1993). 'Gaining ground in Asia/Pacific: ISO 9000 as the Standard', *Chemical Week*, 152(16): 54.

Cohen, M. D. and March, J. G. (1974). *Leadership and Ambiguity. The American College President*. New York: McGraw-Hill.

—— —— and Olsen, J. P. (1972). 'A Garbage Can Model of Organizational Choice', *Administrative Science Quarterly*, 17: 1–25.

Cohen, S. S. (1969). *Modern Capitalist Planning: The French Model*. Berkeley, CA: University of California Press.

Cole, R. E. (1989). *Strategies for Learning*. Berkeley, CA: University of California Press.

Cole, S. (1992). *Making Science*. Cambridge, MA: Harvard University Press.

Coleman, J. S. (1974). *Power and the Structure of Society*. New York: Norton.

—— (1975). 'Social Structure and a Theory of Action', in P. M. Blau (ed.), *Approaches to the Study of Social Structure*. NY: Free Press, pp. 76–93.

—— (1990). *Foundations of Social Theory*. Cambridge, MA: Belknap Press of Harvard University Press.

—— (1991). 'Prologue: Constructed Social Organizations', in P. Bourdieu and J. S. Coleman (eds.), *Social Theory for a Changing Society*. Russell Sage Foundation. Boulder, CO: Westview Press, pp. 1–20.

Collier J. and Wanderley, L. (2002). 'Corporate Responsibility in Brazil: Pride or Prejudice?' Second World Congress of ISBEE Sao Paulo, Brazil January 18, 2002. http://www.Nd.edu/~isbee/papers/Collier.doc

Collins, R. (1979). *The Credential Society*. New York: Academic Press.

Commons, J. R., Wisler, W., Haake, P., Carpenter, O. F., McMullin, T. J., et al. (1921). *Industrial Government*. New York: MacMillan.

Cooper, F. and Packard, R. (1997). *International Development and the Social Sciences: Essays on the History and Politics of Knowledge*. Berkeley, CA: University of California Press.

Crainer, S. and Dearlove, D. (1998). *Gravy Training: Inside the Shadowy World of Business Schools*. Oxford: Capstone.

Creighton, A. (1989). *The Emergence of Incorporation: Standardization and Growth in the Nineteenth Century*. Ph.D. dissertation, Department of Sociology, Stanford University.

Croissant, J. and Restivo, S. (eds.) (2001). *Degrees of Compromise: Industrial Interests and Academic Values*. Albany, NY: SUNY Press.

Croissant, J. L. and Smith-Doerr, L. (Forthcoming/2007). 'Organizational Contexts of Science: Boundaries and Relationships Between University and Industry', in J. Wajeman, E. Hackett, O. Amsterdanska and M. Lynch (eds.) *Handbook of Science and Technology Studies*. Cambridge, MA: MIT Press.

Crook, C. (2005). 'The Good Company', *The Economist*, January 22, 2005: 3–22.

Czarniawska-Joerges, B. and Sevon, G. (eds.) (1996). *Translating Organizational Change*. Berlin: Walter de Gruyter.

—— (eds.) (2005). *Global Ideas: How Ideas, Objects and Practices Travel in the Global Economy*. Lieber.

Dale, B. G. and Oakland, J. S. (1991). *Quality Improvement through Standards*. Cheltenham, UK: Stanley Thorne.

Daniel, C. A. (1998). *MBA: The First Century*. Lewisburg: Bucknell University Press.

Daniels, S. E. (2000). 'Management System Standards Poised for Momentum Boost', *Quality Progress*, 33(3): 31–9.

Datar, S., Feltham, G., and Hughes, J. (1991). 'The Role of Auditor and Audit Quality in Valuing New Issues', *Journal of Accounting and Economics*, 14: 3–49.

Davis, G. (2005). 'New directions in corporate governance', *Annual Review of Sociology*, 31: 143–62.

Davis, G. F. and Greve, H. R. (1997). 'Corporate Elite Networks and Governance Changes in the 1980s', *American Journal of Sociology*, 103(1): 1–37.

DeAngelo, L. E. (1981). 'Auditor Size and Audit Quality', *Journal of Accounting and Economics*, 3 (2): 183–98.

De Greiff, P. and Cronin, C. (eds.) (2002). *Global Justice and Transnational Politics: Essays on the Moral and Political Challenges of Globalization.*

Delacroix, J. and Ragin, C. (1981). 'Structural Blockage: A Cross-National Study of Economic Dependency, State Efficiency, and Underdevelopment', *American Journal of Sociology*, 86:1311–47.

De La Salle University (1997). 'De La Salle University Aspires for ISO-9000 Seal', *Abut-Tanaw: Institutional Publication of the De La Salle University System.* Manila: Philippines 25(2): 20.

Delmas, M. A. (2000). 'Barriers and Incentives to the Adoption of ISO 14001 in the United States', *Duke Environmental Law and Policy Forum*, Fall.

Diamond, L. (1993). 'The Globalization of Democracy', in R. Slater, B. M. Schutz, and S. R. Dorr (eds.), *Global Transformation and the Third World.* Boulder, CO: Lynne Rienner, pp. 31–69.

—— (2005). *Squandered Victory.* Times Books.

—— and Plattner, M. F. (eds.) (2001). *The Global Divergence of Democracies.* Baltimore, MD: Johns Hopkins University Press.

Diehl, P. F. (ed.) (1997). *The Politics of Global Governance: International Organizations in an Interdependent World.* Boulder, CO: Lynn Rienner Pubs.

DiMaggio, P. (ed.) (2001). *The Twenty-First-Century Firm: Changing Economic Organization in International Perspective.* Princeton, NJ: Princeton University Press.

DiMaggio, P. (ed.) and Powell, W. W. (1983). 'The Iron Cage Revisited: Institutional Isomorphism and Collective Rationality in Organizational Fields', *American Sociological Review*, 48 (2): 147–60.

Disclosure Inc. (1996). 'Disclosure/worldscope global [computer file]', Bethesda, MD: Disclosure Inc.

Djelic, M.-L. (1998). *Exporting the American Model: The Postwar Transformation of European Business.* New York: Oxford University Press.

—— and Quack, S. (eds.) (2003). *Globalization and Institutions: Redefining the Rules of the Economic Game.* New York: Edward Elgar.

—— and Sahlin-Andersson, K. (eds.) (2006). *Transnational Governance: Institutional Dynamics of Regulation.* Cambridge, MA: Cambridge University Press.

Dobbin, F. (2000, forthcoming). 'How Institutions Create Ideas: Railroad Finance and the Construction of Public and Private in France and the United States', in W. W. Powell and D. L. Jones (eds.), *Bending the Bars of the Iron Cage: Institutional Dynamics and Processes.* Chicago, IL: University of Chicago Press.

—— and Sutton, J. R. (1998). 'The Strength of the Weak State: The Rights Revolution and the Rise of Human Resources Management Divisions', *American Journal of Sociology*, 104(2): 441–76.

—— —— Meyer, J. W., and Scott, W. R. (1993). 'Equal Opportunity Law and the Construction of Internal Labor Markets', *American Journal of Sociology*, 99(2): 396–427.

Doornbos, M. (2001). " 'Good Governance': The Rise and fall of a Policy Metaphor?' " *Journal of Development Studies*, 37 (6): 93–108.

Drori, G. S. (1993). 'The Relationship Between Science, Technology, and the Economy of Lesser Developed Countries', *Social Studies of Science*, 23: 201–15.

—— (1998). 'A Critical Appraisal of Science Education for Economic Development', in W. W. Cobern (ed.), *Socio-Cultural Perspectives on Science Education: An International Dialogue*. Kluwer, pp. 49–74.

—— (2005). 'United Nations' Dedications: A World Culture in the Making?' *International Sociology*, 20(2): 177–201.

—— Jang, Y. S., and Meyer, J. W. (forthcoming). 'Sources of Rationalized Governance: Cross-National Longitudinal Analyses, 1985–2002', *Administrative Science Quarterly.*

—— and Moon, H. (2001). 'The Changing Nature of Tertiary Education, 1965–95: Shifts in Disciplinary Emphasis', Paper presented at the annual meeting of the American Sociological Association, Anaheim.

—— —— (Forthcoming). 'The Changing Nature of Tertiary Education: Neo-Institutional Perspective onto Cross-National Trends in Disciplinary Enrollment, 1965–1995', in D. P. Baker and A. W. Wiseman (eds.), *The Impact of Comparative Education Research on Institutional Theory*. Elsevier Science.

—— and Meyer, J. W. (2006). 'Scientization: Making a World Safe for Organizing', in M. -L. Djelic and K. Sahlin-Andersson (eds.), *Transnational Governance: Institutional Dynamics of Regulation*. Cambridge, MA: Cambridge University Press.

—— —— Ramirez, F. O., and Schofer, E. (2003). *Science in the Modern World Polity.* Stanford, CA: Stanford University Press, pp. 32–52.

DTI (Department of Trade and Industry) (1982). *Standards, Quality and International Competitiveness*. Command Paper Cmnd 8621. London: HMSO.

Dun and Bradstreet (1996). *ISO 9000 Survey: Comprehensive Data and Analysis of U.S. Registered Companies, 1996*. Chicago, IL: Irwin.

Easterly, W. (2001). *The Elusive Quest for Growth: Economists' Adventure and Misadventure in the Tropics*. Cambridge, MA: MIT Press.

Eastham, J. K. (1964). 'The Turkish Development Plan: The First Five Years', *The Economic Journal*, 74: 132–6.

Economist, The (1999). 'The Burger King', Oct. 23: 78.

Edelman, L. B. (1990). 'Legal Environments and Organizational Governance: The Expansion of Due Process in the American Workplace', *American Journal of Sociology*, 95: 1401–40.

—— (1992). 'Legal Ambiguity and Symbolic Structures: Organizational Mediation of Civil Rights Law', *American Journal of Sociology*, 97: 1531–76.

Edelman, L., Abraham, S., and Erlanger, H. (1992). 'Professional Construction of the Legal Environment: The Inflated Threat of Wrongful Discharge Doctrine', *Law and Society Review*, 26: 47–83.

Education and Training Department, Daewoo Corporation (1991). *Education and Training at Daewoo*. Seoul, Korea.

Ehrlich, P. R. (1971). *The Population Bomb*. New York: Ballantine.

Elliot, J. E. (1958). 'Economic Planning Reconsidered', *Quarterly Journal of Economics*, 72: 55–76.

Elliot, S. (1993). 'Management of Quality in Computing Systems Education: ISO 9000 Series Quality Standards Applied', *Journal of Systems Management*, 44(9): 6–11.

Elliott, R. K. and Jacobson, P. D. (1994). 'Costs and Benefits of Business Information Disclosure', *Accounting Horizons*, 8 (4): 80–96.

Ellul, J. (1975). *The New Demons*. New York: Seabury.

Engwall, L. and Gunnarsson, E. (eds.) (1994). *Management Studies in an Academic Context*. Uppsala: Acta Universitatis Uppsaliensis.

—— and Zamagni, V. (eds.) (1998). *Management Education in Historical Perspective*. Manchester: Manchester University Press.

Environics (2000). *Millennium Poll on Corporate Social Responsibility*. Toronto: Environics International.

Ernst, B. and Kieser, A. (2002). 'In Search of Explanations for the Consulting Explosion', in K. Sahlin-Andersson and L. Engwall (eds.), *The Expansion of Management Knowledge: Carriers, Flows, and Sources*. Stanford, CA: Stanford University Press, pp. 47–73.

Escobar, A. (1992). 'Planning', in W. Sachs (ed.), *The Development Dictionary*. London: Zed Books, pp. 132–45.

—— (1995). *Encountering Development: The Making and Unmaking of the Third World*. Princeton, NJ: Princeton University Press.

Esteva, G. (1992). 'Development', in W. Sachs (ed.), *The Development Dictionary*. London: Zed Books, pp. 6–25.

Etzioni, A. (1968). *The Active Society: A Theory of Societal and Political Processes*. New York: Free Press.

—— (2004). *From Empire to Community: A New Approach to International Relations*, Palgrave Macmillan.

Etzkowitz, H. and Leydesdorff, L. (2000). 'The Dynamics of Innovation: From National Systems and "Mode 2" to a Triple Helix of University-Industry-Government Relations', *Research Policy*, 29: 109–23.

Eurich, N. P. (1985). *Corporate Classrooms: The Learning Business*. Princeton, NJ: Carnegie Foundation for the Advancement of Teaching.

European Commission (1994). *Continuing Training in Enterprises: Facts and Figures— a Report on the Results of the Continuing Vocational Training Survey Carried Out in the Enterprises of the Member States of the European Union in 1994*.

—— (1997). *The European Quality Assurance Standards (EN ISO 9000 and EN 45000) in the Community's New Approach legislation*. Quality Series No.4. Brussels: Directorate General III Industry, Unit III/B/4, Quality Policy, Certification and Conformity Marking.

—— (1998). *Quality Directory: Who Is Doing What in the Quality Field in the European Commission*. Quality Series, The European Quality Promotion Policy. Brussels: Directorate General III Industry, Unit III/B/4, Quality Policy, Certification and Conformity Marking.

—— (2000). *Guide to Implementation of Directives Based on the New Approach and the Global Approach*. Directorate General for Enterprise. Luxembourg: Office for Official Publications of the European Communities.

European University Association (EUA) (2001). *Salamanca Convention 2001. The Bologna Process and the European Higher Education Area*. Geneva: EUA.

—— (2004). *10 Year Anniversary Institutional Evaluation Programme*. Brussels: EUA.

Evans, P. B. (1995). *Embedded Autonomy: States and Industrial Transformation*. Princeton, NJ: Princeton University Press.

—— (1997). 'The Eclipse of the State? Reflections on Stateness in an Era of Globalization', *World Politics*, 50: 62–87

—— (2005). 'Challenges of the "Institutional Turn": New Interdisciplinary Opportunities in Development Theory', in V. Nee and R. Swedberg (eds.), *The Economic Sociology of Capitalism*. Princeton, NJ: Princeton University Press, pp. 90–116.

Evans, P. and Rauch, J. E. (1999). 'Bureaucracy and Growth: A Cross-National Analysis of the Effects of "Weberian" State Structures on Economic Growth', *American Sociological Review*, 64: 748–65.

Feenstra, R. C. (2000). 'World Trade Flows, 1980–1997', Working Paper, National Bureau of Economic Research and Center for International Data, Institute for Governmental Affairs, University of California at Davis.

—— Lipsey, R. E., and Bowen, H. P. (1997). 'World Trade Flows, 1970–1992, with Production and Tariff Data', Working Paper 5910, National Bureau of Economic Research, Cambridge, MA.

Felt, U. and Glanz, M. (2003). 'University Autonomy in Europe: Changing Paradigms in Higher Education Policy', in Observatory for Fundamental University Values and Rights (ed.), *Managing University Autonomy. Collective Decision Making and Human Resources Policy*. Proceedings of the Seminar of the Magna Charta Observatory. 17 September 2002. Bologna: Bononia University Press, pp. 13–104.

Ferguson, J. (1994). *The Anti-Politics Machine: 'Development,' Depoliticization, and Bureaucratic Power in Lesotho*. Minneapolis: University of Minnesota Press.

Ferman, L. A., Cutcher-Gershenfeld, J., Hoyman, M., and Savoie, E. J. (1990). 'Editors Introduction', in L. A. Ferman, J. Cutcher-Gershenfeld, M. Hoyman, and E. J. Savoie (eds.), *New Developments in Worker Training: a Legacy for the 1990s*. Madison, WI: Industrial Relations Research Association.

Fig, D. (2005). 'Manufacturing Amnesia: Corporate Social Responsibility in South Africa', *International Affairs*, 599–617.

Finnemore, M. (1993). 'International Organization as Teachers of Norms: The United Nations Educational, Scientific, and Cultural Organization and Science Policy', *International Organization*, 47: 567–97.

—— (1996). *National Interests in International Society*. Ithaca, NY: Cornell University Press.

—— (1997). 'Redefining Development at the World Bank', in F. Cooper and R. Packard (eds.), *International Development and the Social Sciences: Essays on the History and Politics of Knowledge*. Berkeley, CA: UC Press, pp. 203–27.

—— and Sikkink, K. (1998). 'Norms and International Relations Theory', *International Organization*, 52: 887–917.

Firth, M. (1979). 'The Impact of Size, Stock Market Listing, and Auditors on Voluntary Disclosure in Corporate Annual Reports', *Accounting and Business Research*,
9 (36): 273–80.

Fligstein, N. (1985). 'The Spread of the Multidivisional Form', *American Sociological
Review*, 50: 377–91.

—— (1990). *The Transformation of Corporate Control*. Cambridge, MA: Harvard
University Press.

—— (1996a). 'How to Make a Market: Reflections on the Attempt to Create a Single
Market in the European Union', *American Journal of Sociology*, 102: 1–33.

—— (1996b). 'Markets as Politics: A Political-Cultural Approach to Market Institutions', *American Sociological Review*, 61: 656–73.

—— (2005). 'The Political and Economic Sociology of International Economic
Arrangements', in N. J. Smelser and R. Swedberg (eds.), *The Handbook of Economic
Sociology*, 2nd edn. Princeton, NJ: Princeton University Press, pp. 183–204.

—— and Freeland, R. (1995). 'Theoretical and Comparative Perspectives on Corporate Organization', *Annual Review of Sociology*, 21: 21–44.

—— and Mara-Drita, I. (1993). 'How to Make a Market: Reflections on the Attempt
to Create a Single Unitary Market in the European Community', Paper presented
at the Annual Meetings of the European Community Studies Association,
Washington, DC.

Foucault, M. (1979). *Omnes et Singulatim: Towards a Criticism of 'Political Reason*.
Tanner Lectures on Human Values, Stanford University, 10 October 1979. http://
www.tannerlectures.utah.edu/lectures/foucault81.pdf (accessed 2 June 2005).

—— (1980). *Power/Knowledge*. Brighton: Harvester Press.

—— (1990). *The History of Sexuality*. Vol. 1., Harmondsworth: Penguin.

—— (1991). 'Governmentality', in G. Burchell, C. Gordon, and P. Miller (eds.), *The
Foucault Effect: Studies in Governmentality*. Chicago, IL: University of Chicago
Press, pp. 87–104.

Frank, D. and Gabler, J. Forthcoming (2006). *Reconstructing the University: Global
Changes in the Academic Core over the 20th Century*. Stanford, CA: Stanford
University Press.

Frank, D. J., Hironaka, A., and Schofer, E. (2000). 'The Nation-State and the Natural
Environment over the Twentieth Century', *American Sociological Review*, 65:
96–110.

—— and McEneaney, E. (1999). 'The Individualization of Society and the Liberalization of State Policies on Same-Sex Sexual Relations, 1984–1995', *Social Forces*, 77:
911–44.

—— and Meyer, J. W. (2002). 'The Contemporary Identity Explosion: Individualizing Society in the Post-War Period', *Sociological Theory*, 20(1): 86–105.

—— —— and Miyahara, D. (1995). 'The Individualist Polity and the Prevalence
of Professionalized Psychology: A Cross-National Study', *American Sociological
Review*, 60: 360–77.

—— Hironaka, A., Meyer, J., Schofer, E., and Tuma, N. B. (1999). 'The Rationalization and Organization of Nature in World Culture', in J. Boli and G. Thomas (eds.), *Constructing World Culture*. Stanford, CA: Stanford University Press.

—— Meyer, J. W., Wong, S.-Y., and Ramirez, F. (2000). 'What Counts as History: A Cross-National and Longitudinal Study of University Curricula', *Comparative Education Review*, 44(1): 29–53.

Frazis, H., Joyce, M., Horrigan, M., and Gittleman, M. (1998). 'Results from the 1995 Survey of Employer-Provided Training', *Monthly Labor Review*, June: 3–13.

Freeland, R. F. (2001). *The Struggle for Control of the Modern Corporation: Organizational Change at General Motors, 1924–1970*. New York: Cambridge University Press.

Friedman, E., Johnson, S., Kaufmann, D., and Zoido-Lobatón, P. (2000). 'Dodging the Grabbing Hand: The Determinants of Unofficial Activity in 69 countries', *The Journal of Public Economics*, 76: 459–93.

Friedman, M. (1962). *Capitalism and Freedom*. Chicago, IL: University of Chicago Press.

Friedman, T. (2005). *The World is Flat: A Brief History of the Twenty-First Century*. New York: Farrar, Straus and Giroux, p. 200.

Friedmann, J. (1987). *Planning in the Public Domain: From Knowledge to Action*. Princeton, NJ: Princeton University Press.

Friedrichs, D. O. and Friedrichs, J. (2002). 'The World Bank and Crimes of Globalization: A Case Study', *Social Justice*, 29(1/2): 13–36.

Fuller, B. and Rubinson, R. (1992). *The Political Construction of Mass Education: School Expansion, the State, and Economic Change*. New York: Praeger.

Furusten, S. (1995). *The Managerial Discourse: A Study of the Creation and Diffusion of Popular Management Knowledge*. Published doctoral dissertation, Department of Business Studies, Uppsala University, Sweden.

Galaskiewicz, J. and Burt, R. (1991). 'Interorganization Contagion in Corporate Philanthropy', *Administrative Science Quarterly*, 36(1): 88–105.

Gammal, D. L., Simard, C., Hwang, H., and Powell, W. W. (2005). *Managing Through the Challenges: A Profile of San Francisco Bay Area Nonprofits*. Stanford: Graduate School of Business.

Gambling, T. (1977). 'Magic, Accounting and Morale', *Accounting, Organization and Society*, 2: 141–51.

Geare, A. and Stablein, R. (1995). 'Human Resource Management in New Zealand', in L. F. Moore and P. D. Jennings (eds.), *Human Resource Management on the Pacific Rim: Institutions, Practices, and Attitudes*. New York: Walter de Gruyter.

Geiger, R. L. (1986). *To Advance Knowledge. The Growth of the American Research University, 1900–1940*. New York/Oxford: Oxford University Press.

Gerhards, J. and Haceknbroch, R. (2000). 'Trends and Causes of Cultural Modernization: An Empirical Study of First Names', *International Sociology*, 15(3): 501–31.

Geuna, A. and Martin, B. R. (2003). 'University Research Evaluation and Funding: An International Comparison', *Minerva*, 41: 277–304.

Gibbons, M., Limoge, C., and Nowotny, H. (1994). *The New Production of Knowledge: The Dynamics of Science and Research in Contemporary Societies*. Thousand Oaks, CA: Sage.

—— Limoges, C., Nowotny, H., Schwartzman, S., Scott, P., and Trow, M. (1994). *The New Production of Knowledge*. London: Sage.

Giddens, A. (1984). *The Constitution of Society*. Cambridge: Polity Press.

—— (1990). *The Consequences of Modernity*. Stanford, CA: Stanford University Press.

—— (2000). *Runaway World: How Globalization is Reshaping Our Lives*. London: Brunner Routledge.

—— (2003). *Runaway World: How Globalization is Reshaping Our Lives*. New York: Routledge.

Glick-Schiller, N. and Fouron, G. E. (1999). 'Terrains of Blood and Nation: Haitian Transnational Social Fields', *Ethnic and Racial Studies*, 22: 340–66.

Glynn, P., Kobrin, S. J., and Naim, M. (1997). 'The Globalization of Corruption', in K. A. Elliott (ed.), *Corruption and the Global Economy*. Washington DC: Institute for International Economics, pp. 7–27. http://www.iie.com/publications/chapters preview/12/1iie 2334.pdf (accessed 10 July 2004).

Goedegebuure, L. C. J., Kaiser, F., Maasen, P. A. M., Meek, V. L., van Vught, F. A., and Weert, E. de (1992). *Higher Education Policy in International Comparative Perspective*. Enschede: CHEPS, University of Twente.

Goldsmith, A. A. (1999). 'Africa's Overgrown State Reconsidered: Bureaucracy and Economic Growth', *World Politics*, 51: 520–46.

Goodman, P. (1962). *The Community of Scholars*. New York: Random House.

Gordon, R. A. and Howell, J. E. (1959). *Higher Education for Business*. New York: Columbia University Press.

Gore, C. (2000). 'The Rise and Fall of the Washington Consensus as a Paradigm for Developing Countries', *World Development*, 28: 789–804.

Gouldner, A. W. (1955). *Patterns of Industrial Bureacracy*. Glencoe, IL: Free Press.

Granovetter, M. (1985). 'Economic Action and Social Structure: The Problem of Embeddedness', *American Journal of Sociology*, 91: 481–510.

Gray, S. J., Meek, G. K., and Roberts, C. B. (1995). 'International Capital Market Pressures and Voluntary Annual Report Disclosures by U.S. and U.K. Multinationals', *Journal of International Financial Management and Accounting*, 6(1): 43–68.

Grayson, D. (2004). *Corporate Social Opportunity*. Sheffield: Greenleaf.

Greene, J. H. (1937). *Organized Training in Business*. New York: Harper & Brothers.

Greene, W. H. (1997). *Econometric Analysis*, 3rd edn. Upper Saddle River, New Jersey: Prentice-Hall.

Greenfeld, L. (1992). *Nationalism: Five Roads to Modernity*. Cambridge, MA: Harvard University Press.

Grigorescu, A. (2003). 'International Organizations and Government Transparency: Linking the International and Domestic Realms', *International Studies Quarterly*, 47: 643–67.

Gross, E. (1968). 'Universities as Organizations: A Study of Goals', *American Sociological Review*, 33: 518–44.

Grusky, D. (ed.) (2001). *Social Stratification: Class, Race, and Gender in Sociological Perspectives*, 2nd edn. Boulder, CO: Westview.

Gugler, K, Mueller, D. C., and Yortoglu, B. B. (2004). 'Corporate Governance and Globalization', *Oxford Review of Economic Policy*, 20: 129–56.

Guillén, M. F. (1994). *Models of Management: Work, Authority, and Organization in a Comparative Perspective*. Chicago, IL: University of Chicago Press.

—— (1998). 'International Management and the Circulation of Ideas', in C. L. Cooper and D. M. Rousseau (eds.), *Trends in Organizational Behavior*, Vol. 5. New York: Wiley, pp. 47–63.

—— (2001). 'Is Globalization Civilizing, Destructive or Feeble? A Critique of Five Key Debates in the Social Science Literature', *Annual Review of Sociology*, 27: 235–60.

Guler, I., Guillén, M. F., and MacPherson, J. M. (2002). 'Global Competition, Institutions and the Diffusion of Organizational Practices: The International Spread of ISO 9000 Quality Certificates', *Administrative Science Quarterly*, 47: 207–32.

Haas, P. (1992). 'Epistemic Communities and International Policy Coordination', *International Organization*, 46: 1–35.

Habermas, J. (1993). *Justification and Application*. Cambridge, MA: MIT Press.

Hackett, B. (1997). *The Value of Training in the Era of Intellectual Capital: A Research Report*. Report Number 1199–97-RR, The Conference Board.

Hackett, E. J. (1990). 'Science as a Vocation in the 1990s: The Changing Organizational Culture of Science', *Journal of Higher Education*, 61(3): 241–79.

Hackman, J. R. and Wageman, R. (1995). 'Total Quality Management: Empirical, Conceptual and Practical Issues', *Administrative Science Quarterly*, 40: 309–42.

Haggard, S. (1990). *Pathways from the Periphery: The Politics of Growth in the Newly Industrializing Countries*. Ithaca, NY: Cornell University Press.

Hagigh, S. E. (1992). 'Obtaining EC Product Approvals after 1992: What American Manufacturers Need to Know', *Business America*, 113(4): 30–3.

Hall, P. (1986). *Governing the Economy: The Politics of State Intervention in Britain and France*. New York: Oxford University Press.

—— (ed.) (1989). *The Political Power of Economic Ideas*. Princeton, NJ: Princeton University Press.

Hamann, R. (2004). 'Corporate Responsibility, Partnerships, and Institutional Change: The Case of Mining Companies in South Africa', *Natural Resources Forum*, 28: 1–13.

Handy, C. (2003). 'What's a Business for?' in *Harvard Business Review on Corporate responsibility*. Cambridge, MA: Harvard Business School Press, pp. 27–64.

Hannan, M. T. and Freeman, J. (1977). 'The Population Ecology of Organizations', *American Journal of Sociology*, 82: 929–64.

—— (1989). *Organizational Ecology*. Cambridge, MA: Harvard University Press.

Haraway, D. J. (1996). *Modest-witness @Second-Millenium: FemaleMan-Meets-OncoMouse: Feminism and Technoscience*. New York: Routledge.

Hasse, R. and Krücken, G. (2005). *Neo-Institutionalismus*. Rev. edn. Bielefeld: transcript Verlag.

Hedberg, B. and Jonsson, S. (1978). 'Designing Semi-Confusing Information Systems for Organizations in Changing Environments', *Accounting, Organizations, Society*, 3(1): 47–64.

Hedmo, T. and Sahlin-Andersson, K., and Wedlin, L. (2005). 'The Emergence of a European Regulatory Field of Management Education', Forthcoming in M.-L. Djelic and K. Sahlin-Andersson (eds.), *Transnational Governance: Institutional Dynamics of Regulation*. Cambridge: Cambridge University Press.

—— (2005). 'Fields of Imitation: the Global Expansion of Management Education', in B. Czarniawska and G. Sévon (eds)., *How Ideas, Objects, and Practices Travel in the Global Economy*. Malmö: Liber, pp. 190–212.

Heinz, J. P., Nelson, R. L., and Laumann, E. O. (2001). 'The Scale of Justice: Observations on the Transformation of Urban Law Practice', *Annual Review of Sociology*, 27: 337–62.

Held, D. and McGrew, A. G. (2002*a*). *Globalization/Anti-Globalization*. Malden, MA: Blackwell.

—— (2002*b*). *Governing Globalization: Power, Authority and Global Governance*. Malden, MA: Polity Press.

Held, D., McGrew, A., et al. (1999). *Global Transformations: Politics, Economics and Culture*. Stanford, CA: Stanford University Press.

Heller, K. (1993). 'ISO 9000: A Framework for Continuous Improvement', *Chemical Week*, 153(10): 30–2.

Henderson, D. (2002). *Misquided Virtue: False Notions of Corporate Responsibility*. London: Institute of Economic Affairs.

Hicks, S. R. C. (2004). *Explaining Postmodernism: Skepticism and Socialism from Rousseau to Foucault*. Scholargy Publishing.

Hickson, D. J. and Pugh, D. S. (1995). *Management Worldwide: The Impact of Societal Culture on Organizations around the Globe*. New York: Penguin Books.

Hirschman, A. O. (1981). *Essays in Trespassing: Economics to Politics and Beyond*. Cambridge: Cambridge University Press.

—— (1995). *A Propensity to Self-Subversion*. Cambridge, MA: Harvard University Press.

Hobsbawm, E. J. (1993). *Nations and Nationalism Since 1780*. Cambridge, UK: Cambridge University Press.

Hofstede, G. (1980). *Culture's Consequences: International Differences in Work Related Values*. Newbury Park, CA: Sage.

—— (1991). *Cultures and Organizations: Software of the Mind*. McGraw-Hill.

Hofstede, G. (1994). *Uncommon Sense About Organizations: Cases, Studies and Field Observations*. Thousand Oaks, CA: Sage.

Hopwood, A. G. and Miller, P. (1994). *Accounting as Social and Institutional Practice*. New York: Cambridge University Press.

Houtart, F. and Polet, F. (eds.) (2001). *The Other Davos: The Globalization of Resistance to the World Economic System*.

Huisman, J. and Currie, J. (2004). 'Accountability in Higher Education: Bridge over Troubled water?' *Higher Education*, 48: 529–51.

Huntington, S. (1991). *The Third Wave: Democratization in the Late Twentieth Century*. University of Oklahoma Press.

Hutchins, G. (1993*a*). *ISO 9000: A Comprehensive Guide to Registration, Audit Guidelines, and Successful Certification*. Essex Junction, Vermont: Oliver Wright.

—— (1993*b*). 'ISO 9000 Offers a Global "Mark of Excellence" ', *Public Utilities Fortnightly*, 131(8): 35–6.

Hwang, H. (2003). *Planning Development: State, Globalization, and Shifting Locus of Planning*. Unpublished Ph.D. Dissertation, Stanford University, Department of Sociology.

—— and Powell, W. W. (2005). 'Institutions and Entrepreneurship', in S. Alvarez, R. Agrawal, and O. Sorenson (eds.), *Handbook of Entrepreneurship Research: Disciplinary Perspectives*. Kluwer Publishers, pp. 200–27.

—— and Suarez, D. (2005). 'Lost and Found in the Translation of Strategic Plans and Websites', in B. Czarniawska and G. Sévon (eds.), *How Ideas, Objects, and Practices Travel in the Global Economy*. Malmö: Liber, pp. 71–93.

Industrial Engineering (1993*a*). 'National ISO 9000 Support Group Expands into Europe', 25(8): 10.

—— (1993*b*). 'Support Group Formed for Companies Seeking ISO 9000', 25(3): 8–9.

Inglehart, R. and Baker, W. E. (2000). 'Modernization, cultural change, and the persistence of traditional values', *American Sociological Review*, 65: 19–51.

Inhaber, H. (1977). 'Scientists and Economic Growth', *Social Studies of Science*, 7: 517–24.

Inkeles, A. (1976). 'A Model of the Modern Man: Theoretical and Methodological Issues', in C. E. Black (ed.), *Comparative Modernization: A Reader*. pp. 320–48.

—— and Smith, D. (1974). *Becoming Modern*. Cambridge, MA: Harvard University Press.

Inoue, K. (2003). *Vive la Patiente! Discourse Analysis of the Global Expansion of Health as a Human Right*. Unpublished Ph.D. Dissertation, Stanford University, School of Education.

Inter Documentation Company (Various Years). *National Development Plans*. Zug, Switzerland: Inter Documentation Company.

International Association of Universities (1959–2000). *International Handbook of Universities*. Paris: IAU Press for the Association of Universities.

International Association of University Presidents (IAUP) (2002). *Charter of the International Association of University Presidents*. Sydney.

International Finance Corporation (1988, 1992, 1999). *Emerging Stock Markets Factbook*, Washington, DC: Author.

ISO (International Organization for Standardization) (1988*a*, 1991*a*, 1996*a*, 2000*a*). *ISO Members*, 6th–9th edn. Geneva: ISO Central Secretariat.

ISO (1992*a*). *International Standards for Quality Management—Compendium*, 2nd edn. Geneva: ISO 9000 Central Secretariat.

—— (1992*c*, 1993*c*, 1995*c*). *Directory of Quality System Registration Bodies: Third-party bodies operating quality system registration programmes*, 1st–3rd edn. Geneva: ISO Central Secretariat.

—— (1997). *Historical Record of ISO Membership since its Creation, 1947–1997* [Chart]. Geneva: ISO Central Secretariat.

—— (1999*a*). *The ISO Survey of ISO 9000 and ISO 14000 Certificates—Eighth Cycle.* Paris: ISO Secretariat.

—— (1999*b*). *ISO Annual Report.* Geneva: ISO Central Secretariat.

—— (1999*c*). *ISO Directory of ISO 9000 and ISO 14000 Accreditation and Certification Bodies*, 4th edn. Geneva: ISO Central Secretariat.

—— (2003). *The ISO Survey of ISO 9000 and ISO 14001 Certificates—Twelfth Cycle.* Paris: ISO Secretariat.

Jackson, J. T. (2005). *The Globalizers: Development Workers in Action.* Baltimore, MD: Johns Hopkins University Press.

Jackson, T. (2003). 'Management Ethics and Corporate Policy: A Cross-Cultural Comparison', *Journal of Management Studies*, 37: 349–69.

Jang, Y. S. (2000). 'The Worldwide Founding of Ministries of Science and Technology, 1950–1990', *Sociological Perspectives*, 43: 247–70.

—— (2001). *The Expansion of Modern Accounting as a Global and Institutional Practice.* Unpublished doctoral dissertation, Stanford University.

Jasanoff, S. (1990). *The Fifth Branch: Science Advisers as Policymakers.* Cambridge, MA: Harvard University Press.

Jenkins, C. L. (2005). 'Va. Expands Use of Sentencing Tool for Judges', *Washington Post* Sunday, 24 April 2005: C01.

Jepperson, R. L. (1999). 'Institutional Logics: Two Fundamental Dimensions of Structuration Distinguishing the Modern Nation-State Polities', Paper presented at the annual meetings of the American Sociological Association, August.

—— (2002*a*). 'Political Modernities: Disentangling Two Underlying Dimensions of Institutional Differentiation', *Sociological Theory*, 20: 61–85.

—— (2002*b*). 'The Development and Application of Sociological Neo-Institutionalism', in J. Berger and M. Zelditch Jr. (eds.), *New Directions in Contemporary Sociological Theory.* Lanham, MD: Rowman and Littlefield, pp. 229–66.

—— and Meyer, J. W. (1991). 'The Public Order and the Construction of Formal Organizations', in W. W. Powell and P. J. DiMaggio (eds.), *The New Institutionalism in Organizational Analysis.* Chicago, IL: University of Chicago Press, pp. 204–31.

Jones, G. (2005). *Multinationals and Global Capitalism: From the Nineteenth to the Twenty First Century.* Oxford: Oxford University Press.

Jones, T. M. (1999). 'The Institutional Determinants of Social Responsibility', *Business and Society*, 20: 163–79.

Juran, J. M. (1993). 'Assessing Quality Growth in the US', *Quality*, 32(10): 48–9.

Kagan, A. (1992). 'ISO 9000: Transport Engineering Sectors Move Toward Registration', *Chemical Week*, 151(19): 48–52.

Kanter, R. M. (2003). 'From Spare Change to Real Change: The Social Sector as Beta Site for Business Innovation', in *Harvard Business Review on Corporate responsibility.* Cambridge, MA: Harvard Business School Press, pp. 189–214.

Katz, H. and Keefe, J. (1993). 'Training and Restructuring of Work in Large Unionized Settings', Working paper, Ithaca, NY: Center for Advanced Human Resource Studies, Cornell University.

Keller, G. (1986). *Academic Strategy. The Management Revolution in American Higher Education*, 5th Print. Baltimore, MD: Johns Hopkins University Press.

Kelly, E. and Dobbin, F. (1998). 'How Affirmative Action Became Diversity Management: Employer Response to Antidiscrimination Law, 1961–1996', *American Behavioral Scientist*, 41(7): 960–84.

Kempner, K. and Jurema, A. L. (2002). 'The Global Politics of Education: Brazil and the World Bank', *Higher Education*, 43: 331–54.

Keohane, R. O. and Nye, J. S. Jr. (2000). 'Globalization: What's New? What's Not? (And So What?)', *Foreign Policy*, 118: 104–19.

Kerr, C. (2001). *The Uses of the University*, 5th edn. Cambridge, MA: Harvard University Press.

—— Dunlop, J., Harbison, F., and Myers, C. (1960). *Industrialism and Industrial Man: The Problems of Labor and Management in Economic Growth*. Cambridge, MA: Harvard University Press.

Khagram, S. (2004). *Dams and Development:Transnational Struggles for Water and Power*. Ithaca, NY: Cornell University Press.

—— and Saleem, A. (2005). 'Transnational Transformations: From Government-Centric International Regimes to Multi-Actor Global Governance', Forthcoming in K. Conca (ed.), *Sustainable Global Governance*. Cambridge, MA: MIT Press.

Kieser, A. (1987). 'From Asceticism to Administration of Wealth. Medieval Monasteries and the Pitfalls of Rationalization', *Organization Studies*, 8: 103–24.

—— (1989). 'Organizational, Institutional, and Societal Evolution: Medieval Craft Guilds and the Genesis of Formal Organizations', *Administrative Science Quarterly*, 34: 540–64.

Kim, Y. S., Jang, Y. S., and Hwang, H. (2002). 'Structural Expansion and the Cost of Global Isomorphism: A Cross-National Study of Modern Ministerial Structures, 1950–1990', *International Sociology*, 17(4): 481–504.

Kimberly, J. R. (1984). 'Managerial Innovation', in P. Nystrom and W. Starbuck (eds.), *Handbook of Organizational Design*. New York: Oxford Press, pp. 84–104.

Kipping, M. (1999). 'American Management Consulting Companies in Western Europe, 1920 to 1990: Products, Reputation, and Relationships', *Business History Review*, 73: 190–220.

—— and Engwall, L. (2002). *Management Consulting: Emergence and Dynamics of a Knowledge Industry*. Oxford: Oxford University Press.

Kirk, K. and Mouritsen, J. (1996). 'Spaces of Accountability: Systems of Accountability in a Multinational Firm', in R. Munro and J. Mouritsen (eds.), *Accountability: Power, Ethos, & the Technologies of Managing*. London: International Thomson Business Press, pp. 245–60.

Kirp, D. L. (2004). *Shakespeare, Einstein, and the Bottom Line: The Marketing of Higher Education*. Harvard University Press.

Kleinman, D. L. (2003). *Impure Cultures: University Biology and the World of Commerce.* Madison: University of Wisconsin Press.

Koch, M., Nam, S. H., and Steers, R. M. (1995). 'Human Resource Management in South Korea', in L. F. Moore and P. D. Jennings (eds.), *Human Resource Management on the Pacific Rim: Institutions, Practices, and Attitudes.* New York: Walter de Gruyter.

Kochan, A. (1993). 'ISO 9000: Creating a Global Standardization Process', *Quality,* 32(10): 26–34.

Kochan, T. and Osterman, P. (1991). *Human Resource Development and Utilization: Is There Too Little in the U.S.* Cambridge, MA: Sloan School of Management, Massachusetts Institute of Technology.

Kogut, B. and Parkinson, D. (1993). 'The Diffusion of American Organizing Principles to Europe', in B. Kogut (ed.), *Country Competitiveness: Technology and the Organizing of Work.* Oxford: Oxford University Press, pp. 179–202.

Kooiman, J. (2003). *Governing as Governance.* London: Sage.

Kostera, M. (1995). 'The Modern Crusade: The Missionaries of Management Come to Eastern Europe', *Management Learning,* 26(3): 331–52.

Korea (1986). *The Sixth Five-Year Economic and Social Development plan, 1987–1991.* Seoul: The Government of the Republic of Korea.

Krücken, G. (2002). 'Amerikanischer neo-institutionalismus—europäische perspektiven', *Sociologia Internationalis,* 40: 227–59.

—— Meier, F., and Müller, A. (2005). 'Information, Cooperation, and the Blurring of Boundaries—Technology Transfer in German and American Discourses', *Higher Education* 48 (forthcoming).

LaFree, G. and Morris, N. (2004). 'Corruption as a Global Social Problem', in George Ritzer (ed.), *Handbook of Social Problems: A Comparative International Perspective.* London: Sage, pp. 600–18.

Lamprecht, J. L. (1993). *Implementing the ISO 9000 Series.* New York: Marcel Dekker.

—— (1991). 'ISO 9000 Implementation Strategies', *Quality,* 30(11): 14–17.

LaPalombara, J. (1994). 'Structural and Institutional Aspects of Corruption', *Social Research,* 61: 325–50.

La Porta, R., Lopez-de-Silanes, F., and Shleifer, A. (1998). 'Law and Finance', *Journal of Political Economy,* 106(6): 1113–55.

Lauren, P. (2003). *The Evolution of International Human Rights,* 2nd edn. Philadelphia: University of Pennsylvania Press.

Laurent, A. (1983). 'The Cultural Diversity of Western Conceptions of Management', *International Studies in Management and Organization,* 13(Spr/Sum): 75–96.

Lawler, J. J. and Atmiyanandana, V. (1995). 'Human Resource Management in Thailand', in L. F. Moore and P. D. Jennings (eds.), *Human Resource Management on the Pacific Rim: Institutions, Practices, and Attitudes.* New York: Walter de Gruyter.

Lazarsfeld, P. F. and Sieber, S. D. (1964). *Organizing Educational Research: An Exploration.* Englewood Cliffs: Prentice-Hall.

Leftwitch, A. (2000). *States of Development: On the Primacy of Politics in Development.* Cambridge, UK: Polity Press.

Lesotho (1997). *Sixth National Development Plan, 1996/97–1998/99.* Maseru: The Ministry.

Levine, J. B. (1991). 'It's an Old World in More Ways than One', *Business Week,* Special Edition on Quality: 26–8.

—— (1992). 'Want EC Business? You Have Two Choices', *Business Week,* (3288): 58–9.

Levitt, T. (1958). 'The Dangers of Social Responsibility', *Harvard Business Review,* 36: 41–50.

Lewis, W. A. (1966). *Development Planning: The Essentials of Economic Policy.* New York: Harper & Row.

—— (1955). *The Theory of Economic Growth.* London: Allen and Unwin.

Li, C. (1928). 'A Summer in the Ford Works', *Personnel Journal,* 7: 18–32.

Liao, C. (1991). *Human Resource Management.* Shanghai: Tungchi University Press.

Lindblom, C. E. (1977). *Politics and Markets: The World's Political-Economic Systems.* New York: Basic Books.

Locke, R. (1984). *The End of Practical Man: Entrepreneurship and Higher Education in Germany, France, and Great Britain, 1880–1940.* Greenwich: JAI Press.

—— (1989). *Management and Higher Education Since 1940: The Influence of America and Japan on West Germany, Great Britain and France.* Cambridge: Cambridge University Press.

Lovelock, J. E. (1988). *The Ages of Gaia.* New York: W.W. Norton.

Loya, T. and Boli, J. (1999). 'Standardization in the World Polity: Technical Rationality Over Power', in J. Boli and G. M. Thomas (eds.), *Constructing World Culture: International Nongovernmental Organizations Since 1875.* Stanford, CA: Stanford University Press, pp. 169–97.

Luhmann, N. (1995). *Social Systems,* Trans. E. M. Knodt. Stanford, CA: Stanford University Press.

Lund-Thomsen, P. (2005). 'Corporate Accountability in South Africa: The Role of Community in Mobilizing Environmental Governance', *International Affairs,* 81: 619–33.

Luo, X. (2002). 'From Technical Skills to Personal Development: Employee Training in US Organizations in the Twentieth Century', in K. Sahlin-Andersson and L. Engwall (eds.), *The Expansion of Management Knowledge: Carriers, Ideas and Circulation.* Stanford, CA: Stanford University Press.

Lynch, L. M. (1994). *Training and the Private Sector: International Comparisons.* Chicago, IL: University of Chicago Press.

MacDuffie, J. P. and Kochan, T. A. (1995). 'Do U.S. Firms Invest Less in Human Resources? Training in the World Auto Industry', *Industrial Relations,* 34: 147–68.

Mackay, L., Scott, P., and Smith, D. (1995). 'Restructured and Differentiated? Institutional Responses to the Changing Environment of UK Higher Education', *Higher Education Management,* 7: 193–203.

Maier, C. S. (1970). 'Between Taylorism and Technocracy: European Ideologies and the Vision of Industrial Productivity in the 1920s', *Journal of Contemporary History,* 5(2): 27–61. Reprinted in C. S. Maier (1987), *In Search of Stability: Explorations in Historical Political Economy.* Cambridge: Cambridge University Press.

Maignan, I. and Ralston, D. A. (2002). 'Corporate Responsibility in Europe and the U.S.: Insights From Businesses "Self-Presentations" ', *Journal of International Business Studies*, 33: 497–514.

Mallaby, S. (2004). *The World's Banker.* New York: Penguin Press.

Mander, J. and Goldsmith, E. (1996). *The Case Against the Global Economy . . . and for a Turn Towards the Local.* San Francisco: Sierra Club.

Mann, M. (1993). 'Nation-States in Europe and Other Continents: Diversifying, Developing, Not Dying', *Daedalus*, 122: 115–40.

March, J. G. (1981). 'Decisions in Organizations and Theories of Choice', in A. V. de Ven and W. Joyce (eds.), *Perspectives on Organization Design and Behavior.* New York: Wiley, pp. 205–44.

—— (1987). 'Ambiguity and Accounting: The Elusive Link Between Information and Decision-Making', *Accounting, Organization, and Society*, 12: 153–68.

March, J. G. and Simon, H. A. (1993, 1958). *Organizations*, 2nd edn. Cambridge: Blackwell.

March, J. and Olsen, J. (1976). *Ambiguity and Choice in Organizations.* Bergen: Universitetsforlaget.

—— (1989). *Rediscovering Institutions.* New York: Free Press.

Marginson, S. and Considine, M. (2000). *The Enterprise University. Power, Governance and Reinvention in Australia.* Cambridge: Cambridge University Press.

Margolis, J. D. and Walsh, J. P. (2003). 'Misery Loves Companies: Rethinking Social Initiatives by Business', *Administrative Science Quarterly*, 48: 268–305.

Marquardt, D. W. (1992). 'ISO 9000: A Universal Standard of Quality', *Management Review*, 81(1): 50–2.

Marquette, H. (2003). *Corruption, Politics and Development: The Origins and Development of the World bank's Anti-Corruption Agenda.* Palgrave: Basingstoke.

Marshall, T. H. (1964). *Class, Citizenship, and Social Development.* Garden City, NY: Doubleday.

Martin, J. L. (2003). 'What is Field Theory?', *American Journal of Sociology*, 103: 1–49.

Matten, D. and Crane, A. (2003). 'Corporate Responsibility: Towards an Extended Theoretical Conceptualization', ICRC Working Paper.

—— Crane, A., and Chapple, W. (2003). 'Behind the Mask: Revealing the True Face of Corporate Responsibility', *Journal of Business Ethics*, 45: 109–20.

Mauro, P. (1995). 'Corruption and Growth', *Quarterly Journal of Economics*, 110: 681–712.

Mayo, E. (1945). *The Social Problems of an Industrial Civilization.* Cambridge, MA: Harvard University Press.

McEneaney, E. H. (2003). 'Elemenst of Contemporary Primary School Education', in G. S. Drori, J. W. Meyer, F. O. Ramirez, and E. Schofer (eds.), *Science in the Modern World Polity: Institutionalization and Globalization.* Stanford, CA: Stanford University Press, pp. 136–54.

McEneaney, E. and Meyer, J. (2000). 'The Content of the Curriculum: An Institutionalist Perspective', in M. Hallinan (ed.), *Handbook of Sociology of Education.* New York: Plenum Press, pp. 189–211.

McGregor, D. (1960). *The Human Side of Enterprise*. New York: McGraw-Hill.

McKenna, C. D. (1995). 'The Origins of Modern Management Consulting', *Business and Economic History*, 24: 51–8.

—— Djelic, M.-L., and Ainamo, A. (2000). 'Message and Medium: The Role of Consulting Firms in the Process of Globalization and its Local Interpretation', Paper presented at the 16TH EGOS Colloquium, Helsinki School of Economics and Business Administration, July 2–4.

McNeely, C. L. (1995). *Constructing the Nation-State: International Organization and Prescriptive Action*. Westport: Greenwood Press.

McSweeney, B. (1996). 'The Arrival of an Accountability: Explaining the Imposition of Management by Accounting', in R. Munro and J. Mouritsen (eds.), *Accountability: Power, Ethos, & the Technologies of Managing*. London: International Thomson Business Press, pp. 201–24.

McWilliam, R. C. (1997). Personal Communication with Robert C. McWilliam, Senior Curator-Technology and Standards, The National Museum of Science and Industry, London, October 10.

Mello, S. (1999). 'Business and Social Responsibility: A Study in North East of Brazil'. http://www.rits.org.br/acervo/

Mendel, P. J. (2001). *Global Models of Organization: International Management Standards, Reforms, and Movements*. Doctoral dissertation, Department of Sociology, Stanford University.

—— (2002). 'International Standardization and Global Governance: The Spread of Quality and Environmental Management Standards', in A. J. Hoffman and M. J. Ventresca (eds.), *Organizations, Policy, and the Natural Environment: Institutional and Strategic Perspectives*. Stanford, CA: Stanford University Press, pp. 407–31.

Meridian Securities Markets (1999). *World Stock Exchange Factbook*.

Merlin Falcon Limited (1999). *The Merlin Falcon MBA Guide* [Internet Site]. http://www.merlinfalcon.com/

Merton, R. K. (1940/1957). 'Bureaucratic Structure and Personality', in *Social Theory and Social Structure*, 2nd edn. Glencoe, IL: Free Press, pp. 195–206.

—— (1938/1970). *Science, Technology, and Society in Seventeenth Century England*. New York: Ferting Howard.

—— (1973). *The Sociology of Science*. Chicago, IL: University of Chicago Press.

Metra Consulting (1985). *Handbook of National Development Plans*. London: Graham & Trotman.

Meyer, J. W. (1977). 'Effects of Education as an Institution', *American Journal of Sociology*, 83: 55–77.

—— (1980). 'The World Polity and the Authority of the Nation-State', in A. J. Bergesen (ed.), *Studies of the modern world system*. New York: Academic Press.

—— (1983). 'Institutionalization and the Rationality of Formal Organizational Structure', in J. Meyer and W. R. Scott (eds.), *Organizational Environments*. Beverly Hills: Sage, pp. 261–82.

—— (1986). 'Social Environments and Organizational Accounting', *Accounting, Organizations, and Society*, 11: 345–56.

—— (1992). 'Conclusion: Institutionalization and the Rationality of Formal Organizational Structure', in J. W. Meyer and W. R. Scott (eds.), *Organizational Environments: Ritual and Rationality*. Newbury Park, CA: Sage.

—— (1994). 'Rationalized Environments', in W. R. Scott and J. W. Meyer (eds.), *Institutional Environments and Organizations*. Thousand Oaks, CA: Sage, pp. 28–54.

—— (1996). 'Otherhood: The Promulgation and Transmission of Ideas in the Modern Organizational Environment', in Czarniawska and Sevon. (eds.), *Translating Organizational Change*. Berlin: Walter de Gruyter.

—— (1997). 'Contextual Conditions of Standardization', Paper presented at the SCANCOR/SCORE Seminar on Standardization, Lund, Sweden, September 18–20, 1997.

—— (1998). 'Foreward', in O. Olson, J. Guthrie, and C. Humphry (eds.), *Global Warning: Debating International Developments in New Public Financial Management*. Oslo: Cappenlen Akademisk Forlag AS, pp. 7–13.

—— (2000). 'Globalization: Sources and effects on national states and societies', *International Sociology*, 15(2): 233–48.

—— (2002). 'Globalization and the Expansion and Standardization of Management', in K. Sahlin-Andersson and L. Engwall (eds.), *The Expansion of Management Knowledge: Carriers, Flows and Sources*. Stanford, CA: Stanford Business Books, pp. 44–57.

—— Kamens, D. H., and Benavot, A. (1992). *School Knowledge for the Masses: World Models and National Primary Curricular Categories in the Twentieth Century*. Washington, DC: The Falmer Press.

—— and Jepperson, R. L. (2000). 'The "Actors" of Modern Society: The Cultural Construction of Social Agency', *Sociological Theory*, 18(1): 100–20.

—— and Rowan, B. (1977). 'Institutionalized Organizations: Formal Structure as Myth and Ceremony', *American Journal of Sociology*, 83: 340–63.

—— and Scott, R. W. (1983). *Organizational Environments: Ritual and Rationality*. Beverly Hills: Sage.

—— Boli, J., and Thomas, G. M. (1994). 'Ontology and Rationalization in the Western Cultural Account', in W. R. Scott and J. W. Meyer (eds.), *Institutional Environments and Organizations: Structural Complexity and Individualism*. Thousand Oaks, CA: Sage, pp. 9–27.

Meyer, J. W. Boli-Bennet, J., and Chase-Dunn, C. (1975). 'Convergence and Divergence in Development', *Annual Review of Sociology*, 1: 223–46.

—— Boli, J., Thomas, G., and Ramirez, F. O. (1997). 'World Society and the Nation State'. *American Journal of Sociology*, 103: 144–181.

—— Kamens, D., Benavot, A., Cha, Y.-K., and Wong, S.-Y. (1992). *School Knowledge for the Masses*. London: Falmer.

Meyer, M. W. (1978). *Environments and Organizations*. San Francisco: Jossey-Bass.

Mezias, S. J. (1995). 'Using Institutional Theory to Understand For-Profit Sectors: The Case for Financial Reporting Standards', in W. R. Scott and S. Christensen (eds.), *The Institutional Construction of Organizations: International and Longitudinal Studies*. Thousand Oaks, CA: Sage, pp. 164–96.

Michael, B. (2004). 'Explaining Organizational Change in International Development: The Role of Complexity in Anti-Corruption Work', *Journal of International Development*, 16: 1067–88.

Miller, J. (1993). *The Passion of Michel Foucault*. London: HarperCollins.

Miller, V. A. (1987). 'The History of Training', in R. L. Craig (ed.), *Training & Development Handbook: A Guide to Human Resource Development*, 3rd edn. New York: McGraw-Hill.

Millett, J. D. (1962). *Academic Community: An Essay on Organization*. New York: McGraw-Hill.

Mintzberg, H. (1994). *The Rise and Fall of Strategic Planning*. New York: Free Press.

—— (1989). *Mintzberg on Management: Inside the Strange world of Organizations*. New York: Free Press.

—— Ahlstrand, B., and Lampel, J., (1998). *Strategy Safari: A Guided Tour of the Wilds of Strategic Management*. New York: Free Press.

Mitchell, T. (1988). *Colonizing Egypt*. Cambridge: Cambridge University Press.

—— (1991). 'The Limits of the State', *American Political Science Review*, 85: 77–96.

Mobil Europe, Ltd (1995). 'The Mobil Survey of ISO 9000 Certificates Awarded Worldwide (Fourth Cycle)', *Quality Systems Update*, September, 5(9).

Monahan, S. (1993). Organizational Effects on Jurisdictional Competition: Who Controls Church Work? Unpublished doctoral dissertation, Stanford University.

Monahan, S. C., Meyer, J., and Scott, W. R. (1994). 'Employee Training: The Expansion of Organizational Citizenship', in W. R. Scott and J. Meyer (eds.), *Institutional Environments and Organizations: Structural Complexity and Individualism*. Newbury Park, CA: Sage.

Moon, H. (2002). *The Globalization of Professional Management Education, 1881–2000: Its Rise, Expansion, and Implications*. Unpublished doctoral dissertation, Stanford University.

Moore, K. (1996). 'Organizing Integrity: American Science and the Creation of Public Interest Organizations', *American Journal of Sociology*, 101: 1592–627.

Mörth, U. (ed.) (2004). *Soft law in governance and regulation: An interdisciplinary analysis*. Cheltenham: Edward Elgar.

Mosson, T. M. (1965). *Management Education in Five European Countries*. London: Business Administration.

Mulkay, M. J. (1983). *Science Observed*. London: Sage.

Mullin, R. (1992). 'Service Sector Gets in Line: Still No Rush to Register', *Chemical Week*, 150(17): 46.

Murphy, L. Murphy, L. M. (2005). 'Transitional Advocacy in Education, Changing Roles for NGOs: Examining the Construction of a Global Campaign and its Effects on "Eduction for All" in Uganda. Unpublished Ph.D. Dissertation, Stanford, CH: Stanford University.

Musselin, C. (1999). 'State/University Relations and How to Change Them: The Case of France and Germany', in M. Henkel and B. Little (eds.), *Changing Relationships between Higher Education and the State*. London: Jessica Kingsley, pp. 42–68.

—— (2004a). 'Are Universities Specific Organizations?' Paper presented at the Conference 'Towards a Multiversity? Universities between National Traditions and Global Trends in Higher Education,' Institute for Science and Technology Studies, Bielefeld University, November 11–13, 2004.

—— (2004*b*). *The Long March of French Universities*. New York/London: Routledge and Falmer.

NAO (National Audit Office) (1990). *Department of Trade and Industry: Promotion of Quality and Standards*. House of Commons Paper HC 157 (1989–90). London: HMSO.

National Board of Employment, Education and Training (NBEET) (1990). *Interim Report on the Benchmark Study of Management Development in Australian Private Enterprise*. Canberra: Australian Government Publishing Service.

Nelson, J. M. (1992). 'Poverty, Equity, and the Politics of Adjustment', in S. Haggard and R. R. Kaufman (eds.), *The Politics of Economic Adjustment*. Princeton, NJ: Princeton University Press, pp. 221–169.

Newell, P. (2005). 'Citizenship, Accountability and Community: The Limits of the CR Agenda', *International Affairs*, 81: 541–57.

Nguyen, P.-D. D. (2000). 'A Faster Plan', *Red Herring*, May: 139–46.

Noe, R. A. (2005). *Employee Training and Development*, 3rd edn. Boston: McGraw-Hill/Irwin.

Nowotny, H., Scott, P., and Gibbons, M. (2000). *Re-thinking Science: Knowledge and the Public in an Age of Uncertainty*. Oxford, UK: Polity Press.

NRC (National Research Council) (1995). *Standards, Conformity Assessment, and Trade into the 21st Century*. Washington, DC: National Academy Press.

Nugent, N. (1994). *The Government and Politics of the European Union*. Durham, NC: Duke University Press.

Nyaw, M. (1995). 'Human Resource Management in the People's Republic of China', in L. F. Moore and P. D. Jennings (eds.), *Human Resource Management on the Pacific Rim: Institutions, Practices, and Attitudes*. New York: Walter de Gruyter.

Ohmae, K. (1990). *The Borderless World*. London: Collins.

Oliviero, M. B. and Simmons, A. (2002). 'Who's Mining the Store? Global Civil Society and Corporate Responsibility', *Global Civil Society*, 77–107.

Olson, O., Guthrie, J., and Humphery, C. (eds.) (1998). *Global Warning!: Debating International Developments in New Public Finance Management*. Oslo: Cappelen Akademisk Forlag.

Olzak, S. (1989). 'Analysis of Events in the Study of Collective Action', *Annual Review of Sociology*, 15: 119–41.

Organisation for Economic Co-Operation and Development (OECD) (1999). *Quality and Internationalisation in Higher Education*. Paris: OECD.

—— (2002). *OECD Science, Technology and Industry Outlook 2002*. Paris: OECD.

Olzak, S. (2004). *OECD Principles of Corporate Governance*. Paris: OECD. http://www.oecd.org/dataoe cd/32/18/31557724.pdf (accessed 9 June 2005).

Ó Rian, S. (2000). 'States and Markets in an Era of Globalization', *Annual Review of Sociology*, 26: 187–213.

Osterfeld, D. (1994). 'The World Bank and the IMF: Misbegotten sisters', in P. J. Boettke (ed.), *The Collapse of Development Planning*. New York: New York University Press, pp. 285–209.

Paget, K. (1990). 'Citizen Organizing: Many Movements, no Majority', *The American Prospect*, 1(2) (June): 115–28.

Painter, C. (1994). 'Public Service Reform: Reinventing or Abandoning Government', *Political Quarterly*, 65: 242–62.

Parsons, T. and Platt, G. M. (1973). *The American University*. Cambridge, MA: Harvard University Press.

Pastor, J. C., Meindl, J., and Hunt, R. (1998). 'The Quality Virus: Interorganizational Contagion in the Adoption of Total Quality Management', in J. L. Alvarez (ed.), *Diffusion and Consumption of Business Knowledge*. New York: St. Martin's Press, pp. 201–18.

Peach, R. W. (ed.) (1992). *The ISO 9000 Handbook*. Fairfax, Virginia: CEEM Information Services.

—— (2000*a*). Telephone interview conducted by author, July 14.

—— (2000*b*). Telephone interview conducted by author, August 25.

Pedersen, J. S. and Dobbin, F. (1997). 'The Social Invention of Collective Actors', *American Behavioral Scientist*, 40(4): 431–43.

Perkins, J. A. (ed.) (1973). *The University as an Organization*. New York: McGraw-Hill.

Perks, R. W. (1993). *Accounting and Society*. New York: Chapman & Hall.

Perrow, C. (1970). *Organizational Analysis: A Sociological View*. London: Tavistock.

—— (1986). *Complex Organizations: A Critical Essay*, 3rd edn. New York: Random House.

—— (1991). 'A Society of Organizations', *Theory and Society*, 20: 725–62.

—— (2002). *Organizing America. Wealth, Power, and the Origins of Corporate Capitalism*. Princeton, NJ: Princeton University Press.

Peters, T. and Waterman, R. (1982). *In Search of Excellence*. New York: Harper and Row

Pfeffer, J. (1982). *Organizations and Organization Theory*. Boston: Pitman.

—— (1994). *Competitive Advantage Through People: Unleashing the Power of the Work Force*. Boston: Harvard Business School Press.

—— and Salancik, G. R. (1978). *The External Control of Organizations: A Resource Dependence Perspective*. New York: Harper & Row.

Plessner, H. (1924). 'Zur Soziologie der modernen Forschung und ihrer Organisation in der deutschen Universität', in M. Scheler (ed.), *Soziologie des Wissens*. München and Leipzig: Duncker & Humblodt, pp. 407–25.

Podolny, J. M. (1993). 'A Status-Based Model of Market Competition', *American Journal of Sociology*, 98(4): 829–72.

Polanyi, K. (1944). *The Great Transformation: The Political and Economic Origins of Our Time*. Boston: Beacon Press.

Poon, W. K. (1995). 'Human Resource Management in Hong Kong', in L. F. Moore and P. D. Jennings (eds.), *Human Resource Management on the Pacific Rim: Institutions, Practices, and Attitudes*. New York: Walter de Gruyter.

Port, O. (1993). 'More than a passport to European business', *Business Week, 3343*: 146H–146J.

Porter, M. E. and Kramer, M. R. (2003). 'The Competitive Advantage of Corporate Philanthropy', *Harvard Business Review on Corporate Responsibility*. Cambridge, MA: Harvard Business School Press.

Porter, T. M. (1995). *Trust in Numbers: The Pursuit of Objectivity in Science and Public Life*. Princeton, NJ: Princeton University Press.

Powell, W. W. (2001). 'The Capitalsit Firm in the Twenty-First Century: Emerging patterns in Western Enterprise', in P. DiMaggio (ed.), *The Twenty-First-Century Firm: Changing Economic Organization in International Perspective*. Princeton, NJ: Princeton University Press, pp. 33–68.

—— and Owen-Smith, J. (1998). 'Universities and the Market for Intellectual Property in the Life Sciences', *Journal of Policy Analysis and Management*, 17(2): 253–77.

—— and Snellman, K. (2004). 'The knowledge Economy', *Annual Review of Sociology*, 30: 199–220.

—— and DiMaggio, P. J. (eds.) (1991). *The New Institutionalism in Organizational Analysis*. Chicago, IL: University of Chicago Press.

—— Gammal, D. L., and Simard, C. (2005). 'Close Encounters: The Circulation and Reception of Managerial Practices in the San Francisco Bay Area Nonprofit Community', in B. Czarniawska and G. Sévon (eds.), *How Ideas, Objects, and Practices Travel in the Global Economy*. Malmö: Liber, 233–58.

Power, M. (1997). *The Audit Society*. Oxford: Oxford University Press.

Prahalad, C. K. (2004). *The Fortune at the Bottom of the Pyramid: Eradicating Poverty Through Profits*. New York: Wharton School.

—— and Hammond, A. (2003). 'Serving the World's Poor, Profitably', in *Harvard Business Review on Corporate Responsibility*. Cambridge, MA: Harvard Business School Press, pp. 1–26.

Pritchett, H. S. (1905). 'Shall The University Become a Business Corporate?' *Atlantic Monthly*, 96: 289–99.

Quality Systems Update (1996). 'Hospital's Quality System Gets Clean Bill of Health', *Quality Systems Update: A Global ISO 9000 & ISO 14000 Information Service*, 6(3): 1, 6.

Quazi, A. H. and O'Brien, D. (2000). 'An Empirical Test of a Cross-National Model of Corporate Responsibility', *Journal of Business Ethics*, 25: 33–51.

Ramirez, F. O. (2001). 'Eyes Wide Shut: University, State and Society', A keynote address presented at University of Frankfurt, Frankfurt, Germany.

—— and Boli, J. (1987). 'Global Patterns of Educational Institutionalization', in Thomas et al. (eds.), *Institutional Structure: Constituting State, Society, and the Individual*. Newbury Park: Sage, pp. 150–72.

—— Luo, X., Schofer, E., and Meyer, J. W. (Forthcoming). 'Does Academic Achievement Lead to Economic Development?' *American Journal of Education*.

—— and Meyer, J. W. (2002). *Expansion and Impact of the World Human Rights Regime*. Proposal to the National Science Foundation, Stanford University.

Ramirez, F. O. Soysal, Y., and Shanahan, S. (1998). 'The Changing Logic of Political Citizenship: Cross-National Acquisition of Women's Suffrage', *American Sociological Review*, 62: 735–45.

—— and Wotipka, C. M. (2001). 'Slowly But Surely? The Global Expansion of Women's Participation in Science and Engineering Field of Study, 1972–1992', *Sociology of Education*, 74 (July): 231–51.

Reed Reference Electronic Publishing (1994, 1998). *Corporate Affiliations PLUS* [CD-ROM database]. New Providence, NJ.

Reif, K. and Marlier, E. (1998). *Eurobarometer 44.0: Cancer, Education Issues, and the Single European Currency.* [Computer file]. Conducted by INRA (Europe), Brussels. Koeln, Germany: Zentralarchiv fuer Empirische Sozialforschung [producer]. 3rd ZA edn. Koeln, Germany: Zentralarchiv fuer Empirische Sozialforschung/Ann Arbor, MI: Inter-university Consortium for Political and Social Research [distributors] (1995).

Reimann, C. W. and Hertz, H. S. (1994). 'The Malcolm Baldrige National Quality Award and ISO 9000 Registration: Understanding Their Many Important Differences', Report from the Office of Quality Programs, National Institute of Standards and Technology, Gaithersburg, MD.

Rhoades, G. and Sporn, B. (2002). 'New Models of Management and Shifting Modes and Costs of Production: Europe and the United States', *Tertiary Education and Management*, 8: 3–28.

Rhodes, R. A. W. (1994). 'The Hollowing Out of the State: The Changing Nature of the Public Service in Britain', *Political Quarterly*, 65: 138–51.

Riddle, P. (1989). *University and State: Political Competition and the Rise of Universities, 1200–1985.* Unpublished doctoral dissertation, Stanford University.

Ritzer, G. (ed.) (2004a). *The Handbook of Social Problems: A Comparative International Perspective.* Sage.

—— (2004b). *The Globalization of Nothing.* Thousand Oaks, CA: Pine Forge Press.

Roberts, J. and Scapens, R. (1985). 'Accounting Systems and Systems of Accountability— Understanding Accounting Practices in their Organizational Contexts', *Accounting, Organizations and Society*, 10 (4): 443–56.

Roberts, W. T. (2005). 'The Uneven Globalization of Civil Society Organizations and the Consequences for Cross-National Disparities in Human Development', *International Journal of Sociology and Social Policy*, 25(1/2) 118–44.

Robertson, R. (1992). *Globalization.* London: Sage.

—— (1994). 'Globalization and Glocalization', *Journal of International Communication*, 1: 33–52.

Romanelli, E. and Schoonhoven, C. B. (2001). 'The Local Origins of New Firms', in C. B. Schoonhoven and E. Romanelli (eds.), *The Entrepreneurship Dynamic: Origins of Entrepreneurship and the Evolution of Industries.* Stanford, CA: Stanford University Press, pp. 40–67.

Rose, N. (1996). 'Governing "Advanced" Liberal Democracies', in Barry et al. (eds.), *Foucault and Political Reason.* Chicago, IL: University of Chicago Press, pp. 37–64.

—— (1999). *Powers of Freedom: Reframing Political Thought.* Cambridge: Cambridge University Press.

Rothblatt, S. and Wittrock, B. (eds.) (1993). *The European and American University since 1800. Historical and Sociological Essays.* Cambridge: Cambridge University Press.

Rothery, B. (1993). *ISO 9000*, 2nd edn. Brookfield, Vermont: Gower.

Rourke, F. E. and Brooks, G. E. (1966). *The Managerial Revolution in Higher Education.* Baltimore, MD: Johns Hopkins Press.

Roy, W. G. (1997). *Socializing Capital: The Rise of the Large Industrial Corporation in America.* Princeton, NJ: Princeton University Press.

Ruef, M. (2002). 'At the Interstices of Organizations: The Explosion of the Management Consulting Profession, 1933–1997', in K. Sahlin-Andersson and L. Engwall (eds.), *The Expansion of Management Knowledge: Carriers, Flows, and Sources.* Stanford, CA: Stanford University Press, pp. 74–95.

Ruggie, J. (1982). 'International Regimes, Transactions, and Change: Embedded Liberalism in the Postwar Economic Order', *International Organization*, 36: 379–415.

Sachs, W. (ed.) (1992). *The Development Dictionary: A Guide to Knowledge as Power.* London: Zed Books.

Sagasti, F. (1973). 'Underdevelopment, Science and Technology: The Point of View of the Underdeveloped Countries', *Science Studies*, 3: 47–59.

—— and Alcalde, G. (1999). *Development Cooperation in a Fractured Global Order: An Arduous Transition.* Ottawa: International Development Research Center.

Sahlin-Andersson, K. and Engwall, L. (eds.) (2002). *The Expansion of Management Knowledge: Carriers, Flows and Sources.* Stanford, CA: Stanford Business Books.

Salamon, L. M. (1987). 'Partners in Public Service: The Scope and Theory of Government-Nonprofit Relations', in W. W. Powell (ed.), *The Nonprofit Sector: A Research Handbook.* New Haven: Yale University Press, pp. 99–117.

—— (1994). 'The Rise of the Nonprofit Sector', *Foreign Affairs*, 73 (July–August): 109–22.

Salamon, L., Anheier, H., List, R., and Toepler, S. S. (1999). *Global Civil Society: Dimensions of the Nonprofit Sector.* Johns Hopkins Center for Civil Society Studies.

Sarewitz, D. (1996). *Frontiers of Illusion: Science, Technology, and the Politics of Progress.* Philadelphia, PA: Temple University Press.

Sass, S. A. (1982). *The Pragmatic Imagination: A History of the Wharton School, 1881–1981.* Philadelphia, PA: University of Philadelphia Press.

Saunders, M. (1992). 'ISO 9000 and Marketing in Europe: Should U.S. Manufacturers be Concerned?', *Business America*, 113(8): 24–5.

Saxenian, A. (2002). 'Transnational Communities and the Evolution of Global Production Networks: The Cases of Taiwan, China and India', *Industry and Innovation*, 9(3): 183–202.

Schimank, U. (2001). 'Festgefahrene Gemischtwarenläden. Die deutschen Hochschulen als erfolgreich scheiternde Organisationen', in E. Stölting and U. Schimank (eds.), *Die Krise der Universitäten.* Wiesbaden: Westdeutscher Verlag Leviathan Special Issue 20/2001, pp. 223–42.

Schipper, K. (1981). 'Discussion of Voluntary Corporate Disclosure: The Case of Interim Reporting', *The Journal of Accounting Research*, 19 (Supplement): 621–32.

Schissler, H. and Soysal, Y. N. (2005). *The Nation, Europe, and the World: Textbooks and Curricula in Transition*. Oxford: Berghahn Books.

Schofer, E. (1999). 'The Rationalization of Science and the Scientization of Society: International Science Organizations, 1870–1995', in J. Boli and G. Thomas (eds.), *Constructing World Culture: International Nongovernmental Organization since 1985*. Stanford, CA: Stanford University Press, pp. 249–66.

—— and Meyer, J. W. (2005). 'The World-Wide Expansion of Higher Education in the Twentieth Century', with E. Schofer. Dept. of Sociology, University of Minnesota.

Schwarz, S. and Westerheijden, D. F. (2004). *Accreditation and Evaluation in the European Higher Education Area*. Dordrecht: Kluwer.

Scott, J. (1991). 'The Evidence of Experience', *Critical Inquiry*, 17: 773–97.

Scott, W. R. (1991). 'Unpacking Institutional Arguments', in W. W. Powell and P. J. DiMaggio (eds.), *The New Institutionalism in Organizational Analysis*. Chicago, IL: University of Chicago Press, pp. 164–82.

—— (1992). *Organizations: Rational, Natural, and Open Systems*, 3rd edn. Englewood Cliffs, NJ: Prentice-Hall.

—— (1994). 'Institutions and organizations: toward theoretical synthesis', in W. R. Scott and J. W. Meyer (eds.), *Institutional Environments and Organizations*. London: Sage, 55–80.

—— (1995). *Institutions and Organizations*. Thousand Oaks, CA: Sage.

—— (2001). *Institutions and Organizations*, 2nd edn. Thousand Oaks, CA: Sage.

—— (2003). *Organizations: Rational, Natural, and Open Systems*, 4th edn. New Jersey, NJ: Prentice-Hall.

—— and Meyer, J. W. (1994). *Institutional Environments and Organizations: Structural Complexity and Individualism*. Thousand Oaks, CA: Sage.

—— —— (1994). 'The Rise of Training Programs in Firms and agencies: An institutional perspective', in R. W. Scott and J. W. Meyer (eds.), *Institutional Environments and Organizations*. Thousand Oaks, CA: Sage, pp. 228–54.

—— Ruef, M., Mendel, P. J., and Caronna, C. A. (2000). *Institutional Change and Healthcare Organizations*. Chicago, IL: University of Chicago Press.

Segev, E., Raveh, A., and Farjoun, M. (1999). 'Conceptual Maps of the Leading MBA Programs in the US: Core Courses, Concentration Areas, and the Ranking of the School', *Strategic Management Journal*, 20: 549–65.

Selznick, P. (1957). *Leadership in Administration*. Evanston, IL: Row, Peterson.

Sen, A. (2000). *Development as Freedom*. New York: Anchor Books.

Sethi, S. P. (2003). 'Globalization and the Good Corporation: A Need for Proactive Co-Existence', *Journal of Business Ethics*, 43: 21–31.

Shamir, R. (2004). 'The De-radicalization of Corporate Responsibility', *Critical Sociology*, 30: 669–89.

Shelton, D. (1995). 'Humman Resource Management in Australia', in L. F. Moore and P. D. Jennings (eds.), *Human Resource Management on the Pacific Rim: Institutions, Practices, and Attitudes*. New York: Walter de Gruyter, pp. 31–60.

Shenav, Y. (1995). 'From Chaos to Systems: The Engineering Foundations of Organization Theory', *Administrative Science Quarterly*, 40: 557–85.

Shenhav, Y. and Kamens, D. (1991). 'The "Costs" of Institutional Isomorphism in Non-Western Countries', *Social Studies of Science*, 21: 427–545.

Short, D. G. (1993). *Fundamentals of Financial Accounting*, 7th edn. Boston: Irwin.

Siegel, D. S., Waldman, D., and Link, A. (2003). 'Assessing the Impact of Organizational Practices on the Relative Productivity of University Technology Transfer Offices: An Exploratory Study', *Research Policy*, 32: 27–48.

Sinclair, A. (1995). 'The Chameleon of Accountability: Forms and Discourses', *Accounting, Organizations, and Society*, 20 (2/3): 219–37.

Sinclair, T. J. (1994). 'Passing Judgment: Credit Rating Processes as Regulatory Mechanisms of Governance in the Emerging World Order', *Review of International Political Economy*, 1(1): 133–59.

Singer, J. D. and Small, M. (1977). *Diplomatic Exchange Data, 1815–1970 [Computer file]*. Ann Arbor, MI: Inter-university Consortium for Political and Social Research.

Singh, A. (1995). 'The State and Industrialization in India: Successes and Failures and the Lessons for the Future', in Chang and Rowthorn (eds.), *The Role of the State in Economic Change*. Oxford: Claredon Press, pp. 170–86.

Sklair, L. (2001). *The Transnational Capitalist Class*. Oxford: Blackwell.

Slaughter, S. and Leslie, L. (1997). *Academic Capitalism: Politics, Policies, and the Entrepreneurial University*. Baltimore, MD: Johns Hopkins University Press.

—— and Rhoades, G. (2004). *Academic Capitalism and the New Economy: Markets, State, and Higher Education*. Baltimore, MD: Johns Hopkins University Press.

—— Campbell, T. I. D., Holleman, P., and Morgan, E. (2002). 'The Traffic in Students: Graduate Students as Tokens of Exchange Between Industry and Academe'. *Science, Technology and Human Values*, 27(2): 282–313.

Smith, C. (2003). 'The New Corporate Philanthropy', in *Harvard Business Review on Corporate responsibility*. Cambridge, MA: Harvard Business School Press, pp. 157–88.

Smith, J., Chatfield, C., and Pagnucco, R. (eds.) (1997). *Transnational Social Movements and Global Politics: Solidarity Beyond the State*. Syracuse: Syracuse University Press.

Soo, M. and Carson, C. (2004). 'Managing the Research University. Clark Kerr and the University of California', *Minerva*, 42: 215–36.

Soysal, Y. N. (1994). *Limits of Citizenship: Migrants and Postnational Membership in Europe*. Chicago, IL: University of Chicago Press.

Spizizen, G. (1992). 'The ISO 9000 Standards: Creating a Level Playing Field for International Quality', *National Productivity Review*, 11(3): 331.

Stata Corporation (1999). *Stata Statistics and Data Analysis, Release 6.0 [statisticial computer application]*. College Station, Texas: Stata Press.

—— (2000). *Stata Reference Manual*. College Station, Texas: Stata Press.

Stepan, N. (1978). 'The Interplay Between Socio-Economic Factors and Medical Science: Yellow Fever Research, Cuba, and the United States', *Social Studies of Science*, 8: 397–423.

Stichweh, R. (1984). *Zur Entstehung des modernen Systems wissenschaftlicher Disziplinen: Physik in Deutschland 1740–1890*. Frankfurt a.M.: Suhrkamp.

Stiglitz, J. E. (1994). *Wither Socialism?* Cambridge, MA: MIT Press.

Stinchcombe, A. L. (1965). 'Social structures and Organizations', in J. March (ed.), *Handbook of Organizations*. Chicago, IL: Rand McNally, pp. 142–93.

—— (1990). *Information and Organizations*. Berkeley, CA: University of California Press.

Stopford, J. and Strange, S. (1991). *Rival States, Rival Firms: Competition for World Market Shares*. Cambridge: Cambridge University Press.

Strang, D. (1990). 'From Dependency to Sovereignty: An Event History Analysis of Decolonization 1870–1987', *American Sociological Review*, 55: 846–60.

—— (1991). 'Adding Social Structure to Diffusion Models: An Event History Framework', *Sociological Methods and Research*, 19: 324–53.

—— (1997). 'Cheap Talk: Managerial Discourse on Quality Circles as an Organizational Innovation', Technical Report 97–1, Department of Sociology, Cornell University, Revised July 1997.

—— and Chang, P. M. Y. (1993). 'The International Labor Organization and the Welfare State: Institutional Effects on National Welfare Spending, 190–1980', *International Organization*, 47: 235–62.

—— and Meyer, J. W. (1993). 'Institutional Conditions for Diffusion', *Theory and Society*, 22: 487–511.

—— —— (1994). 'Institutional Conditions for Diffusion', in *Institutional Environments and Organizations*. Thousand Oaks, CA: Sage, pp. 100–12.

—— and Soule, S. A. (1998). 'Diffusion in Organizations and Social Movements: From Hybrid Corn to Poison Pill', *Annual Review of Sociology*, 24: 265–90.

Stratton, B. (1993). 'A Few Words About the Last Word', *Quality Progress*, 26(10): 63–5.

Sutton, J. R., Dobbin, F., Meyer, J. W., and Scott, W. R. (1994). 'The Legalization of the Workplace', *American Journal of Sociology*, 99: 944–71.

Swanson, D. L. (1999). 'Toward and Integrative Theory of Business and Society: A Research Strategy for Corporate Social Performance', *Academy of Management Review*.

Swedberg, R. (1994). 'The Idea of "Europe" and the Origin of the European Union— A Sociological Approach', *Zeitschrift fur Soziologie*, 23(5): 378–87.

Sweet, J. (1938). 'Training to improve work', *Personnel Journal*, 17: 109–15.

Swidler, A. (1985). 'Culture in Action: Symbols and Strategies', *American Journal of Sociology*, 51: 273–86.

Swift, T. and Zadek, S. (2002). *Corporate Responsibility and the Competitive Advantage of Nations*. London: Institute of Social and Ethical Accountability with the Copenhagen Centre.

Tamm-Hallstrom, K. (1996). 'The Production of Management Standards', *Revue D'Economie Industrielle*, 75(1): 61–76.

Tanzi, V. and Davoodi, H. (1997). 'Corruption, Public Investment, and Growth', IMF Working Paper 97/139, Washington, DC: IMF.

Task Force on Higher Education and Society (2000). *Higher Education in Developing Countries. Peril and Promise*. Washington, DC: The International Bank for Reconstruction and Development and The World Bank.

Tattum, L. (1992). 'ISO 9000 in Europe: The Competitive Edge is Dulled', *Chemical Week*, 151(19): 37–8.

Taylor, F. W. (1911). *The Principles of Scientific Management*.

Teferra, D. and Altbach, P. G. (2004). 'African Higher Education: Challenges for the 21st Century', *Higher Education*, 47: 21–50.

Thomas, A. (2004). 'The Rise of Social Cooperatives in Italy', *Voluntas: International Journal of Voluntary and Nonprofit Organization*, 15(3): 243–63.

Thomas, G., Meyer, J. W., Ramirez, F. O., and Boli, J. (1987). *Institutional Structure: Constituting State, Society, and the Individual*. Newbury Park: Sage.

Thomas, G. M. and Meyer, J. W. (1984). 'The Expansion of the State', *Annual Review of Sociology*, 10: 461–82.

Thompson, J. D. (1967). *Organizations in Action*. New York: McGraw-Hill.

Tiessen, J. H. (1997). 'Individualism, Collectivism, and Entrepreneurship: A Framework for International Comparative Research', *Journal of Business Venturing*, 12(5): 367–84.

Tilly C. (1990). *Coercion, Capital and European States, AD 990–1990*. Cambridge, UK: Blackwell.

Tinbergen, J. (1967). *Development Planning*. New York: McGraw-Hill.

—— (1968). 'Wanted: A World Development Plan', *International Organization*, 22: 417–431.

Tocqueville, A. de (1969 [1836]). *Democracy in America*. J. P. Maier (ed.), Trans. G. Lawrence. Garden City, New York: Anchor Books, pp. 513–17.

Tolbert, P. S. and Zucker, L. G. (1983). 'Institutional Sources of Change in the Formal Structure of Organizations: The Diffusion of Civil Service Reform, 1880–1935', *Administrative Science Quarterly*, 30: 20–39.

Toulmin, S. E. (1990). *Cosmopolis: The Hidden Agenda of Modernity*. New York: Free Press.

Triandis, H. C. (1995). *Individualism and Collectivism*. Boulder, CO: Westview Press.

Trow, M. (1996). 'Trust, Markets and Accountability in Higher Education: A Comparative Perspective', *Higher Education Policy*, 9: 309–24.

Truth and Reconciliation Commission (TRC) (2003). *Truth and Reconciliation Commission of South Africa Report*, March 21, 2003.

Tsoukalis, L. (1993). *The New European Economy*. New York: Oxford University Press.

Tuma, N. B. and Hannan, M. (1984). *Social Dynamics: Models and Methods*. San Diego: Academic Press.

Turkey. (1996). *Seventh Five-year Development Plan*. Ankara: Ekonomik ve Sosyal Dokumantasyon ve Arastirma A.S.

Turner, C. H. and Trompenaars, F. (1993). *The Seven Cultures of Capitalism: Value Systems for Creating Wealth in the United States, Britain, Japan, Germany, France and the Netherlands*. New York: Doubleday.

Turner, J. H. (1991). 'Structuration Theory of Anthony Giddens', in *The Structure of Sociological Theory*, 5th edn. California: Wadsworth, pp. 519–39.

Tyack, D. (1974). *The One Best System*. Cambridge, MA: Harvard University Press.

United Nations (1994–1999). *World Investment Report* [several annual issues]. New York: United Nations.

United Nations Development Programme (1999). *Human Development Report.* New York: Oxford University Press.

—— (2000). *Human Development Report.* New York: Oxford University Press.

—— (Various Years). *Human Development Report.* New York: Oxford University Press.

United Nations Education Science and Culture Organization (1998, 1999, 2000). *The Statistical Yearbook.* Paris: Author.

Union of International Associations (2000). *Yearbook of International Organizations.* Brussels: Author.

Useem, M. (1993). *Executive Defense: Shareholder Power and Corporate Reorganization.* Cambridge: Harvard University Press.

Ventresca, M. (1996). When States Count: International and Political Dynamics in Modern Census Establishment, 1800–1993. Ph.D. dissertation, Stanford University.

Viola, M. and Agrawal, J. P. (1979). A Directory of Graduate Degree Programs in Business Administration and Related Fields at Postsecondary Institutions Outside the United States. Boston, MA: Northwestern University.

Vogel, S. C. (1996). *Freer Markets, More Rules.* Ithaca, NY: Cornell University Press.

Wade, R. (2000). 'Wheels within Wheels: Rethinking the Asian Crisis and the Asian Model', *Annual Review of Political Science*, 3: 85–115.

—— and Veneroso, F. (1998). 'The Asian Crisis: The High Debt Model Versus the Wall Street-Treasury-IMF Complex', *New Left Review*, 228: 3–23.

Walgenbach, P. (1996). 'The Institutionalization of Total Quality Management', Presentation to the Stanford Workshop on Comparative Systems.

—— (1997). 'Show Biz Hype or Rowing on the Galley', Working paper, Department of Business Administration and Organization Theory, University of Mannheim.

—— (2001). 'The Production of Distrust by a Means of Producing Trust', *Organization Studies*, 22: 693–714.

Wallerstein, I. (1974). *The Modern World System*, Vol. 1. New York: Academic Press.

—— (2000). 'Globalization or Age of Transition? A Long-Term View of the Trajectory of the World-System', *International Sociology*, 15(2): 249–65.

Waters, M. (1995). *Globalization.* London: Routledge.

Waterston, A. (1965). *Development Planning: Lessons of Experience.* Baltimore, MD: Johns Hopkins Press.

Watts, R. L. and Zimmerman, J. L. (1986). *Positive Accounting Theory.* Englewood Cliffs, NJ: Prentice-Hall.

Weber, E. J. (1976). *Peasants into Frenchmen : the Modernization of Rural France, 1870–1914.* Stanford, CA: Stanford University Press.

Weber, M. (1968). *Economy and Society: An Outline of Interpretive Sociology.* New York: Bedminster Press.

—— (1978). *Economy and Society.* Berkeley, CA: University of California Press.

WebInfoCo. (2000). 'MBA Program Information Site.' http://www.mbainfo.com/.

Weick, K. E. (1976). 'Educational Organizations as Loosely Coupled Systems', *Administrative Science Quarterly*, 21: 1–19.

—— (1995). *Sensemaking in Organizations.* Thousand Oaks, CA: Sage.

Weingart, P. (2004). 'Impact of Bibliometrics upon the Science System: Inadvertent Consequences?' *Scientometrics*, 62: 67–85.

Went, R. (2003). 'Globalization in the Perspective of Imperialism', *Science and Society*, 66(4): 473–97.

White, H. C. (1992). *Identity and Control. A Structural Theory of Social Action.* Princeton, NJ: Princeton University Press.

Whitley, R., Thomas, A., and Marceau, J. (1981). *Masters of Business? Business Schools and Business Graduates in Britain and France.* London: Tavistock.

Whittington, G. (1993). 'Corporate Governance and the Regulation of Financial Reporting', *Accounting and Business Research*, 23(91A): 311–19.

Wilensky, H. (1964). 'The Professionalization of Everyone?' *The American Journal of Sociology*, 70: 137–158.

Wilford, J. N. (1981). *The Mapmakers.* New York: Knopf.

Williamson, J. (1993). 'Democracy and the Washington Consensus', *World Development*, 21: 1329–36.

—— (2000). 'What Should the World Bank Think about the Washington Consensus?' *World Bank Research Observer*, 15: 251–64.

Williamson, O. E. (1975). *Markets and Hierarchies: Analysis and Antitrust Implications.* New York: Free Press.

—— (1985). *The Economic Institutions of Capitalism.* New York: Free Press.

Wilson, J. Q. (1989). *Bureaucracy: What Government Agencies Do and Why They Do It.* New York: Basic Books.

Wissenschaftsrat (2004). 'Leitfaden zur institutionellen Akkreditierung', July 2004 (Drucksache 6189/04). Cologne.

Wittrock, B. and Elzinga, A. (eds.) (1985). *The University Research System: The Public Policies of the Home of Scientists.* Stockholm: Almquist and Wiksell.

Wolf, M. (2004). *Why Globalization Works?* New Haven: Yale University Press.

Wolfe, D. (1972). *The Home of Science: The Role of the University.* New York: McGraw-Hill.

Wong, S.-Y. (1991). 'The Evolution of Social Science Instruction, 1900–1980', *Sociology of Education*, 64(1): 33–47.

Woo, J. (1991). *Race to the Swift: State and Finance in Korean Industrialization.* New York: Columbia University Press.

Woods, N. (1999). 'Good Governance in International Organizations', *Global Governance*, 5: 39–61.

World Bank (1973). *List of National Development Plans*, 4th edn. Washington, DC: International Bank for Reconstruction and Development.

—— (1994). *Higher Education. The Lessons of Experience.* Washington: International Bank for Reconstruction and Development/The World Bank.

—— (1996). *World Development Report (computer file).* Hong Kong: Published for the World Bank by Asia 2000 Ltd.

—— (1997). *The World Development Report 1997.* Oxford: Oxford University Press.

—— (1998). *World Development Report.* Washington, DC: Author.

—— (1999). *World Development Indicators* [CD-ROM]. Washington, DC: Development Data Group of the World Bank's International Economics Department.

World Bank (2000*a*). *World Development Indicators* [CD-ROM]. Washington, DC: Development Data Group of the World Bank's International Economics Department.

—— (2000*b*). *World Bank, Data Group* [Internet Site]. http://www.worldbank.org/ data/databytopic/class.htm

—— (2000*c*). *World Development Report.* Washington, DC: Author.

—— (2002). 'World Development Report 2002: Building Institutions for Markets'. Washington DC: The World Bank.

—— (Various Years). *World Development Report.* New York: Oxford University Press.

World Business Council for Sustainable Development (2000). *Corporate Responsibility: Making Good Business Sense.* Geneva: WBCSD.

World Conference on Higher Education (1998). *World Declaration on Higher Education for the Twenty-first Century: Vision and Action.* Paris.

Wuthnow, R. (1980). 'The World-Economy and the Institutionalization of Science in Seventeenth Century Europe', in A. Bergesen (ed.), *Studies in the Modern World System.* New York: Academic Press, pp. 25–55.

Yuen, C. and Yeo, K. (1995). 'Human Resource Management Practices in Singapore', in L. F. Moore and P. D. Jennings (eds.), *Human Resource Management on the Pacific Rim: Institutions, Practices, and Attitudes.* New York: Walter de Gruyter.

Zaciewski, R. (1993). 'Shifting the Process Control Paradigm—Automotive Standards to ISO 9000', *Quality,* 32(4): 38–9.

Zucker, L. (1977). 'The Role of Institutionalization in Cultural Persistence', *American Journal of Sociology,* 42: 726–43.

Zuckerman, A. (1997). *International Standards Desk Reference.* New York: AMACOM American Management Association.

Zuckerman, H. (1989). 'The Sociology of Science', in N. Smelser (ed.), *Handbook of Sociology.* Newbury Park: Sage, pp. 511–74.

Index